FOUR PLAYS

OF

OUR TIME

Edited by

HERMAN VOADEN, M.A., C.D.A.

Former Director of English
Central High School of Commerce
Toronto

TORONTO
THE MACMILLAN COMPANY OF CANADA LIMITED

FOUR PLAYS OF OUR TIME

FOREWORD

The four plays in this volume were chosen after more than
a year's search. At least two hundred plays were considered;
scores were read carefully; many teachers and theatre experts
were consulted. Some well-known plays were not available
because they are the property of other publishers; many more
were not included because they are already published in
educational editions. Allowing for these unavoidable omis-
sions, the editor believes that this is as challenging and satisfying a collection of plays as can be assembled today in Canada
—the best available to Canadian students. He has great hopes
that the volume will play the same significant role in the study
of the full-length play that *On Stage** has played for many
years in the one-act field.

The principle that proved to be effective in *On Stage* has
been followed. The notes contain a wealth of material touching on every aspect of the theatre as it relates to the four plays.
There is much more material than can be used in normal
classroom study, and still more material is available in the
supplementary notes which the publishers will provide, at no
extra cost, for teachers. Different aspects of this varied material will appeal to different teachers and classes, depending
on the approach that is made to the plays. The intelligent
student will realize that he has not exhausted the possibilities
of the book in his classroom study, and will treasure it as a
valuable item for his permanent library.

A major advantage which *Four Plays of Our Time* has over
single-play volumes is that it makes possible the comparative
study of plays. Teachers are aware of the new trend in teaching the novel in Grade XII, in which from three to seven
works of fiction are studied for their relative treatment of such

*Published by Macmillan of Canada, edited by Herman Voaden.

elements as plot, character, theme, and setting. Our volume makes possible a similar comparative study of drama. And with the supplementary notes provided by the publisher the teacher is encouraged to push the comparative study farther—to the relationship between drama and fiction, as exemplified in *I Remember Mama* and the short stories on which it was based, and in *The Teahouse of the August Moon* and the source novel of the same name. A further study is suggested in these notes concerning the relationship between Ibsen's drama, *An Enemy of the People*, and Arthur Miller's contemporary version of that play.

There is abundant material in the volume to provide a two-year course in drama. But if the book is to be used for one year only, the following suggestions are made for non-academic, average and gifted classes. Non-academic classes might study two of the plays, using only such material in the notes as is of interest and can be absorbed. It would be best for such classes to concentrate on a dramatic approach, stressing simple story and character values. *Flight Into Danger* might be the first play studied. It can be read easily in two periods. *I Remember Mama* is perhaps the next choice for such a class.

The "average" class could read two of the plays in a fairly thorough manner, either presenting them as class plays or studying them from a literary point of view. If only two plays are read, the supplementary notes leading to a comparative study with the source material could also be used. As an alternative, three or four of the plays could be studied, with emphasis on dramatic interpretation, or with a less intensive literary analysis.

The gifted class should be able to study most or all of the plays and read the notes dealing with them, including the publisher's supplementary material.

The arrangement of material follows the pattern of *On Stage*. Before each play the editor has sought to arouse the interest and to stir the enthusiasm of the student reader-actor.

There are discussions of the origin and history of the play, and of its merits and appeal. The student is told what to look for; he is told what has delighted audiences, as shown in the appreciation of the public and the praise of critics. There are simple directions for rehearsing and staging the plays, with ideas about design, interpretation and direction.

After each play there is biographical material about the authors: what they have written, and their writing philosophies and techniques. There are some character studies, and discussions of some of the challenging issues raised by the dramatists.

An exception to this pattern is the fourth play, *An Enemy of the People*. Here Arthur Miller's brilliant *Preface* was available as a logical introduction, and the discussions that would normally precede the play follow it.

At the back of the book there are notes and questions about each play. The notes are not merely explanatory. Both notes and questions are designed to stimulate thought and to give new understanding of character, story and idea values, and of dramatic techniques through which these are presented.

The notes have been written out of a great love of the theatre, a lifelong devotion to it, and a tremendous belief in its role as one of the great civilizing and enriching forces in our lives. The editor hopes that this love, devotion and faith will confirm and strengthen his readers in a comparable dedication to the theatre—that they will create an enthusiasm for the theatre that will last a lifetime. As with *On Stage*, he has sought to create a mood of adventure and enjoyment, confident that in such a mood knowledge and understanding will follow. He has sought to widen horizons and to open up new vistas, new avenues of study in all aspects of the theatre: problems of interpretation and production, types of plays, dramatic trends. He has sought to lead the student in a spirit of adventure to significant books and important dramas by other playwrights. He hopes that this volume will help to create a greater interest in drama in Canada; that *Four Plays of Our Time* will make a significant contribution to the development of both school and community theatre, and that among those who read, study and act these plays, there will be some who will provide the intelligent and gifted leadership which the theatre in Canada will need in the years to come.

The editor wishes to acknowledge his indebtedness to the many individuals who have aided him, both directly and indirectly, in preparing this volume. He is particularly indebted to Mr. Arthur Hailey for his co-operation, kindness and help; to all those, notably Mr. Charles Rittenhouse, Mr. Harding Greenwood, and Mr. Ernest Winter, whose comments were of invaluable assistance to the editor in the final selection of the plays; to the editorial staff of The Macmillan Company, and particularly to Miss Gladys Neale, Manager of the School Book Department.

PUBLISHER'S NOTE

Herman Voaden, the editor of this volume, is well known as teacher, leader in the arts, theatre director, and playwright. At the Central High School of Commerce, Toronto, where he was Director of the English Department for many years, he pioneered in progressive educational methods, including the "play approach" to drama. He recently resigned from this post to devote all his time to writing. In April, 1965, he was given the English Centennial Award by the English Section of the Ontario Educational Association.

Mr. Voaden has long been in the forefront of the movement to create a more favourable climate for the arts, and to bring them closer to the people of Canada. He was the first president of the Canadian Arts Council (now the Canadian Conference of the Arts), and has been active in this organization throughout the twenty years of its existence.

For the Toronto Play Workshop, a centre he founded for the writing and production of Canadian plays and for experimentation with new stage techniques, Mr. Voaden wrote and produced five "symphonic" plays, *Rocks*, *Earth-Song*, *Hill-Land*, *Murder Pattern*, and *Ascend as the Sun*; two dance dramas, *Romeo and Juliet*, and *The Masque of the Red Death*; and also a dramatization of *Maria Chapdelaine*. He presented the first Canadian productions of T. S. Eliot's *Murder in the Cathedral* at Queen's University, Kingston, and at Massey Hall, Toronto, and was given the Canadian Drama Award for outstanding contributions to the Canadian theatre.

In recent years Mr. Voaden has had a wide range of interests, but has continued his activities as a playwright and dramatist in his writing of an opera libretto, *The Prodigal Son*; an oratorio based on the Book of Esther; and a play about Emily Carr, the noted British Columbia painter and writer, which was one of the top ten in the Stratford–Globe and Mail Playwriting Competition. He is now at work on another play.

ABOUT THE PICTURES ON THE END-PAPERS

Top Left: *An Enemy of the People*, Act I, Scene 2.

Dr. Stockmann is about to attack his brother Peter, who has accused him of being an enemy of the community. His daughter Petra and his wife restrain him.

Bottom Left: *The Teahouse of the August Moon*, Act III, Scene 1.

Lotus Blossom performs for her guests a traditional dance "of infinite grace and delicacy" in the new teahouse. The pagoda roof can be seen, and the coloured paper panels with their lovely Japanese designs through which soft lights glow. In the foreground, watching the dance, are, from left to right, Sakini, Captain McLean and Captain Fisby.

Top Right: *Flight Into Danger*, Act III.

George Spencer, truck salesman and pilot of World War II, in a tense moment at the controls of the passenger aircraft he is attempting to land. With him is the Stewardess.

Bottom Right: *I Remember Mama*, Act I.

Uncle Chris is about to drive Dagmar, accompanied by Nels and Mama, to the hospital in his old Ford car. Jessie is beside him. Aunt Jenny pushes Aunt Sigrid after them, dragging Mr. Thorkelson. Aunt Trina follows him. To the right is a lamp-post; in the background are the dim shapes of the houses of San Francisco.

CONTENTS

FOUR PLAYS OF OUR TIME

INTRODUCTION

To Teachers and Interested Students

In his second autobiography, *The Widening Circle*, John van Druten, author of the play *I Remember Mama*, told how the theatre offered him "a greater degree of excitement than any other art". There was a magic in the theatre which held him to it. As a writer and director he sought always for this magic, "a strange and elusive thing that descends from nowhere". He describes it as "a miraculous bringing together of the magic qualities in everyone connected with the production, that will hold the audience, transferring its quality to them."

All four plays in our volume have woven this spell over audiences—*Flight Into Danger* in repeated television performances, and the other three night after night in the theatre. If you are fortunate enough to have known this magic you will be able to re-create it, as you read or act these plays. Even if you have not known the miracle in a living theatre you will be able to make it come true for yourself—if you believe in it—as you read the plays, silently or aloud, or read or act them with your friends, or hear them read by your teacher.

The plays represent an interesting range of dramatic types and moods: melodrama, folk comedy, satiric Oriental fable, and problem play. *Flight Into Danger* is a thriller, constructed with great skill. It supplies something that is not in any of the other plays in the volume—a quality of sheer physical excitement, sustained and built through a series of breathless climaxes. Students and teachers will be caught up in its spell. They will be fascinated by the printed form of a television play. TV drama is an increasingly important form of theatre, and this superb example illuminates the technique of writing for the new medium. We are happy and

1

proud to include *Flight Into Danger*—a play that has had the greatest popular success of any Canadian play.

I Remember Mama, dominated by the warm femininity of Mama, balances the strong masculinity of *Flight Into Danger*. Here is a gentle, charming, durable, memorable comedy, rich in character values and appealing in its simple, forthright telling of episodes in the life of a Norwegian family in San Francisco. *The Teahouse of the August Moon* adds two new notes to the volume—a broadly comic, even farcical mood and a mood of oriental fantasy. These seemingly contrasting moods are blended in a singularly successful fashion. Finally we have the drama of ideas, exemplified by Ibsen's powerful play, *An Enemy of the People*—re-written for contemporary audiences by one of the most distinguished of American dramatists.

What a wide range of scene, character, and thought! We start with Canada today, with the air age. Here are airline personnel on the ground in Vancouver; others in a plane, miles above the prairies and mountains, taking a group of fellow Canadians to the Grey Cup match. Danger strikes, and one of these passengers unexpectedly becomes a hero! Then we have Europe in America, a portrait of a Norwegian family making the new world its own at the turn of the century in San Francisco—a portrait in which the simple but lasting virtues of love, courage, understanding, and sympathy are notably exhibited. Next we have America in Okinawa during World War II. This is our own world again, a shrinking world that is moving toward the "one world" to come. Here are the problems arising from the meeting of East and West, dealt with wisely and humorously. Here is the sly and wonderful rogue Sakini, and the frail Lotus Blossom, and the Americans, some partly wise like Fisby and McLean, and others forever foolish, like Colonel Purdy. Finally, we go back to a Norwegian town seventy years ago, where the scientist, Dr. Stockmann, at the outposts of truth, battles against the compact and stupid majority, led by his wily brother, Peter Stockmann. Ibsen's play, re-written by Arthur Miller, throws a searchlight on the unsolved problems of democracy which face us.

In its search for more expressive forms the theatre has been influenced by the new techniques of film, radio, and television which are able to tell a story in a swift succession of changing scenes, from many points of view. It has sought to break away from the rigid three-act pattern and to achieve the greater freedom of these newer media. It has also been influenced by the example of plays written in the great periods of play-writing that preceded the nineteenth century, notably the dramas of Molière and Shakespeare, with their many scenes and greater freedom of construction. *I Remember Mama* and *The Teahouse of the August Moon* are both interesting because they show these influences. *I Remember Mama* has four stage areas, on which twenty-eight scenes are played. These scenes move swiftly from one area to the other. *The Teahouse of the August Moon* has ten scenes. The action flows from one area to another, as bamboo panels are raised and lowered.

Both *I Remember Mama* and *The Teahouse of the August Moon* are interesting because they employ a narrator. When the curtains open on the average play you are confronted with people you don't know. The novelist can tell you all about his characters—who they are and what they have done thus far. But the playwright must convey this background information by devious means, which must seem natural and lifelike. Typical devices used are servants discussing their master's business or past, or a stranger arriving and being told about the household. Even a telephone conversation is useful. You will be interested, as you read *An Enemy of the People*, to see how this background information is skilfully conveyed to us, item by item, without blocking the flow of the story.

The Greeks jumped this hurdle by using a Chorus which had dramatic foreknowledge of the events to come. Shakespeare used prologues, and a Chorus in *Henry the Fifth*. In their soliloquies and asides his characters tell us a great deal about themselves. Oriental dramas often employ narrators. Of our three new media, radio drama uses a narrator almost consistently to introduce scenes and characters and to advance the story.

In *Playwright at Work* John van Druten spoke of his relief and pleasure at being able to convey this background information directly by using Katrin as a narrator in *I Remember Mama*. It is she who tells the story, recalling the past with the aid of her diary. She does not acknowledge the audience; she is a writer, talking aloud to herself. She is a participant as well as a narrator, slipping in and out of the action at will.

Equally interesting is the narrator in *The Teahouse of the August Moon*, Sakini. He resembles the Stage Manager in Thornton Wilder's beautiful and moving play, *Our Town*, a play which you will enjoy reading if you have not already done so. He explains the characters and action; he takes part himself; above all he sets the mood of the play, establishing a warm and friendly relationship with the audience. He talks to us between each of the ten scenes and speaks the opening and closing words. Like a god he is able to bring the puppets who are "frozen", to life. His wise philosophy and unending good humour delight audiences and send them home happy.

Here, then, are four significant plays of our time. It is the editor's hope that as you read and act them the excitement and magic of the theatre will descend upon you "from nowhere", as John van Druten said, and that there will be born in you a love of the stage that will last a lifetime. Moreover, he hopes that you will see more clearly the kind of life you want to lead. Beyond the present lives, in each of us, a dream of what life may be for us and for our fellowmen. Patterns of behaviour are set before you in these plays: the courage of an ex-pilot; the warm tenderness and love of life of a Norwegian immigrant; the gentle, wise humour of an oriental rogue and philosopher; the burning zeal for truth of a scientist. Let us hope that these examples will quicken your dreams and spur you to a stronger acceptance of life's challenge.

STAGE DIRECTIONS

There are two points to remember in reading and following stage directions:

1. "Right" and "left" mean the actor's right and left.

2. The old stage floors were "raked"; they sloped *down* toward the audience. Hence "down stage" means *toward* the audience; "up stage" means *away* from the audience.

SEVEN POSSIBLE PROCEDURES IN CLASSROOM DRAMA

1. A reading by the teacher, who explains and discusses the play as he does so.

2. A reading by students. Parts are assigned, and read without preparation. They are changed frequently, to maintain interest. The teacher may read one part. The reading should be as spirited and vital as possible. Students can be at the four corners of the room or at the front of the class.

3. A classroom reading in which there is preparation but no memorization. The parts are assigned ahead of time. (If effort can be rewarded in this and the following procedures, perhaps by a mark which is part of the student's literature mark, the results will be encouraging.)

4. A prepared reading from raised desks or lecterns—perhaps with desk lights, which are turned on when the character is taking part in a scene.

5. A prepared radio reading with microphones, if a public address system is available.

6. A staged performance of a scene or act—with movements and perhaps with costumes and make-up. This should be rehearsed. Books in hand; no memorization.

7. A memorized and costumed performance of a scene or act.

FLIGHT INTO DANGER

ARTHUR HAILEY

HAILEY'S COMET

One night in 1955 Arthur Hailey was flying home from Vancouver to Toronto on a Trans-Canada Air Lines flight. He had been on a business trip to the coast. He was day-dreaming. In the war he had been a pilot himself. "I got to wondering what would happen if both pilots became sick," he told me, "and whether I could bring the plane down." Half-waking, half-dozing, more for mental exercise than anything else, he thought the story through from beginning to conclusion.

So our play was born—one of the most successful Canadian plays yet written.

It took Hailey roughly ten days, working evenings, to complete the script. The play required less rewriting than anything he has written since. Having finished it, he checked it carefully with a test pilot for accuracy of detail and then mailed it to the CBC script department.

Despite the production hazards, CBC bought *Flight Into Danger* on February 20, 1956, and David Greene, CBC producer, launched into an eighteen-thousand-dollar production, one of the most expensive hour dramas the CBC had done. To get a control panel Greene borrowed a salvaged North Star cockpit from the RCAF in Trenton. It was eight feet high, nine feet wide and eleven feet long; it weighed 1,500 pounds. He had to get a permit from the Ontario Department of Highways to transport it to Toronto, and caused a traffic jam on Highway 401 bringing it in!

Greene and his cameraman, Len Macdonald, spent several days both at the RCAF base at Trenton and at Malton Airport. The opening and closing sequences of the plane departing and landing were filmed at Malton; the film clips of the North Star in flight were photographed at Trenton. Avro fire engines and emergency equipment in action were also filmed.

On April 3, 1956, *Flight Into Danger* was presented on CBC's General Motors Theatre. The producer and his associates were confident that they had a good show, but they never dreamed that the response would be so overwhelming. The studio was flooded with telephone calls and letters. A viewer in Toronto called *Flight* ". . . the most gripping, tension-packed play I have ever seen on TV". From Montreal came the comment: ". . . one of the finest productions I have ever seen on television—be it English, American or Canadian . . . it was a good feeling for us as viewers to see a Canadian story unfold and we felt the utmost pride in having shared in the excitement of that flight." And from Detroit ". . . three of us at our house were spellbound for an hour by this production. . . ." Five months later the CBC arranged for a repeat showing.

The American NBC production was directed by Herbert Hirschman. He was so impressed with the Canadian kinescope that he used all of David Greene's film clips and based many of his "shots" on the CBC presentation. The production again was a phenomenal success. It hit viewers with such impact that *Variety*, the show business trade paper, nicknamed it *Hailey's Comet*. Hirschman reported: "The show caused a stir such as rarely occurs in this business." Jack Gould, of the *New York Times*, perhaps the best known TV critic in America, wrote, "A superb thriller. One of the finest ever done on live television. . . . Mr. Hailey wrote his play with masterful tautness and highly effective understatement." Suddenly, overnight, Arthur Hailey's name became a household word.

There was the same overwhelming response when the BBC screened the kinescope of the original CBC production. The studio switchboard was jammed by enthusiastic callers for fifteen minutes. The *Daily Telegraph* described it as "one of the most exciting dramas television has yet shown us", and the *News Chronicle* called it "rare and outstanding".

Following the NBC performance the motion picture rights were sold and Hailey spent six weeks in Hollywood working on the screen play. The picture, called *Zero Hour*, was released by Paramount in November, 1957. Dana Andrews played Spencer, Linda Darnell was the Stewardess and Sterling Hayden was Treleaven.

The next step in this amazing story is that *Flight Into Danger* was turned into a novel. The adaptation was done by John Castle (really a pseudonym for two authors). As a novel *Flight Into Danger* has duplicated its success as a television thriller. It has been published in fifteen countries, including translations into eleven languages. In North America serialization rights to the novel were acquired by *The Ladies' Home Journal* and there have been nine other serializations overseas. A soft-cover edition is also to be published.

The next chapter in the story is that a stage version of *Flight Into Danger* is now available. Moreover, our television version is included in an anthology of some of the author's TV plays. And we are proud to present it here, in distinguished company, in an anthology of plays for Canadian schools, as an example of television playwriting at its highest level.

Two ideas emerge from this fable-like account. The first is that the entertainment arts are drawing more closely together and are borrowing increasingly from one another. Here is a dramatic idea which started as a television play, and then became in turn a film, a novel, and a stage play!

The second impression is a sense of wonder, almost amounting to disbelief, at the success of the idea that was born on the plane on that night ride from Vancouver.

It is your turn to read one of the best television plays yet written.

CAST

Aboard Flight 714:

The Passengers: George Spencer
Dr. Frank Baird
Seven Male Passengers
Two Women Passengers

The Crew: Captain
First Officer
Stewardess

At Vancouver Airport:

Captain Martin Treleaven   Switchboard Operator
Airport Controller   Radio Operator
Harry Burdick   Tower Controller

At Winnipeg Airport:

First Passenger Agent   Second Passenger Agent

FLIGHT INTO DANGER

ACT I

FADE IN: *the passenger lobby of Winnipeg Air Terminal at night. At the departure counter of Cross-Canada Airlines a male passenger agent in uniform* (FIRST AGENT) *is checking a manifest. He reaches for p.a. mike.*

FIRST AGENT. Flight 98, direct fleet-liner service to Vancouver, with connections for Victoria, Seattle and Honolulu, leaving immediately through gate four. No smoking. All aboard, please.

> (*During the announcement* GEORGE SPENCER *enters through the main lobby doorway. About 35, he is a senior factory salesman for a motor truck manufacturer.* SPENCER *pauses to look for the Cross-Canada counter, then hastens toward it, arriving as the announcement concludes.*)

SPENCER. Is there space on Flight 98 for Vancouver?

FIRST AGENT. Sorry, sir, that flight is full. Did you check with Reservations?

SPENCER. Didn't have time. I came straight out on the chance you might have a "no show" seat.

FIRST AGENT. With the big football game on tomorrow in Vancouver, I don't think you'll have much chance of getting out before tomorrow afternoon.

SPENCER. That's no good. I've got to be in Vancouver tomorrow by midday.

FIRST AGENT (*hesitates*). Look, I'm not supposed to tell you this, but there's a charter flight in from Toronto. They're going out to the coast for the game. I did hear they were a few seats light.

SPENCER.   Who's in charge? Where do I find him?

FIRST AGENT.   Ask at the desk over there. They call themselves Maple Leaf Air Charter. But mind, *I* didn't send you.

SPENCER (*smiles*). Okay, thanks.

> (SPENCER *crosses to another departure counter which has a cardboard sign hanging behind it—Maple Leaf Air Charter. Behind the desk is an agent in a lounge suit. He is checking a manifest.*)

SPENCER.   Excuse me.

SECOND AGENT.   Yes?

SPENCER.   I was told you might have space on a flight to Vancouver.

SECOND AGENT.   Yes, there's one seat left. The flight's leaving right away though.

SPENCER.   That's what I want.

SECOND AGENT.   Very well, sir. Your name, please?

SPENCER.   Spencer—George Spencer.

SECOND AGENT.   That'll be fifty-five dollars for the one-way trip.

SPENCER.   Will you take my air travel card?

SECOND AGENT.   No sir. Just old-fashioned cash.

SPENCER.   All right.

> (*Produces wallet and counts out bills.*)

SECOND AGENT (*handing over ticket*). Do you have any bags?

SPENCER.   One. Right here.

SECOND AGENT.   All the baggage is aboard. Would you mind keeping it with you?

SPENCER.   Be glad to.

SECOND AGENT.   Okay, Mr. Spencer. Your ticket is your

boarding pass. Go through gate three and ask the commissionaire for Flight 714. Better hurry.

SPENCER.   Thanks a lot. Good night.

SECOND AGENT.   Good night.

> (*Exit* SPENCER. *Enter* STEWARDESS.)

SECOND AGENT.   Hi, Janet. Did the meals get aboard?

STEWARDESS.   Yes, they've just put them on. What was the trouble?

SECOND AGENT.   Couldn't get service from the regular caterers here. We had to go to some outfit the other side of town. That's what held us up.

STEWARDESS.   Are we all clear now?

SECOND AGENT.   Yes, here's everything you'll need.

> (*Hands over papers.*)

There's one more passenger. He's just gone aboard. So that's 56 souls in your lovely little hands.

STEWARDESS.   I'll try not to drop any.

SECOND AGENT (*reaching for coat*).   Well, I'm off home.

STEWARDESS (*as she leaves*). 'Night.

SECOND AGENT (*pulling on coat*). 'Night, Janet.

> (*Calls after her.*)

Don't forget to cheer for the Blue Bombers tomorrow.

> (STEWARDESS *waves and smiles.*)

DISSOLVE TO: *the passenger cabin of a DC-4 liner. There is one empty aisle seat. Seated next to it is* DR. FRANK BAIRD, M.D., *55.* GEORGE SPENCER *enters, sees the unoccupied seat and comes toward it.*

SPENCER.   Pardon me, is this anyone's seat?

BAIRD.   No.

SPENCER.   Thanks.

> (SPENCER *sheds his topcoat and puts it on the rack above the seats. Meanwhile the plane's motors can be heard starting.*)

CUT TO: FILM INSERT—*four-engined airplane exterior, night: the motors starting.*

CUT TO: *the passenger cabin.*

BAIRD. I presume you're going to the big game like the rest of us.

SPENCER. I'm ashamed to admit it, but I'd forgotten about the game.

BAIRD. I wouldn't say that too loudly if I were you. Some of the more exuberant fans might tear you limb from limb.

SPENCER. I'll keep my voice down.

> (*Pleasantly.*)

Matter of fact, I'm making a sales trip to the coast.

BAIRD. What do you sell?

SPENCER. Trucks.

BAIRD. Trucks?

SPENCER. That's right. I'm what the local salesmen call the son-of-a-gun from head office with the special prices. Need any trucks? How about forty? Give you a real good discount today.

BAIRD (*laughs*). I couldn't use that many, I'm afraid. Not in my line.

SPENCER. Which is?

BAIRD. Medicine.

SPENCER. You mean you're a doctor?

BAIRD. That's right. Can't buy one truck, leave alone forty. Football is the one extravagance I allow myself.

SPENCER. Delighted to hear it, Doctor. Now I can relax.

> (*As he speaks, the run-up of the aircraft engines begins, increasing to a heavy roar.*)

BAIRD (*raising his voice*). Do you think you can in this racket? I never can figure out why they make all this noise before take-off.

SPENCER (*shouting, as noise increases*). It's the normal run-up of the engines. Airplane engines don't use battery ignition like you have in your car. They run on magneto ignition, and each of the magnetos is tested separately. If they're okay and the motors are giving all the power they should— away you go!

BAIRD.   You sound as if you know something about it.

SPENCER.   I'm pretty rusty now. I used to fly fighters in the air force. But that was ten years ago. Reckon I've forgotten most of it. Well, there we go.

> (*The tempo of the motors increases.* BAIRD *and* SPENCER *lean toward the window to watch the take-off, although it is dark outside.*)

CUT TO: *the passenger cabin. The noise of the motor is reduced slightly and the two men relax in their seats.* SPENCER *reaches for cigarettes.*

SPENCER.   Smoke?

BAIRD.   Thank you.

> (*They light up.* STEWARDESS *enters from aft of airplane and reaches for two pillows from the rack above.*)

STEWARDESS.   We were held up at Winnipeg, sir, and we haven't served dinner yet. Would you care for some?

SPENCER.   Yes, please.

> (STEWARDESS *puts a pillow on his lap.*)

STEWARDESS (*to* BAIRD).   And you, sir?

BAIRD.   Thank you, yes.

> (*To* SPENCER.)

It's a bit late for dinner, but it'll pass the time away.

STEWARDESS.   There's lamb chops or grilled halibut.

BAIRD.   I'll take the lamb.

SPENCER.   Yes, I'll have that, too.

STEWARDESS.   Thank you, sir.

BAIRD (*to* SPENCER).   Tell me . . . By the way, my name is Baird.

SPENCER. Spençer. George Spencer.

(*They shake hands.*)

BAIRD. How'd'do. Tell me, when you make a sales trip like this do you . . .

(*Fade voices and pan with the* STEWARDESS *returning aft. Entering the airplane's tiny galley she picks up a telephone and presses a call button.*)

VOICE OF FIRST OFFICER. Flight deck.

STEWARDESS. I'm finally serving the dinners. What'll "you-all" have—lamb chops or grilled halibut?

VOICE OF THE FIRST OFFICER. Just a minute.

(*Pause.*)

Skipper says he'll have the lamb . . . Oh, hold it! . . . No, he's changed his mind. Says he'll take the halibut. Make it two fish, Janet.

STEWARDESS. Okay.

(STEWARDESS *hangs up the phone and begins to arrange meal trays.*)

CUT TO: SPENCER AND BAIRD.

SPENCER. No, I hadn't expected to go west again this quickly.

BAIRD. You have my sympathy. I prescribe my travel in small doses.

(STEWARDESS *enters and puts meal tray on pillow.*)

Oh, thank you.

STEWARDESS. Will you have coffee, tea or milk, sir?

BAIRD. Coffee, please.

STEWARDESS. I'll bring it later.

BAIRD. That'll be fine. (*To* SPENCER.) Tell me, do you follow football at all?

SPENCER. A little. Hockey's my game, though. Who are you for tomorrow?

BAIRD. The Argos, naturally.

(*As the* STEWARDESS *brings second tray.*)

Thank you, dear.

STEWARDESS.   Will you have coffee, tea or . . .

SPENCER.   I'll have coffee too. No cream.

(STEWARDESS *nods and exits.*)

(*To* BAIRD.)

Must be a calm night outside. No trouble in keeping the dinner steady.

BAIRD (*looking out of window*). It *is* calm. Not a cloud in sight. Must be a monotonous business flying these things once they're off the ground.

SPENCER.   It varies, I guess.

AUDIO: *fades up the roar of motors.*

DISSOLVE TO: FILM INSERT—*airplane in level flight, night.*

DISSOLVE TO: *the aircraft flight deck. The* CAPTAIN *is seated on left,* FIRST OFFICER *on right. Neither is touching the controls.*

FIRST OFFICER (*into radio mike*). Height 16,000 feet. Course 285 true. ETA Vancouver 0505 Pacific Standard. Over.

RADIO VOICE.   Flight 714. This is Winnipeg Control. Roger. Out.

(*The* FIRST OFFICER *reaches for a log sheet and makes a notation, then relaxes in his seat.*)

FIRST OFFICER.   Got any plans for Vancouver?

CAPTAIN.   Yes, I'm going to sleep for two whole days.

(*The* STEWARDESS *enters with a meal tray.*)

STEWARDESS.   Who's first?

CAPTAIN.   You take yours, Harry.

(STEWARDESS *produces a pillow and the* FIRST OFFICER *slides back his seat, well clear of control column. He places the pillow on his knees and accepts the tray.*)

FIRST OFFICER.   Thanks, honey.

CAPTAIN.   Everything all right at the back, Janet? How are the football fans?

STEWARDESS.   They tired themselves out on the way from Toronto. Looks like a peaceful, placid night.

Dialogue FIRST OFFICER (*with mouth full of food, raising fork for emphasis*). Aha! Those are the sort of nights to beware of. It's in the quiet times that trouble brews. I'll bet you right now that somebody's getting ready to be sick.

STEWARDESS.   That'll be when you're doing the flying. Or have you finally learned how to hold this thing steady?

(*To* CAPTAIN.)

How's the weather?

CAPTAIN.   General fog east of the mountains, extending pretty well as far as Manitoba. But it's clear to the west. Should be rockaby smooth the whole way.

STEWARDESS.   Good. Well, keep Junior here off the controls while I serve coffee.

(*Exits.*)

FIRST OFFICER (*calling after her*). Mark my words, woman! Stay close to that mop and pail.

CAPTAIN.   How's the fish?

FIRST OFFICER (*hungrily*). Not bad. Not bad at all. If there were about three times as much it might be a square meal.

AUDIO: *fade voices into roar of motors.*

DISSOLVE TO: *the passenger cabin.* SPENCER *and* BAIRD *are concluding their meal.* BAIRD *puts down a coffee cup and wipes his mouth with a napkin. Then he reaches up and presses a call button over his head. There is a soft "ping" and the* STEWARDESS *enters.*

STEWARDESS.   Yes, sir?

BAIRD.   That was very enjoyable. Now if you'll take the tray I think I'll try to sleep.

STEWARDESS. Surely.

> (*To* SPENCER.)

Will you have more coffee, sir?

SPENCER. No thanks.

> (STEWARDESS *picks up the second tray and goes aft.*
> SPENCER *yawns.*)

Let me know if the noise keeps you awake. If it does, I'll have the engines stopped.

BAIRD (*chuckles*). Well, at least there won't be any night calls—I hope.

> (BAIRD *reaches up and switches off the overhead read-*
> *ing lights so that both seats are in semi-darkness.*
> *The two men prepare to sleep.*)

DISSOLVE TO: FILM INSERT—*airplane in level flight, night.*

DISSOLVE TO: *the passenger cabin. The* CAPTAIN *emerges from the flight deck and strolls aft, saying "Good evening" to one or two people who glance up as he goes by. He passes* SPENCER *and* BAIRD *who are sleeping. As the* CAPTAIN *progresses, the* STEWARDESS *can be seen at the rear of the cabin. She is bending solicitously over a woman passenger, her hand on the woman's forehead. The* CAPTAIN *approaches.*

CAPTAIN. Something wrong, Miss Burns?

STEWARDESS. This lady is feeling a little unwell. I was going to get her some aspirin.

> (*To the* WOMAN PASSENGER.)

I'll be back in a moment.

CAPTAIN. Sorry to hear that. What seems to be the trouble?

> (*The* WOMAN PASSENGER *has her head back and her*
> *mouth open. A strand of hair has fallen across her*
> *face and she is obviously in pain.*)

FIRST WOMAN PASSENGER (*speaking with effort*). I'm sorry

to be such a nuisance, but it hit me all of a sudden . . . just a few minutes ago . . . dizziness and nausea and a sharp pain . . . (*indicating abdomen*) down here.

CAPTAIN.   Well, I think the Stewardess will be able to help you.

> (STEWARDESS *returns.*)

STEWARDESS.   Now, here you are; try these.

> (*She hands over two aspirins and a cup of water. The* PASSENGER *takes them, then puts her head back on the seat rest.*)

FIRST WOMAN PASSENGER.   Thank you very much.

> (*She smiles faintly at the* CAPTAIN.)

CAPTAIN (*quietly, taking* STEWARDESS *aside*).   If she gets any worse you'd better let me know and I'll radio ahead. But we've still five hours' flying to the coast. Is there a doctor on board, do you know?

STEWARDESS.   There was no one listed as a doctor on the manifest. But I can go round and ask.

CAPTAIN (*looks around*).   Well, most everybody's sleeping now. We'd better not disturb them unless we have to. See how she is in the next half-hour or so.

> (CAPTAIN *bends down and puts a hand on the* WOMAN's *shoulder.*)

Try to rest, madam, if you can. Miss Burns will take good care of you.

> (*The* CAPTAIN *nods to* STEWARDESS *and begins his return to the flight deck. The* STEWARDESS *arranges blanket around the* WOMAN PASSENGER. SPENCER *and* BAIRD *are still sleeping as the* CAPTAIN *passes.*)

DISSOLVE TO: FILM INSERT—*airplane in level flight, night.*

DISSOLVE TO: *the passenger cabin.* SPENCER *stirs and wakes. Then he glances forward to where the* STEWARDESS *is leaning over another section of seats and her voice can be heard softly.*

STEWARDESS.   I'm sorry to disturb you, but we're trying to find out if there's a doctor on board.

FIRST MALE PASSENGER.   Not me, I'm afraid. Is something wrong?

STEWARDESS.   One of the passengers is feeling unwell. It's nothing too serious.

>   (*Moving on to the next pair of seats.*)

I'm sorry to disturb you, but we're trying to find out if there's a doctor on board.

>   (*There is an indistinct answer from the two people just questioned, then* SPENCER *sits forward and calls the* STEWARDESS.)

SPENCER.   Stewardess!

>   (*Indicating* BAIRD, *who is still sleeping.*)

This gentleman is a doctor.

STEWARDESS.   Thank you. I think we'd better wake him. I have two passengers who are quite sick.

SPENCER.   All right.

>   (*Shaking* BAIRD's *arm.*)

Doctor! Doctor! Wake up!

BAIRD.   Um. Um. What is it?

STEWARDESS.   Doctor, I'm sorry to disturb you. But we have two passengers who seem quite sick. I wonder if you'd take a look at them.

BAIRD (*sleepily*).   Yes . . . yes . . . of course.

>   (SPENCER *moves out of seat to permit* BAIRD *to reach the aisle.* BAIRD *then follows the* STEWARDESS *aft to the* FIRST WOMAN PASSENGER. *Although a blanket is around her, the woman is shivering and gasping, with her head back and eyes closed. The* DOCTOR *places a hand on her forehead and she opens her eyes.*)

STEWARDESS.   This gentleman is a doctor. He's going to help us.

FIRST WOMAN PASSENGER.   Oh, Doctor . . . !

BAIRD.   Now just relax.

> (*He makes a quick external examination, first checking pulse, then taking a small pen-type flashlight from his pocket and looking into her eyes. He then loosens the blanket and the* WOMAN'S *coat beneath the blanket. As he places a hand on her abdomen she gasps with pain.*)

BAIRD.   Hurt you there?

> (*With an effort she nods.*)

There?

FIRST WOMAN PASSENGER.   Oh yes! Yes!

> (BAIRD *replaces the coat and blanket, then turns to* STEWARDESS.)

BAIRD (*with authority*).   Please tell the Captain we must land at once. This woman has to be gotten to hospital immediately.

STEWARDESS.   Do you know what's wrong, Doctor?

BAIRD.   I can't tell. I've no means of making a proper diagnosis. But it's serious enough to land at the nearest city with hospital facilities. You can tell your Captain that.

STEWARDESS.   Very well, Doctor. (*Moving across the aisle and forward.*) While I'm gone will you take a look at this gentleman here? He's also complained of sickness and stomach pains.

> (BAIRD *goes to a* MALE PASSENGER *indicated by the* STEWARDESS. *The man is sitting forward and resting his head on the back of the seat ahead of him. He is retching.*)

BAIRD.   I'm a doctor. Will you put your head back, please? (*The man groans, but follows the doctor's instruction.*

He is obviously weak. BAIRD *makes another quick examination, then pauses thoughtfully.*)

BAIRD.   What have you had to eat in the last twenty-four hours?

SECOND MALE PASSENGER (*with effort*). Just the usual meals . . . breakfast . . . bacon and eggs . . . salad for lunch . . . couple of sandwiches at the airport . . . then dinner here.

(*The* STEWARDESS *enters, followed by the* CAPTAIN.)

BAIRD (*to* STEWARDESS). Keep him warm. Get blankets around him.

(*To* CAPTAIN.)

How quickly can we land, Captain?

CAPTAIN.   That's the trouble. I've just been talking to Calgary. There was light fog over the prairies earlier, but now it's thickened and everything is closed in this side of the mountains. It's clear at the coast and we'll have to go through.

BAIRD.   Is that faster than turning back?

CAPTAIN.   It would take us longer to go back now than to go on.

BAIRD.   Then how soon do you expect to land?

CAPTAIN.   At about five a.m. Pacific time.

(*As* BAIRD *glances at his watch.*)

You need to put your watch on two hours because of the change of time. We'll be landing in three hours forty-five minutes from now.

BAIRD.   Then I'll have to do what I can for these people. Can my bag be reached? I checked it at Toronto.

CAPTAIN.   We can get it. Let me have your tags, Doctor.

(BAIRD *takes out a wallet and selects two baggage tags which he hands to* CAPTAIN.)

BAIRD.   There are two bags. It's the small overnight case I want.

(*As he finishes speaking the airplane lurches violently.* BAIRD *and the* STEWARDESS *and the* CAPTAIN *are thrown sharply to one side. Simultaneously the telephone in the galley buzzes several times. As the three recover their balance the* STEWARDESS *answers the phone quickly.*)

STEWARDESS. Yes?

FIRST OFFICER'S VOICE (*under strain*). Come forward quickly. I'm sick!

STEWARDESS. The First Officer is sick. He says come quickly.

CAPTAIN (*to* BAIRD). You'd better come too.

(*The* CAPTAIN *and* BAIRD *move quickly forward, passing through the flight deck door.*)

CUT TO: *the flight deck. The* FIRST OFFICER *is at the controls on the right-hand side. He is retching and shuddering, flying the airplane by will-power and nothing else. The* CAPTAIN *promptly slides into the left-hand seat and takes the controls.*

CAPTAIN. Get him out of there!

(*Together* BAIRD *and the* STEWARDESS *lift the* FIRST OFFICER *from his seat and, as they do, he collapses. They lower him to the floor and the* STEWARDESS *reaches for a pillow and blankets.* BAIRD *makes the same quick examination he used in the two previous cases. Meanwhile the* CAPTAIN *has steadied the aircraft and now he snaps over a button to engage the automatic pilot. He releases the controls and turns to the others, though without leaving his seat.*)

CAPTAIN. He must have been changing course when it happened. We're back on auto pilot now. Now, Doctor, what is it? What's happening?

BAIRD. There's a common denominator in these attacks. There has to be. And the most likely thing is food.

(*To* STEWARDESS.)

How long is it since we had dinner?

STEWARDESS.   Two-and-a-half to three hours.

BAIRD.   Now then, what did you serve?

STEWARDESS.   Well, the main course was a choice of fish or meat.

BAIRD.   I remember that. I ate meat.

>   (*Indicating* FIRST OFFICER.)

What did he have?

STEWARDESS (*faintly, with dawning alarm*).   Fish.

BAIRD.   Do you remember what the other two passengers had?

STEWARDESS.   No.

BAIRD.   Then go back quickly and find out, please.

>   (*As the* STEWARDESS *exits* BAIRD *kneels beside* FIRST
>   OFFICER *who is moaning.*)

BAIRD.   Try to relax. I'll give you something in a few minutes to help the pain. You'll feel better if you stay warm.

>   (BAIRD *arranges the blanket around the* FIRST OFFICER.
>   Now the STEWARDESS reappears.*)

STEWARDESS (*alarmed*).   Doctor, both those passengers had fish. And there are three more cases now. And they ate fish too. Can you come?

BAIRD.   Yes, but I need that bag of mine.

CAPTAIN.   Janet, take these tags and get one of the passengers to help you.

>   (*Hands over* BAIRD'*s luggage tags.*)

Doctor, I'm going to get on the radio and report what's happening to Vancouver. Is there anything you want to add?

BAIRD.   Yes. Tell them we have three serious cases of suspected food poisoning and there appear to be others. When we land we'll want ambulances and medical help waiting, and the hospitals should be warned. Tell them we're not sure, but we suspect the poisoning may have been caused by fish served on board. You'd better suggest they put a ban on serving all food which originated wherever ours came from until we've established the source for sure.

CAPTAIN. Right.

> (*He reaches for the radio mike and* BAIRD *turns to go aft. But suddenly a thought strikes the* CAPTAIN.)

Doctor, I've just remembered . . .

BAIRD. Yes.

CAPTAIN (*quietly*). I ate fish.

BAIRD. When?

CAPTAIN. I'd say about half an hour after he did.

> (*Pointing to* FIRST OFFICER.)

Maybe a little longer. Is there anything I can do?

BAIRD. It doesn't follow that everyone will be affected. There's often no logic to these things. You feel all right now?

CAPTAIN. Yes.

BAIRD. You'd better not take any chances. Your food can't be completely digested yet. As soon as I get my bag I'll give you something to help you get rid of it.

CAPTAIN. Then hurry, Doctor. For God's sake, hurry!

> (*Into mike.*)

Vancouver Control. This is Maple Leaf Charter Flight 714. I have an emergency message. Do you read? Over.

VOICE ON RADIO (VANCOUVER OPERATOR). Go ahead 714.

CAPTAIN. We have serious food poisoning on board. Several passengers and the First Officer are seriously ill . . .

DISSOLVE TO: *the luggage compartment below the flight deck. A passenger is hurriedly passing up bags to the* STEWARDESS. BAIRD *is looking down from above.*

BAIRD. That's it! That's it down there! Let me have it!

FADE OUT

ACT II

FADE IN: *the Control Room, Vancouver Airport. At a radio panel an* OPERATOR, *wearing headphones, is transcribing a message on a typewriter. Part way through the message he presses a button on the panel and a bell rings stridently, signalling an emergency. At once an* AIRPORT CONTROLLER *appears behind the* OPERATOR *and reads the message as it continues to come in. Nearby is a telephone switchboard manned by an operator, and a battery of teletypes clattering noisily.*

CONTROLLER (*over his shoulder, to* SWITCHBOARD OPERATOR). Get me area traffic control, then clear the teletype circuit to Winnipeg. Priority message.

(*Stepping back to take phone.*)

Vancouver Controller here. I've an emergency report from Maple Leaf Charter Flight 714, ex-Winnipeg for Vancouver. There's serious food poisoning among the passengers and the First Officer is down too. They're asking for all levels below them to be cleared, and priority approach and landing. ETA is 0505. . . . Roger. We'll keep you posted.

(*To a* TELETYPE OPERATOR, *who has appeared.*)

Got Winnipeg?

(*As* TELETYPE OPERATOR *nods.*)

Send this message. Controller Winnipeg. Urgent. Maple Leaf Charter Flight 714 reports serious food poisoning among passengers believed due to fish dinner served on flight. Imperative check source and suspend all other food service originating same place. That's all.

(*To* SWITCHBOARD OPERATOR.)

Get me the local agent for Maple Leaf Charter. Burdick's his name—call his home. And after that I want the city police—the senior officer on duty.

(CONTROLLER *crosses to radio control panel and reads message which is just being completed.*)

(*To* RADIO OPERATOR.)

Acknowledge. Say that all altitudes below them are being cleared and they'll be advised of landing instructions here. Ask them to keep us posted on condition of the passengers.

SWITCHBOARD OPERATOR.   Mr. Burdick is here at the airport. I have him on the line now.

CONTROLLER.   Good. Controller here. Burdick, we've got an emergency message on one of your flights—714, ex-Toronto and Winnipeg. (*Pause.*) No, the aircraft is all right. There's food poisoning among the passengers and the First Officer has it too. You'd better come over.

(*Replaces phone. Then to* SWITCHBOARD OPERATOR.)

Have you got the police yet?

(*As* OPERATOR *nods.*)

Right, put it on this line. Hullo, this is the Controller, Vancouver Airport. Who am I speaking to, please? (*Pause.*) Inspector, we have an emergency on an incoming flight. Several of the passengers are seriously ill and we need ambulances and doctors out here at the airport. (*Pause.*) Six people for sure, maybe more. The flight will be landing at five minutes past five local time—that's in about three and a half hours. Now, will you get the ambulances, set up traffic control and alert the hospitals? Right. We'll call you again as soon as there's anything definite.

(*During the* above, HARRY BURDICK, *local manager of Maple Leaf Air Charter, has entered.*)

BURDICK.   Where's the message?

(RADIO OPERATOR *hands him a copy which* BURDICK *reads.*)

BURDICK (*to* RADIO OPERATOR).   How's the weather at Calgary? It might be quicker to go in there.

CONTROLLER.   No dice! There's fog down to the deck everywhere east of the Rockies. They'll have to come through.

BURDICK.   Let me see the last position report.

(*As* CONTROLLER *passes a clip board.*)

You say you've got medical help coming?

CONTROLLER.   The city police are working on it now.

BURDICK.   That message! They say the First Officer is down. What about the Captain? Ask if he's affected, and ask if there's a doctor on board. Tell them we're getting medical advice here in case they need it.

CONTROLLER.   I'll take care of that.

BURDICK (*to* SWITCHBOARD OPERATOR).   Will you get me Doctor Knudsen, please. You'll find his home number on the emergency list.

CONTROLLER (*into radio mike*).   Flight 714, this is Vancouver.

DISSOLVE TO: *the airplane passenger cabin.* BAIRD *is leaning over another prostrate passenger. The main lighting is on in the cabin and other passengers, so far not affected, are watching with varying degrees of concern and anxiety. Some have remained in their seats, others have clustered in the aisle. The* DOCTOR *has obtained his bag and it is open beside him. The* STEWARDESS *is attending to another passenger nearby.*

BAIRD (*to* STEWARDESS).   I think I'd better talk to everyone and tell them the story.

(*Moving to centre of cabin, he raises his voice.*)

Ladies and gentlemen, may I have your attention, please? If you can't hear me, perhaps you would come a little closer.

(*Pause, as passengers move in.*)

My name is Baird and I am a doctor. I think it's time that everyone knew what is happening. So far as I can tell, we have several cases of food poisoning and we believe that the cause of it was the fish which was served for dinner.

SECOND WOMAN PASSENGER (*with alarm, to man beside her*).   Hector! We both had fish!

BAIRD.   Now, there is no immediate cause for alarm or panic, and even if you did eat fish for dinner, it doesn't follow that you are going to be affected too. There's seldom any logic to these things. However, we *are* going to take some precautions and the Stewardess and I are coming around to everyone, and I want you to tell us if you ate fish. If you did we'll tell you what to do to help yourselves. Now, if you'll go back to your seats we'll begin right away.

> (*To* STEWARDESS, *as passengers move back to their seats.*)

All we can do now is to give immediate first aid.

STEWARDESS. What should that be, Doctor?

BAIRD. Two things. First, everyone who ate fish must drink several glasses of water. That will help to dilute the poison. After that we'll give an emetic. I have some emetic pills in my bag, and if there aren't enough we'll have to rely on salt. Do you have salt in the galley?

STEWARDESS. A few small packets which go with the lunches, but we can break them open.

BAIRD. All right. We'll see how far the pills will go first. I'll start at the back here. Meanwhile you begin giving drinking water to the passengers already affected and get some to the First Officer too. I'll ask someone to help you.

FIRST MALE PASSENGER. Can I help, Doctor?

BAIRD. What did you eat for dinner—fish or meat?

FIRST MALE PASSENGER. Meat.

BAIRD. All right. Will you help the Stewardess bring glasses of water to the people who are sick? I want them to drink at least three glasses each—more if they can.

STEWARDESS (*going to galley*). We'll use these cups. There's drinking water here and at the rear.

FIRST MALE PASSENGER. All right, let's get started.

BAIRD (*to* STEWARDESS). The Captain! Before you do anything else you'd better get him on to drinking water, and give him two emetic pills. Here.

> (*Takes bottle from his bag and shakes out the pills.*)

Tell him they'll make him feel sick, and the sooner he is, the better.

STEWARDESS. Very well, Doctor.

SECOND WOMAN PASSENGER (*frightened*). Doctor! Doctor! I heard you say the pilots are ill. What will happen to us if they can't fly the plane? Hector, I'm frightened.

THIRD MALE PASSENGER. Take it easy, my dear. Nothing has happened so far and the doctor is doing all he can.

BAIRD. I don't think you'll have any reason to worry, madam. It's quite true that both of the pilots had the fish which we believe may have caused the trouble. But only the First Officer is affected. Now, did you and your husband eat fish or meat?

THIRD MALE PASSENGER. Fish. We both ate fish.

BAIRD. Then will you both drink at least—better make it four—of those cups of water which the other gentleman is bringing around. After that, take one of these pills each.

(*Smiling.*)

I think you'll find there are little containers under your seat. Use those.

(*Goes to rear of plane.*)

FOURTH MALE PASSENGER (*in broad English Yorkshire accent*). How's it comin', Doc? Everything under control?

BAIRD. I think we're holding our own. What did you have for dinner?

FOURTH PASSENGER. Ah had the bloomin' fish. Didn't like it neither. Fine how-d'you-do this is. Coom all this way t'see out team win, and now it looks like Ah'm headed for a mortuary slab.

BAIRD. It really isn't as bad as that, you know. But just as a precaution, drink four cups of water—it's being brought around now—and after that take this pill. It'll make you feel sick.

FOURTH MALE PASSENGER (*pulling carton from under seat and holding it up*). It's the last time I ride on a bloomin' airplane! What a service! They give you your dinner and then coom round and ask for it back.

BAIRD.   What did you have for dinner, please—meat or fish?

FIFTH MALE PASSENGER.   Meat, Doctor.

BAIRD.   All right, we won't worry about you.

SIXTH MALE PASSENGER.   I had meat, Doctor.

SEVENTH MALE PASSENGER.   I had fish.

DOCTOR.   Very well. Will you drink at least four cups of water, please? It'll be brought round to you. Then take this pill.

SIXTH MALE PASSENGER (*slow speaking. A little dull witted*). What's caused this food poisoning, Doctor?

BAIRD.   Well, it can either be caused through spoilage of the food, or some kind of bacteria—the medical word is staphylococcus poisoning.

SIXTH MALE PASSENGER (*nodding knowledgeably*). Oh, yes . . . staphylo . . . I see.

BAIRD.   Either that, or some toxic substance may have gotten into the food during its preparation.

SEVENTH MALE PASSENGER.   Which kind do you think this is, Doctor?

BAIRD.   From the effect I suspect a toxic substance.

SEVENTH MALE PASSENGER.   And you don't know what it is?

BAIRD.   We won't know until we make laboratory tests. Actually, with modern food-handling methods—the chances of this happening are probably a million to one against.

STEWARDESS (*entering*). I couldn't get the First Officer to take more than a little water, Doctor. He seems pretty bad.

BAIRD.   I'll go to him now. Have you checked all the passengers in the front portion?

STEWARDESS.   Yes, and there are two more new cases— the same symptoms as the others.

BAIRD.   I'll attend to them—after I've looked at the First Officer.

STEWARDESS.   Do you think . . .

(*Before the sentence is completed the galley telephone buzzes insistently.* BAIRD *and the* STEWARDESS *exchange glances quickly, then, without waiting to answer the phone, race to the flight deck door.*)

CUT TO: *the flight deck. The* CAPTAIN *is in the left-hand seat. Sweat pouring down his face, he is racked by retching and his right hand is on his stomach. Yet he is fighting against the pain and attempting to reach the radio transmitter mike. But he doesn't make it and, as* BAIRD *and the* STEWARDESS *reach him, he falls back in his seat.*

CAPTAIN (*weakly*). I did what you said . . . guess it was too late. . . . You've got to give me something, Doctor . . . so I can hold out . . . till I see this airplane on the ground. . . . You understand? . . . It'll fly itself on this course . . . but I've got to take it in. . . . Get on the radio. . . . Tell control . . .

(*During the above* BAIRD *and the* STEWARDESS *have been helping the* CAPTAIN *from his seat. Now he collapses into unconsciousness and* BAIRD *goes down beside him. The* DOCTOR *has a stethoscope now and uses it, then makes the other checks quickly and efficiently.*)

BAIRD.   Get blankets over him. Keep him warm. There's probably a reaction because he tried to fight it off so long.

STEWARDESS (*alarmed*). Can you do what he said? Can you bring him round long enough to land?

BAIRD (*bluntly*). You're part of this crew, so I'll tell you how things are. Unless I can get him to a hospital quickly I'm not even sure I can save his life. And that goes for the others too.

STEWARDESS.   But . . .

BAIRD.   I know what you're thinking, and I've thought of it too. How many passengers are there on board?

STEWARDESS.   Fifty-six.

BAIRD. And how many fish dinners did you serve?

STEWARDESS (*composing herself*). Probably about fifteen. More people ate meat than fish, and some didn't eat at all because it was so late.

BAIRD. And you?

STEWARDESS. I had meat.

BAIRD (*quietly*). My dear, did you ever hear the term "long odds"?

STEWARDESS. Yes, but I'm not sure what it means.

BAIRD. I'll give you an example. Out of a total field of 55, our chance of safety depends on there being one person back there who not only is qualified to land this airplane, but who didn't choose fish for dinner tonight.

> (*After her initial alarm the* STEWARDESS *is calm now, and competent. She looks* BAIRD *in the eye and even manages a slight smile.*)

STEWARDESS. Then I suppose I should begin asking.

BAIRD (*thoughtfully*). Yes, but there's no sense in starting a panic. (*Decisively.*) You'd better do it this way. Say that the First Officer is sick and the Captain wondered if there's someone with flying experience who could help him with the radio.

STEWARDESS. Very well, Doctor.

> (*She turns to go.*)

BAIRD. Wait! The man who was sitting beside me! He said something about flying in the war. And we both ate meat. Get him first! But still go round the others. There may be someone else with more experience.

> (STEWARDESS *exits and* BAIRD *busies himself with the* FIRST OFFICER *and the* CAPTAIN. *After a moment,* GEORGE SPENCER *enters.*)

SPENCER. The Stewardess said . . .

> (*Then, as he sees the two pilots.*)

. . . No! Not both pilots!

BAIRD. Can *you* fly this airplane—and land it?

SPENCER. No! No! Not a chance! Of course not!

BAIRD. But you told me you flew in the war.

SPENCER. So I did. But that was fighters—little combat airplanes, not a great ship like this. I flew airplanes which had one engine. This has four. Flying characteristics are different. Controls don't react the same way. It's another kind of flying altogether. And besides that, I haven't touched an airplane for over ten years.

BAIRD (*grimly*). Then let's hope there's someone else on board who can do the job . . . because neither of these men can.

(STEWARDESS *enters and pauses.*)

STEWARDESS (*quietly*). There's no one else.

BAIRD. Mr. Spencer, I know nothing of flying. I have no means of evaluating what you tell me. All I know is this: that among the people on this airplane who are physically able to fly it, you are the only one with any kind of qualifications to do so. What do you suggest?

SPENCER (*desperately*). Isn't there a chance—of either pilot recovering?

BAIRD. I'll tell you what I just told the Stewardess here. Unless I can get them to hospital quickly, I can't even be sure of saving their lives.

(*There is a pause.*)

SPENCER. Well—I guess I just got drafted. If either of you are any good at praying, you can start any time.

(*He slips into the left-hand seat.*)

Lets take a look. Altitude 16,000. Course 290. The ship's on automatic pilot—we can be thankful for that. Air speed 210 knots.

(*Touching the various controls.*)

Throttles, pitch, mixture, landing gear, flaps, and the flap indicator. We'll need a check list for landing, but we'll get that on the radio. . . . Well, maybe we'd better tell the world about our problems.

(*To* STEWARDESS.)

Do you know how to work this radio? They've added a lot of gizmos since my flying days.

STEWARDESS (*pointing*). It's this panel up here they use to talk to the ground, but I'm not sure which switches you have to set.

SPENCER. Ah yes, here's the channel selector. Maybe we'd better leave it where it is. Oh, and here we are—"transmit".

(*He flicks a switch and a small light glows on the radio control panel.*)

Now we're in business.

(*He picks up the mike and headset beside him, then turns to the other two.*)

Look, whatever happens I'm going to need another pair of hands here. Doc, I guess you'll be needed back with the others, so I think the best choice is Miss Canada here. How about it?

STEWARDESS. But I know nothing about all this!

SPENCER. Then that'll make us a real good pair. But I'll tell you what to do ahead of time. Better get in that other seat and strap yourself in. That all right with you, Doc?

BAIRD. Yes, do that. I'll take care of things in the back. And I'd better go there now. Good luck!

SPENCER. Good luck to *you*. We're all going to need it.

(BAIRD *exits.*)

SPENCER. What's your first name?

STEWARDESS. Janet.

SPENCER. Okay, Janet. Let's see if I can remember how to send out a distress message. . . . Better put on that headset beside you.

(*Into mike.*)

Mayday! Mayday! Mayday!

(*To* STEWARDESS.)

What's our flight number?

STEWARDESS.   714.

SPENCER (*into mike*). This is Flight 714, Maple Leaf Air Charter, in distress. Come in anyone. Over.

VOICE ON RADIO (*immediately, crisply*). This is Calgary, 714. Go ahead!

VOICE ON RADIO (VANCOUVER OPERATOR). Vancouver here, 714. All other aircraft stay off the air. Over.

SPENCER.   Thank you Calgary and Vancouver. This message is for Vancouver. This aircraft is in distress. Both pilots and some passengers . . .

(*To* STEWARDESS.)

How many passengers?

STEWARDESS.   It was seven a few minutes ago. It may be more now.

SPENCER.   Correction. At least seven passengers are suffering from food poisoning. Both pilots are unconscious and in serious condition. We have a doctor on board who says that neither pilot can be revived. Did you get that, Vancouver? (*Pause.*) Now we come to the interesting bit. My name is Spencer, George Spencer. I am a passenger on this airplane. Correction: I *was* a passenger. I have about a thousand hours' total flying time, but all of it was on single-engine fighters. And also I haven't flown an airplane for ten years. Now then, Vancouver, you'd better get someone on this radio who can give me some instructions about flying this machine. Our altitude is 16,000, course 290 magnetic, air speed 210 knots. We are on automatic pilot. Your move, Vancouver. Over.

(*To* STEWARDESS.)

You want to take a bet that that stirred up a little flurry down below?

(*The* STEWARDESS *shakes her head, but does not reply.*)

DISSOLVE TO: *the Control Room, Vancouver.*

> (*The* CONTROLLER *is putting down a phone as the* RADIO OPERATOR *brings a message to him. He reads the message.*)

CONTROLLER. Oh, no!

> (*To* RADIO OPERATOR.)

Ask if . . . No, let me talk to them.

> (CONTROLLER *goes to panel and takes the transmitter mike. The* RADIO OPERATOR *turns a switch and nods.*)

CONTROLLER (*tensely*). Flight 714. This is Vancouver Control. Please check with your doctor on board for any possibility of either pilot recovering. Ask him to do everything possible to revive one of the pilots, even if it means neglecting other people. Over.

SPENCER'S VOICE ON RADIO. Vancouver, this is 714, Spencer speaking. I understand your message. But the doctor says there is no possibility whatever of either pilot recovering to make the landing. He says they are critically ill and may die unless they get hospital treatment soon. Over.

CONTROLLER. All right 714. Stand by please.

> (*He pauses momentarily to consider the next course of action. Then briskly to* SWITCHBOARD OPERATOR.)

Get me area traffic control—fast.

> (*Into phone.*)

Vancouver Controller. The emergency we had!—right now it looks like it's shaping up for a disaster.

FADE OUT

ACT III

FADE IN: *the Control Room, Vancouver. The atmosphere is one of restrained pandemonium. The* RADIO OPERATOR *is typing a message. The teletypes are busy. The* CONTROLLER *is on one telephone and* HARRY BURDICK *on another. During what follows cut back and forth from one to the other.*

CONTROLLER (*into phone*). As of right now, hold everything taking off for the east. You've got 45 minutes to clear any traffic for south, west or north. After that, hold everything that's scheduled outwards. On incoming traffic, accept anything you can get on the deck within the next 45 minutes. Anything you can't get down by then for sure, divert away from this area. Hold it.

> (*A* MESSENGER *hands him a message which he scans. Then to* MESSENGER.)

Tell the security officer.

> (*Into phone.*)

If you've any flights coming in from the Pacific, divert them to Seattle. And any traffic inland is to stay well away from the east-west lane between Calgary and Vancouver. Got that? Right.

BURDICK (*into phone*). Is that Cross-Canada Airlines? . . . Who's on duty in operations? . . . Let me talk to him. (*Pause.*) Mr. Gardner, it's Harry Burdick of Maple Leaf Charter. We have an incoming flight that's in bad trouble and we need an experienced pilot to talk on the radio. Someone who's flown DC-4's. Can you help us? (*Pause.*) Captain Treleaven? Yes, I know him well. (*Pause.*) You mean he's with you now? (*Pause.*) Can he come over to Control right away? (*Pause.*) Thank you. Thank you very much.

> (*To* SWITCHBOARD OPERATOR.)

Get me Montreal. I want to talk with Mr. Barney Whitmore. You may have to try Maple Leaf Air Charter office first, and someone there'll have his home number. Tell them the call is urgent.

SWITCHBOARD OPERATOR. Right. (*To* CONTROLLER.) I've got the fire chief.

CONTROLLER (*into phone*). Chief, we have an emergency. It's Flight 714, due here at 0505. It may be a crash landing. Have everything you've got stand by. If you have men off duty call them in. Take your instructions from the Tower. They'll tell you which runway we're using. And notify the city fire department. They may want to move equipment into this area. Right.

(*To* SWITCHBOARD OPERATOR.)

Now get me the city police again—Inspector Moyse.

SWITCHBOARD OPERATOR. I have Seattle and Calgary waiting. They both received the message from Flight 714 and want to know if we got it clearly.

CONTROLLER. Tell them thank you, yes, and we're working the aircraft direct. But ask them to keep a listening watch in case we run into any reception trouble.

(*Another message is handed him. After reading, he passes it to* BURDICK.)

There's bad weather moving in. That's all we need.

(*To* SWITCHBOARD OPERATOR.)

Have you got the police? Right! (*Into phone.*) It's the Airport Controller again, Inspector. We're in bad trouble and we may have a crash landing. We'll need every spare ambulance in the city out here—and doctors and nurses too. Will you arrange it? (*Pause.*) Yes, we do—56 passengers and a crew of three. (*Pause.*) Yes, the same time—0505. That's less than three hours.

BURDICK (*to* SWITCHBOARD). Is Montreal on the line yet? Yes, give it to me. Hullo. Hullo. Is that you, Barney? It's Harry Burdick in Vancouver. I'll give you this fast, Barney. Our flight from Toronto is in bad trouble. They have food › poisoning on board and both pilots and a lot of the passengers have passed out. There's a doctor on board and he says there's no chance of recovery before they get to hospital. (*Pause.*) It's a passenger doing the flying. He's just been on the radio. (*Pause.*) No, he isn't qualified. He flew single-engine fighters in the war, nothing since. (*Pause.*) I've asked him that. This doctor on board says there isn't a chance. (*Pause.*) What else can we do? We've got to talk him down. Cross-Canada are lending us a pilot. It's Captain Treleaven, one of their senior men. He's here now, just arrived. We'll get on the radio with a check list and try to bring him in. (*Pause.*) We'll do the best we can. (*Pause. Then impatiently.*) Of course it's a terrible risk, but can you think of something better? (*Pause.*) No, the papers aren't on to it yet, but don't worry, they will be soon. We can't help that now. (*Pause. Anxious to get off phone.*) That's all we know, Barney. It only just happened, I called you right away. ETA is 0505 Pacific time; that's just under two hours. I've got a lot to do, Barney. I'll have to get on with it. (*Pause. Nodding impatiently.*) I'll call you. I'll call you as soon as I know anything more. . . . G'bye.

> (*During the foregoing* CAPTAIN MARTIN TRELEAVEN, *45, has entered. He is wearing airline uniform. As* BURDICK *sees* TRELEAVEN, *he beckons him, indicating that he should listen. To* TRELEAVEN.)

Did you get that?

TRELEAVEN (*calmly*). Is that the whole story?

BURDICK. That's everything we know. Now what I want you to do is get on the horn and talk this pilot down. You'll have to help him get the feel of the airplane on the way. You'll have to talk him round the circuit. You'll have to give him the cockpit check for landing, and—so help me!—you'll have to talk him on to the ground.

> (CAPTAIN TRELEAVEN *is a calm man, not easily perturbed. While* BURDICK *has been talking, the* CAPTAIN *has been filling his pipe. Now, with methodi-*

cal movements, he puts away his tobacco pouch and begins to light the pipe.)

TRELEAVEN (*quietly*). You realize, of course, that the chances of a man who has only flown fighter airplanes, landing a four-engine passenger ship safely are about nine to one against.

BURDICK (*rattled*). Of course I know it! You heard what I told Whitmore. But do *you* have any other ideas?

TRELEAVEN. No. I just wanted to be sure you knew what we are getting into, Harry. All right. Let's get started. Where do I go?

CONTROLLER. Over here.

(They cross to the radio panel and the OPERATOR *hands him the last message from the aircraft. When he has read it he takes the transmitter mike.)*

TRELEAVEN. How does this thing work?

RADIO OPERATOR (*turning a switch*). You're on the air now.

TRELEAVEN (*calmly*). Hullo Flight 714. This is Vancouver and my name is Martin Treleaven. I am a Cross-Canada Airlines captain and my job right now is to help fly this airplane in. First of all, are you hearing me okay? Over.

VOICE OF SPENCER. Yes, Captain, loud. and clear. Go ahead, please.

TRELEAVEN. Where's that message?

(As OPERATOR *passes it. Into mike.)*

I see that I'm talking to George Spencer. Well, George, I don't think you're going to have much trouble. These DC-4s handle easily, and we'll give you the drill for landing. But first of all, please tell me what your flying experience is. The message says you have flown single-engine fighters. What kind of airplanes were these, and did you fly multi-engine airplanes at all? Let's hear from you, George. Over.

CUT TO: *the flight deck.*

SPENCER (*into mike*). Hullo, Vancouver, this is 714. Glad

to have you along, Captain. But let's not kid each other, please. We both know we need a lot of luck. About my flying. It was mostly on Spitfires and Mustangs. And I have around a thousand hours total. And all of that was ten years ago. Over.

CUT TO: *the Control Room.*

TRELEAVEN (*into mike*). Don't worry about that, George. It's like riding a bicycle. You never forget it. Stand by.

CONTROLLER (*to* TRELEAVEN). The air force has picked up the airplane on radar and they'll be giving us courses to bring him in. (*Hands over paper.*) Here's the first one. See if you can get him on that heading.

TRELEAVEN (*nods. Then into mike*). 714, are you still on automatic pilot? If so, look for the auto-pilot release switch. It's a push-button on the control yoke and is plainly marked. Over.

CUT TO: *the flight deck.*

SPENCER (*into mike*). Yes, Vancouver. I see the auto-pilot switch. Over.

CUT TO: *the Control Room.*

TRELEAVEN (*into mike*). Now, George, in a minute you can unlock the automatic pilot and get the feel of the controls, and we're going to change your course a little. But first listen carefully. When you use the controls they will seem very heavy and sluggish compared with a fighter airplane. But don't worry, that's quite normal. You must take care, though, to watch your air speed carefully and do not let it fall below 120 knots while your wheels and flaps are up. Otherwise you will stall. Now, do you have someone up there who can work the radio to leave you free for flying? Over.

CUT TO: *the flight deck.*

SPENCER (*into mike*). Yes, Vancouver. I have the Stewardess here with me and she will take over the radio now. I am going to unlock the automatic pilot. Over.

(*To* STEWARDESS *as he depresses the auto-pilot release.*)

Well, here we go.

(*Feeling the controls,* SPENCER *eases into a left turn. Then straightening out, he eases the control column slightly forward and back.*)

CUT TO: *the Control Room.*

TRELEAVEN'S VOICE.   Hullo 714. How are you making out, George? Have you got the feel of her yet?

CUT TO: *the flight deck.*

SPENCER.   Tell him I'm on manual now and trying out some gentle turns.

STEWARDESS (*into mike*). Hullo Vancouver. We are on manual now and trying out some gentle turns.

CUT TO: *the Control Room.*

TRELEAVEN (*into mike*).   Hullo George Spencer. Try the effect of fore-and-aft control on your air speed. To begin with, close your throttles slightly and bring your air speed back to 160. Adjust the trim as you go along. But watch that air speed closely. Remember to keep it well above 120. Over.

CUT TO: *the flight deck.*

SPENCER (*tensely. Still feeling out the controls*). Tell him okay.

STEWARDESS (*into mike*).   Okay Vancouver. We are doing as you say.

TRELEAVEN'S VOICE (*after a pause*). Hullo 714. How does she handle, George?

SPENCER (*disgustedly*). Tell him sluggish like a wet sponge.

STEWARDESS.   Sluggish like a wet sponge, Vancouver.

CUT TO: *the Control Room. There is a momentary relaxing of tension as* CAPTAIN TRELEAVEN *and the group around him exchange grins.*

TRELEAVEN (*into mike*).   Hullo George Spencer. That

would be a natural feeling because you were used to handling smaller airplanes. The thing you have got to remember is that there is a bigger lag in the effect of control movements on air speed, compared with what you were used to before. Do you understand that? Over.

CUT TO: *the flight deck.*

SPENCER. Tell him I understand.

STEWARDESS (*into mike*). Hullo Vancouver. Yes, he understands. Over.

CUT TO: *the Control Room.*

TRELEAVEN (*into mike*). Hullo George Spencer. Because of that lag in air speed you must avoid any violent movements of the controls, such as you used to make in your fighter airplanes. If you *do* move the controls violently, you will overcorrect and be in trouble. Is that understood? Over.

CUT TO: *the flight deck.*

SPENCER (*nodding, beginning to perspire*). Tell him—yes, I understand.

STEWARDESS (*into mike*). Yes Vancouver. Your message is understood. Over.

CUT TO: *the Control Room.*

TRELEAVEN (*into mike*). Hullo George Spencer. Now I want you to feel how the ship handles at lower speeds when the flaps and wheels are down. But don't do anything until I give you the instructions. Is that clear? Over.

CUT TO: *the flight deck.*

SPENCER. Tell him okay: let's have the instructions.

STEWARDESS (*into mike*). Hullo Vancouver. Yes, we understand. Go ahead with the instructions. Over.

TRELEAVEN'S VOICE. First of all, throttle back slightly, get your air speed steady at 160 knots, and adjust your trim to maintain level flight. Then tell me when you're ready. Over.

SPENCER. Watch that air speed, Janet. You'll have to call

if off to me when we land, so you may as well start practising.

STEWARDESS. It's 200 now . . . 190 . . . 185 . . . 180 . . . 175 . . . 175 . . . 165 . . . 155 . . . 150 . . . (*Alarmed.*) That's too low! He said 160!

SPENCER (*tensely*). I know. I know. Watch it! It's that lag on the air speed I can't get used to.

STEWARDESS. 150 . . . 150 . . . 155 . . . 160 . . . 160 . . . It's steady on 160.

SPENCER. Tell them.

STEWARDESS (*into mike*). Hullo Vancouver. This is 714. Our speed is steady at 160. Over.

CUT TO: *the Control Room.*

TRELEAVEN (*into mike*). Okay 714. Now, George, I want you to put down 20 degrees of flap. But be careful not to make it any more. The flap lever is at the base of the control pedestal and is plainly marked. Twenty degrees will mean moving the lever down to the second notch. Over.

CUT TO: *the flight deck.*

SPENCER. Janet, *you*'ll have to put the flaps down. (*Pointing.*) There's the lever.

TRELEAVEN'S VOICE. Can you see the flap indicator, George? It's near the centre of the main panel.

SPENCER. Here's the indicator he's talking about. When I tell you, push the lever down to the second notch and watch the dial. Okay?

STEWARDESS. Okay.

(*Then with alarm.*)

Oh, look at the air speed! It's down to 125!

(SPENCER *grimaces and pushes the control column forward.*)

SPENCER (*urgently*). Call off the speed! Call off the speed!

STEWARDESS. 140 . . . 150 . . . 160 . . . 170 . . . 175 . . . Can't you get it back to 160?

SPENCER (*straining*). I'm trying! I'm trying! (*Pause.*) There it is.

CUT TO: *the passenger cabin.*

SECOND WOMAN PASSENGER (*frightened*).   Hector! Hector! We're going to crash! I know it! Oh, do something! Do something!

BAIRD.   (*He appears at her elbow.*) Have her take this. It'll help calm her down.

(*Gives pill and cup to* THIRD MALE PASSENGER.)

Try not to worry. That young man at the front is a very experienced pilot. He's just what they call "getting the feel" of the airplane.

(*He moves aft in the cabin.*)

FIRST MALE PASSENGER.   Doctor!

BAIRD.   Yes.

FIRST MALE PASSENGER.   Tell us the truth, Doctor. Have we got a chance? Does this fellow know how to fly this thing?

BAIRD.   We've got all kinds of chances. He's a very experienced pilot, but it's just that he's not used to flying this particular type and he's getting the feel of it.

FOURTH MALE PASSENGER.   You didn't need none of them pills to make me sick. Never mind me dinner. Now Ah'm worried about yesterday's breakfast.

CUT TO: *the flight deck.*

STEWARDESS (*into mike*).   Hullo Vancouver. Air speed is 160 and we are ready to put down the flaps. Over.

CUT TO: *the Control Room.*

TRELEAVEN (*into mike*).   Okay 714. Go ahead with your flaps. But be careful—only 20 degrees. Then, when you have 20 degrees down, bring back the air speed to 140, adjust your trim, and call me again. Over.

CUT TO: *the flight deck.*

SPENCER.   Okay Janet—flaps down! 20 degrees.

(*The* STEWARDESS *pushes down the flap lever to its second notch.*)

Tell them we've got the flaps down, and the air speed's coming to 140.

STEWARDESS (*into mike*). Hullo Vancouver. This is 714. The flaps are down and our air speed is 140.

CUT TO: *the Control Room.*

TRELEAVEN.   All right 714. Now the next thing is to put the wheels down. Are you still maintaining level flight?

CUT TO: *the flight deck.*

SPENCER.   Tell him—more or less.

STEWARDESS (*into mike*). Hullo Vancouver. More or less.

CUT TO: *the Control Room.*

RADIO OPERATOR.   This guy's got a sense of humour.

BURDICK.   That's a *real* help.

TRELEAVEN (*into mike*).   Okay 714. Try to keep your altitude steady and your speed at 140. Then when you *are* ready, put down the landing gear and let your speed come back to 120. You will have to advance your throttle setting to maintain that air speed, and also adjust your trim. Is that understood? Over.

CUT TO: *the flight deck.*

SPENCER.   Ask him—what about the propeller controls and mixture?

STEWARDESS (*into mike*). Hullo Vancouver. What about the propeller controls and mixture?   Over.

CUT TO: *the Control Room.*

CONTROLLER.   He's thinking, anyway.

TRELEAVEN (*into mike*).   Leave them alone for the time being. Just concentrate on holding that air speed steady with the wheels and flaps down. Over.

CUT TO: *the flight deck.*

SPENCER.   Wheels down, Janet, and call off the air speed.

STEWARDESS. (*Puts landing gear down.*) 140 . . . 145 . . . 140 . . . 135 . . . 130 . . . 125 . . . 120 . . . 115. . . . The speed's too low!

SPENCER. Keep calling it!

STEWARDESS. 115 . . . 120 . . . 120. . . . Steady on 120.

CUT TO: *the Control Room.*

TRELEAVEN (*into mike*). Hullo George Spencer. Your wheels should be down by now and look for three green lights to show that they're locked. Over.

CUT TO: *the flight deck.*

SPENCER. Are they on?

STEWARDESS. Yes—all three lights are green.

SPENCER. Tell them.

STEWARDESS (*into mike*). Hullo Vancouver. Yes, there are three green lights.

CUT TO: *the Control Room.*

TRELEAVEN. Okay 714, now let's put down full flap so that you can feel how the airplane will handle when you're landing. As soon as full flap is down, bring your air speed back to 110 knots and trim to hold it steady. Adjust your throttle setting to hold your altitude. Is that understood? Over.

CUT TO: *the flight deck.*

SPENCER. Tell him "yes".

STEWARDESS (*into mike*). Yes Vancouver. That is understood.

SPENCER. Full flap, Janet! Push the lever all the way down, and call off the air speed.

STEWARDESS. 120 . . . 115 . . . 115 . . . 110 . . . 110 . . .

SPENCER. Okay, tell 'em we've got full flap and air speed 110, and she still handles like a sponge, only more so.

STEWARDESS (*into mike*). Hullo Vancouver. We have full flap, and air speed is 110. And the pilot says she still handles like a sponge, only more so.

CUT TO: *the Control Room. Again there is a momentary sense of relief.*

TRELEAVEN (*into mike*). That's nice going, George. Now I'm going to give you instructions for holding your height and air speed while you raise the flaps and landing gear. Then we'll run through the whole procedure again.

CUT TO: *the flight deck.*

SPENCER.   Again! I don't know if my nerves'll stand it.

    (*Pause.*)

All right. Tell him okay.

DISSOLVE TO: *Control Room clock showing 2:55.*

DISSOLVE TO: *Control Room clock showing 5:20.*

DISSOLVE TO: *the Control Room.* CAPTAIN TRELEAVEN *is still seated in front of the transmitter, but has obviously been under strain. He now has his coat off and his tie loosened and there is an empty carton of coffee beside him.* BURDICK *and the* CONTROLLER *are in background, watching tensely. A phone rings and the* CONTROLLER *answers it. He makes a note and passes it to* TRELEAVEN.

TRELEAVEN (*into mike*). Hullo Flight 714. Our flying practice has slowed you down and you are later than we expected. You are now 12 minutes' flying time from Vancouver Airport, but it's getting light, so your landing will be in daylight. You should be able to see us at any minute. Do you see the airport beacon? Over.

STEWARDESS' VOICE.   Yes, we see the airport beacon. Over.

TRELEAVEN.   Okay George, now you've practised everything we need for a landing. You've flown the ship with wheels and flaps down, and you know how she handles. Your fuel feeds are checked and you're all set to come in. You won't hear from me again for a few minutes because I'm moving to the Control Tower so I'll be able to see you on the circuit and approach. Is that clear? Over.

STEWARDESS' VOICE.   Yes, Vancouver, that is understood. Over.

TRELEAVEN.   All right, George.   Continue to approach at two thousand feet on your present heading and wait for instructions.   We'll let you know the runway to use at the last minute because the wind is shifting.   Don't forget we want you to do at least one dummy run, and then go round again so you'll have practice in making the landing approach.   Over.

>   (*He mops his forehead with a crumpled handkerchief.*)

CUT TO: *the flight deck.* SPENCER, *too, has his coat off and tie loosened.   His hair is ruffled and the strain is plainly beginning to tell on him.   The* STEWARDESS *is still in the co-pilot's seat and* BAIRD *is standing behind them both.   The* STEWARDESS *is about to acknowledge the last radio message, but* SPENCER *stops her.*

SPENCER.   I'll take it, Janet.

>   (*Into mike.*)

No dice, Vancouver.   We're coming straight in and the first time is "it".   Dr. Baird is here beside me.   He reports two of the passengers and the First Officer are in critical condition, and we must land in the next few minutes.   The doctor asks that you have stomach pumps and oxygen equipment ready. Over.

CUT TO: *the Control Room.*

BURDICK.   He mustn't!   We need time!

TRELEAVEN.   It's his decision.   By all the rules he's in command of the airplane.

>   (*Into mike.*)

714, your message is understood.   Good luck to us all.   Listening out.

>   (*To* BURDICK *and* CONTROLLER.)

Let's go!

DISSOLVE TO: *the flight deck.*

SPENCER. This is it, Doctor. You'd better go back now and make sure everybody's strapped in tight. Are both the pilots in seats?

BAIRD. Yes.

SPENCER. How about the passengers who aren't sick? Are they worried?

BAIRD. A little, but there's no panic. I exaggerated your qualifications. I'd better go. Good luck.

SPENCER (*with ironic grin*). Thanks.

DISSOLVE TO: *the Control Tower, Vancouver Airport. It is a glass-enclosed area, with radio panels and other equipment, and access is by a stairway from below. It is now daylight and the* TOWER CONTROLLER *is looking skywards, using binoculars. There is the sound of hurried feet on the stairway and* TRELEAVEN, *the* CONTROLLER *and* BURDICK *emerge in that order.*

TOWER CONTROLLER. There he is!

    (TRELEAVEN *picks up a second pair of binoculars, looks through them quickly, then puts them down.*)

TRELEAVEN. All right—let's make our decision on the runway. What's it to be?

TOWER CONTROLLER. Zero eight. It's pretty well into wind now, though there'll be a slight cross-wind from the right. It's also the longest.

TRELEAVEN (*into mike*). Hullo Flight 714. This is Martin Treleaven in Vancouver Tower. Do you read me? Over.

CUT TO: *the flight deck.*

STEWARDESS (*into mike*). Yes, Vancouver Tower. Loud and clear. Over.

CUT TO: *the Tower.*

TRELEAVEN (*crisply, authoritatively, yet calmly*). From here on, do not acknowledge any further transmissions unless you wish to ask a question. You are now ready to join the airport circuit. The runway for landing is zero eight. That means you are now cross-wind and will shortly make a left turn on to the down-wind leg. Begin now to lose height to one thousand feet. Throttle back slightly and make your descent at 400 feet a minute. Let your air speed come back to 160 knots and hold it steady there. . . . Air speed 160.

CONTROLLER (*reaching for phone*). Runway is zero eight. All vehicles stand by near the extreme south end. Do not, repeat not, go down the runway until the aircraft has passed by you because it may swing off. Is that clear? (*Pause.*) Right.

CUT TO: FILM INSERT—*fire trucks and ambulances are manned and move away with sirens wailing.*

CUT TO: *the flight deck.* SPENCER *is pushing the throttles forward and the tempo of the motors increases.*

SPENCER.   Tell them we're at one thousand feet and levelling off.

STEWARDESS (*into mike*). Vancouver Tower. We are now at one thousand feet and levelling off. Over.

TRELEAVEN'S VOICE.   Now let's have 20 degrees of flap. Do not acknowledge this message.

SPENCER.   20 degrees of flap, Janet.

(*The* STEWARDESS *reaches for flap lever and pushes it down while she watches the flap indicator.*)

TRELEAVEN'S VOICE.   When you have your flaps down, bring your air speed back slowly to 140 knots, adjust your trim, and begin to make a left turn on to the down-wind leg. When you have turned, fly parallel with the runway you see on your left. I repeat—air speed 140 and begin a left turn.

CUT TO: *close-up of instrument panel showing artificial horizon and air-speed indicator. The air speed first comes back to 140, goes slightly below it, then returns to 140. The artificial horizon tilts so that the airplane symbol is banked to the left.*

CUT TO: *the flight deck.* SPENCER *has control yoke turned to the left and is adjusting the throttles.*

CUT TO: *the Tower.*

TRELEAVEN. Watch your height! Don't make that turn so steep! Watch your height! More throttle! Keep the air speed on 140 and the nose up! Get back that height! You need a thousand feet!

CUT TO: *the flight deck.* SPENCER *eases the throttles open and the tempo of the motors increases. He eases the control column forward, then pulls back again.*

CUT TO: *close-up of climb and descent indicator. The instrument first shows a descent of 500 feet per minute drop, then a climb of 600 feet, and then gradually begins to level off.*

CUT TO: *the Control Tower.* (CAPTAIN TRELEAVEN *is looking out through binoculars, the others anxiously behind him.*)

TRELEAVEN (*angrily*). He can't fly the bloody thing! Of course he can't fly it! You're watching fifty people going to their deaths!

BURDICK (*shouting*). Keep talking to him! Keep talking! Tell him what to do!

TRELEAVEN (*urgently, into mike*). Spencer, you can't come straight in! You've got to do some circuits, and practise that approach. You've enough fuel left for three hours' flying. Stay up, man! Stay up!

CUT TO: *the flight deck.*

SPENCER. Give it to me!

(*taking the mike. Then tensely.*)

Listen, down there! I'm coming in! Do you hear me?—I'm coming in. There are people up here who'll die in less than an hour, never mind three. I may bend your precious airplane a bit, but I'll get it down. Now get on with the landing check. I'm putting the gear down now.

(*To* STEWARDESS.)

Wheels down, Janet!

> (*The* STEWARDESS *selects landing gear "down" and*
> SPENCER *reaches for the throttles.*)

CUT TO: *airplane in flight, daylight. Its landing wheels come down.*

CUT TO: *the flight deck.*

STEWARDESS (*looks out of window, then back to* SPENCER.)
Wheels down and three green lights.

CUT TO: *the Tower.*

BURDICK.   He may not be able to fly worth a damn, but he's sure got guts.

TRELEAVEN (*into mike*). Increase your throttle setting slightly to hold your air speed now that the wheels are down. Adjust your trim and keep that height at a thousand feet. Now check your propeller setting and your mixture—propellers to fully fine; mixture to full rich. I'll repeat that. Propellers to fully fine; mixture to full rich.

CUT TO: *the flight deck.*

SPENCER (*to himself, as he moves controls*). Propellers fully fine. Mixture full rich. (*To* STEWARDESS.) Janet, let me hear the air speed.

STEWARDESS.   130 . . . 125 . . . 120 . . . 125 . . . 130 . . .

CUT TO: *the Tower.*

TRELEAVEN (*into mike*). You are well down-wind now. You can begin to make a left turn on the cross-wind leg. As you turn, begin losing height to 800 feet and let your air speed come back to 120. I'll repeat that. Start a left turn. Lose height to 800. Air speed 120.

> (*He picks up binoculars, then puts them down hurriedly*
> *and takes mike again.*)

You are losing height too fast! You are losing height too fast! Open up! Open! Hold your height now! Keep your air speed at 120.

CUT TO: *the flight deck.*

STEWARDESS. 110 . . . 110 . . . 105 . . . 110 . . . 110 . . . 120 . . . 120. . . . Steady at 120.

SPENCER. What a miserable insensitive wagon this is! It doesn't respond! It doesn't respond at all!

STEWARDESS. 125 . . . 130 . . . 130. . . . Steady on 130.

CUT TO: *the Tower.*

TRELEAVEN. Start your turn into wind now to line up with the runway. Make it a gentle turn—you've plenty of time. As you turn, begin losing height, about 400 feet a minute. But be ready to correct if you lose height too fast. Adjust your trim as you go. That's right! Keep turning! As soon as you've completed the turn, put down full flap and bring your air speed to 115. I'll repeat that. Let down 400 feet a minute. Full flap. Then air speed 115.

> (*To the others.*)

Is everything ready on the field?

CONTROLLER. As ready as we'll ever be.

TRELEAVEN. Then this is it. In sixty seconds we'll know.

CUT TO: *the flight deck.*

SPENCER (*muttering*). Not quite yet . . . a little more . . . that should do it.

> (*As he straightens out of the turn.*)

Janet, give me full flap!

> (*The* STEWARDESS *reaches for the flap control, pushes it down and leaves it down.*)

Height and air speed!

STEWARDESS. 700 feet, speed 130 . . . 600 feet, speed 120 . . . 500 feet, speed 105. . . . We're going down too quickly!

SPENCER. I know! I know!

> (*He pushes throttle forward and the tempo of the motors increases.*)

Keep watching it!

STEWARDESS. 450 feet, speed 100 . . . 400 feet, speed 100 . . .

CUT TO: FILM INSERT—*airplane (DC-4) with wheels and flaps down, on a landing approach.*

CUT TO: *the Tower.*

TRELEAVEN (*urgently into mike*). Open up! Open up! You're losing height too fast! (*Pause.*) Watch the air speed! Your nose is too high! Open up quickly or she'll stall! Open up, man! open up!

BURDICK. He heard you. He's recovering.

TRELEAVEN (*into mike*). Maintain that height until you get closer in to the runway. But be ready to ease off gently. . . . You can start now. . . . Let down again. . . . That looks about right. . . . But watch the air speed. Your nose is creeping up. . . . (*More steadily.*) Now listen carefully, George. There's a slight cross-wind on the runway and your drift is to the right. Straighten up just before you touch down, and be ready with more right rudder as soon as you *are* down. And remember to cut the switches if you land too fast. (*Pause.*) All right, your approach is good. . . . Get ready to round out—now! (*Pause. Then urgently.*) You're coming in too fast! Lift the nose up!

CUT TO: *the flight deck.*

TRELEAVEN'S VOICE. Lift the nose up! Back on the throttles! Throttles right back! Hold her off! Not too much! Not too much! Be ready for that cross-wind! Ease her down, *now*! Ease her down!

CUT TO: FILM INSERT—*a landing wheel skimming over a runway and about to touch down. As it makes contact, rock picture to show instability.*

CUT TO: *the flight deck. There is a heavy thud and* SPENCER *and the* STEWARDESS *are jolted in their seats. There is another, another, and another. Everything shakes.*

SPENCER (*shouting*). Cut the switches! Cut the switches!

(*The* STEWARDESS *reaches upward and pulls down the cage of the master switches. Instantly the heavy roar of motors stops, but there is still a whistling because the airplane is travelling fast.* SPENCER *stretches out his legs as he puts his full strength into applying the airplane toe brakes, at the same time pulling back on the control column. There is a screaming of rubber on pavement, and* SPENCER *and the* STEWARDESS *are thrown violently to the left. Then, except for the hum of the radio and gyros, there is silence as the airplane stops.*)

SPENCER (*disgustedly*). I groundlooped! I did a lousy stinking groundloop! We're turned right around the way we came!

STEWARDESS. But we're all right! We're all right! You did it! You did it!

(*She leans over and kisses him.* SPENCER *pulls off his radio headset. Outside there is a rising note of approaching sirens. Then, from the headset we hear* CAPTAIN TRELEAVEN's *voice.*)

TRELEAVEN'S VOICE (*exuberantly*). Hullo George Spencer. That was probably the lousiest landing in the history of this airport. So don't ever ask us for a job as a pilot. But there are some people here who'd like to shake you by the hand, and later on we'll buy you a drink. Stay right where you are, George! We're coming over.

FADE OUT.

THE END

SUCCESS STORY

Arthur Hailey was born in 1920 in Luton, England; he had his schooling there. He was a Royal Air Force pilot during World War II, and after the war served as an Air Ministry Staff Officer in London. Finding peace-time military service dull, he resigned from the RAF in 1947 to emigrate to Canada. For six years he was associate editor, then editor, of *Bus and Truck Transport*, a trade magazine. Then he became sales promotion manager for a truck company. (Note that Spencer in *Flight Into Danger* was a truck salesman.) On May 1, 1956, he set up his own advertising agency. He disposed of it in 1958 in order to devote all his time to writing.

In January, 1955, while he was sales promotion manager, he took the step which led him into creative writing. He had an interesting, well-paid job, but there were moments when he had a sense of "something lacking". One day, on impulse, he dropped into a firm of industrial placement consultants and arranged for a series of psychological aptitude tests. The tests cost him a hundred dollars but he does not regret the expenditure. One paragraph in the report read as follows: "The subject has a marked flair for the unusual and dramatic. He has a great deal of creativity which seeks expression and he needs an outlet for this either in the work area or avocationally. He would do well as a writer and may be wasted in industry." For some time he did nothing about this. Then he decided to write a play for television. *Flight Into Danger* was the result.

In the next three years Hailey wrote a dozen successful television plays. Typical of these were *Time Lock* (1956) which is about a boy locked in a bank vault sealed with a time lock; *Course for Collision* (1957) about a mythical U.S. president on a desperate mission to Moscow, who orders his plane to collide with a Soviet bomber in order to save New York from an atomic bomb; and *Death Minus One* (1958) which had its source in news stories about unexploded bombs and about two children trapped for hours beneath the ruins of a bombed-out church.

As this is being written, Hailey's latest endeavour is a novel entitled *The Final Diagnosis*, which has been chosen as the October, 1959, selection of the Literary Guild of America. He is now at work on a novel, with a western Canada setting, to be published in 1960.

Here is surely an almost incredible success story of our time. At thirty-five years of age a young advertising executive, with no university education, with limited writing experience save in a technical field, and no knowledge of the theatre or of television save that gained by occasional playgoing and by watching TV drama in his own living-room, suddenly turns to creative writing. He skyrockets to fame with his first play. For a while he thinks his initial successes may be only a flash in the pan; he gives a part of his time to writing and keeps on with his advertising business. But now, after three and a half years, his reputation is still as high, and he is beginning to make a name for himself in the field of fiction. He is a full-time writer. *Time Magazine* has described him as "one of the six top television playwrights in the world", and the *Radio Times* as "the television writer *par excellence*". He has maintained a gross income of between $50,000 and $100,000 a year since he started to write. He has sold everything that he has written. He feels secure and confident now, as he looks toward the future. He is doing what he wants most to do.

A WRITER'S WAY OF LIFE

Has his success changed Arthur Hailey? As I write this, he is living in a comfortable ranch house in Scarborough, a suburb of Toronto, with his wife, Sheila, and three children, Jane, Steven and Diane. "Our standard of living has not changed very much," he told me. "We travel a little more. We have built a cottage in Haliburton which we love. But we have no desire to move; we like our neighbours and our children are happy here. I could earn more if I did certain other kinds of writing, but money is not all that important."

"I am glad we feel like this," he went on. "Both my wife and I came from humble circumstances. We want our children to have the university education and many other advantages that we missed. But we try not to spoil them. We want to encourage the sense of thrift in them."

As he talked Arthur Hailey was neither humble nor proud. He was modestly confident, pleased with his new security and grateful for it; he was looking forward to years of creative work ahead of him. "I am doing the job I love doing," he said. "I wasn't before."

"MY PLAYS ARE MEANT TO ENTERTAIN"

Arthur Hailey is a born story-teller. He believes that television plays are meant to entertain. "In the course of entertainment there is no reason why you cannot make a valid point or say something you feel strongly about. This adds feeling and conviction to the story. But you must not moralize. The story must not take second place."

By entertainment Hailey does not mean an escape from life. "A story should reflect life, but should not moralize about it, at least in an obvious way."

One reason why Arthur Hailey's plays give a sense of reality and truth is that he likes to tell a story in which he himself can take part as one of the characters, or sit beside the character as he tells it.

This is one of the reasons why *Flight Into Danger* has such a tremendous appeal. The hero complex is deep in all of us. We see ourselves in George Spencer's place, in the same tense situation. We dream of doing better deeds than we are able to do in real life. We suffer and shine in heroic effort and achievement.

As Hailey reaches full stature as a TV dramatist and, more recently, as a novelist, and as he researches his materials ever more thoroughly and allows his characters and incidents to grow from this authentic material, it is my belief that his insistence on "entertainment" as a criterion of his art will be increasingly difficult to defend. For while he will always remain a born story-teller, the point of his story and the truth of his characters and setting will at least be as appealing to the reader as the story that is told—perhaps in time more meaningful.

For the present, however, Arthur Hailey maintains that his primary purpose is to entertain. And this is the chief reason why he will not write for the theatre. The theatre, to him, is too "discursive". He believes that the story in a play takes second place to "moralizing" about problems and ideas.

TIPS FOR WRITERS

In his early plays, like *Flight Into Danger*, a dramatic situation flashed suddenly into Hailey's consciousness. *Time Lock* was born in the moment when his neighbour, a bank manager, showed him the vault in a new bank and Hailey asked what would happen if a child were trapped within it. Very little research was needed for *Flight Into Danger* since Hailey had been a pilot himself; but with *Time Lock* he spent two weeks interviewing bank managers, welders, a doctor and a retired vault expert. The actual writing took only four days.

In his later work Hailey has followed a different pattern. He does a great deal of research in a given field, reading all he can and interviewing (with his tape recorder) as many people as possible who can supply him with valuable material. On one story project he spent an entire week-end in the home of a Scotland Yard detective and his family to find out what a policeman was really like off duty. On another occasion he went shopping with an atomic scientist who was buying his wife's groceries.

His plan is "to dig, dig, and keep on digging around the general subject matter". At first, he warns, the going will be slow. "But invariably, before long, ideas, incidents and characters will reveal themselves like successive veins of gold, proving once more the hoary adage that truth has the edge on fiction."

Hailey is a master in the art of creating suspense, and his advice on the subject is interesting. He suggests that one should never consciously strive to create tension. Suspense is achieved by "mild statements, underplaying and calmness." Excitement may often appear ridiculous and destroy suspense. "If a story is told in sequence, tidily, and with the ultimate issue left in doubt, suspense will usually create itself."

Finally a word of advice to the would-be writer about dialogue. It cannot be taught, says our author. Each writer must learn how to create his own effective dialogue—"patiently, by listening, by surreptitious note-taking, and by practice."

"Surreptitious note-taking" suggests George Bernard Shaw's delightful satire at Shakespeare's expense, *The Dark Lady of the Sonnets*, in which he accuses the bard of securing his most famous lines by eavesdropping, scribbling into his notebook the words of his Dark Lady, a Beefeater, and even Her Majesty Queen Elizabeth. The idea of one of Shakespeare's most famous scenes was born, according to Shaw, when he saw the Queen walk in her sleep; he merely set down the words she spoke!

So if you want to be a writer you must begin to listen to the patterns of speech around you. Patiently you must study and practise the delicate and difficult art of dialogue. You must learn to choose words and cadences which are true to the character and mood of each speaker in each situation. "The trick—if you can do it—," says Hailey, "is to keep in mind a constant mental picture of your characters, then have them interpret each basic thought in the manner you think they might: warmly, acidly, indifferently—whichever fits."

I REMEMBER MAMA

JOHN van DRUTEN

Adapted from Kathryn Forbes' **book**
Mama's Bank Account

MAMA'S BANK ACCOUNT

Our second play is a dramatization of six of the short stories in *Mama's Bank Account*, Kathryn Forbes' beguiling volume of sketches of life in San Francisco early in the century.

Mama's Bank Account had a modest beginning. In the Toronto *Star Weekly* of January 18, 1941, there appeared a short story called *Mama and Her Bank Account*. Ten weeks later, in the issue of March 29, a second one was printed called *Mama and the Idle Roomer*. The *Reader's Digest* reprinted both of these.

The response was immediate and tremendous. Thousands wrote, asking for more of these stories of Mama and her family, and in the spring of 1943 *Mama's Bank Account* was published.

The author, Kathryn Forbes, was born in San Francisco, March 20, 1909. She took her pen name, Forbes, from her paternal grandmother; her real name before her marriage in 1926 to Robert Edward McLean was Kathryn Anderson. Her grandmother on her mother's side was a Norwegian immigrant; the young Kathryn had the blue eyes and fair hair of her Viking forebears. She was a housewife, looking after her husband and two children and writing short stories and radio plays in her spare time, when the sudden and unexpected success of these first two stories, based on reminiscences of her childhood, encouraged her to write the series which brought her fame.

After the Broadway opening of *I Remember Mama* an interviewer asked Miss Forbes what her family thought of the book. "Well," she replied, "one of my aunts said, 'It's a very nice book, Kathryn, but I don't see what all the shouting is about. Anyone in the family could have written it.'"

In a letter to the editor Miss Forbes tells of her activities since writing *Mama's Bank Account*. Her second novel, *Transfer Point*, was published in 1947; she is now working on a third. Her short stories—including two more dealing with Mama— have been published in several national magazines. For seven years she was busy with the television serialization of her famous book, starring Peggy Wood as Mama.

In her letter Miss Forbes answered two specific questions. She confirmed the fact that the Toronto *Star Weekly* "in your beautiful Canada" published the first "Mama" stories. The second question was whether she drew Mama from her grandmother or from her mother. Her answer: "My maternal grandmother was mainly the prototype of Mama, but there was a lot of my own mother in the book."

If you have not already done so, I hope you will read *Mama's Bank Account*. If possible, read it soon after you have read the play. It is a fascinating experience to compare the two books. Not only will you learn more about Mama and her family—for there are seventeen short stories, and, as already noted, only six of them are used in the play—but you will also gain new insight into the two literary types, fiction and drama, and the opportunities that each offers for the imaginative revelation of the laughter, bravery, beauty and tenderness of life.

THE PLAY'S HISTORY

An interesting chain of events brought *Mama* to the stage. Everyone has heard of the famous musical comedy team of Rodgers and Hammerstein. In 1944 they were enjoying great success with their first hit, *Oklahoma!*. As the story is told, Mary Rodgers, oldest daughter of Richard Rodgers, the composer, read *Mama's Bank Account* and was thrilled by it. She persuaded her mother to read it, who in turn urged Mrs. Oscar Hammerstein II to do so. Soon the husbands and everyone in the two families had read the book and agreed that it should be turned into a play. The producing firm of Rodgers and Hammerstein was formed to stage it.

One of the best-known playwrights of the English-speaking stage, John van Druten, was asked to make the dramatization. He was not anxious to do so; he was basking in the phenomenal success of his play, *The Voice of the Turtle*. But he agreed to read the book. He, too, was enthusiastic. However, he felt that if the play was to succeed it needed the great actress, Mady Christians, to play Mama. He doubted that she would be interested. This was an older part than any she had attempted; it was also lighter than the classical and serious roles in which she had made her name.

Here was an extraordinary coincidence! Richard Rodgers showed van Druten a letter from Mady Christians in which she urged him (Rodgers) to read *Mama's Bank Account* and asked him, if the book should ever be turned into a play, to recommend her for the title role!

So the play was written, cast and rehearsed. The critics, on the whole, were most enthusiastic, and the play was a tremendous popular success, running for 714 performances.

Included in the distinguished cast, along with Mady Christians and the famous Austrian-born actor Oscar Homolka, who played Uncle Chris, was a young actor named Marlon Brando in the role of Nels, the son.

I Remember Mama had the distinction of being the first stage success brought to radio with its Broadway cast. You can read the hour-long radio version in *Theatre Guild on the Air*, a collection of radio plays which is available in many libraries. You will find the comparison between the stage and radio versions engrossing.

In 1948 RKO Pictures released a widely-acclaimed film version of the play, with Irene Dunne as Mama, Oscar Homolka in his original role of Uncle Chris, Barbara Bel Geddes as Katrin, Sir Cedric Hardwicke as Mr. Hyde and Edgar Bergen as the timid lover, Mr. Thorkelson.

What did the author of *Mama's Bank Account* think of the play and its performance? "I claim," writes Miss Forbes, "the unique distinction of being one author who was very happy with the adaptation, interpretation and presentation of her literary child."

STAGING THE PLAY

The Broadway setting was elaborate, as you can see from the picture on the inside front and back covers. But it can be adapted easily to little theatre and school productions, and to classroom presentations. Basically there are four stages: the stage itself, two small areas down right and left, and the area in front of the curtain.

On the stage we have the kitchen, which is the centre of the family's life. It is a real kitchen, with dresser, chest, window and door, designed to make us believe that it is part of a real home in which real people live, and to give us a sense of permanence and of continuing life.

Notice that the kitchen does not occupy the entire stage. The back door of the house is in the left wall, and we can see people coming and going from the street. In the picture, for example, we have Uncle Chris' ancient automobile and its occupants.

This combination of indoor and outdoor settings is being used increasingly by playwrights to give another dimension to their drama, to increase the sense of reality, and to make possible a dual life on the stage which we in the audience can see and hear, but in which the actors of each group are aware only of what goes on in their own area.

Notice also that the front of the house itself rises above the kitchen, with windows lighted at night, and that behind it (on a painted cloth or backdrop) we can see the houses, telephone poles and hills of San Francisco.

The main stage is used for two other big scenes. It becomes the hospital corridor and Uncle Chris' bedroom. Too many characters appear in both these settings to be crowded on the smaller stages down right and left. Both sets are shallow; they are placed in front of the kitchen wall and its permanent chest, window and dresser.

The settings on the smaller stages, down right and left, are changed swiftly. The scenery used for them merely suggests a place; it is less realistic than that used in the kitchen. A desk makes Katrin's study; a section of wall with roller skates hanging on it and a small kitchen stepladder represents Christine's boudoir. The scenery for these stages, we say, is "indicative"; it merely indicates the locale.

The down right area is Katrin's study. It is here that she writes in her diary and reads from it. It is here that she recalls the scenes which make the play, herself entering into them as a younger girl.

In the Broadway production this area also became Christine's boudoir, a hospital waiting-room, the school stage dressing-room, a telephone booth for Mama and the verandah of Uncle Chris' ranch. These are all associated with the family, or with Uncle Chris. The aunts and strangers appear on the opposite stage, down left. There we have Jenny's kitchen and parlour, Arne's hospital bedroom, the drug store, park bench and hotel lobby.

The most fascinating of the four stage areas is the one down stage, in front of the main curtain. It is a no man's land; it is everyone's land. It has no scenery. Our imaginations must create the settings: the approach to Katrin's study, the street leading to the drug store, the lawn beside the porch of Uncle Chris' ranch house, the verandah before his front door.

This area has qualities of ritual. Katrin sits on the front steps while Mr. Hyde reads to the family, and moves easily into her world of recollection and dreams. Here she shares with us her thoughts and memories.

Thus in one production we have three kinds of staging: the realistic scenes in the kitchen; the semi-realistic scenes on the small stages down right and down left; and the non-realistic scenes down stage. As you read or act the play decide for yourself whether these three styles merge successfully. One critic, in reviewing the Broadway production, said that they didn't, but I have not met anyone who saw the play in New York who agreed with him.

If you are acting the play in the classroom, set out the areas carefully. The main stage is, of course, at the front of the classroom. The best way to provide for the down right and down left areas is to remove one or two desks or chairs at the head of the inner and outer rows; if this cannot be done, an area at the extreme right and left at the front of the room will have to be used. The chairs at the second desks from the front in each row can be removed to provide the down stage area.

A HEART-WARMING PLAY

In 1944, when *I Remember Mama* was produced on Broadway, the Second World War was in progress. Unlike most of the plays presented that year, it made no reference to the war. One critic labelled it "escapist entertainment", and another "a pleasantly undisturbing evening in the theatre".

The fact that while seeing it one "escaped" from the tensions of the war may have been one of the reasons why it was popular when it first appeared. But there was a deeper reason why the play appealed in war time. In a violent and chaotic world, the family is a rock to cling to. *I Remember Mama* celebrates the family. It celebrates the homely virtues of honesty, courage, sympathy, understanding and love. The best critics have recognized from the first its glowing warmth, its humanity and simplicity.

These are qualities which are just as important in peace as in war. The play's continued and increasing popularity is proof of this. It grows on us with the years. It endures.

A famous theatre critic, John Gassner, has pointed out that *I Remember Mama* adds to our "spiritual armoury", particularly with its portraits of Mama and Uncle Chris. Mama is a gallant figure, with her great tenderness of heart, her forthrightness, her wit and wisdom. She is completely endearing. She is the rudder of the family boat, steering it through the most troubled waters. Her resourcefulness, her bluntness, her near unscrupulousness prevent the portrait from becoming sentimental. For example, having seen Dagmar once in the hospital, she will not try to see her again because it is "against the rules". She is brave, amusing, lovable. Her wisdom often is intuitive. We are stronger and better for knowing her.

As striking in a different way is the terrifying, lonely Uncle Chris, that black Norwegian, "with his black hair and fierce mustache". He is overwhelmingly gifted for life, larger than life. With his pain, his tragic loneliness, his kindliness to crippled children, and his fierce blustering humour, he is a memorable figure.

Thus the critics who labelled *I Remember Mama* merely as "escapist" and "pleasantly undisturbing" were surely wrong. The simple and humble qualities of life are the enduring ones; you have to be mature to appreciate them. As Wilella Waldorf wrote of the play in the New York *Post*, ". . . Mr. van Druten has seen to it that it has quality and a certain quiet distinction that arises from Mama herself and her way of living and bringing up a family."

The play performs a service for us, also, in disarming the prejudices against newcomers of those of us who have lived in the new world for one or more generations. The strength of the new world is that it has attracted the best folk from many lands, people who have come because they are strong in spirit and have courage and idealism. There are no finer people than Mama and her family; in manners alone they have much to teach us, with their Old-World courtesy, the obedience of the children to their parents, and their respect for their elders; they and others like them have made and are making a rich contribution to our civilization.

Finally, before you start to read the play, I should like to suggest that one of its qualities which will, I hope, make a deep impression on you is its statement of the importance of literature and of the great tradition of beauty, imagination and idealism that is enshrined in our finest books. This is one reason we are particularly happy to have *I Remember Mama* included in our collection. You will realize, with Mama, that there is "so much we can learn". She recognizes the riches that are in the great books. At the climax of the dramatic scene when she finds out that Mr. Hyde's cheque is worthless, she touches the books he has left and says, "No, he owed us nothing." And later, "He pay with better things than money."

CAST

I Remember Mama was first produced by Messrs. Richard Rodgers and Oscar Hammerstein II at the Shubert Theatre, New Haven, Connecticut, on September 28, 1944, and subsequently at the Music Box Theatre, New York City, on October 19, 1944, with the following cast:

KATRIN	Joan Tetzel
MAMA	Mady Christians
PAPA	Richard Bishop
DAGMAR	Carolyn Hummel
CHRISTINE	Frances Heflin
MR. HYDE	Oswald Marshall
NELS	Marlon Brando
AUNT TRINA	Adrienne Gessner
AUNT SIGRID	Ellen Mahar
AUNT JENNY	Ruth Gates
UNCLE CHRIS	Oscar Homolka
A WOMAN	Louise Lorimer
MR. THORKELSON	Bruno Wick
DR. JOHNSON	William Pringle
ARNE	Robert Antoine
A NURSE	Marie Gale
ANOTHER NURSE	Dorothy Elder
SODA CLERK	Frank Babcock
MADELINE	Cora Smith
DOROTHY SCHILLER	Ottilie Kruger
FLORENCE DANA MOORHEAD	Josephine Brown
BELL-BOY	Herbert Kenwith

Scrub woman, nurses, doctors, and hotel guests.

The action passes in and around San Francisco some years ago.

Staged by Mr. van Druten
Settings and lighting by George Jenkins
Costumes designed by Lucinda Ballard

I REMEMBER MAMA

ACT I

(The stage directions in this script are a description of the method of presentation used in the production at The Music Box Theatre, New York City. It is possible that these could be altered or simplified in the case of other productions, if necessary.)

The period of the play is around 1910.

On either side of the stage, down front, are two small turntables, left and right, on which the shorter front scenes are played against very simplified backgrounds. As each scene finishes the lights dim and the table revolves out, leaving an unobstructed view of the main stage. The main stage is raised by two steps, above which traveller curtains open and close.

When the curtain rises, KATRIN, *in a spotlight, is seated at a desk on the right turntable, facing the audience. She is writing and smoking a cigarette.* KATRIN *is somewhere in her early twenties. She should be played by an actress who is small in stature, and capable of looking sufficiently a child not to break the illusion in subsequent scenes. She is a blonde. Her hair, when we see her first, is in a modern "up" style, capable of being easily loosened to fall to shoulder length for the childhood scenes. She wears a very short dress, the skirt of which is concealed for the prologue by the desk behind which she is seated.*

KATRIN *writes in silence for a few moments, then puts down her pen, takes up her manuscript, and begins to read aloud what she has written.*

KATRIN *(reading).* "For as long as I could remember, the house on Steiner Street had been home. Papa and Mama had both been born in Norway, but they came to San Francisco because Mama's sisters were here. All of us were born here. Nels, the oldest and the only boy—my sister Christine—and the littlest sister, Dagmar."

(She puts down her manuscript and looks out front.)

It's funny, but when I look back, I always see Nels and Christine and myself looking almost as we do today. I guess that's because the people you see all the time stay the same age in your head. Dagmar's different. She was always the baby—so I see her as a baby. Even Mama—it's funny, but I always see Mama as around forty. She couldn't *always* have been forty.

(She puts out her cigarette, picks up her manuscript and starts to read again.)

"Besides us, there was our boarder, Mr. Hyde. Mr. Hyde was an Englishman who had once been an actor, and Mama was very impressed by his flowery talk and courtly manners. He used to read aloud to us in the evenings. But first and foremost, I remember Mama."

(The light dims down, leaving KATRIN *only faintly visible. Lights come up on the main stage, revealing the house on Steiner Street—a kitchen room. It has a back flat, with a dresser C., holding china. On either side of the dresser is a door; the one to the R. leads to the pantry; the one to the L. to the rest of the house. The L. wall is a short one. It is the wall of the house, and contains a door upstage leading into the street, being presumably the back door of the*

*house, but the one most commonly used as the
entry-door. Beyond it the street is visible, with a
single lamp-post L., just outside the house. Behind
the room rises the house itself with upper windows
lighted, and behind it a painted backdrop of the San
Francisco hills, houses, and telegraph posts.*

*The furniture of the kitchen is simple. A table C.,
with two chairs above it, armchairs at either end,
and a low bench below it. Against the R. wall upstage, a large stove; below it another armchair. The
window is below the door in the L. wall and has a
low Norwegian chest under it.*)

KATRIN'S VOICE (*continuing in the half-dark, as the scene
is revealed*). "I remember that every Saturday night Mama
would sit down by the kitchen table and count out the money
Papa had brought home in the little envelope."

(*By now the tableau is revealed in full, and the light
on* KATRIN *dwindles further. The picture is as she
described.* MAMA—*looking around forty—is in the
armchair R. of the table, emptying the envelope of
its silver dollars and smaller coins.* PAPA—*looking
a little older than* MAMA—*stands above her. His
English throughout is better than hers, with less
accent.*)

MAMA. You call the children, Lars. Is good they should
know about money.

(PAPA *goes to door back L., and calls.*)

PAPA. Children! Nels—Christine—Katrin!

CHILDREN'S VOICES (*off, answering*). Coming, Papa!

MAMA. You call loud for Katrin. She is in her study,
maybe.

PAPA. She is where?

MAMA. Katrin make the old attic under the roof into a
study.

PAPA (*amused*). So? (*Shouting*) Katrin! Katrin!

KATRIN (*still at her desk, down front*). Yes, Papa. I heard.

PAPA (*returning to the room*). A study now, huh? What does Katrin study?

MAMA. I think Katrin wants to be author.

PAPA. Author?

MAMA. Stories she will write. For the magazines. And books, too, maybe, one day.

PAPA (*taking out his pipe*). Is good pay to be an author?

MAMA. I don't know. For magazines, I think maybe yes. For books, I think no.

PAPA. Then she become writer for magazines.

MAMA. Maybe. But I like she writes books. Like the ones Mr. Hyde reads us.

> (DAGMAR *enters from the pantry. She is a plump child of about eight and carries an alley cat in her arms.*)

Dagmar, you bring that cat in again?

DAGMAR. Sure, she's my Elizabeth—my beautiful Elizabeth!

> (*She crosses to the chest under the window, and sits, nursing the cat.*)

PAPA. Poor Elizabeth looks as if she had been in fight again.

DAGMAR. Not poor Elizabeth. *Brave* Elizabeth. Elizabeth's a Viking cat. She fights for her honour!

PAPA (*exchanging an amused glance with* MAMA). And just what is a cat's honour, little one?

DAGMAR. The honour of being the bravest cat in San Francisco.

> (CHRISTINE *comes back in L. She, like* KATRIN, *should be played by a small young actress, but not a child. Her hair is to her shoulders—her dress short—her age indeterminate. Actually, she is about 13 at this time. She is the cool, aloof, matter-of-fact one of the family.*)

Aren't you, Elizabeth?

CHRISTINE (*sitting above the table*).   That disgusting cat!

DAGMAR.   She's not disgusting. She's beautiful. Beautiful as the dawn!

CHRISTINE.   And when have *you* ever seen the dawn?

DAGMAR.   I haven't seen it, but Mr. Hyde read to us about it.

> (*Mr. Hyde comes in from door back L. He is a slightly seedy, long-haired man in his fifties. Rather of the old-fashioned English "laddie" actor type. He wears a very shabby long overcoat, with a deplorable fur collar, and carries his hat. His accent is English.*)

Didn't you, Mr. Hyde?   Didn't you read to us about the dawn?

MR. HYDE.   I did, my child of joy. The dawn, the rosy-finger-tipped Aurora. . . .

DAGMAR.   When can I get to *see* the dawn, Mama?

MAMA.   Any morning you get up early.

DAGMAR.   Is there a dawn every morning?

MAMA.   Sure.

DAGMAR (*incredulous*).   It's all that beautiful, and it happens every *morning*? Why didn't anyone *tell* me?

MR. HYDE.   My child, that is what the poets are for. To tell you of *all* the beautiful things that are happening every day, and that no one sees until they tell them.

> (*He starts for the door L.*)

MAMA.   You go out, Mr. Hyde?

MR. HYDE.   For a few moments only, dear Madam. To buy myself a modicum of that tawny weed, tobacco, that I lust after, as Ben Jonson says. I shall be back in time for our nightly reading.

> (*He goes out and disappears down the street, into the wings, off L.*)

MAMA (*who has gone to the door back L., calls with a good*

deal of sharpness and firmness). Nels! Katrin! You do not hear Papa call you?

NELS *(from off, upstairs).* Coming, Mama!

KATRIN *(at her desk).* Yes, Mama. I'm coming.

> *(She rises. In her few moments in the dark, she has loosened her hair to her shoulders, and we see that her skirt is short as she walks from her desk, and up the steps into the set. As soon as she has left it, the turntable revolves out. Immediately after her,* NELS *comes in back L. He is a tall, strapping young fellow—old enough to look 18 or 19, or 15 or 16, according to his dress, or demeanour. Now, he is about 15.)*

PAPA. So now all are here.

MAMA. Come, then.

> *(*CHRISTINE, NELS *and* KATRIN *gather around the table.* DAGMAR *remains crooning to* ELIZABETH.*)*

> *(Sorting coins.)*

First, for the landlord.

> *(She makes a pile of silver dollars. It gets pushed down the table from one member of the family to the next, each speaking as he passes it.* PAPA *comes last.)*

NELS *(passing it on).* For the landlord.

KATRIN *(doing likewise).* For the landlord.

CHRISTINE *(passing it to* PAPA*).* The landlord.

PAPA. For the landlord.

> *(He dumps the pile at his end of the table, writing on a piece of paper, which he wraps around the pile.)*

MAMA *(who has been sorting).* For the grocer.

> *(The business is repeated. During this repeat, Dagmar's crooning to the cat becomes audible, contrapuntally to the repetitions of "For the grocer".)*

DAGMAR (*in a crescendo*).   In all the United States no cat was as brave as Elizabeth.

(*Fortissimo.*)

In all the *world* no cat was as brave as Elizabeth!

MAMA (*gently*).   Hush, Dagmar. Quietly. You put Elizabeth back into the pantry.

DAGMAR (*in a loud, stage whisper, as she crosses to pantry*). In Heaven or HELL no cat was as brave as Elizabeth.

(*She goes out with the cat.*)

MAMA.   For Katrin's shoes to be half-soled. (*She passes a half dollar.*)

NELS.   Katrin's shoes.

KATRIN (*proudly*).   *My* shoes!

CHRISTINE (*contemptuously*).   Katrin's old shoes.

PAPA.   Katrin's shoes.

CHRISTINE.   Mama, Teacher says this week I'll need a new notebook.

MAMA.   How much will it be?

CHRISTINE.   A dime.

MAMA (*giving her a dime*).   For the notebook. You don't lose it.

CHRISTINE.   I won't lose it.

(*She wraps it in her handkerchief.*)

MAMA.   You take care when you blow your nose.

CHRISTINE.   I'll take care.

PAPA.   Is all, Mama?

MAMA.   Is all for this week. Is good. We do not have to go to the Bank.

(*She starts to gather up the few remaining coins.* KATRIN *leaves the group, comes and sits on the steps, front.*)

NELS.   Mama. . . .

(*She looks up, catching an urgency in his tone.* PAPA *suspends smoking for a moment.*)

Mama, I'll be graduating from grammar school next month.
Could I . . . could I go on to High, do you think?

MAMA (*pleased*).   You want to go to High School?

NELS.   I'd like to . . . if you think I could.

MAMA.   Is good.

(PAPA *nods approvingly*.)

NELS (*awkwardly*).   It . . . it'll cost a little money. I've got
it all written down.

(*Producing a piece of paper from his pocket.*)

Carfare, clothes, notebooks, things I'll really need. I figured
it out with Cy Nichols. He went to High last year.

(MAMA *and* PAPA *come closer together, to look at the
paper he puts before them.*)

MAMA.   Get the *Little* Bank, Christine.

(CHRISTINE *gets a small box from the dresser.*)

KATRIN (*from the steps—herself again, in the present—
looking out front*).   The Little Bank! That was the most
important thing in the whole house. It was a box we used to
keep for emergencies—like the time when Dagmar had croup
and Papa had to go and get medicine to put in the steam kettle.
I can *smell* that medicine now! The things that came out of
the Little Bank! Mama was always going to buy herself a
warm coat out of it, when there was enough, only there never
was.

(*Meanwhile,* MAMA *has been counting the contents.*)

NELS (*anxiously*).   Is there enough, Mama?

MAMA (*shaking her head*).   Is not much in the Little Bank
right now. We give to the dentist, you remember? And for
your roller-skates?

NELS (*his face falling*).   I know. And there's your warm
coat you've been saving for.

MAMA.   The coat I can get another time. But even so . . .

(*She shakes her head.*)

CHRISTINE. You mean Nels can't go to High?

MAMA. Is not enough here. We do not want to have to go to the Bank, do we?

NELS. No, Mama, no. I'll work in Dillon's grocery after school.

> (MAMA *writes a figure on the paper and starts to count on her fingers.* PAPA *looks over, and does the sum in his head.*)

PAPA. Is not enough.

MAMA (*finishing on her fingers against her collarbone*). No, is not enough.

PAPA (*taking his pipe out of his mouth and looking at it a long time*). I give up tobacco.

> (MAMA *looks at him, almost speaks, then just touches his sleeve, writes another figure and starts on her fingers again.*)

CHRISTINE. I'll mind the Maxwell children Friday nights. Katrin can help me.

> (MAMA *writes another figure.* PAPA *looks over—calculates again, nods with satisfaction.*)

MAMA (*triumphantly*). Is good! Is enough!

NELS. Gee!

MAMA. We do not have to go to the Bank.

> (DAGMAR *returns, without the cat.*)

DAGMAR (*hearing the last line*). Where is the Bank?

CHRISTINE. Downtown.

DAGMAR. What's it look like?

CHRISTINE. Just a building.

DAGMAR. Like a prison?

CHRISTINE (*sharply*). No, nothing like a prison.

DAGMAR. Well, then, why does Mama always say "We don't want to go to the Bank"?

CHRISTINE. Because . . . well, because no one ever wants to go to the Bank.

DAGMAR. Why not?

CHRISTINE. Because if we went to the Bank all the time, there'd be no money left there. And then if we couldn't pay our rent, they'd turn us out like Mrs. Jensen down the street.

DAGMAR. You mean, it's like saving some of your candy for tomorrow?

MAMA. Yes, my Dagmar. Is exactly like saving your candy.

DAGMAR. But if . . . if all the other people go to the Bank, then there won't be any money left for us, either.

NELS (*kindly*). It isn't like that, Dagmar. Everyone can only get so much.

DAGMAR. How much?

NELS. However much you've got there . . . put away. You see, it's *our* money that we put there, to keep safe.

DAGMAR. When did we put it there?

NELS. I . . . I don't know when. A long time back, I guess. Wasn't it, Mama?

MAMA. Is enough about the Bank.

DAGMAR. How much money have we got in the Bank?

NELS. I don't know. How much, Mama?

MAMA. Enough.

> (*During the last speeches* AUNT TRINA *appears from the wings down front L. She is a timid, mouselike little woman of about 40, with some prettiness about her. She wears her hat and coat, and a pathetic feather boa. She comes up the street and knocks on the house door.*)

MAMA (*hearing the knock*). Was the door?

CHRISTINE (*quickly*). If it's the Aunts, I'm going to my boodwar.

KATRIN (*rising, entering the scene*). And I'm going to my study.

MAMA (*stopping them*). You cannot run away. We must be polite to the Aunts.

(PAPA *has opened the door.*)

Why, is Trina!

PAPA. Trina, and all by herself!

MAMA. Say good evening to Aunt Trina, children.

CHILDREN (*together*). Good evening, Aunt Trina.

TRINA. Good evening, children. How well they all look.

MAMA. You have a feather boa. Is new. (*Inspecting it.*) Beautiful.

TRINA (*simpering a little*). It was a present.

MAMA (*smiling*). A present! Look, Lars. Trina has a present.

PAPA (*feeling it*). Is fine.

> (*He puts Trina's hat, coat and boa on the chest under the window.*)

MAMA. Jenny and Sigrid don't come with you, Trina?

TRINA (*embarrassed*). No, I . . . I didn't tell them I was coming. I want to talk to you, Marta.

MAMA (*smiling*). So? Sit then, and we talk.

TRINA (*nervously agitated*). Could we talk alone?

MAMA. Alone?

TRINA. If you wouldn't mind.

MAMA (*going to the stove*). Children, you leave us alone a little. I call you. Dagmar, you go with Katrin.

KATRIN (*protesting*). Oh, but Mama . . .

MAMA (*firmly*). Katrin, you take Dagmar!

KATRIN. Yes, Mama. (*Pushing* DAGMAR, *resentfully.*) Come on.

> (*The* CHILDREN *go out back L.*)

MAMA. Now—what is it, Trina?

TRINA (*looking down, embarrassed*). Marta . . .

MAMA (*helpfully*). Yes?

TRINA. Oh, no, I can't say it.

MAMA (*anxiously*). Trina, what is it?

TRINA. It's . . . something very personal.

MAMA. You want Lars should go outside?

TRINA. Would you mind, Lars? Just for a minute?

PAPA (*good-humouredly*). No, I go. I know what women's secrets are.

> (*Teasing.*)

As your Uncle Chris says—"Vomen! Pff!"

MAMA. You have your pipe, Lars? Is fine night.

> (PAPA *takes out his pipe—then lays it down.*)

What is it?

PAPA. I forget. I give up tobacco.

MAMA. Is still some tobacco in your pouch?

> (PAPA *nods.*)

Then you do not give up tobacco till you have finish. You give up *more* tobacco—not the tobacco you already have.

PAPA. Is not right, Marta.

> (*He pats her, takes his pipe, and goes out L., standing outside the house, under the lamp-post, and looking up at the stars, smoking.*)

MAMA. So, Trina. Now. What is it.

TRINA. Marta. . . . I want to get married.

MAMA. You mean . . . you want to get married, or there is someone you want to marry?

TRINA. There's someone I want to marry.

MAMA. Does *he* want to marry *you*?

TRINA. He says he does.

MAMA (*delighted*). Trina! Is wonderful!

TRINA (*crying a little*). *I* think it is.

MAMA. Who is?

TRINA. Mr. Thorkelson.

MAMA. From the Funeral Parlor?

> (TRINA *nods.* MAMA *nods, speculatively, but with less enthusiasm.*)

TRINA. I know he isn't very handsome or . . . or tall. I

know it isn't what most people would think a very nice profession, but . . .

MAMA.   You love him, Trina?

(TRINA *nods ecstatically.*)

Then is good. (*She pats* TRINA'S *hand.*)

TRINA.   Marta, will you . . . will you help me tell the others?

MAMA.   Oh . . . Jenny and Sigrid . . . they do not know?

TRINA.   No. I was afraid they'd laugh at me. But if *you* tell them . . .

MAMA.   Jenny will not like you tell me first.

TRINA (*desperately*).   I can't help that. You've got to tell them not to laugh at me. If they laugh at me, I'll . . . I'll kill myself.

MAMA (*with decision*).   Jenny and Sigrid will not laugh. I promise you, Trina.

TRINA.   Oh, thank you, Marta. And . . . Uncle Chris?

MAMA (*with some seriousness*).   Ah!

TRINA.   Will you talk to him?

MAMA.   It is Mr. Thorkelson who must talk to Uncle Chris. Always it is the husband who must talk to the head of the family.

TRINA.   Yes. I know, but . . . well, Uncle Chris is so very frightening. He's so big and black, and he shouts so. And Mr. Thorkelson is . . . well, kind of timid, really.

MAMA (*gently*).   But, Trina, if he is to be your husband, he must learn not to be timid. You do not want husband should be timid. *You* are timid. Is not good when *both* are timid.

(*Then firmly.*)

No! Jenny and Sigrid I speak to, but Mr. Thorkelson must go to Uncle Chris.

PAPA (*re-enters the house*).   Marta, Trina, I do not want to interrupt your talk, but Jenny and Sigrid are coming.

TRINA (*alarmed*).   Oh, dear!

PAPA.   I see them get off the cable-car. They come up the hill.

TRINA (*in a flurry*).   I'd better go to your room for a minute.

> (*She starts for the door, turns back, gets her things from the chest, and runs out, carrying them, back L. Meanwhile, MAMA has been whispering the news to PAPA.*)

MAMA.   The coffee is ready—I get more cups.

> (*During the above, AUNTS JENNY and SIGRID have entered from the wings L., front. JENNY is a domineering woman in her fifties; SIGRID, whining and complaining.*)

SIGRID (*in the street*).   Wait, Jenny, I must get my breath. This hill kills me every time I climb it.

JENNY.   You climbed bigger hills than that in the old country.

SIGRID.   I was a *girl* in the old country.

> (*They march to the door and knock—SIGRID following JENNY.*)

MAMA (*opening the door to them*).   Jenny. Sigrid. Is surprise.

> (*To SIGRID.*)

Where's Ole?

SIGRID.   Working. He's always working. I never see anything of him at all.

MAMA (*crossing to the stove for coffee-pot*).   Is good to work.

SIGRID.   It's good to see your husband once in a while, too.

JENNY.   (*No nonsense about her.*) Has Trina been here?

MAMA.   Trina?

JENNY.   She's gone somewhere. And she doesn't know anyone but *you* . . .

MAMA.   That is what *you* think.

JENNY.   What do you mean by that?

MAMA.   Give Lars your coat. I give you some coffee. Then we talk about Trina.

SIGRID (*as* PAPA *helps with coats*).   She *has* been here?

MAMA.   Yes, she has been here. (*Pouring coffee and passing cups.*)

JENNY.   What did Trina want?

MAMA.   She want to talk to me.

JENNY.   What about?

MAMA.   Marriage.

SIGRID.   What?

MAMA (*pouring calmly*).   Marriage.

(*Passing* SIGRID's *cup.*)

Trina wants to get married.

JENNY.   That's no news. Of course she wants to get married. Every old maid wants to get married.

MAMA.   There is someone who wants to marry Trina.

JENNY.   Who'd want to marry Trina?

MAMA.   Mr. Thorkelson.

SIGRID.   Peter Thorkelson? Little Peter? (*She gestures a midget.*)

MAMA.   He is not so little.

SIGRID.   He's hardly bigger than my Arne—and Arne is not ten yet.

MAMA.   So he is hardly bigger than your Arne. Does every husband have to be big man?

JENNY.   Trina's making it up. That happens with old maids, when they get to Trina's age.

MAMA (*firmly*).   No, Jenny—it is true. Mr. Thorkelson wants to marry Trina.

JENNY (*changing her tactics slightly*).   Mr. Thorkelson. She'd be the laughing stock. (*She laughs.*)

MAMA (*moving to her*).   Jenny, Trina is here. She will

come in a minute. This is serious for her. You will not laugh
at her.

JENNY.   I shall do what I please.

MAMA.   No, Jenny, you will not.

JENNY.   And why won't I?

MAMA.   Because I will not let you.

JENNY.   And how will you stop me?

MAMA.   If you laugh at Trina, I will tell her of the time
before your wedding when your husband try to run away.

SIGRID.   What is that?

JENNY.   Who told you that?

MAMA.   I know.

SIGRID (*intrigued*).   Erik . . . tried to run away?

JENNY.   It's not true.

MAMA.   Then you do not mind if I tell Trina.

JENNY.   Uncle Chris told you.

SIGRID (*tenaciously*).   Tried to run away?

MAMA.   It does not matter, Sigrid. Jenny will not laugh
at Trina now. Nor will you! For if *you* laugh at her, I will
tell of your wedding night with Ole, when you cry all the
time, and he bring you home to Mother.

PAPA (*with sudden enjoyment*).   This I do *not* know.

MAMA (*reprovingly*).   Is no need you should know. I do
not tell these stories for spite—only so they do not laugh at
Trina. Call her, Lars. You like more coffee, Jenny? Sigrid?

> (PAPA *goes to the door back L., calls, "Trina."* MAMA
> *pours coffee for* JENNY. MR. HYDE *reappears down
> front L., and lets himself into the house.*)

MR. HYDE (*seeing company*).   Oh, I beg your pardon. I
was not aware . . .

MAMA.   Mr. Hyde, these are my sisters.

MR. HYDE.   Enchanted, ladies. Madame. Madame. The
Three Graces.

> (*He bows.* SIGRID *giggles coyly. He goes to the door
> back L.*)

You will excuse me?

MAMA.   Sure, Mr. Hyde.

MR. HYDE.   I shall be in my room. (*He goes out.*)

JENNY.   So *that's* your famous boarder. Has he paid you his rent yet? Three months he's been here, hasn't he?

MAMA.   Is hard to ask. Surely he will pay soon.

JENNY (*with a snort*).   Surely he won't! If I ran my boarding house the way you run this place . . .

PAPA.   Maybe your boarders wouldn't always leave you.

JENNY.   If Marta thinks she's going to get the warm coat she's always talking about out of *that* one . . .

MAMA.   Jenny, Mr. Hyde is a gentleman. He reads to us aloud. Wonderful books . . . Longfellow, and Charles Dickens, and Fenimore Kipling.

(TRINA *steals back.*)

MAMA (*seeing her hesitant in the doorway*).   Come in, Trina. The coffee is getting cold.

(*She pours a cup. There is a silence.*)

I tell them.

JENNY.   Why did you come to Marta first?

PAPA.   She thought Marta would understand.

JENNY.   Aren't Sigrid and I married women, too?

PAPA.   You have been married longer than Marta. She think maybe you forget.

JENNY.   What sort of a living does Mr. Thorkelson make?

TRINA.   I . . . I haven't asked.

SIGRID.   Can he keep you?

TRINA.   I don't think he would have asked me to marry him if he couldn't.

JENNY.   Maybe he thinks you are going to keep *him.*

MAMA (*warningly*).   Jenny!

SIGRID.   Maybe he thinks Trina will have a dowry like the girls at home.

TRINA.   Well, why shouldn't I? You all had dowries. . . .

JENNY. We were married in Norway. And our parents were alive. Where would your dowry come from, I'd like to know?

TRINA. Uncle Chris. He's head of the family.

JENNY. And who will ask him?

TRINA. He won't need asking. When Mr. Thorkelson goes to see him . . .

JENNY. Uncle Chris will eat him!

SIGRID (*giggling maliciously*). Little Peter and Uncle Chris!

MAMA (*with meaning*). Maybe Uncle Chris will tell him some family stories. He knows many, does Uncle Chris.

(*The* AUNTS *put down their cups, discomfited.*)

JENNY (*to change the subject*). Where are the children? Aren't we going to see them before we go?

PAPA. Of course, I'll call them.

(*He goes to the door and does so, shouting.*)

Children! Your aunts are *leaving!*

CHILDREN'S VOICES (*eagerly*). Coming, Papa!

JENNY. You come with us, Trina?

MAMA. I think maybe Trina like to stay here and listen to Mr. Hyde read to us. You like, Trina?

TRINA. Well, if I wouldn't be in the way. I asked Mr. Thorkelson to call for me here. He'll see me home. I'll help you with the coffee things.

(*She takes the tray of coffee cups and goes into the pantry.*)

(KATRIN *returns, back L. She carries her diary,* DAGMAR *follows her, and behind them,* CHRISTINE.)

KATRIN *and* DAGMAR (*curtseying*). Good evening, Aunt Sigrid. Good evening, Aunt Jenny.

(CHRISTINE *sketches a perfunctory curtsey without speaking.*)

JENNY.   Where have *you* all been hiding yourselves?

DAGMAR (*going into the pantry*).   We've been in Christine's boodwar.

JENNY.   Her *what?*

MAMA.   Christine makes the little closet into a boudoir. I give her those bead portières, Jenny, that you lend us when we come from the old country.

SIGRID.   And what does she do there?

CHRISTINE (*impertinently*).   What people usually do in boudoirs.

MAMA.   Christine, that is rude. It is her little place to herself.

(NELS *enters, back L.*)

NELS.   Hello, Aunt Sigrid. Hello, Aunt Jenny.

SIGRID (*shaking hands*).   Good evening, Nels. My, how tall he is getting!

MAMA (*proudly*).   Yes, is almost as tall as his Papa.

SIGRID.   He looks to me as if he was outgrowing his strength. Dagmar was looking pale, too.

(DAGMAR *returns now, carrying the cat again.*)

SIGRID (*jumping*).   Goodness, what a horrid-looking cat.

DAGMAR.   She's not. She's beautiful.

PAPA.   Is her new friend. She goes with Dagmar everywhere.

CHRISTINE.   She does. First thing you know, she'll have the cat sleeping with her.

DAGMAR (*eagerly*).   Oh, Mama, can I? Can I, Mama?

JENNY.   Certainly not. Don't you know a cat draws breath from a sleeping child? You wouldn't want to wake up some morning *smothered*, would you?

DAGMAR.   I wouldn't care. Elizabeth can have *all* my breath!

(*She blows into the cat's face.*)

There!

JENNY (*putting on gloves*). Elizabeth—what a very silly name for a cat.

NELS. It's a very silly name for *that* cat. It's a Tom.

MAMA. Nels, how do you know?

NELS. I looked!

DAGMAR. How can you tell?

NELS. You can.

DAGMAR. But how?

MAMA (*quickly warning*). Nels, you do not say how!

NELS (*to* DAGMAR). So you'd better think up another name for him.

DAGMAR. I won't. He's Elizabeth. And he's going to *stay* Elizabeth.

PAPA. We could call him *Uncle* Elizabeth.

DAGMAR (*laughing delightedly*). Uncle Elizabeth! Do you hear, Elizabeth? You're called *Uncle* Elizabeth now!

JENNY. Such foolishness! Well, good-bye, all. Marta. Lars.

(*Good-byes are exchanged all around, the* CHILDREN *curtseying formally.*)

MAMA. Good-bye, Jenny. Good-bye, Sigrid. Nels, you go tell Mr. Hyde we are ready for the reading.

(NELS *goes off, back L. The* AUNTS *leave and walk down L.* MAMA *stands in the doorway, waving good-bye.*)

SIGRID (*as they go*). Well, I never thought we'd live to see the day Trina gets married.

JENNY. She's not married yet. She's got Uncle Chris to deal with first.

(*They disappear into wings L.*)

MAMA (*returning to the room and calling into the pantry*). Trina, they have gone. Dagmar, you put Elizabeth out for the night now.

DAGMAR (*correcting her*). *Uncle* Elizabeth!

MAMA. *Uncle* Elizabeth!!

> (DAGMAR *goes out into the pantry with the cat.* TRINA *comes in as* MR. HYDE *and* NELS *return back L.*)

Mr. Hyde, this is my sister Trina.

MR. HYDE (*bowing*). Enchanted!

MAMA (*seating herself R. of the table*). Mr. Hyde reads to us "The Tales From Two Cities." Is a beautiful story. But sad.

TRINA (*brightly*). I like sad stories. (*She gets out her handkerchief.*)

> (*The whole family group themselves around the table,* DAGMAR *returning and seating herself on the floor below* MAMA. MR. HYDE *takes the armchair L. of table.* KATRIN *is on the steps R. front.*)

MR. HYDE. Tonight, I would like to finish it.

MAMA. Is good.

MR. HYDE. Are you ready?

CHILDREN. Yes, please, Mr. Hyde.

MR. HYDE. I will go on from where we left off. (*He starts to read.*)

"In the black prison of the Conciergerie, the doomed of the day awaited their fate. They were in number as the weeks of the year. Fifty-two were to roll that afternoon on the life-tide of the City to the boundless, everlasting sea. . . ."

> (*The lights dim down slowly, leaving spots on* KATRIN *and* MR. HYDE *only.*)

KATRIN. I don't think I shall ever forget that night. It was almost midnight when he came to the end, and none of us had noticed.

MR. HYDE (*reading from the last page*).

"It is a far, far better thing that I do than I have ever done; it is a far, far better rest that I go to than I have ever known."

> (*He closes the book.*)

"The End."

(*The R. turntable revolves in again.* KATRIN *rises from the step, and crosses to her desk on the turntable.*)

KATRIN. I wrote in my diary that night before I went to bed.

(*She reads aloud from it.*)

"Tonight Mr. Hyde finished 'The Tale of Two Cities.' The closing chapters are indeed superb. How beautiful a thing is self-sacrifice. I wish there were someone *I* could die for."

(*She sits looking out front.*)

Mr. Hyde read us all kinds of books. He thrilled us with "Treasure Island," and terrified us with "The Hound of the Baskervilles." I can still remember the horror in his voice as he read. . . .

MR. HYDE (*still on the main stage in his spot, reading*). "Dr. Mortimer looked strangely at us for an instant, and his voice sank almost to a whisper as he answered: 'Mr. Holmes, they were the footprints of a gigantic *hound!*' "

(*He closes the book.*)

We will continue tomorrow night. If you are interested.

KATRIN (*looking out front*). If we were interested! You couldn't have kept us from it. It meant a lot to Mama, too, because Nels stopped going nights to the street corner to hang about with the neighbourhood boys. The night they got into trouble for breaking into Mr. Dillon's store, Nels was home with us. And sometimes Mr. Hyde read us poetry. "The Lady of the Lake" . . . and the "Rime of the Ancient Mariner."

MR. HYDE (*reading*).

> "About, about, in reel and rout
> The death-fires danced at night.
> The water, like a witch's oils,
> Burnt green and blue and white."

(*His spot goes out, and the traveller curtains close on the kitchen scene.*)

KATRIN.   There were many nights I couldn't sleep for the way he had set my imagination dancing.

(*Reading from her diary again.*)

"What a wonderful thing is literature, transporting us to realms unknown."

(*To herself.*)

And all the time my school teacher kept telling me that I ought to write about things I knew. I did write a piece for her once about Uncle Chris, and she said it wasn't nice to write like that about a member of one's own family. Papa called Mama's Uncle Chris a black Norwegian, because of his dark hair and fierce moustache, but there were others in the family who claimed that he was black in a different way. The Aunts, for example.

(*Spot goes up on L. front turntable, representing Jenny's kitchen.* JENNY *and* TRINA *are discovered.* JENNY *is rolling pastry.* TRINA *is crocheting.*)

JENNY.   Black! I'll say he's black. Black in his heart. Cursing and swearing. . .

TRINA.   Marta says that's only because it hurts him to walk.

JENNY.   Rubbish. I know all about his limp and the accident back in the old country—but has anyone ever heard him complain? Marta's always making excuses for him.

TRINA.   I know . . . but he *is* good to the children. All those oranges he's always sending them. . . .

JENNY.   Oranges! What good is oranges? Turn 'em yellow. They're the only things he's ever been known to give away, anyway. He's got other uses for his money.

TRINA.   What do you mean?

JENNY.   Bottles! And that woman he lives with!

TRINA.   He *says* she's his housekeeper.

JENNY.   Well, he couldn't very well come right out and call her what she is, could he? Though *I* will one of these days. And to his face, too.

(SIGRID *comes through the curtains C. She crosses to*
JENNY *and* TRINA.)

SIGRID. Jenny. Trina. What do you think? What do you
think Uncle Chris has done now?

TRINA. What?

JENNY. Tell us.

SIGRID. You know my little Arne's knee—that fall he had
two months ago? The man at the drugstore said it was only
a bruise, but today it was hurting him again, so I left him home
when I went to do the marketing. I asked Mrs. Schultz next
door to keep an eye on him, and who should turn up, not ten
minutes after I'd gone, but Uncle Chris. And what do you
think?

JENNY. Well, tell us, if you're going to. Don't keep *asking* us.

SIGRID. He took one look at Arne's knee, bundled him
into that rattletrap old automobile of his, and rushed him
straight off to the hospital. I've just come from there . . . and
what do you think? They've operated! They've got him
in Plaster of Paris!

JENNY. Without consulting you?

SIGRID. It seems the doctor is a friend of his . . . that's why
he did it. No, this time he's gone too far. To put a child of
Arne's age through all that pain! They wouldn't even let me
see Arne. I'm going to tell Uncle Chris exactly what I think
of him. . . .

JENNY. That's right.

SIGRID. I'm going to tell him right now.

(*Weakening a little.*)

Come with me, Jenny.

JENNY. Well, I . . . No, I can't leave my baking.

SIGRID. You must, Jenny. We must stand together. You
come, too, Trina, and ask about your dowry. *Make* him give
it to you.

TRINA. Oh, but . . . Marta said Mr. Thorkelson should do that. . . .

JENNY. Well, then, go and get Mr. Thorkelson. Go down to the mortuary and get him now. Sigrid's quite right. We girls have got to stand together!

(*Blackout. Turntable revolves out.*)

KATRIN (*at her desk*). Nobody knew where Uncle Chris lived. That was part of the mystery about him. He used to roam up and down the state buying up farms and ranches that had gone to pieces, and bullying them back into prosperity. Then he'd sell at a profit and move on again. Two or three times a year he'd descend on the city in his automobile and come roaring and stamping into our house.

(*Her light dims.*)

(*The sound of a very old and noisy Ford car changing gears is heard off L. A grinding and screaming as it comes to a standstill. Then* UNCLE CHRIS' VOICE, *shouting.*)

UNCLE CHRIS' VOICE. Marta, Lars! Children—vere are you?

(*The curtains part on the kitchen again. Outside in the street is Uncle Chris' car—an antique model. A woman is seated beside the empty driver's seat.* UNCLE CHRIS *is knocking on the house door. He is an elderly, powerful, swarthy man with a limp. In the kitchen,* NELS *and* CHRISTINE *are cowering.*)

UNCLE CHRIS. Marta! Lars!

CHRISTINE (*scared*). It's Uncle Chris.

NELS (*equally so*). I know.

CHRISTINE. What'll we do?

UNCLE CHRIS. Is nobody home? Hey, there—is nobody home?

(*Banging on the door.*)

Hey—someone—answer the door.

(*He tries the door handle; it opens and he strides,
limpingly, in. He has a strong accent, and uses the
Norwegian pronunciation of the children's names.*)

So, vat is—you do not answer the door? You do not hear
me calling?

(*The* CHILDREN *cower silently.*)

I say, you do not hear me calling? I do not call loud enough?

CHRISTINE.   Y-yes, Uncle Chris.

UNCLE CHRIS.   Which yes? Yes, you do not hear me—or
yes I do not call loud enough?

NELS.   We heard you, Uncle Chris.

UNCLE CHRIS.   Then why you do not come?

NELS.   We . . . we were just going to.

(KATRIN *has left her desk and come up the steps.*)

UNCLE CHRIS.   Let me look at you. You too, Katrinë, do
not stand there—come and let me look at you.

(*They line up as though for inspection. He thumps*
NELS *between the shoulder blades.*)

Stand tall!

(*They all straighten up.*)

Um-hum. By the dresser, where the marks are.

(NELS *goes to the wall by the dresser.* UNCLE CHRIS
*compares his mark with the previous one—and
makes a new one on the wall, writing by it*)

Two inches. Two inches in . . .

(*Examining the date*)

Six months. Is good. Christinë.

(CHRISTINE *replaces* NELS.)

Show me your teeth.

(*She does so.*)

You brush them goot?

(*She nods.*)

Nils, there is a box of oranges in the automobile. You fetch them in.

> (NELS *goes out L.* UNCLE CHRIS *measures* CHRISTINE.)

Where is the little von? Dagmar?

KATRIN.   She's sick, Uncle Chris.

UNCLE CHRIS (*arrested*).   Sick? What is the matter with her?

KATRIN.   It's her ear. She's had an earache for two days. Bad earache. Mama sent for the doctor.

UNCLE CHRIS.   Goot doctor? What he say?

KATRIN.   He's in there now.

> (*She points off, back L. Meanwhile* CHRISTINE *has remained standing by the wall, afraid to move.*)

UNCLE CHRIS.   I go in.

> (*He starts to the door back L., but* MAMA *and* DR. JOHNSON *come into the room as he does so. During this* NELS *has gone to the car, and with nervous smiles at the woman seated by the driver's seat, has heaved out a huge box of oranges. He returns with the oranges during the ensuing scene.*)

MAMA (*greeting him*).   Uncle Chris.

UNCLE CHRIS.   How is with Dagmar?

MAMA.   Is bad. Doctor, this is my Uncle, Mr. Halvorsen.

DOCTOR.   How do you do, sir?

UNCLE CHRIS.   What is with the child?

DOCTOR.   We must get her to a hospital. At once. We'll have to operate.

MAMA.   Operate?

DOCTOR.   I'm afraid so.

MAMA.   Can wait? Until my husband comes home from work?

DOCTOR.   I'm afraid not. Her best chance is for us to operate immediately.

MAMA (*after a second*).   We go.

(*She goes to the dresser for the Little Bank.*)

UNCLE CHRIS (*who has watched her decision with approval, turns to the doctor*). What is with the child?

DOCTOR. I'm afraid it's a mastoid.

UNCLE CHRIS. Ah . . . then you operate immediately.

DOCTOR (*resenting this*). That's what I said.

UNCLE CHRIS. Immediately!

MAMA (*who has poured the contents of the Little Bank onto the table*). Doctor . . . is enough?

DOCTOR. I was thinking of the County Hospital.

MAMA. No. No. We pay. Is enough?

KATRIN. If there isn't, we can go to the Bank.

CHRISTINE. We've got a Bank Account.

MAMA. Is enough without we go to the Bank, Doctor? My husband is carpenter. Make good money.

UNCLE CHRIS. If there is need of money, *I* pay.

DOCTOR (*mainly in dislike of Uncle Chris*). It'll be all right. We'll take her to the Clinic. You pay what you can afford.

UNCLE CHRIS. Goot. Goot. I have a patient there already. My nephew, Arne. They operate this morning on his knee.

DOCTOR. Are you a physician, sir?

UNCLE CHRIS. I am better physician than most doctors. Nils, there, my other nephew, he become doctor when he grow up.

(NELS *looks up, surprised.*)

DOCTOR (*chillily*). Oh, indeed . . . very interesting. Well, now, if you will have the child at the Clinic in . . . shall we say an hour's time. . . .

UNCLE CHRIS. The child will be at the Clinic in *ten minutes*' time. I haf my automobile.

DOCTOR. I can hardly make arrangements in ten minutes.

UNCLE CHRIS. *I* make arrangements. I know doctors.

MAMA. Uncle Chris, Dr. Johnson arrange. He is good doctor.

DOCTOR (*ironically*). Thank you, Madam.

MAMA. You go, Doctor. We come.

DOCTOR. Very well, in an hour, then. And Dagmar will be well taken care of, I promise you. I will do the operation myself.

UNCLE CHRIS. I watch.

DOCTOR. You will do no such thing, sir.

UNCLE CHRIS. Always I watch operations. I am head of family.

DOCTOR. I allow no one to attend my operations.

UNCLE CHRIS. Are so bad?

DOCTOR (*to* MAMA). Mrs. Hanson, if I am to undertake this operation and the care of your child, it must be on the strict understanding that this gentleman does not come near either me or my patient.

MAMA. Yes, Doctor, I talk to him. . . . You go to hospital now, please.

DOCTOR. Very well. But you understand . . . nowhere near me, or I withdraw from the case. (*He goes.*)

UNCLE CHRIS. I go see Dagmar.

MAMA. Wait. Uncle Chris, is kind of you, but Dagmar is sick. You frighten her.

UNCLE CHRIS. I frighten her?

MAMA. Yes, Uncle Chris. You frighten everyone. . . .

UNCLE CHRIS (*amazed*). I??

MAMA. Everyone but me. Even the girls. . . . Jenny, Sigrid, Trina . . . they are frightened of you.

UNCLE CHRIS. The girls! Vomen! Pff!

MAMA. And the children, too. So Nels and I get Dagmar. You drive us to hospital in your automobile, but you do not frighten Dagmar. And you leave Doctor alone. Dr. Johnson is *fine* doctor. You come with me, Nels. You carry Dagmar.

(NELS *and* MAMA *go out back* L. UNCLE CHRIS *stands in amazement and puzzlement. The* TWO GIRLS *watch him, hardly daring to move.*)

UNCLE CHRIS.   Is true? I frighten you? Christinë . . .
Katrinë . . . you are frightened of me? Come, I ask you.
Tell me the truth. You are frightened of me?

KATRIN (*tremulously*).   A . . . a little, Uncle Chris.

UNCLE CHRIS.   No? And you, Christinë?

CHRISTINE.   Y . . . yes, Uncle Chris.

UNCLE CHRIS.   But Nils . . . Nils is a boy . . . he is not
frightened?

CHRISTINE.   Not . . . not as much as we are. . . .

UNCLE CHRIS.   But he is frightened?

CHRISTINE.   Yes, Uncle Chris.

UNCLE CHRIS.   But, why? What is there to be frightened
of? I am your Uncle Chris . . . why do I frighten you?

CHRISTINE.   I don't know.

UNCLE CHRIS.   But that is bad. Very bad. The Aunts, yes,
I like to frighten them.

(THE GIRLS *giggle*.)

That makes you laugh. You do not like the Aunts? Come,
tell me. You do not like the Aunts? Say!

KATRIN.   Not . . . very much, Uncle Chris.

UNCLE CHRIS.   And which do you not like the most? Jenny
. . . Sigrid . . . Trina. . . . Tell me—huh?

KATRIN.   I think I like Aunt Jenny least. She's so . . . so
bossy.

CHRISTINE.   I can't stand Aunt Sigrid. Always whining
and complaining.

UNCLE CHRIS (*with a great roar of laughter*).   Is good.
Jenny, bossy. Sigrid, whining. Is true! But your Mama, she
is different. And she cook goot. The Aunts, they cannot cook
at all. Only you do not tell your Mama we have talked of
them so. It is a secret, for us. Then you cannot be frightened
of me any more . . . when we have secret. I tell you my
secret, too. *I* do not like the Aunts. And so that they do not
bother me, I frighten them and shout at them. You I do not

shout at if you are goot children, and clean your teeth goot, and eat your oranges.

> (*He takes out a snuff-box and partakes of its contents.*)

> (*On the cue "You I do not shout at" the posse of* AUNTS *appears, in outdoor clothes, accompanied by* MR. THORKELSON, *a terrified little man. They come in down L. and start up to the house.*)

SIGRID (*stopping in the street*).   Jenny. Do you see what I see? A woman, in his automobile.

JENNY.   How shameful.

SIGRID.   Ought we to bow?

JENNY.   Bow? To a woman like that? We cut her. That's what we do. I'll show you.

> (*She strides to the front door, ignoring the woman in the car, and enters the house. The others follow.*)

JENNY (*entering*).   Uncle Chris, Sigrid has something to say to you.

SIGRID (*with false bravery*).   Uncle Chris, you took Arne to the hospital. . . .

UNCLE CHRIS.   Yes, I take Arne to the hospital. And now we take Dagmar to the hospital, so you do not clutter up the place.

JENNY.   What's the matter with Dagmar?

CHRISTINE.   It's her ear. Dr. Johnson's going to operate.

SIGRID (*catching her favourite word*).   Operate? This is some more of Uncle Chris' doings. Did you hear what he did to Arne?

UNCLE CHRIS (*turning on her*).   Sigrid, you are a whining old fool, and you get out of here. . . .

SIGRID (*deflating*).   We'd better go, Jenny. . . . .

JENNY (*stoutly*).   No . . . there has been enough of these high-handed goings-on. . . .

UNCLE CHRIS.   And you, Jenny . . . you are a bossy old

fool, and you get out of here, too, and we take Dagmar to hospital.

> (NELS *enters, carrying* DAGMAR *in his arms, wrapped in a blanket.*)

You got her goot, Nils?

NELS. Sure, Uncle Chris.

UNCLE CHRIS. We go.

JENNY (*getting between them and the door*). No! You are going to hear me out. (*Weakening.*) That is, you are going to hear *Sigrid* out. . . .

UNCLE CHRIS. If you do not get out of the way of the door before I count three, I trow you out. And Sigrid, too, as big as she is. Von. . . .

> (SIGRID *moves.*)

Two. . . .

> (JENNY *moves. He looks back at the children with a wink and a smile.*)

Is goot! You put her in back of the car, Nils.

> (NELS *goes out, carrying* DAGMAR, *and lifts her into the car.* UNCLE CHRIS *follows and starts cranking.*)

TRINA (*running to the door after him, with* MR. THORKELSON). But, Uncle Chris, I want to introduce Mr. Thorkelson. . . .

> (*But* UNCLE CHRIS *ignores her, continuing to crank. She returns crestfallen into the room with* MR. THORKELSON. MAMA *re-enters back L., wearing hat and coat and carrying a cheap little overnight case.*)

MAMA. Jenny . . . Trina, we go to hospital.

> (*She goes to* KATRIN *and* CHRISTINE.)

You will be good children until Mama comes home?

THE GIRLS. Sure, Mama.

UNCLE CHRIS (*calling from the car*). Marta, we go!

MAMA (*calling back*). I come.

(*She turns to the children again.*)

There is milk in the cooler, and fruit and cookies for your lunch.

CHRISTINE. We'll be all right, Mama. Don't worry.

MAMA. I go now. (*She starts for the door.*)

SIGRID (*stopping her*). Marta!

MAMA. What is it?

SIGRID. You *can't* go in his automobile.

MAMA. Why not?

UNCLE CHRIS (*calling again*). Marta, we go!

MAMA. I come.

SIGRID. Because . . . because *she's* in it. The . . . the woman!

MAMA. So it will kill me, or Dagmar, if we sit in the automobile with her? I have see her. She looks nice woman.

(*Calling off, as she goes*)

I come!

UNCLE CHRIS. We go!

(*She climbs into the rear of the car, which backs noisily off during the next speeches.*)

MR. THORKELSON (*in a low whisper to* TRINA). Is that woman his wife?

TRINA (*nervously*). Yes. . . .

MR. THORKELSON. Yes?

TRINA (*whispering back, loudly*). No!

JENNY (*to* THE GIRLS). Don't stand there gaping like that, girls.

(*She shoos them into the pantry.*)

Go away! Go away!

(THE GIRLS *go.* JENNY *turns and sees the disappearing car through the open door.*)

Oh! They've gone! We go after them! Sigrid, you lead the way!

(*She gives* SIGRID *a push and the four go out, with* JENNY *dragging* MR. THORKELSON, *and* TRINA *following. Blackout. The travellers close.*)

(*Spot on R. turntable, representing a kind of closet-room. Roller skates hanging on the wall.* KATRIN *and* CHRISTINE *are seated on a small kitchen step-ladder with glasses of milk, and cookies on plates.*)

KATRIN. How long have they been gone now?

CHRISTINE. About three hours. And I wish you wouldn't keep asking that.

KATRIN. How long do operations take? I heard Aunt Sigrid telling about Mrs. Bergman who was five hours on the table.

CHRISTINE. Aunt Sigrid's friends always have everything worse than anyone else. And it gets worse each time she tells it, too.

(KATRIN *smiles—drinks some milk and eats a cookie.*)

KATRIN (*with a certain melancholy enjoyment*). The house feels lonesome, doesn't it—without Mama? It's like in a book. "The sisters sat huddled in the empty house, waiting for the verdict that was to spell life or death to the little family."

CHRISTINE. Oh, don't talk such nonsense.

KATRIN. It's not nonsense.

CHRISTINE. It is, too. In the first place, we're not a little family. We're a big one. And who said anything about life or death anyway? Always trying to make everything so dramatic!

KATRIN. Well, it *is* dramatic.

CHRISTINE. It's not. It's just . . . well, worrying. But you don't have to make a tragedy out of it.

(*Pause.*)

KATRIN. You're not eating anything.

CHRISTINE. I know that.

KATRIN. You're not drinking your milk, either. Aren't you hungry?

CHRISTINE. No. And you wouldn't be, either, if you'd any feeling for Mama and Dagmar, instead of just heartlessly sitting there eating and enjoying making a story out of it.

KATRIN. Oh, Chris, I'm not heartless. I do have feeling for them. I can't help it if it goes into words like that. Everything always does with me. But it doesn't mean I don't feel it. And I think we *ought* to eat. I think Mama would want us to.

(*Pause.* CHRISTINE *hesitates a moment, then takes a bite of a cookie. They both eat in silence. The light dims on them, and the turntable revolves out.*)

(*The travellers part on the hospital corridor. A main back flat representing the wall, running diagonally up from the front of the main stage L. towards the back. Down front L. is a bench, on which* MAMA *and* NELS *are sitting, holding hands, looking off. Below the bench is the elevator, and above the bench, set back a little, is a closet for brooms and mops, etc. The reception desk, at which a nurse is sitting, is R.C., towards the front. The wall goes up into darkness, and behind the nurse's desk is darkness.*

As the curtains open, there is a hubbub down front by the nurse's desk, where the AUNTS *are haranguing* UNCLE CHRIS. MR. THORKELSON *stands slightly in back of them.*)

SIGRID. But, Uncle Chris, I tell you I must see him!

UNCLE CHRIS (*storming*). You don't understand English? No visitors for twenty-four hours.

SIGRID. But *you've* seen him.

UNCLE CHRIS. I am not visitor. I am exception.

SIGRID. Well, then, his mother should be an exception, too. I'll see the doctor.

UNCLE CHRIS. *I* have seen doctor. I have told him you are not goot for Arne.

SIGRID. Not good for my own son. . . .

UNCLE CHRIS. Not goot at all. You cry over him. I go now.

(*He starts to do so, but* JENNY *pushes* TRINA *forward.*)

TRINA (*with desperate courage*). Uncle Chris . . . Uncle Chris . . . I *must* speak to you.

UNCLE CHRIS. I have business.

TRINA. But, Uncle Chris. . . . I want to get married.

UNCLE CHRIS. Well, then, *get* married. (*He starts off again.*)

TRINA. No, wait, I . . . I want to marry Mr. Thorkelson. Here.

(*She produces him from behind her.*)

Peter, this is Uncle Chris. Uncle Chris, this is Mr. Thorkelson.

UNCLE CHRIS (*staring at him*). So?

MR. THORKELSON. How are you, sir?

UNCLE CHRIS. Busy. (*He turns again.*)

TRINA. Please, Uncle Chris. . . .

UNCLE CHRIS. What is? You want to marry him? All right, marry him. I have other things to think about.

TRINA (*eagerly*). Then . . . then you give your permission?

UNCLE CHRIS. Yes, I give my permission. If you want to be a fool, I cannot stop you.

TRINA (*gratefully*). Oh, thank you, Uncle Chris.

UNCLE CHRIS. So. Is all?

TRINA (*anxious to escape*). Yes, I think is all.

JENNY (*firmly*). No!!

UNCLE CHRIS. No?

(MR. THORKELSON *is pushed forward again.*)

MR. THORKELSON. Well, there . . . there was a little something else. You see, Trina mentioned . . . well, in the old country it was always usual . . . and after all, we do all come from the old country. . . .

UNCLE CHRIS. What is it? What you want?

MR. THORKELSON. Well, it's a question of Trina's . . . well, not to mince matters . . . her dowry.

UNCLE CHRIS (*shouting*). Her what?

MR. THORKELSON (*very faintly*). Her dowry. . . .

UNCLE CHRIS. Ah! Her dowry. Trina wants a dowry. She is forty-two years old. . . .

TRINA (*interrupting*). No, Uncle Chris. . . .

UNCLE CHRIS (*without pausing*). And it is not enough she gets a husband. She must have dowry.

NURSE (*who has been trying to interrupt, now bangs on her desk*). Please! Would you mind going and discussing your family matters somewhere else? This is a hospital, not a marriage bureau!

UNCLE CHRIS (*after glaring at the* NURSE, *turns to* MR. THORKELSON). You come into the waiting room. I talk to you about dowry.

> (*He strides off into the darkness behind the nurse's desk.* MR. THORKELSON, *with an appealing look back at* TRINA, *follows him. The* AUNTS *now remember* MAMA, *sitting on the bench, and cross to her.*)

JENNY. Did you hear that, Marta?

MAMA (*out of a trance*). What?

JENNY. Uncle Chris.

MAMA. No, I do not hear. I wait for doctor. Is two hours since they take Dagmar to operating room. More.

SIGRID. Two hours? That's nothing! When Mrs. Bergman had her gall bladder removed she was *six* hours on the table.

MAMA. Sigrid, I do not want to hear about Mrs. Bergman. I do not want to hear about anything. I wait for doctor. Please, you go away now. You come this evening.

TRINA. But, Marta, you can't stay here all by yourself.

MAMA. I have Nels. Please, Trina . . . I wait for doctor . . . you go now.

JENNY. We go.

TRINA. Oh, but I must wait for Peter and Uncle Chris. . . .

JENNY. We'll go next door and have some coffee. Sigrid, do you have money?

SIGRID. Yes, I . . . I have a little.

JENNY. Good. Then I treat you. We'll be next door if you want us, Marta.

> (MAMA *nods without looking at them, her eyes still fixed on the elevator door. The* AUNTS *leave, going down the steps from the stage as though they were the hospital steps, and off L.*
>
> *For a moment, the stage is quiet. Then a* SCRUB-WOMAN *enters from down R., carrying a mop and pail which she puts into the closet, and then leaves. The elevator door opens and a doctor in white coat comes out, followed by an orderly, carrying a tray of dressings. They disappear up R. behind the desk.* MAMA *rises, agitatedly, looking after them. Then* DR. JOHNSON *returns from R. front, carrying his hat and bag. He sees* MAMA *and crosses to her, C.*)

DOCTOR. Oh, Mrs. Hanson. . . .

MAMA. Doctor. . . .

DOCTOR. Well, Dagmar's fine. She came through it beautifully. She's back in bed now, sleeping off the anaesthetic.

MAMA. Thank you, Doctor. (*She shakes hands with him.*)

DOCTOR. You're very welcome.

MAMA. Is good of you, Doctor. (*She shakes hands with him again.*) Where is she? I go to her now.

DOCTOR. Oh, I'm sorry, but I'm afraid that's against the rules. You shall see her tomorrow.

MAMA. Tomorrow? But, Doctor, she is so little. When she wakes she will be frightened.

DOCTOR. The nurses will take care of her. Excellent care. You needn't worry. You see, for the first twenty-four hours, clinic patients aren't allowed to see visitors. The wards must be kept quiet.

MAMA. I will not make a sound.

DOCTOR. I'm very sorry. Tomorrow. And now . . . (*He glances at his watch.*) Good afternoon.

> (*He puts on his hat and goes out L., down the steps and off.*)

> (MAMA *stands still a moment, looking after him.*)

MAMA. Come, Nels. We go find Dagmar.

NELS. But, Mama, the doctor said . . .

MAMA. We find Dagmar.

> (*She looks vaguely around her. Then goes to the nurse's desk.*)

You tell me, please, where I can find my daughter?

NURSE. What name?

MAMA. Dagmar.

NELS. Dagmar Hanson.

NURSE (*looking at her record book*). Hanson, Ward A. Along there.

> (*She points upstage.* MAMA *starts to go up.*)

Oh, just a moment.

> (MAMA *returns.*)

When did she come in?

MAMA. This morning. They just finish operation.

NURSE. Oh, well, then I'm afraid you can't see her today. No visitors for the first twenty-four hours.

MAMA. Am not visitor. I am her Mama.

NURSE. I'm sorry, but it's against the rules.

MAMA. Just for one minute. Please.

NURSE. I'm sorry. It's against the rules.

(MAMA *stands staring.* NELS *touches her arm. She looks at him, nods, trying to smile, then turns and walks with him to L. and down the steps.*)

MAMA. We must think of some way.

NELS. Mama, they'll let you see her tomorrow. They said so.

MAMA. If I don't see her today how will I know that all is well with her? What can I tell Papa when he comes home from work?

NELS. The nurses will look after her, Mama. Would you like to come next door for some coffee?

MAMA (*shaking her head*). We go home. We have coffee at home. But I must see Dagmar today.

(*She plods off L. with* NELS.) (*The travellers close.*)

(*Spot goes up on R. turntable.* UNCLE CHRIS *and* MR. THORKELSON *are seated on a bench and chair, as in a waiting-room. A table with a potted plant is between them. A clock on the wall points to 2:30.*)

UNCLE CHRIS. Well, it comes then to this. You love my niece, Trina?

(MR. THORKELSON, *very scared, gulps and nods.*)

You want to marry her?

(MR. THORKELSON *nods again.*)

You are in position to support her?

(MR. THORKELSON *nods again.*)

Why, then, you want dowry?

(*No answer. He shouts.*)

What for you want dowry?

MR. THORKELSON. Well . . . well, it would be a nice help. And it is customary.

UNCLE CHRIS. Is not customary. Who give dowries? Parents. Why? Because they are so glad they will not have to support their daughters any more, they pay money. I do not support Trina. I do not care if Trina gets married. Why then should I pay to have her married?

MR. THORKELSON. I never thought of it like that.

UNCLE CHRIS. Is insult to girl to pay dowry. If I do not give dowry, will you still marry Trina?

MR. THORKELSON. I . . . I don't know.

UNCLE CHRIS. You don't know? You don't know?? You think I let Trina marry a man who will not take her without dowry?

MR. THORKELSON. No, I suppose you wouldn't.

UNCLE CHRIS. What kind of man would that be? I ask you, what kind of man would that be?

MR. THORKELSON (*fascinated—helpless*). Well, not a very nice kind of man.

UNCLE CHRIS. And are you that kind of man?

MR. THORKELSON. I . . . I don't think so.

UNCLE CHRIS (*conclusively*). Then you don't want dowry!!

MR. THORKELSON (*giving up*). No, I . . . I guess I don't.

UNCLE CHRIS (*slapping his back*). Goot. Goot. You are goot man. I like you. I give you my blessing. And I send you vedding present. I send you box of oranges.

> (*While he is boisterously shaking Mr. Thorkelson's hand, blackout. Turntable revolves out.*)

> (*The curtains open on the kitchen. It is empty.* MAMA *and* NELS *come up the hill from the L. and let themselves into the house. There is silence as they take off their hats and coats.*)

MAMA (*after a moment*). Where are the girls?

NELS. I guess they're upstairs.

> (*Goes to door back L. and calls*)

Chris! Katrin!

GIRLS' VOICES. Coming!

NELS. Shall I make you some coffee?

> (MAMA *shakes her head.*)

You said you'd have coffee when you got home.

MAMA.   Later. First I must think.

NELS.   Mama, please don't worry like that. Dagmar's all right. You know she's all right.

(THE GIRLS *come in back L.*)

CHRISTINE (*trying to be casual*).   Well, Mama, everything all right?

MAMA (*nodding*).   Is all right. You have eaten?

KATRIN.   Yes, Mama.

MAMA.   You drink your milk?

CHRISTINE.   Yes, Mama.

MAMA.   Is good.

CHRISTINE (*seeing her face*).   Mama, something's the matter.

KATRIN (*over-dramatically*).   Mama, Dagmar's not—? She isn't—? Mama!

MAMA.   No, Dagmar is fine. The doctor say she is fine.

(*She rises.*)

What is time?

NELS.   It's three o'clock.

MAMA.   Three hours till Papa come.

(*She looks around and then goes slowly into the pantry, back R.*)

KATRIN.   Nels, what is it? There *is* something the matter.

NELS.   They wouldn't let Mama see Dagmar. It's a rule of the hospital.

CHRISTINE.   But Dagmar's all right?

NELS.   Oh, yes, she's all right.

CHRISTINE (*impatiently*).   Well, then . . .!

NELS.   But Mama's very upset. She started talking to me in Norwegian in the street-car.

KATRIN (*emotionally*).   What can we do?

CHRISTINE (*coldly*).   You can't do anything. When will they let her see Dagmar?

NELS.   Tomorrow.

CHRISTINE.   Well, then, we'll just have to wait till tomorrow.

KATRIN.   Chris, how can you be so callous? Can't you see that Mama's heart is breaking?

CHRISTINE.   No, I can't. And you can't either. People's hearts don't break.

KATRIN.   They do, too.

CHRISTINE.   Only in books.

(MAMA *comes back; she wears an apron, and carries a scrub brush and a bucket of hot water.*)

Why, Mama, what are you going to do?

MAMA.   I scrub the floor. (*She gets down on her knees.*)

CHRISTINE.   But you scrubbed it yesterday.

MAMA.   I scrub it again. (*She starts to do so.*)

KATRIN.   But, Mama . . .

MAMA (*bending low*).   Comes a time when you've got to get down on your knees.

KATRIN (*to* CHRISTINE).   Now do you believe me?

(CHRISTINE, *suddenly unendurably moved, turns and rushes from the room.*)

NELS.   Mama, don't. Please don't. You must be tired.

KATRIN (*strangely*).   Let her alone, Nels.

(*They stand in silence watching* MAMA *scrub. Suddenly she stops.*)

What is it, Mama? What is it?

MAMA (*sitting back on her haunches*).   I think of something!

(*Slowly.*)

I think I think of something.

(*The lights dim and the curtains close on the kitchen.*)

(*From down front L.* UNCLE CHRIS' VOICE *singing. The lights slowly come up on the L. turntable, showing* ARNE *(a child of about eight) in a hospital bed, with* UNCLE CHRIS *beside him.)*

UNCLE CHRIS *(singing)*.
    "Ten t'ousand Svedes vent t'rough de veeds
        At de battle of Coppen-hagen.
    Ten t'ousand Svedes vent t'rough de veeds
        Chasing vun Nor-ve-gan!"

ARNE. Uncle Chris!

UNCLE CHRIS. Yes, Arne?

ARNE. Uncle Chris, does it *have* to hurt like this?

UNCLE CHRIS. If you vant it to be vell, and not to valk always like Uncle Chris, it does . . . for a little. Is very bad?

ARNE. It is . . . kinda. . . . Oo—oo . . .!

UNCLE CHRIS. Arne, don't you know any svear vords?

ARNE. W-what?

UNCLE CHRIS. Don't you know any svear words?

ARNE. N-no, Uncle Chris. Not real ones.

UNCLE CHRIS. Then I tell you two fine vons to use when pain is bad. Are "Damn" and "Damittohell." You say them?

ARNE. N-now?

UNCLE CHRIS. No, not now. When pain comes again. You say them then. They help plenty. I know. I haf pain, too. I say them all the time. And if pain is *very* bad, you say, "*God*-damittohell." But only if is *very* bad. Is bad now?

ARNE. No, it's . . . it's a little better.

UNCLE CHRIS. You sleep some now, maybe?

ARNE. I'll try. Will . . . will you stay here, Uncle Chris?

UNCLE CHRIS. Sure. Sure. I stay here. You are not frightened of Uncle Chris?

ARNE. No. Not any more.

UNCLE CHRIS. Goot. Goot. You like I sing some more?

ARNE. If you wouldn't mind. But maybe something a little . . . well, quieter.

UNCLE CHRIS *(tenderly)*. Sure. Sure.

(*He begins quietly to sing a Norwegian lullaby; in the midst,* ARNE *cries out.*)

ARNE. Oo—oo. . . . Oh, *damn*. Damn. Damittohell!

UNCLE CHRIS (*delighted*). Goot! It helps—eh?

ARNE (*with pleased surprise*). Yes—yes.

UNCLE CHRIS. Then you sleep some!

(*He fixes* ARNE's *pillows for him, and resumes the lullaby, seated on his chair beside the bed. After another verse, he leans over, assuring himself that the child is asleep, and then very quietly, without interrupting his singing, takes a flask from his pocket and lifts it to his lips, as the light dims. The table revolves out.*)

(*The curtains part on the hospital corridor again. There is a different* NURSE *now at the reception desk, talking on the telephone as* MAMA *and* KATRIN *come in from L. and up the steps.*)

MAMA (*as they come up, in an undertone*). Is not the same nurse. Katrin, you take my hat and coat.

(*She takes them off, revealing that she still wears her apron.*)

KATRIN. But, Mama, won't they . . .

MAMA (*interrupting, finger to lips*). Ssh! You let me go ahead. You wait on bench for me.

(*She goes to the closet door above the bench and opens it.* KATRIN *stares after her in trepidation.* MAMA *takes out a damp mop and pail, and gets down on her knees in front of the nurse's desk, starting to clean the floor. The* NURSE *looks up.* MAMA *catches her eye.*)

MAMA (*brightly*). Very dirty floors.

NURSE. Yes, I'm glad they've finally decided to clean them. Aren't you working late?

MAMA (*quickly, lowering her head*). Floors need cleaning.

> (*She pushes her way, crawling on hands and knees, up behind the desk, and disappears up the corridor, still scrubbing.* KATRIN *steals to the bench, where she sits, still clutching* MAMA's *hat and coat, looking interestedly around her. The light dims, leaving her in a single spot, as she starts to talk to herself.*)

KATRIN (*to herself*). "The Hospital" . . . A poem by Katrin Hanson.

> (*She starts to improvise.*)

> "She waited, fearful, in the hall,
> And held her bated breath."

Breath—yes, that'll rhyme with death.

> (*She repeats the first two lines.*)

> "She waited fearful in the hall
> And held her bated breath.
> She trembled at the least footfall,
> And kept her mind on death."

> (*She gets a piece of paper and pencil from her pocket and begins to scribble, as a* NURSE *comes out of the elevator, carrying some charts, which she takes to the desk, and then goes out down R.* KATRIN *goes on with her poem.*)

> "Ah, God, 'twas agony to wait.
> To wait and watch and wonder. . . ."

Wonder—under—bunder—funder—sunder. Sunder!

> (*Nods to herself and goes on again.*)

> "To wait and watch and wonder,
> About her infant sister's fate,
> If Death life's bonds would sunder."

> (*Then, to herself again, looking front.*)

That's beautiful. Yes, but it isn't true. Dagmar isn't dying.

It's funny—I don't want her to die—and yet when Mama said she was all right, I was almost—well, almost disappointed. It wasn't exciting any more. Maybe Christine's right, and I haven't any heart. How awful! "The girl without a heart." That'd be a nice title for a story. "The girl without a heart sat in the hospital corridor. . . ."

> (*The lights come up again as* UNCLE CHRIS *appears, up R. behind the desk. He wears his hat and is more than a little drunk. He sees* KATRIN.)

UNCLE CHRIS.   Katrinë. What you do here?

> (*He sits on the bench beside her.*)

KATRIN (*nervously*).   I'm waiting for Mama.

UNCLE CHRIS.   Where is she?

KATRIN (*scared*).   I . . . I don't know.

UNCLE CHRIS.   What you mean . . . you don't know?

KATRIN (*whispering*).   I think . . . I think she's seeing Dagmar.

UNCLE CHRIS (*shaking his head*).   Is first day. They do not allow visitors first day.

KATRIN (*trying to make him aware of the* NURSE).   I know. But I think that's where she is.

UNCLE CHRIS.   Where *is* Dagmar?

KATRIN.   I don't know.

> (UNCLE CHRIS *rises and goes to the* NURSE *at the desk.*)

UNCLE CHRIS.   In what room is my great-niece, Dagmar Hanson?

NURSE (*looking at her book*).   Hanson . . . Hanson . . . when did she come in?

UNCLE CHRIS.   This morning.

NURSE.   Oh, yes. Were you wanting to see her?

UNCLE CHRIS.   What room is she in?

NURSE.   I asked were you wanting to see her.

UNCLE CHRIS.   And *I* ask what room she is in.

NURSE. We don't allow visitors the first day.

UNCLE CHRIS. Have I said I vant to visit her? I ask what room she is in.

NURSE. Are you by chance, Mr. . . . (*looking at her book*) Halvorsen?

UNCLE CHRIS (*proudly, and correcting her pronunciation*) Christopher Halvorsen.

NURSE. Did you say you were her uncle?

UNCLE CHRIS. Her great-uncle.

NURSE. Well, then, I'm afraid I can't tell you anything about her.

UNCLE CHRIS. Why not?

NURSE. Orders.

UNCLE CHRIS. Whose orders?

NURSE. Dr. Johnson's. There's a special note here. Patient's uncle, Mr. Halvorsen, not to be admitted or given information under any circumstances.

UNCLE CHRIS (*after a moment's angry stupefaction*). Goddamittohell!

> (*He strides away down L., taking out his flask, and shaking it, only to find it empty.* MAMA *returns from up R., carrying the mop and pail, walking now and smiling triumphantly.*)

MAMA (*to the* NURSE). Thank you.

> (*She replaces the mop and pail in the closet, and then sees* UNCLE CHRIS).

Uncle Chris, Dagmar is fine!

UNCLE CHRIS (*coming back to her, amazed*). You see her?

MAMA. Sure, Uncle Chris, I see her.

UNCLE CHRIS (*reiterating, incredulous*). You see Dagmar?!

MAMA. Sure.

> (*She takes her hat from* KATRIN *and starts to put it on.*)

Is fine hospital. But such floors! A mop is never good. Floors should be scrubbed with a brush. We go home. Uncle Chris, you come with us? I make coffee.

UNCLE CHRIS.   Pah! Vot good is coffee? I go get drink.

MAMA (*reprovingly*).   Uncle Chris!

UNCLE CHRIS.   Marta, you are fine voman. Fine. But I go get drink. I get drunk.

MAMA (*quickly aside to* KATRIN).   His leg hurts him.

UNCLE CHRIS.   And you do not make excuses for me! I get drunk because I like it.

MAMA (*conciliating him*).   Sure, Uncle Chris.

UNCLE CHRIS (*shouting*).   I like it!

(*Then, with a change.*)

No, is not true. You know is not true. I do not like to get drunk at all. But I do not like to come home with you, either.

(*Growing slightly maudlin.*)

You have family. Is fine thing. You do not know how fine. Katrinë, one day when you grow up, maybe you know what a fine thing a family is. I haf no family.

KATRIN.   But, Uncle Chris, Mama's always said you were the *head* of the family.

UNCLE CHRIS.   Sure. Sure. I am head of the family, but I haf no family. So I go get drunk. You understand, Marta?

MAMA.   Sure, Uncle Chris. You go get drunk.

(*Sharply.*)

But don't you feel sorry for yourself!

(UNCLE CHRIS *glares at her a moment, then strides off R., boisterously singing his song of "Ten Thousand Swedes."* MAMA *watches him go, then takes her coat from* KATRIN.)

Is fine man. Has fine ideas about family.

(KATRIN *helps her on with her coat.*)

I can tell Papa now that Dagmar is fine. She wake while I am with her. I explain rules to her. She will not expect us now until tomorrow afternoon.

KATRIN. You won't try and see her again before that?

MAMA (*gravely*). No. That would be against the rules! Come. We go home.

(*They go off L.*)

CURTAIN

ACT II

SCENE: *Opening, exactly as in Act One.* KATRIN *at her desk.*

KATRIN (*reading*).   "It wasn't very often that I could get Mama to talk—about herself, or her life in the old country, or what she felt about things. You had to catch her unawares, or when she had nothing to do, which was very, very seldom. I don't think I can ever remember seeing Mama unoccupied."

(*Laying down the manuscript and looking out front.*)

I do remember one occasion, though. It was the day before Dagmar came home from the hospital. And as we left, Mama suggested treating me to an ice-cream soda.

(*She rises, gets her hat from beside her—a school-girl hat—puts it on and crosses C. while she speaks the next lines.*)

She had never done such a thing before, and I remember how proud it made me feel—just to sit and talk to her quietly like a grown-up person. It was a kind of special *treat*-moment in my life that I'll always remember—quite apart from the soda, which was *wonderful.*

(*She has reached C. stage now.* MAMA *has come from between the curtains, and starts down the steps.*)

MAMA.   Katrin, you like we go next door, and I treat you to an ice-cream soda?

KATRIN (*young now, and overcome*).   Mama—do you mean it?

MAMA.   Sure. We celebrate. We celebrate that Dagmar is well, and coming home again.

(*They cross to the L., where the turntable represents a drugstore, with a table and two chairs at which they seat themselves.*)

What you like to have, Katrin?

KATRIN.   I think a chocolate . . . no, a strawberry . . . no, a chocolate soda.

MAMA (*smiling*).   You are sure?

KATRIN (*gravely*).   I think so. But, Mama, can we *afford* it?

MAMA.   I think this once we can afford it.

(*The* SODA CLERK *appears from L.*)

SODA CLERK.   What's it going to be, ladies?

MAMA.   A chocolate ice-cream soda, please—and a cup of coffee.

(*The* SODA CLERK *goes.*)

KATRIN.   Mama, he called us "ladies"!

(MAMA *smiles.*)

Why aren't you having a soda, too?

MAMA.   Better I like coffee.

KATRIN.   When can I drink coffee?

MAMA.   When you are grown up.

KATRIN.   When I'm eighteen?

MAMA.   Maybe before that.

KATRIN.   When I graduate?

MAMA.   Maybe. I don't know. Comes the day you are grown up. Papa and I will know.

KATRIN.   Is coffee really nicer than a soda?

MAMA.   When you are grown up, it is.

KATRIN.   Did you use to like sodas better . . . before you were grown up?

MAMA.   We didn't have sodas before I was grown up. It was in the old country.

KATRIN (*incredulous*).   You mean they don't have sodas in Norway?

MAMA.   Now, maybe. Now I think they have many things from America. But not when I was a little girl.

(*The* SODA CLERK *brings the soda and the coffee.*)

SODA CLERK.   There you are, folks. (*He sets them down and departs.*)

KATRIN (*after a good pull at the soda*).   Mama, do you ever want to go back to the old country?

MAMA.   I like to go back once to look, maybe. To see the mountains and the fjords. I like to show them once to you all. When Dagmar is big, maybe we all go back once . . . one summer . . . like tourists. But that is how it would be. I would be a tourist there now. There is no one I would know any more. And maybe we see the little house where Papa and I live when we first marry. And . . .

(*Her eyes grow misty and reminiscent.*)

something else I would look at.

KATRIN.   What is that?

(MAMA *does not answer.*)

What would you look at, Mama?

MAMA.   Katrin, you do not know you have brother? Besides Nels?

KATRIN.   No! A brother? In Norway? Mama. . . .

MAMA.   He is my first baby. I am eighteen when he is born.

KATRIN.   Is he there now?

MAMA (*simply*).   He is dead.

KATRIN (*disappointed*).   Oh. I thought you meant . . . I thought you meant a real brother. A long-lost one, like in stories. When did he die?

MAMA.   When he is two years old. It is his grave I would like to see again.

(*She is suddenly near tears, biting her lip and stirring her coffee violently, spilling a few drops on her suit. She gets her handkerchief from her pocketbook, dabs at her skirt, then briefly at her nose, then she returns the handkerchief and turns to* KATRIN *again.*)

(*Matter-of-factly.*)

Is good, your ice-cream soda?

KATRIN (*more interested now in* MAMA *than in it*).   Yes.
Mama . . . have you had a very *hard* life?

MAMA (*surprised*).   Hard? No. No life is easy all the
time. It is not meant to be.

KATRIN.   But . . . rich people . . . aren't *their* lives easy?

MAMA.   I don't know, Katrin. I have never known rich
people. But I see them sometimes in stores and in the streets,
and they do not *look* as if they were easy.

KATRIN.   Wouldn't you like to be rich?

MAMA.   I would like to be rich the way I would like to be
ten feet high. Would be good for some things—bad for others.

KATRIN.   But didn't you come to America to get rich?

MAMA (*shocked*).   No. We come to America because
they are all here—all the others. Is good for families to be
together.

KATRIN.   And did you like it right away?

MAMA.   Right away. When we get off the ferry boat and
I see San Francisco and all the family, I say: "Is like Norway," only it is better than Norway. And then you are all
born here, and I become American citizen. But not to get
rich.

KATRIN.   *I* want to be rich. Rich and famous. I'd buy
you your warm coat. When are you going to get that coat,
Mama?

MAMA.   Soon now, maybe—when we pay doctor, and Mr.
Hyde pay his rent. I think now I *must* ask him. I ask him
tomorrow, after Dagmar comes home.

KATRIN.   When I'm rich and famous, I'll buy you lovely
clothes. White satin gowns with long trains to them. And
jewellery. I'll buy you a pearl necklace.

MAMA.   We talk too much!

(*She signs to the* SODA CLERK.)

Come, finish your soda. We must go home.

(*The* SODA CLERK *comes.*)

How much is it, please?

SODA CLERK.   Fifteen cents.

MAMA.   Here are two dimes. You keep the nickel. And thank you. Was good coffee.

>   (*They start out and up the steps towards the curtains C.*)

Tomorrow Dagmar will be home again. And, Katrin, you see Uncle Elizabeth is there. This afternoon again she was asking for him. You keep Uncle Elizabeth in the house all day until she comes home.

>   (*They disappear behind the curtains.*)

>   (*After a second, the howls of a cat in pain are heard from behind the curtains—low at first, then rising to a heart-rending volume, and then diminishing again as the curtains part on the kitchen once more.* MAMA, PAPA, *and* DAGMAR *are entering the house.*)

DAGMAR (*standing on threshold, transfixed*).   It's Uncle Elizabeth, welcoming me home! That's his song of welcome. Where is he, Mama?

>   (*She looks around for the source of the howls.*)

MAMA.   He is in the pantry. . . .

>   (*As* DAGMAR *starts to rush thither.*)

But wait . . . wait a minute, Dagmar. I must tell you. Uncle Elizabeth is . . . sick.

DAGMAR.   Sick? What's the matter with him?

PAPA.   He has been in fight. Last night. He come home this morning very sick indeed.

>   (DAGMAR *starts for the pantry door, back R., as* NELS *comes out.*)

MAMA.   Nels, how is Uncle Elizabeth? Nels has been doctoring him.

NELS.   He's pretty bad, Mama. I've dressed all his wounds again with boric acid, but . . .

(*As* DAGMAR *tries to get past him.*)

I wouldn't go and see him now, baby.

DAGMAR.   I've got to. He's *my* cat. I haven't seen him in a whole month. More.

(*She runs into the pantry and disappears.*)

MAMA.   Nels, what you think?

NELS.   I think we ought to have had him put away before she came home.

MAMA.   But she would have been so unhappy if he was not here *at all*.

NELS.   She'll be unhappier still if he dies.

(*Another howl is heard from the pantry, and then* DAGMAR *comes rushing back.*)

DAGMAR.   Mama, what happened to him? What happened to him? Oh, Mama . . . when I tried to pick him up, his bandage slipped over his eye. It was bleeding. Oh, Mama, it looked awful. Oh . . .

(*She starts to cry.*)

MAMA (*fondling her*).   He look like that all over. Nels, you go see to his eye again.

(*Wearily,* NELS *returns to the pantry.*)

Listen, Dagmar . . . *Lille Ven* . . . would it not be better for the poor thing to go quietly to sleep?

DAGMAR.   You mean—go to sleep and never wake up again?

(MAMA *nods gently.*)

No.

PAPA.   I think he die anyway. Nels try to make him well. But I do not think he can.

DAGMAR.   Mama can. Mama can do everything.

> (*Another howl from offstage. She clutches* MAMA
> *agonizedly.*)

Make him live, Mama. Make him well again. *Please!*

MAMA. We see. Let us see how he gets through the night.
And now, Dagmar, you must go to bed. I bring you your
supper.

DAGMAR. But you will fix Uncle Elizabeth? You promise,
Mama?

MAMA. I promise I try. Go now.

> (DAGMAR *goes out, back L.*)

I must fix her supper.

> (*She starts for the pantry. Howls again. She and*
> PAPA *stand and look at each other.* NELS *comes*
> *out.*)

NELS. Mama, it's just cruelty, keeping that cat alive.

MAMA. I know.

PAPA (*as another howl, the loudest yet, emerges*). You
say we see how the cat get through the night. I ask you how
do *we* get through the night? Is no use, Marta. We must put
the cat to sleep. Nels, you go to the drug-store, and get
something. Some chloroform, maybe.

> (*He gives him a coin.*)

NELS. How much shall I get?

PAPA. You ask the man. You tell him it is for a cat. He
knows.

> (NELS *goes out L. and down the street into the wings.*)

> (*Looking at* MAMA's *face.*)

Is best. Is the only thing.

MAMA. I know. But poor Dagmar. It is sad homecoming
for her. And she has been so good in hospital. Never once
she cry.

> (*She pulls herself together.*)

I get her supper.

(*Another howl from offstage.*)

And I take the cat outside. Right outside, where we . . . where *Dagmar* cannot hear him.

> (*She goes into the pantry.* PAPA *takes a folded newspaper from his pocket, puts on his glasses and starts to read. The door, back L., opens gently and* MR. HYDE *peeps out. He wears his hat and coat and carries his suitcase and a letter.* PAPA *has his back to him.* MR. HYDE *lays the letter on the dresser and then starts to tiptoe across to the door. Then* PAPA *sees him.*)

PAPA.   You go out, Mr. Hyde?

MR. HYDE (*pretending surprise*).   Oh. . . . Oh, I did not see you, Mr. Hanson.

> (*He puts down the suitcase.*)

I did not know you were back. As a matter of fact, I . . . I was about to leave this letter for you.

> (*He fetches it.*)

The fact is . . . I . . . have been called away.

PAPA.   So?

MR. HYDE.   A letter I received this morning necessitates my departure. My immediate departure.

PAPA.   I am sorry.

> (MAMA *returns with a tray, on which are milk, bread, butter, and jelly.*)

Mama, Mr. Hyde says he goes away.

MAMA (*coming to the table with the tray*).   Is true?

MR. HYDE.   Alas, dear Madam, yes. 'Tis true, 'tis pity. And pity 'tis, 'tis true. You will find here . . .

> (*He presents the letter.*)

my cheque for all I owe you, and a note expressing my profoundest thanks for all your most kind hospitality. You will say good-bye to the children for me?

(*He bows, as* MAMA *takes the letter.*)

MAMA (*distressed*).   Sure. Sure.

MR. HYDE (*bowing again*).   Madam, my deepest gratitude.

(*He kisses her hand.* MAMA *looks astonished. He bows to* PAPA.)

Sir—my sincerest admiration!

(*He opens the street door.*)

It has been a privilege. Ave Atque Vale! Hail and farewell!

(*He makes a gesture and goes.*)

MAMA.   Was wonderful man! Is too bad.

(*She opens the letter, takes out the cheque.*)

PAPA.   How much is the cheque for?

MAMA.   Hundred ten dollar! Is four months.

PAPA.   Good. Good.

MAMA.   Is wonderful. Now we pay doctor everything.

PAPA.   And you buy your warm coat. With fur now, maybe.

MAMA (*sadly*).   But there will be no more reading. You take the cheque, Lars. You get the money?

PAPA (*taking it*).   Sure, I get it. What does he say in his letter?

MAMA.   You read it while I fix supper for Dagmar.

(*She starts to butter the bread, and spread jelly, while* PAPA *reads.*)

PAPA (*reading*).   "Dear Friends, I find myself compelled to take a somewhat hasty departure from this house of happiness. . . ."

MAMA.   Is beautiful letter.

PAPA (*continuing*).   "I am leaving you my library for the children. . . ."

MAMA.   He leaves his books?

PAPA.   He says so.

MAMA. But is wonderful. Go see, Lars. See if they are in his room.

(PAPA *lays down the letter and goes out back L.* NELS *and* CHRISTINE *appear down L., coming up to the house.* CHRISTINE *carries schoolbooks.*)

CHRISTINE. I'm sure it was him, Nels. Carrying his suitcase, and getting on the cable-car. I'm sure he's going away.

NELS. Well, I hope he's paid Mama.

(*They open the street door.*)

CHRISTINE (*bursting in*). Mama, I saw Mr. Hyde getting on the cable-car.

MAMA. I know. He leave.

CHRISTINE. Did he pay you?

MAMA. Sure, he pay me. Hundred ten dollar. . . .

NELS. Gee. . . .

MAMA (*smiling*). Is good.

CHRISTINE. Are you going to put it in the Bank?

MAMA. We need it right away.

(PAPA *returns, staggering under an armload of books.*)

Mr. Hyde leaves his books, too. For you.

NELS. Say!

(PAPA *stacks them on the table.* NELS *and* CHRISTINE *rush to them, reading the titles.*)

The Pickwick Papers, The Complete Shakespeare . . .

CHRISTINE. Alice in Wonderland, The Oxford Book of Verse . . .

NELS. The Last of the Mohicans, Ivanhoe . . .

CHRISTINE. We were right in the middle of that.

MAMA. Nels can finish it. He can read to us now in the evenings. He has fine voice, too, like Mr. Hyde.

(NELS *flushes with pleasure.*)

Is wonderful. So much we can learn.

(*She finishes the supper-making.*)

Christine, you take the butter back to the cooler for me, and the yelly, too.

(CHRISTINE *does so.*)

I go up to Dagmar now.

(*She lifts the tray, then pauses.*)

You get it, Nels?

NELS.　What? . . . Oh. . . .

(*Taking a druggist's small bottle from his pocket.*)

Here.

MAMA.　You put it down. After I come back, we do it. You know how?

NELS.　Why, no, Mama, I . . .

MAMA.　You do not ask?

NELS.　No, I . . . I thought Papa . . .

MAMA.　You know, Lars?

PAPA.　No, I don't *know* . . . but it cannot be difficult. If you *hold* the cat . . .

MAMA.　And watch him die? No! I think better you get rags . . . and a big sponge, to soak up the chloroform. You put it in the box with him, and cover him over. You get them ready out there.

NELS.　Sure, Mama.

MAMA.　I bring some blankets.

(NELS *goes off to the pantry, as* CHRISTINE *comes back. Again* MAMA *lifts the tray and starts for the door back L. But there is a knock on the street door from* AUNT JENNY, *who has come to the house from down L. in a state of some excitement.*)

MAMA (*agitated*).　So much goes on! See who it is, Christine.

CHRISTINE (*peeping*).　It's Aunt Jenny.

(*She opens the door.*)

MAMA.　Jenny. . . .

JENNY (*breathless*).   Marta . . . has he gone?

MAMA.   Who?

JENNY.   Your boarder . . . Mr. Hyde. . . .

MAMA.   Yes, he has gone. Why?

JENNY.   Did he pay you?

MAMA.   Sure he pay me.

JENNY.   How?

MAMA.   He give me a cheque. Lars has it right there.

JENNY (*with meaning*).   A cheque!

MAMA.   Jenny, what is it? Christine, you give Dagmar her supper. I come soon.

> (CHRISTINE *takes the tray from her and goes out back L.*)

What is it, Jenny? How do you know that Mr. Hyde has gone?

JENNY.   I was at Mr. Kruper's down the street . . . you know, the restaurant and bakery, . . . and he told me Mr. Hyde was there today having his lunch, and when he left he asked if he would cash a cheque for him. For fifty dollars.

> (*She pauses.*)

PAPA.   Well, go on.

JENNY.   Your fine Mr. Hyde didn't expect Mr. Kruper to take it to the bank until tomorrow, but he did. And what do you think? Mr. Hyde hasn't even an *account* at that bank!

> (NELS *returns and stands in the pantry doorway.*)

MAMA.   I don't understand.

PAPA (*taking the cheque from his pocket*).   You mean the cheque is no good?

JENNY.   No good at all.

> (*Triumphantly.*)

Your Mr. Hyde was a crook, just as I always thought he was, for all his reading and fine ways. Mr. Kruper said he'd been cashing them all over the neighbourhood.

(MAMA *stands quite still, without answering.*)
How much did he owe you? Plenty, I'll bet.

(*Still no answer.*)

Eh? Marta, I said I bet he owed you plenty. Didn't he?

MAMA (*looks around, first at* NELS *and then down at the books on the table. She touches them.*)
No. No, he owed us nothing.

(*She takes the cheque from* PAPA, *tearing it.*)
Nothing.

JENNY (*persistently*). How much was that cheque *for*?

(*She reaches her hand for it.*)

MAMA (*evading her*). It does not matter. He pay with better things than money.

(*She goes to the stove, where she throws in the cheque, watching it burn.*)

JENNY. I told you right in the beginning that you shouldn't trust him. But you were so sure . . . just like you always are. Mr. Hyde was a gentleman. A gentleman! I bet it must have been a hundred dollars that he rooked you of. Wasn't it?

MAMA (*returning*). Jenny, I cannot talk now. Maybe you don't have things to do. I have.

JENNY (*sneeringly*). What? What have *you* got to do that's so important?

MAMA (*taking up the medicine bottle*). I have to chloroform a cat!

(JENNY *steps back in momentary alarm, almost as though* MAMA *were referring to her, as she goes out into the pantry with the medicine bottle, not so very unlike Lady Macbeth with the daggers.*)

(*Blackout and curtains close.*)

(*After a moment, the curtains part again on the kitchen, the next morning. The books have been taken off the table, and* MAMA *is setting the break-*

fast dishes, with PAPA *helping her.* DAGMAR *comes bursting into the room, back L.*)

DAGMAR. Good morning, Mama. 'Morning, Papa. Is Uncle Elizabeth all better?

MAMA. Dagmar, there is something I must tell you.

DAGMAR. I want to see Uncle Elizabeth first.

(*She runs into the pantry.* MAMA *turns helplessly to* PAPA.)

MAMA. Do something! Tell her!

PAPA. If we just let her think the cat die . . . by itself. . . .

MAMA. No. We cannot tell her lies.

(PAPA *goes to the pantry door, opening it.*)

DAGMAR (*heard in pantry, off*). What a funny, funny smell. Good morning, my darling, my darling Elizabeth.

(MAMA *and* PAPA *stand stricken.* DAGMAR *comes in, carrying the cat, wrapped in an old shirt, with its head covered.*)

My goodness, you put enough blankets on him! Did you think he'd catch cold?

MAMA (*horror-stricken*). Dagmar, you must not. . . .

(*She stops at the sight of the cat, whose tail is twitching, quite obviously alive.*)

Dagmar, let me see . . . Let me see the cat!

(*She goes over to her, and uncovers its head.*)

DAGMAR (*overjoyed*). He's well. Oh, Mama, I *knew* you'd fix him.

MAMA (*appalled*). But, Dagmar, I didn't. I . . .

DAGMAR (*ignoring her*). I'm going to take him right up and show him to Nels.

(*She runs off back L., calling*)

Nels! Nels! Uncle Elizabeth's well again!

MAMA (*turning to* PAPA). Is a miracle!

PAPA (*shrugging*). You cannot have used enough chloroform. You just give him good sleep, and that cures him. We rechristen the cat, Lazarus!

MAMA. But, Lars, we must tell her. Is not *good* to let her grow up believing I can fix *everything!*

PAPA. Is best thing in the world for her to believe.

(*He chuckles.*)

Besides, I know *exactly* how she feels.

(*He lays his hand on hers.*)

MAMA (*turning with embarrassment from his demonstrativeness*). We finish getting breakfast.

(*She turns back to the table. The curtains close.*)

(*Lights up down front R.* KATRIN *and* CHRISTINE *enter from the wings, in school clothes, wearing hats.* CHRISTINE *carries schoolbooks in a strap.* KATRIN *is reciting.*)

KATRIN.

"The quality of mercy is not strained,
It droppeth as the gentle rain from heaven
Upon the place beneath: it is twice blest;
It blesseth him that gives, and him that takes. . . ."

(*She dries up.*)

". . . him that takes. It blesseth him that gives and him that takes. . . ."

(*She turns to* CHRISTINE.)

What comes after that?

CHRISTINE. I don't know. And I don't care.

KATRIN. Why, Chris!

CHRISTINE. I don't. It's all I've heard for weeks. The school play, and your graduation, and going on to High. And never a thought of what's happening at home.

KATRIN. What do you mean?

CHRISTINE. You see—you don't even know!

KATRIN. Oh, you mean the strike?

CHRISTINE.   Yes, I mean the strike. Papa hasn't worked
for four whole weeks, and a lot you care. Why, I don't believe you even know what they're striking *for*. Do you? All
you and your friends can talk about is the presents you're
going to get. You make me ashamed of being a girl.

(*Two girls,* MADELINE *and* DOROTHY, *come through
the curtains C., talking.*)

MADELINE (*to* DOROTHY).   Thyra Walsh's family's going
to add seven pearls to the necklace they started for her when
she was a baby. Oh, hello, Katrin! Did you hear about
Thyra's graduation present?

KATRIN (*not very happily*).   Yes, I heard.

MADELINE.   I'm getting an onyx ring, with a diamond in it.

KATRIN.   A real diamond?

MADELINE.   Yes, of course. A *small* diamond.

DOROTHY.   What are *you* getting?

KATRIN.   Well . . . well, they haven't actually told me, but
I think . . . I think I'm going to get that pink celluloid dresser
set in your father's drug-store.

DOROTHY.   You mean that one in the window?

KATRIN (*to* MADELINE).   It's got a brush and comb and
mirror . . . and a hair-receiver. It's genuine celluloid!

DOROTHY.   I wanted Father to give it to me, out of stock,
but he said it was too expensive. Father's an awful tightwad.
They're giving me a bangle.

MADELINE.   Oh, there's the street-car. We've got to fly.
'Bye, Katrin. 'Bye, Christine. See you tomorrow. Come on,
Dorothy.

(*The* TWO GIRLS *rush off L.*)

CHRISTINE.   Who said you were going to get the dresser
set?

KATRIN.   Nobody's said so . . . for certain. But I've sort of
hinted, and . . .

CHRISTINE.   Well, you're not going to get it.

KATRIN. How do you know?

CHRISTINE. Because I know what you *are* getting. I heard Mama tell Aunt Jenny. Aunt Jenny said you were too young to appreciate it.

KATRIN. What is it?

CHRISTINE. Mama's giving you her brooch. Her *solje*.

KATRIN. You mean that old silver thing she wears that belonged to Grandmother? What would I want an old thing like that for?

CHRISTINE. It's an heirloom. Mama thinks a lot of it.

KATRIN. Well, then, she ought to keep it. You don't really mean that's *all* they're going to give me?

CHRISTINE. What more do you want?

KATRIN. I want the dresser set. My goodness, if Mama doesn't realize what's a suitable present . . . why, it's practically the most important time in a girl's life, when she graduates.

CHRISTINE. And you say you're not selfish!

KATRIN. It's not selfishness.

CHRISTINE. Well, I don't know what else you'd call it. With Papa not working, we need every penny we can lay our hands on. Even the Little Bank's empty. But you'll devil Mama into giving you the dresser set somehow. So why talk about it? I'm going home.

(*She turns and goes up the steps and through the curtains.*)

(KATRIN *stands alone with a set and stubborn mouth, and then sits on the steps.*)

KATRIN. Christine was right. I got the dresser set. They gave it to me just before supper on graduation night. Papa could not attend the exercises because there was a strike meeting to decide about going back to work. I was so excited that night, I could hardly eat, and the present took the last remnants of my appetite clean away.

(*The curtains part on the kitchen.* PAPA, MAMA *and* DAGMAR *at table, with coffee.* CHRISTINE *is clearing dishes.*)

CHRISTINE. I'll just stack the dishes now, Mama. We'll wash them when we come home.

(*She carries them into the pantry.*)

PAPA (*holding up a cube of sugar*). Who wants coffee-sugar?

(*He dips it in his coffee.*)

Dagmar?

(*He hands it to her.*)

Katrin?

(*She rises from the step, coming into the scene for the sugar.*)

MAMA. You get your coat, Katrin; you need it.

(KATRIN *goes out back L.*)

DAGMAR. Aunt Jenny says if we drank black coffee like you do at our age, it would turn our complexions dark. I'd like to be a black Norwegian. Like Uncle Chris. Can I, Papa?

PAPA. I like you better blonde. Like Mama.

DAGMAR. When do you get old enough for your complexion *not* to turn dark? When can we drink coffee?

PAPA. One day, when you are grown up.

(JENNY *and* TRINA *have come to the street door L.* JENNY *knocks.*)

MAMA. There are Jenny and Trina.

(*She goes to the door.*)

Is good. We can start now.

(*She opens the door.* JENNY *and* TRINA *come in.*)

JENNY. Well, are you all ready? Is Katrin very excited?

PAPA (*nodding*). She ate no supper.

(MAMA *has started to put on her hat, and to put on*
DAGMAR's *hat and coat for her.* CHRISTINE *comes*
back from the pantry. PAPA *gives her a dipped*
cube of sugar.)

JENNY. Is that *black* coffee you dipped that sugar in?
Lars, you shouldn't. It's not good for them. It'll . . .

PAPA (*finishing for her*). Turn their complexions black.
I know. Well, maybe it is all right if we have *one* coloured
daughter.

JENNY. Lars, really!

(KATRIN *returns with her coat.*)

KATRIN. Aunt Jenny, did you see my graduation present?

(*She gets it from a chair.* CHRISTINE *gives her a dis-*
gusted look, and goes out back L. KATRIN *displays*
the dresser set.)

Look! It's got a hair-receiver.

JENNY. But I thought . . . Marta, I thought you were going
to give her . . .

MAMA. No, you were right, Jenny. She is too young to
appreciate that. She like something more gay . . . more
modern.

JENNY. H'm. Well, it's very pretty, I suppose, but . . .

(*She looks up as* MAMA *puts on her coat.*)

You're not wearing your *solje!*

MAMA (*quickly*). No. I do not wear it tonight. Come,
Trina, we shall be late.

TRINA. Oh, but Peter isn't here yet.

MAMA. Katrin has her costume to put on. He can follow.
Or do you like to wait for Peter?

TRINA. I think . . . if you don't mind . . .

MAMA. You can stay with Lars. He does not have to go
yet.

JENNY. I hope Katrin knows her part.

PAPA. Sure she knows it. *I* know it, too.

TRINA.   It's too bad he can't see Katrin's debut as an actress.

MAMA.   You will be back before us, Lars?

PAPA (*nodding*).   I think the meeting will not last long.

MAMA.   Is good. We go now.

> (*She goes out with* JENNY *and* DAGMAR. CHRISTINE *and* NELS *return from back L., and follow, waiting outside for* KATRIN, *while the others go ahead.* KAT-RIN *puts on her hat and coat and picks up the dresser set.*)

PAPA (*to* TRINA).   You like we play a game of checkers while we wait?

TRINA.   Oh, I haven't played checkers in years.

PAPA.   Then I beat you. (*He rises to get the checker set.* KATRIN *kisses him.*)

KATRIN.   Good-bye, Papa.

PAPA.   Good-bye, daughter. I think of you.

KATRIN.   I'll see you there, Aunt Trina.

TRINA.   Good luck!

PAPA.   I get the checkers.

> (KATRIN *goes out L.,* PAPA *gets the checker set from a cupboard under the dresser, brings it to the table and sets it up during the ensuing scene, which is played outside in the street.*)

CHRISTINE (*contemptuously*).   Oh, bringing your cheap trash with you to show off?

KATRIN.   It's not trash. It's beautiful. You're just jealous.

CHRISTINE.   I told you you'd devil Mama into giving it to you.

KATRIN.   I didn't. I didn't devil her at all. I just showed it to her in Mr. Schiller's window. . . .

CHRISTINE.   And made her go and sell her brooch that her very own mother gave her.

KATRIN.   What?

NELS. Chris . . . you weren't supposed to tell that!

CHRISTINE. I don't care. I think she ought to know.

KATRIN. Is that true? Did Mama—Nels—?

NELS. Well, yes, as a matter of fact, she did. Now, come on.

KATRIN. No, no, I don't believe it. I'm going to ask Papa.

NELS. You haven't time.

KATRIN. I don't care.

> (*She rushes back to the house and dashes into the kitchen.* CHRISTINE *goes off down L.,* NELS *follows her.*)

Papa—Papa—Christine says— Papa, did Mama sell her brooch to give me this?

PAPA. Christine should not have told you that.

KATRIN. It's true, then?

PAPA. She did not sell it. She traded it to Mr. Schiller for your present.

KATRIN (*near tears*). Oh, but she shouldn't. . . . I never meant . . .

PAPA. Look, Katrin. You wanted the present. Mama wanted your happiness; she wanted it more than she wanted the brooch.

KATRIN. But I never meant her to do *that.* (*Crying.*) She *loved* it so. It was all she had of Grandmother's.

PAPA. She always meant it for you, Katrin. And you must not cry. You have your play to act.

KATRIN (*sobbing*). I don't want to act in it now.

PAPA. But you must. Your audience is waiting.

KATRIN (*as before*). I don't care.

PAPA. But you must care. Tonight you are not Katrin any longer. You are an actress. And an actress must act, whatever she is feeling. There is a saying—what is it—

TRINA (*brightly*). The mails must go through!

PAPA. No, no. The show must go on. So you stop crying, and go and act your play. We talk of this later. Afterwards.

KATRIN (*pulling herself together*).   All right. I'll go.

(*Sniffling a good deal, she picks up the dresser set and goes back to the street and off down L. PAPA and TRINA exchange glances, and then settle down to their checkers.*)

PAPA.   Now we play.

(*The lights fade and the curtains close.*)

(*Spot up on stage R. turntable. The two girls from the earlier scene are dressing in costumes for "The Merchant of Venice" before a plank dressing table.*)

DOROTHY.   I'm getting worried about Katrin. If anything's happened to *her* . . .

MADELINE (*pulling up her tights*).   I'll forget my lines. I know I will. I'll look out and see Miss Forrester sitting there, and forget every single line.

(*KATRIN rushes in from the L. She carries the dresser set, places it on the dressing table.*)

We thought you'd had an accident, or something . . .

KATRIN.   Dorothy, is your father here tonight?

DOROTHY.   He's going to be. Why?

KATRIN.   I want to speak to him.

(*As she pulls off her hat and coat*)

Will you tell him . . . please . . . not to go away without speaking to me? After. After the exercises.

DOROTHY.   What on earth do you want to speak to Father for?

KATRIN.   I've got something to say to him. Something to ask him. It's important. *Very* important.

MADELINE.   Is that the dresser set? (*Picking it up.*) Can I look at it a minute?

KATRIN (*snatching it from her, violently*).   No!

MADELINE.   Why, what's the matter? I only wanted to look at it.

KATRIN (*emotionally*). You can't. You're not to touch it. Dorothy, you take it and put it where I can't see it.

(*She thrusts it at her.*)

Go on. . . . Take it! Take it! Take it!!

(*Blackout.*)

(*Curtains part on the kitchen.* MAMA *and* PAPA *in conclave at the table with cups of coffee.*)

MAMA. I am worried about her, Lars. When it was over, I see her talking with Mr. Schiller—and then she goes to take off her costume and Nels tells me that he will bring her home. But it is long time, and is late for her to be out. And in the play, Lars, she was not good. I have heard her practise it here, and she was good, but tonight, no. It was as if . . . as if she was thinking of something else all the time.

PAPA. I think maybe she was.

MAMA. But what? What can be worrying her?

PAPA. Marta . . . tonight, after you leave, Katrin found out about your brooch.

MAMA. My brooch? But how? Who told her?

PAPA. Christine.

MAMA (*angry*). Why?

PAPA. I do not know.

MAMA (*rising with a sternness we have not seen before, and calling*). Christine! Christine!

CHRISTINE (*emerging from the pantry, wiping a dish*). Were you calling me, Mama?

MAMA. Yes. Christine, did you tell Katrin tonight about my brooch?

CHRISTINE (*frightened but firm*). Yes.

MAMA. Why did you?

CHRISTINE. Because I hated the smug way she was acting over that dresser set.

MAMA. Is no excuse. You make her unhappy. You make her not good in the play.

CHRISTINE.   Well, she made *you* unhappy, giving up your brooch for her selfishness.

MAMA.   Is not your business. I choose to give my brooch. Is not for you to judge. And you know I do not want you to tell. I am angry with you, Christine.

CHRISTINE.   I'm sorry. But I'm not sorry I told.

> (*She goes back to the pantry with a set, obstinate face.*)

PAPA.   Christine is the stubborn one.

> (NELS *and* KATRIN *have approached the house outside L. They stop and look at each other in the lamplight.* KATRIN *looks scared. Then* NELS *pats her, and she goes in,* NELS *following.* MAMA *looks up inquiringly and searchingly into Katrin's face.* KATRIN *turns away, taking off her hat and coat, and taking something from her pocket.*)

NELS.   What happened at the meeting, Papa?

PAPA.   We go back to work tomorrow.

NELS.   Gee, that's bully. Isn't it, Mama?

MAMA (*absently*).   Yes, is good.

KATRIN (*coming to* MAMA).   Mama . . . here's your brooch.

> (*She gives it to her.*)

I'm sorry I was so bad in the play. I'll go and help Christine with the dishes.

> (*She turns and goes into the pantry.*)

MAMA (*unwrapping the brooch from tissue paper*).   Mr. Schiller give it back to her?

NELS.   We went to his house to get it. He didn't want to. He was planning to give it to his wife for her birthday. But Katrin begged and begged him. She even offered to go and work in his store during her vacation if he'd give it back.

PAPA (*impressed*).   So? So!

MAMA.   And what did Mr. Schiller say?

NELS.   He said that wasn't necessary.   But he gave her a
job all the same.   She's going to work for him, afternoons, for
three dollars a week.

MAMA.   And the dresser set—she gave that back?

NELS.   Yes.   She was awful upset, Mama.   It was kinda
hard for her to do.   She's a good kid.   Well, I'll say good night.
I've got to be up early.

PAPA.   Good night, Nels.

NELS.   Good night, Papa.   (*He goes out back L.*)

MAMA.   Good night, Nels.

PAPA.   Nels is the kind one.

> (*He starts to re-fill Mama's coffee cup.   She stops
> him, putting her hand over her cup.*)

No?

MAMA (*rising, crossing R. and calling*).   Katrin! Katrin!

KATRIN (*coming to the pantry door*).   Yes, Mama?

MAMA.   Come here.

> (KATRIN *comes to her.* MAMA *holds out the brooch.*)

You put this on.

KATRIN.   No . . . it's yours.

MAMA.   It is your graduation present.   I put it on for you.

> (*She pins the brooch on* KATRIN's *dress.*)

KATRIN (*near tears*).   I'll wear it always.   I'll keep it forever.

MAMA.   Christine should not have told you.

KATRIN.   I'm glad she did.   Now.

PAPA.   And I am glad, too.

> (*He dips a lump of sugar and holds it out to her.*)

Katrin?

KATRIN (*tearful again, shakes her head*).   I'm sorry, Papa.
I . . . I don't feel like it.

> (*She moves away and sits on the chest under the
> windows, with her back to the room.*)

PAPA. So? So? (*He goes to the dresser.*)

MAMA. What you want, Lars?

(*He does not answer, but takes a cup and saucer, comes to the table and pours a cup of coffee, indicating* KATRIN *with his head.* MAMA *nods, pleased, then checks his pouring and fills up the cup from the cream pitcher which she empties in so doing.* PAPA *puts in sugar, and moves to* KATRIN.)

PAPA. Katrin.

(*She turns. He holds out the cup.*)

KATRIN (*incredulous*). For me?

PAPA. For our grown-up daughter.

(MAMA *nods.* KATRIN *takes the cup, lifts it—then her emotion overcomes her. She thrusts it at* PAPA *and rushes from the room.*)

PAPA. Katrin is the dramatic one! Is too bad. Her first cup of coffee, and she does not drink it.

MAMA. It would not have been good for her, so late at night.

PAPA (*smiling*). And you, Marta, you are the practical one.

MAMA. You drink the coffee, Lars. We do not want to waste it.

(*She pushes it across to him.*)

(*Lights dim. Curtains close.*)

(*Lights up on L. turntable, representing the parlour of Jenny's house. A telephone on a table, at which* TRINA *is discovered, talking.*)

TRINA (*into phone*). Yes, Peter. Yes, Peter. I know, Peter, but we don't know where he is. It's so long since we heard from him. He's sure to turn up soon. Yes, I know, Peter. I know, but . . .

(*Subsiding obediently.*)

Yes, Peter. Yes, Peter.

> (*Sentimentally.*)

Oh, Peter, you know I do. Good-bye, Peter.

> (*She hangs up, and turns, to see* JENNY, *who has come in behind her, eating a piece of toast and jam.*)

JENNY.   What was all that about?

TRINA.   Peter says we shouldn't wait any longer to hear from Uncle Chris. He says we should send the wedding invitations out right away. He was quite insistent about it. Peter can be very masterful, sometimes . . . when he's alone with *me!*

> (*The telephone rings again.* JENNY *answers it, putting down the toast, which* TRINA *takes up and nibbles at during the scene.*)

JENNY.   This is Mrs. Stenborg's boarding house. Mrs. Stenborg speaking. Oh, yes, Marta . . . what is it?

> (*She listens.*)

> (*Spot up on R. turntable, disclosing* MAMA *standing at a wall telephone booth. She wears hat and coat, and has an opened telegram in her hand.*)

MAMA.   Jenny, is Uncle Chris. I have a telegram. It says if we want to see him again we should come without delay.

JENNY.   Where is he?

MAMA (*consulting the telegram*).   It comes from a place called Ukiah. Nels says it is up north from San Francisco.

JENNY.   Who is the telegram from?

MAMA.   It does not say.

JENNY.   That . . . woman?

MAMA.   I don't know, Jenny. I think maybe.

JENNY.   I won't go.

> (SIGRID *comes in through the curtains C., dressed in hat and coat, carrying string marketing bags, full of vegetables.* JENNY *speaks to her, whisperingly, aside.*)

It's Uncle Chris. Marta says he's dying.

> (*Then, back into phone.*)

Why was the telegram sent to *you?* I'm the eldest.

MAMA. Jenny, is not the time to think of who is eldest. Uncle Chris is dying.

JENNY. I don't believe it. He's too mean to die. Ever.

> (NELS *comes to booth from wings, R., and hands* MAMA *a slip of paper.*)

I'm not going.

MAMA. Jenny, I cannot stop to argue. There is a train at eleven o'clock. It takes four hours. You call Sigrid.

JENNY. Sigrid is here now.

MAMA. Good. Then you tell her.

JENNY. What do you say the name of the place is?

MAMA. Ukiah. (*Spelling in Norwegian*) U.K.I.A.H.

JENNY. I won't go.

MAMA. That *you* decide. (*She hangs up. Her spot goes out.*)

SIGRID. Uncle Chris dying!

JENNY. The wages of sin.

TRINA. Oh, he's old. Maybe it is time for him to go.

JENNY. Four hours by train, and maybe have to stay all night. All that expense to watch a wicked old man die of the D.T.'s.

SIGRID. I know, but . . . there is his will. . . .

JENNY. Huh, even supposing he's anything to leave— you know who he'd leave it *to*, don't you?

SIGRID. Yes. But all the same, he's dying now, and blood is thicker than water. Especially when it's Norwegian. I'm going. I shall take Arne with me. Uncle Chris was always fond of children.

TRINA. I agree with Sigrid. I think we *should* go.

JENNY. Well, *you* can't go, anyway.

TRINA. Why not?

JENNY.   Because of that woman. You can't meet a woman like that.

TRINA.   Why not? If you two can . . .

SIGRID.   We're married women.

TRINA.   I'm engaged!

JENNY.   That's not the same thing.

SIGRID.   Not the same thing at all!

TRINA.   Nonsense. I've never met a woman like that. Maybe I'll never get another chance. Besides, if he's going to change his will, there's still my dowry, remember. Do you think we should take Peter?

JENNY.   Peter Thorkelson? Whatever for?

TRINA.   Well, after all, I mean . . . I mean, his profession . . .

JENNY.   Trina, you always were a fool. Anyone would know the last person a dying man wants to see is an undertaker!

(*Blackout.*)   (*Turntable revolves out.*)

(*Spot up on* KATRIN, *standing down front, R.C. She wears her school-girl hat.*)

KATRIN.   When Mama said I was to go with her, I was excited and I was frightened. It was exciting to take sandwiches for the train, almost as though we were going on a picnic. But I was scared at the idea of seeing death, though I told myself that if I was going to be a writer, I had to experience everything. But all the same, I hoped it would be all over when we got there.

(*She starts to walk toward C. and up the steps.*)

It was afternoon when we arrived. We asked at the station for the Halvorsen ranch, and it seemed to me that the man looked at us strangely. Uncle Chris was obviously considered an odd character. The ranch was about three miles from the town; a derelict, rambling old place. There was long grass, and tall trees, and a smell of honeysuckle. We made quite a cavalcade, walking up from the gate.

> (*The procession comes in from the R., behind* KATRIN. MAMA, JENNY, TRINA, SIGRID, *and* ARNE.)

The woman came out on the steps to meet us.

> (*The procession starts towards the C., moving upwards. The* WOMAN *comes through the curtains, down one step. The* AUNTS *freeze in their tracks.* MAMA *goes forward to her.*)

MAMA. How is he? Is he—?

WOMAN (*with grave self-possession*). Come in, won't you?

> (*She holds the curtains slightly aside.* MAMA *goes in.* KATRIN *follows, looking curiously at the* WOMAN. *The* AUNTS *walk stiffly past her,* SIGRID *clutching* ARNE *and shielding him from contact with the* WOMAN. *They disappear behind the curtains. The* WOMAN *stands a moment, looking off into the distance. Then she goes in behind the curtains, too.*)

> (*The curtains draw apart, revealing Uncle Chris' bedroom. It is simple, and shabby. The door to the room is at the back, L. In the L. wall is a window, with curtains, drawn aside now. In front of it, a wash-stand. The afternoon sunlight comes through the windows, falling onto the big double bed, in which* UNCLE CHRIS *is propped up on pillows. Beside him, R., on a small table is a pitcher of water. He has a glass in his hand.* MAMA *stands to the R. of him:* JENNY *to the L. The others are ranged below the window. The* WOMAN *is not present.*)

UNCLE CHRIS (*handing* MAMA *the empty glass*). I want more. You give me more. Is still some in the bottle.

MAMA. Uncle Chris, that will not help now.

UNCLE CHRIS. It always help.

(*With a glance at* JENNY.)

Now especially.

JENNY (*firmly*). Uncle Chris, I don't think you realize . . .

UNCLE CHRIS. What I don't realize? That I am dying? Why else do I think you come here? Why else do I think you stand there, watching me?

(*He sits upright.*)

Get out. Get out. I don't want you here. Get out!

JENNY. Oh, very well. Very well. We'll be outside on the porch, if you want us.

(*She starts towards the door.*)

UNCLE CHRIS. That is where I want you—on the porch!

(JENNY *goes out.* TRINA *follows.* SIGRID *is about to go, too, when* UNCLE CHRIS *stops her.*)

Wait. That is Arne. Come here, Arne.

(ARNE, *propelled by* SIGRID, *advances toward the bed.*)

How is your knee?

ARNE. It's fine, Uncle Chris.

UNCLE CHRIS. Not hurt any more? You don't use svear vords any more?

ARNE. N-no, Uncle Chris.

UNCLE CHRIS. You walk goot? Quite goot? Let me see you walk. Walk around the room.

(ARNE *does so.*)

Fast. Fast. Run! Run!

(ARNE *does so.*)

Is goot.

SIGRID (*encouraged and advancing*). Uncle Chris, Arne has always been so fond of you. . . .

UNCLE CHRIS (*shouting*). I tell you all to get out. Except Marta.

(*As* KATRIN *edges with the* AUNTS *to the door*)

And Katrinë. Katrinë and I haf secret. You remember, Katrinë?

KATRIN. Yes, Uncle Chris.

MAMA. Uncle Chris, you must lie down again.

UNCLE CHRIS. Then you give me drink.

MAMA. No, Uncle Chris.

UNCLE CHRIS. We cannot waste what is left in the bottle. You do not drink it . . . who will drink it when I am gone? What harm can it do . . . now? I die, anyway. . . . You give it to me.

> (MAMA *goes to the wash-stand, pours him a drink of whiskey and water, and takes it to him, sitting on the bed beside him. He drinks, then turns to her, leaning back against her arm and the pillows.*)

Marta, I haf never made a will. Was never enough money. But you sell this ranch. It will not bring moch. I have not had it long enough. And there is mortgage. Big mortgage. But it leave a little. Maybe two, tree hundred dollars. You give to Yessie.

MAMA. Yessie?

UNCLE CHRIS. Yessie Brown. My housekeeper. No, why I call her that to you? You understand. She is my voman. Twelve years she has been my voman. My wife, only I cannot marry her. She has husband alive somewhere. She was trained nurse, but she get sick and I bring her to the country to get well again. There will be no money for *you*, Marta. Always I wanted there should be money to make Nils doctor. But there were other things . . . quick things. And now there is no time to make more. There is no money, but you make Nils doctor, all the same. You like?

MAMA. Sure, Uncle Chris. It is what Lars and I have always wanted for him. To help people who suffer. . . .

UNCLE CHRIS. Is the greatest thing in the world. It is to have a little of God in you. Always I wanted to be doctor myself. Is the only thing I have ever wanted. Nils must do it for me.

MAMA.   He will, Uncle Chris.

UNCLE CHRIS.   Is goot.

> (*He strokes her hand.*)

You are the goot one. I am glad you come, *Lille Ven.*

> (*He moves his head restlessly.*)

Where is Yessie?

MAMA.   I think she wait outside.

UNCLE CHRIS.   You do not mind if she is here?

MAMA.   Of course not, Uncle Chris.

UNCLE CHRIS.   You call her. I like you both be here.

> (MAMA *goes, with a quick glance at* KATRIN. UNCLE
> CHRIS *signs to* KATRIN *to come closer. She sits on
> the chair beside the bed.*)

Katrinë, your Mama write me you drink coffee now?

> (*She nods. He looks at her affectionately.*)

Katrinë, who will be writer. . . . You are not frightened of me now?

KATRIN.   No, Uncle Chris.

UNCLE CHRIS.   One day maybe you write story about Uncle Chris. If you remember.

KATRIN (*whispering*).   I'll remember.

> (MAMA *returns with the* WOMAN. *They come to the
> side of his bed.*)

UNCLE CHRIS (*obviously exhausted and in pain*).   I like you both stay with me . . . now. I think best now maybe Katrinë go away. Good-bye, Katrinë.

> (*Then he repeats it in Norwegian.*)

Farvell, Katrinë.

KATRIN.   Good-bye, Uncle Chris.

UNCLE CHRIS.   You say it in Norwegian, like I do.

KATRIN (*in Norwegian*).   Farvell, Onkel Chris.

(*She slips out, in tears.*)

UNCLE CHRIS. Yessie! Maybe I should introduce you to each other. Yessie, this is my niece, Marta. The only von of my nieces I can stand. Marta, this is Yessie, who have give me much happiness. . . .

(*The* TWO WOMEN *shake hands.*)

MAMA. I am very glad to meet you.

JESSIE. I am, too.

UNCLE CHRIS (*as they shake*). Is goot. And now you give me von more drink. You have drink with me . . . both of you. That way we finish the bottle. Yes?

(JESSIE *and* MAMA *look at each other.*)

MAMA. Sure, Uncle Chris.

UNCLE CHRIS. Goot. Yessie, you get best glasses.

(*With a chuckle to* MAMA.)

Yessie does not like to drink, but this is special occasion.

(JESSIE *gets three glasses from a wall shelf.*)

What is the time?

MAMA. It is about half past four, Uncle Chris.

UNCLE CHRIS. The sun comes around this side the house in afternoon. You draw the curtain a little maybe. Is strong for my eyes.

(MAMA *goes over and draws the curtains over the window. The stage darkens.* JESSIE *pours three drinks, filling two of the glasses with water. She is about to put water in the third when* UNCLE CHRIS *stops her.*)

No, no, I take it now without water. Always the last drink without water. Is Norwegian custom.

(*To* MAMA, *with a smile.*)

True?

(JESSIE *sits on the bed beside him, about to feed his drink to him, but he pushes her aside.*)

No. No, I do not need you feed it to me. I can drink myself.

(*He takes the glass from her.*)

Give Marta her glass.

(JESSIE *hands a glass to* MAMA. *The two women stand on either side of the bed, holding their glasses.*)

So. . . . Skoal!

JESSIE (*clinking glasses with him*).   Skoal.

MAMA (*doing likewise*).   Skoal.

(*They all three drink. Slow dim to blackout. Curtains close.*)

(*Spot up on R. turntable. A porch with a bench, and a chair, on which the three* AUNTS *are sitting.* JENNY *is dozing.*)

SIGRID (*flicking her handkerchief*).   These gnats are awful. I'm being simply eaten alive.

TRINA.   Gnats are always worse around sunset.   (*She catches one.*)

JENNY (*rousing herself*).   I should never have let you talk me into coming. To be insulted like that . . . turned out of his room . . . and then expected to sit here hour after hour without as much as a cup of coffee. . . .

SIGRID.   I'd make coffee if I knew where the kitchen was.

JENNY.   *Her* kitchen? It would poison me.

(*Rising.*)

No, I'm going home. Are you coming, Trina?

TRINA.   Oh, I think we ought to wait a little longer. After all, you can't *hurry* these things. . . . I mean . . .

(*She breaks off in confusion at what she has said.*)

JENNY (*to* SIGRID).   And all your talk about his will! A lot of chance we got to say a word!

TRINA.   Maybe Marta's been talking to him.

(MAMA *comes from between the curtains C.*)

JENNY. Well?

MAMA. Uncle Chris has . . . gone.

(*There is a silence.*)

JENNY (*more gently than is her wont*). Did he . . . say anything about a will?

MAMA. There is no will.

JENNY. Well, then, that means . . . we're his nearest relatives. . . .

MAMA. There is no money, either.

SIGRID. How do you know?

MAMA. He told me. (*She brings out a small notebook that she is carrying.*)

JENNY. What's that?

MAMA. Is an account of how he spent the money.

JENNY. Bills from a liquor store.

MAMA. No, Jenny. No. I read it to you.

(JENNY *sits again.*)

You know how Uncle Chris was lame . . . how he walked always with limp. It was his one thought . . . lame people. He would have liked to be a doctor and help them. Instead, he help them other ways. I read you the last page. . . .

(*She reads from the notebook.*)

"Joseph Spinelli. Four years old. Tubercular left leg. Three hundred thirty-seven dollars, eighteen cents."

(*Pause.*)

"Walks now. Esta Jensen. Nine years. Club-foot. Two hundred seventeen dollars, fifty cents. Walks now."

(*Then, reading very slowly.*)

"*Arne* Solfeldt. . . ."

SIGRID (*startled*). *My* Arne?

MAMA (*reading on*). "Nine years. Fractured kneecap. Four hundred forty-two dollars, sixteen cents."

(KATRIN *and* ARNE *come running in from the L. across
the stage.*)

ARNE (*calling as he comes running across*).　Mother . . .
Mother . . . Are we going to eat soon?

(*He stops, awed by the solemnity of the group, and
by* MAMA, *who puts out her hand gently, to silence
him.*)

What is it? Is Uncle Chris . . .?

MAMA (*to the* AUNTS).　It does not tell the end about Arne.
I like to write "Walks now." Yes?

SIGRID (*very subdued*).　Yes.

MAMA (*taking a pencil from the book*).　Maybe even . . .
"runs"?

(SIGRID *nods, moist-eyed.* TRINA *is crying.* MAMA
writes in the book, and then closes it.)

So. Is finished. Is all.

(*She touches* JENNY *on the shoulder.*)

It was good.

JENNY (*after a gulping moment*).　I go and make some
coffee.

(*The woman,* JESSIE, *appears from between the curtains on the steps.*)

JESSIE.　You can go in and see him now, if you want.

(JENNY *looks back, half-hesitant, at the others. Then
she nods and goes in.* TRINA *follows her, mopping
her eyes.* SIGRID *puts her arm suddenly around* ARNE
*in a spasm of maternal affection, and they, too, go
in.* MAMA, KATRIN, *and* JESSIE *are left alone.*)

I'm moving down to the hotel for tonight . . . so that you can
all stay.

(*She is about to go back, when* MAMA *stops her.*)

MAMA.　Wait. What will you do now . . . after he is buried?
You have money?

(JESSIE *shakes her head.*)

Where you live?

JESSIE.   I'll find a room somewhere. I'll probably go back to nursing.

MAMA.   You like to come to San Francisco for a little? To our house? We have room. Plenty room.

JESSIE (*touched, moving to* MAMA).   That's very kind of you, but . . .

MAMA.   I like to have you. You come for a little as our guest. When you get work you can be our boarder.

JESSIE (*awkwardly grateful*).   I don't know why you should bother. . . .

MAMA (*touching her*).   You were good to Uncle Chris.

(JESSIE *grasps her hand, deeply moved, then turns and goes quickly back through the curtains.* MAMA *turns to* KATRIN.)

Katrin, you come and see him?

KATRIN (*scared*).   See him? You mean . . .

MAMA.   I like you see him. You need not be frightened. He looks . . . happy and at peace. I like you to know what death looks like. Then you are not frightened of it, ever.

KATRIN.   Will you come with me?

MAMA.   Sure.

(*She stretches out her hand, puts her arm around her, and then leads her gently in through the curtains.*)

(*Spot up on L. turntable, representing a park bench against a hedge.* TRINA, *and* MR. THORKELSON, *in outdoor clothes, are seated together.* TRINA *is cooing over a baby-carriage.*)

TRINA.   Who's the most beautiful Norwegian baby in San Francisco? Who's going to be three months old tomorrow? Little Christopher Thorkelson!

(*To* MR. THORKELSON.)

Do you know, Peter, I thing he's even beginning to *look* a

little like Uncle Chris! Quite apart from his black curls--
and those, of course, he gets from *you*.

(*To baby again.*)

He's going to grow up to be a black Norwegian, isn't he, just
like his daddy and his Uncle Chris?

(*Settling down beside* MR. THORKELSON.)

I think there's something about his mouth . . . a sort of . . .
well . . . *firmness*. Of course, it's *your* mouth, too. But then
I've always thought you had quite a lot of Uncle Chris about
you.

(*She looks back at the baby.*)

Look—he's asleep.

MR. THORKELSON.   Trina, do you know what next Thurs-
day is?

TRINA (*nodding, smiling*).   Our anniversary.

MR. THORKELSON.   What would you think of our giving a
little party?

TRINA.   A party?

MR. THORKELSON.   Oh, quite a modest one. Nothing
showy or ostentatious—but, after all, we have been married
a year, and with your having been in mourning and the baby
coming so soon and everything, we've not been able to entertain. I think it's time you . . . took your place in society.

TRINA (*scared*).   What . . . sort of a party?

MR. THORKELSON.   An evening party.

(*Proudly.*)

A soirée! I should say about ten people . . . some of the
Norwegian colony . . . and Lars and Marta, of course. . . .

TRINA (*beginning to count on her fingers*).   And Jenny
and Sigrid. . . .

MR. THORKELSON.   Oh . . . I . . . I hadn't thought of asking
Jenny and Sigrid.

TRINA.   Oh, we'd have to. We couldn't leave them out.

MR. THORKELSON.   Trina, I hope you won't be offended

if I say that I have never really felt . . . well, altogether comfortable with Jenny and Sigrid. They have always made me feel that they didn't think I was . . . well . . . *worthy* of you. Of course, I know I'm not, but . . . well . . . one doesn't like to be reminded of it . . . *all* the time.

TRINA (*taking his hand*). Oh, Peter.

MR. THORKELSON. But you're quite right. We must ask them. Now, as to the matter of refreshments . . . what would you suggest?

TRINA (*flustered*). Oh, I don't know. I . . . what would you say to . . . ice cream and cookies for the ladies . . . and coffee, of course . . . and . . . perhaps port wine for the gentlemen?

MR. THORKELSON (*anxiously*). Port wine?

TRINA. Just a little. You could bring it in already poured out, in *little* glasses. Jenny and Sigrid can help me serve the ice cream.

MR. THORKELSON (*firmly*). No. If Jenny and Sigrid come, they come as guests, like everyone else. You shall have someone in to help you in the kitchen.

TRINA. You mean a waitress?

(MR. THORKELSON *nods, beaming.*)

Oh, but none of us have *ever* . . . do you really think . . . I mean . . . you did say we shouldn't be ostentatious. . . .

MR. THORKELSON (*nervously*). Trina, there's something I would like to say. I've never been very good expressing myself or my . . . well . . . *deeper* feelings—but I want you to know that I'm not only very fond of you, but very . . . well . . . very *proud* of you as well, and I want you to have the best of everything, as far as it's in my power to give it to you.

(*As a climax.*)

I want you to have a waitress!

TRINA (*overcome*). Yes, Peter.

(*They hold hands.*)

(*The lights fade and the turntable revolves out.*)

(*Curtains part on kitchen, slightly changed, smartened and refurnished now.* MAMA *and* PAPA *seated as usual.* DAGMAR, *looking a little older, is seated on the chest, reading a solid-looking book.* NELS *enters from back L. door, carrying a newspaper. He wears long trousers now, and looks about seventeen.*)

NELS. Hello! Here's your evening paper, Papa.

(PAPA *puts down the morning paper he is reading, and takes the evening one from* NELS.)

PAPA. Is there any news?

NELS. No.

(*He takes out a package of cigarettes with elaborate unconcern.* MAMA *watches with disapproval. Then, as he is about to light his cigarette, he stops, remembering something.*)

Oh, I forgot. There's a letter for Katrin. I picked it up on the mat as I came in.

(*Going to door back L., and calling*)

Katrin! Katrin! There's a letter for you.

KATRIN (*answering from off stage*). Coming!

MAMA. Nels, you know who the letter is from?

NELS. Why, no, Mama.

(*Hands it to her.*)

It looks like her own handwriting.

MAMA (*gravely inspecting it*). Is bad.

PAPA. Why is bad?

MAMA. She get too many like that. I think they are stories she send to the magazines.

DAGMAR (*closing her book loudly, rising*). Well, I'll go and see if I have any puppies yet. Mama, I've just decided something.

MAMA.   What have you decided?

DAGMAR.   If Nels is going to be a doctor, when I grow up, I'm going to be a— (*looking at the book-title, and stumbling over the word*) vet-vet-veterinarian.

MAMA.   And what is that?

DAGMAR.   A doctor for animals.

MAMA.   Is good. Is good.

DAGMAR.   There are far more animals in the world than there are human beings, and far more human doctors than animal ones. It isn't fair.

> (*She goes to the pantry door.*)

I suppose we couldn't have a horse, could we?

> (*This only produces a concerted laugh from the family. She turns, sadly.*)

No. . . . I was afraid we couldn't.

> (*She goes into the pantry.* KATRIN *comes in, back L. She wears a slightly more adult dress than before. Her hair is up and she looks about eighteen.*)

KATRIN.   Where's the letter?

MAMA (*handing it to her*).   Here.

> (KATRIN *takes it, nervously. She looks at the envelope, and her face falls. She opens it, pulls out a manuscript and a rejection slip, looks at it a moment, and then replaces both in the envelope. The others watch her covertly. Then she looks up, with determination.*)

KATRIN.   Mama . . . Papa . . . I want to say something.

PAPA.   What is it?

KATRIN.   I'm not going to go to college.

PAPA.   Why not?

KATRIN.   Because it would be a waste of time and money. The only point in my going to college was to be a writer. Well, I'm not going to be one, so . . .

MAMA.   Katrin, is it your letter that makes you say this?
It is a story come back again?

KATRIN.   Again is right. This is the tenth time. I made
this one a test. It's the best I've ever written, or ever shall
write. I know that. Well, it's no good.

NELS.   What kind of a story is it?

KATRIN.   Oh . . . it's a story about a painter, who's a
genius, and he goes blind.

NELS.   Sounds like "The Light That Failed."

KATRIN.   Well, what's wrong with that?

NELS (*quickly*).   Nothing. Nothing!

KATRIN.   Besides, it's not like that. My painter gets better.
He has an operation and recovers his sight, and paints better
than ever before.

MAMA.   Is good.

KATRIN (*bitterly unhappy*).   No, it isn't. It's rotten. But
it's the best I can do.

MAMA.   You have asked your teachers about this?

KATRIN.   Teachers don't know anything about writing.
They just know about literature.

MAMA.   If there was someone we could ask . . . for advice
. . . to tell us . . . tell us if your stories are good.

KATRIN.   Yes. Well, there isn't. And they're *not*.

PAPA (*looking at the evening paper*).   There is something
here in the paper about a lady writer. I just noticed the head-
line. Wait.

(*He looks back for it and reads*)

"Woman writer tells key to literary success."

KATRIN.   Who?

PAPA.   A lady called Florence Dana Moorhead. It gives
her picture. A fat lady. You have heard of her?

KATRIN.   Yes, of course. Everyone has. She's terribly
successful. She's here on a lecture tour.

MAMA.   What does she say is the secret?

PAPA.   You read it, Katrin. (*He hands her the paper.*)

KATRIN (*gabbling the first part*). "Florence Dana Moorhead, celebrated novelist and short story writer . . . blah-blah-blah . . . interviewed today in her suite at the Fairmont . . . blah-blah-blah . . . pronounced sincerity the one essential quality for success as a writer."

(*Throwing aside the paper.*)

A lot of help that is.

MAMA. Katrin, this lady . . . maybe if you sent her your stories, *she* could tell you what is wrong with them?

KATRIN (*wearily*). Oh, Mama, don't be silly.

MAMA. Why is silly?

KATRIN. Well, in the first place because she's a very important person . . . a celebrity . . . and she'd never read them. And in the second, because . . . you seem to think writing's like. . . . well, like cooking, or something. That all you have to have is the recipe. It takes a lot more than that. You have to have a gift for it.

MAMA. You have to have a gift for cooking, too. But there are things you can learn, if you have the gift.

KATRIN. Well, that's the whole point. I haven't. I *know* . . . now. So, if you've finished with the morning paper, Papa, I'll take the want ad. section, and see if I can find myself a job.

(*She takes the morning paper and goes out R.*)

MAMA. Is bad. Nels, what you think?

NELS. I don't know, Mama. Her stories seem all right to me, but I don't know.

MAMA. It would be good to know. Nels, this lady in the paper . . . what else does she say?

NELS (*taking up the paper*). Not much. The rest seems to be about *her* and her home. Let's see. . . .

(*He reads*)

"Apart from literature, Mrs. Moorhead's main interest in life is gastronomy."

MAMA. The stars?

NELS. No—eating. "A brilliant cook herself, she says that she would as soon turn out a good soufflé as a short story, or find a new recipe as she would a first edition."

MAMA (*reaching for the paper*). I see her picture?

> (*She looks at it.*)

Is kind face.

> (*Pause while she reads a moment. Then she looks up and asks*)

What is first edition?

> (*Blackout.*)

> (*Lights up on L. turntable, representing the lobby of the Fairmont hotel. A couch against a column with a palm behind it. An orchestra plays softly in the background.* MAMA *is discovered seated on the couch, waiting patiently. She wears a hat and a suit, and clutches a newspaper and a bundle of manuscripts. A couple of guests come through the curtains and cross, disappearing into the wings L.* MAMA *watches them. Then* FLORENCE DANA MOORHEAD *enters through the curtains. She is a stout, dressy, good-natured, middle-aged woman. A* BELL-BOY *comes from the R., paging her.*)

BELL-BOY. Miss Moorhead?

F. D. MOORHEAD. Yes?

BELL-BOY. Telegram.

F. D. MOORHEAD. Oh. . . . Thank you.

> (*She tips him, and he goes.* MAMA *rises and moves towards her.*)

MAMA. Please . . . Please . . . Miss Moorhead . . . Miss Moorhead.

F. D. MOORHEAD (*looking up from her telegram, on the steps*). Were you calling me?

MAMA. Yes. You are . . . Miss Florence Dana Moorhead?

F. D. MOORHEAD. Yes.

MAMA. Please . . . might I speak to you for a moment?

F. D. MOORHEAD. Yes—-what's it about?

MAMA. I read in the paper what you say about writing.

F. D. MOORHEAD (*with a vague social smile*). Oh, yes?

MAMA. My daughter, Katrin, wants to be a writer.

F. D. MOORHEAD (*who has heard that one before*). Oh, really? (*She glances at her watch on her bosom.*)

MAMA. I bring her stories.

F. D. MOORHEAD. Look, I'm afraid I'm in rather a hurry. I'm leaving San Francisco this evening. . . .

MAMA. I wait two hours here for you to come in. Please, if I may talk to you for one, two minutes. That is all.

F. D. MOORHEAD (*kindly*). Of course, but I think I'd better tell you that if you want me to read your daughter's stories, it's no use. I'm very sorry, but I've had to make it a rule never to read anyone's unpublished material.

MAMA (*nods—then after a pause*). It said in the paper you like to collect recipes . . . for eating.

F. D. MOORHEAD. Yes, I do. I've written several books on cooking.

MAMA. I, too, am interested in gastronomy. I am good cook. Norwegian. I make good Norwegian dishes. Lutefisk. And Kjödboller. That is meat-balls with sauce.

F. D. MOORHEAD. Yes, I know. I've eaten them in Christiania.

MAMA. I have a special recipe for Kjödboller . . . my mother give me. She was best cook I ever knew. Never have I told this recipe, not even to my own sisters, because they are not good cooks.

F. D. MOORHEAD (*amused*). Oh?

MAMA. But . . . if you let me talk to you . . . I give it to you. I promise it is good recipe.

F. D. MOORHEAD (*vastly tickled now*).   Well, that seems
fair enough. Let's sit down.

(*They move to the couch and sit.*)

Now, your daughter wants to write, you say? How old is she?

MAMA.   She is eighteen. Just.

F. D. MOORHEAD.   *Does* she write, or does she just . . .
want to write?

MAMA.   Oh, she writes all the time. Maybe she should
not be author, but it is hard to give up something that has
meant so much.

F. D. MOORHEAD.   I agree, but . . .

MAMA.   I bring her stories. I bring twelve.

F. D. MOORHEAD (*aghast*).   Twelve!

MAMA.   But if you could read maybe just one . . . To know
if someone is good cook, you do not need to eat a whole
dinner.

F. D. MOORHEAD.   You're very persuasive. How is it your
daughter did not come herself?

MAMA.   She was too unhappy. And too scared . . . of you.
Because you are celebrity. But I see your picture in the
paper. . . .

F. D. MOORHEAD.   That frightful picture!

MAMA.   Is the picture of a woman who like to eat good. . . .

F. D. MOORHEAD (*with a rueful smile*).   It certainly is.
Now, tell me about the Kjödboller.

MAMA.   When you make the meat-balls you drop them in
boiling stock. Not water. That is one of the secrets.

F. D. MOORHEAD.   Ah!

MAMA.   And the cream sauce. That is another secret.
It is half *sour* cream, added at the last.

F. D. MOORHEAD.   That sounds marvellous.

MAMA.   You must grind the meat six times. I could write
it out for you. And . . . (*tentatively*) while I write, you could
read?

F. D. MOORHEAD (*with a laugh*). All right. You win. Come upstairs to my apartment.

> (*She rises.*)

MAMA. Is kind of you.

> (*They start out L.*)

Maybe if you would read *two* stories, I could write the recipe for Lutefisk as well. You know Lutefisk . . .?

> (*They have disappeared into the wings, and the turntable revolves out.*)

> (*Spot up, R. turntable.* KATRIN *at her desk.*)

KATRIN. When Mama came back, I was sitting with my diary, which I called my Journal now, writing a Tragic Farewell to my Art. It was very seldom that Mama came to the attic, thinking that a writer needed privacy, and I was surprised to see her standing in the doorway.

> (*She looks up.* MAMA *is standing on the steps, C.*)

Mama!

MAMA. You are busy, Katrin?

KATRIN (*jumping up*). No, of course not. Come in.

MAMA (*coming down*). I like to talk to you.

KATRIN. Yes, of course.

MAMA (*seating herself at the desk*). You are writing?

KATRIN. No. I told you, that's all over.

MAMA. That is what I want to talk to you about.

KATRIN. It's all right, Mama. Really, it's all right. I was planning to tear up all my stories this afternoon, only I couldn't find half of them.

MAMA. They are here.

KATRIN. Did *you* take them? What for?

MAMA. Katrin, I have been to see Miss Moorhead.

KATRIN. Who's Miss . . .? You don't mean Florence Dana Moorhead?

> (MAMA *nods.*)

You don't mean . . . Mama, you don't mean you took her my stories?

MAMA.   She read five of them. I was two hours with her. We have glass of sherry. Two glass of sherry.

KATRIN.   What . . . what did she say about them?

MAMA (*quietly*).   She say they are not good.

KATRIN (*turning away*).   Well, I knew that. It was hardly worth your going to all that trouble just to be told that.

MAMA.   She say more. Will you listen, Katrin?

KATRIN (*trying to be gracious*).   Sure. Sure. I'll listen.

MAMA.   I will try and remember. She say you write now only because of what you have read in other books, and that no one can write good until they have felt what they write about. That for years she write bad stories about people in the olden times, until one day she remember something that happen in her own town . . . something that only she could know and understand . . . and she feels she must tell it . . . and that is how she write her first good story. She say you must write more of things you know. . . .

KATRIN.   That's what my teacher always told me at school.

MAMA.   Maybe your teacher was right. I do not know if I explain good what Miss Moorhead means, but while she talks I think I understand. Your story about the painter who is blind . . . that is because . . . forgive me if I speak plain, my Katrin, but it is important to you . . . because you are the dramatic one, as Papa has said . . . and you think it would feel good to be a painter and be blind and not complain. But never have you imagined how it would really be. Is true?

KATRIN (*subdued*).   Yes, I . . . I guess it's true.

MAMA.   But she say you are to go on writing. That you have the gift.

(KATRIN *turns back to her, suddenly aglow.*)

And that when you have written story that is real and true . . . then you send it to someone whose name she give me.

(*She fumbles for a piece of paper.*)

It is her . . . agent . . . and say she recommend you. Here.
No, that is recipe she give me for goulash as her grandmother
make it . . . here . . .

    (*She hands over the paper.*)

It helps, Katrin, what I have told you?

    KATRIN (*subdued again*). Yes, I . . . I guess it helps.
Some. But what have *I* got to write about? I haven't seen
anything, or been anywhere.

    MAMA. Could you write about San Francisco, maybe? Is
fine city. Miss Moorhead write about her home town.

    KATRIN. Yes, I know. But you've got to have a central
character or something. She writes about her grandfather . . .
he was a wonderful old man.

    MAMA. Could you maybe write about Papa?

    KATRIN. Papa?

    MAMA. Papa is fine man. Is wonderful man.

    KATRIN. Yes, I know, but . . .

    MAMA (*rising*). I must go fix supper. Is late. Papa will
be home.

    (*She goes up the steps to the curtains, and then turns
      back.*)

I like you should write about Papa.

    (*She goes inside.*)

    KATRIN (*going back to her seat behind the desk*). Papa.
Yes, but what's he ever done? What's ever happened to him?
What's ever happened to *any* of us? Except always being poor
and having illnesses, like the time when Dagmar went to
hospital and Mama . . .

    (*The idea hits her like a flash.*)

Oh. . . . Oh. . . .

    (*Pause—then she becomes the* KATRIN *of today.*)

And that was how it was born . . . suddenly in a flash . . . the
story of "Mama and the Hospital" . . . the first of all the

stories. I wrote it . . . oh, quite soon after that. I didn't tell
Mama or any of them. But I sent it to Miss Moorhead's
agent. It was a long time before I heard anything . . . and
then one evening the letter came.

> (*She takes an envelope from the desk in front of her.*)

For a moment I couldn't believe it. Then I went rushing
into the kitchen, shouting. . . .

> (*She rises from the desk, taking some papers with her,
> and rushes upstage, crying, "Mama, Mama." The
> curtains have parted on the kitchen—and the fam-
> ily tableau—*MAMA, PAPA, CHRISTINE, *and* NELS.
> DAGMAR *is not present.* KATRIN *comes rushing in,
> up the steps. The R. turntable revolves out as soon
> as she has left it.*)

Mama . . . Mama . . . I've sold a story!

MAMA.   A story?

KATRIN.   Yes, I've got a letter from the agent . . . with a
cheque for . . . (*gasping*) five hundred dollars!

NELS.   No kidding?

MAMA.   Katrin . . . is true?

KATRIN.   Here it is. Here's the letter. Maybe I haven't
read it right.

> (*She hands the letter.* PAPA *and* MAMA *huddle and
> gloat over it.*)

CHRISTINE.   What will you *do* with five hundred dollars?

KATRIN.   I don't know. I'll buy Mama her warm coat, I
know that.

CHRISTINE.   Coats don't cost five hundred dollars.

KATRIN.   I know. We'll put the rest in the Bank.

NELS (*kidding*).   Quick. Before they change their mind,
and stop the cheque.

KATRIN.   Will you, Mama? Will you take it to the Bank
downtown tomorrow?

> (MAMA *looks vague.*)

What is it?

MAMA. I do not know how.

NELS. Just give it to the man and tell him to put it in your account, like you always do.

(MAMA *looks up at* PAPA.)

PAPA. You tell them . . . now.

CHRISTINE. Tell us what?

MAMA (*desperately*). Is no Bank Account. Never in my life have I been inside a bank.

CHRISTINE. But you always told us . . .

KATRIN. Mama, you've always said . . .

MAMA. I know. But was not true. I tell a lie.

KATRIN. But why, Mama? Why did you pretend?

MAMA. Is not good for little ones to be afraid . . . to not feel secure. But now . . . with five hundred dollar . . . I think I can tell.

KATRIN (*going to her, emotionally*). Mama!

MAMA (*stopping her, quickly*). You read us the story. You have it there?

KATRIN. Yes.

MAMA. Then read.

KATRIN. Now?

MAMA. Yes. No— Wait. Dagmar must hear.

(*She opens pantry door and calls.*)

Dagmar.

DAGMAR (*off*). Yes, Mama?

MAMA (*calling*). Come here, I want you.

DAGMAR (*off*). What is it?

MAMA. I want you. No, you leave the rabbits!

(*She comes back.*)

What is it called . . . the story?

KATRIN (*seating herself in the chair that Mr. Hyde took in the opening scene*). It's called "Mama and the Hospital."

PAPA (*delighted*).   You write about Mama?

KATRIN.   Yes.

MAMA.   But I thought . . . I thought you say . . . I tell you . . .

(*She gestures at* PAPA, *behind his back.*)

KATRIN.   I know, Mama, but . . . well, that's how it came out.

(DAGMAR *comes in.*)

DAGMAR.   What is it?   What do you want?

MAMA.   Katrin write story for magazine. They pay her five hundred dollar to print it.

DAGMAR (*completely uninterested*).   Oh.

(*She starts back for the pantry.*)

MAMA (*stopping her*).   She read it to us. I want you should listen. You are ready, Katrin?

KATRIN.   Sure.

MAMA.   Then read.

(*The group around the table is now a duplicate of the grouping around* MR. HYDE *in the first scene, with* KATRIN *in his place.*)

KATRIN (*reading*).   "For as long as I could remember, the house on Steiner Street had been home. All of us were born there. Nels, the oldest and the only boy . . ."

(NELS *looks up, astonished to be in a story.*)

"my sister, Christine . . ."

(CHRISTINE *does likewise.*)

"and the littlest sister, Dagmar. . . ."

DAGMAR.   Am I in the story?

MAMA.   Hush, Dagmar. We are all in the story.

KATRIN.   "But first and foremost, I remember Mama."

(*The lights begin to dim and the curtain slowly to fall. As it descends, we hear her voice continuing*)

"I remember that every Saturday night Mama would sit down by the kitchen table and count out the money Papa had brought home in the little envelope. . . ."

(*By now, the curtain is down.*)

THE END

THE PLAYWRIGHT
AND THE NEED FOR SINCERITY

I should like to recommend two autobiographies which John van Druten wrote. The first is *The Way to the Present*. It appeared in 1938 and is a vividly written account of his childhood, adolescence and early manhood. He was born in London in 1901, of a Dutch father and an English mother. Trained as a lawyer, he lectured in English law and legal history at University College in Wales. It was there that he started to write plays. With the death of his mother (his father had died when he was young), he resolved to give up teaching law and make a living for himself in the theatre in the United States.

The second autobiography, *The Widening Circle*, was published just before his death in 1957. It was written at his home in the Coachella Valley in Southern California. He had lived there for fifteen years. This second book brought the story of his life up to date.

For those who are directly interested in the problems of writing—especially writing for the theatre—John van Druten published a wise and interesting book, already referred to, *Playwright at Work*. It is an old saying that dramatists are born, not made; but if you are keenly interested in writing for the stage, you should read books like this, written by men who have lived their life in the theatre. You can then try your hand at writing, and if you have talent and determination, the life of a writer is open to you.

John van Druten wrote four novels and twenty-four plays in

addition to the three books referred to. Others of his famous stage successes include *Young Woodley, There's Always Juliet, The Distaff Side, Old Acquaintance, The Damask Cheek, The Voice of the Turtle, Bell, Book and Candle,* and *I am a Camera.* He was also a brilliant director, having directed most of his later plays as well as the famous musical, *The King and I.* He wrote the story and dialogue for many Hollywood films.

In both *The Way to the Present* and *Playwright at Work,* John van Druten mentioned an experience which is significant for understanding *I Remember Mama.* When he was eighteen —the same age as Katrin—and a law student, he took thirty of his poems to the great poet John C. Squire—later Sir John Squire. Squire read them. His comment was, "No artist has ever produced a genuine work of art unless he were first sin-cerely moved by its subject," and he added that it was no use "pumping up emotion" for the sake of writing about it. In an article published in the *Writer,* van Druten said that Sir John's advice made him "not only a better writer, but a better person". "It was my first lesson in the difficult art of sincerity, without which nothing of real and lasting value is ever produced."

The same advice was given to him by his play agent, J. L. Campbell, who told him that he should never write a play unless the idea fascinated him and he couldn't leave it alone. He said that he should never write anything in which he did not genuinely believe, that he should write about the kind of peo-ple he knew, the kind of background he knew; that he should write wholly from within himself. "It may take a long time," he ended. "I don't think your work will ever be sensational or set the Thames on fire, but I do believe, if you are honest and sincere with it, that you can be a good and successful play-wright."

This search for sincerity, for a deeper truth, you will find in the three books which I have urged you to read. As you read them, you will see why Katrin in our play is treated with such understanding; why we are able to enter into her problem with sympathy and conviction; and why the climax is genuine and moving. John van Druten's life and art were marked by sin-cerity. Cyrano de Bergerac's words might be his:

> "Never to make a line I have not heard
> In my own heart."

THE TEAHOUSE OF THE AUGUST MOON

JOHN PATRICK

Adapted from the novel
by Vern Sneider

ONE OF THE MOST DELIGHTFUL PLAYS IN YEARS

From a score of teachers and theatre experts whom we consulted in choosing the plays for this volume, there was an almost unanimous chorus of approval and pleasure when we suggested *The Teahouse of the August Moon*. Only *I Remember Mama* approached it in popularity.

Teahouse is a fantasy, completely unlike the average American play. When it appeared, it was hailed as one of the funniest and most captivating comedies to appear on Broadway in many seasons. In the whole history of the New York stage, only twenty plays and musicals have had longer runs. It played for 1,027 performances.

William Hawkins of the *New York World-Telegram & Sun*, wrote, ". . . an enchanting play, filled with the most extraordinary good sense about human and international relations". And Brooks Atkinson, the famous drama critic of the *New York Times* said, ". . . completely captivating . . . a piece of exotic make-believe in a style as intimate as a fairy story. What Mr. Patrick says is interesting. How he says it is imaginative and original." The delight of the play, he wrote, goes beyond its "pleasantly ironic" story. "As a piece of theatre writing it is extraordinarily fresh. In the theory of art, form and content are identical, i.e., the content provides the form. But the marriage of form and content is seldom as happy as it is in the case of this comedy."

This fable of the West meeting the East is deftly and skilfully contrived. It is told with sparkling satire and with humour that is sometimes broad and hilarious—sometimes subtle and gentle.

The central situation is rich in irony. The American Occupation Forces attempt to inculcate the ideals of democracy in an oriental village. Applying these democratic principles in a topsy-turvy, but logical, way, the natives vote to build themselves a teahouse rather than the pentagon-shaped school house which is called for in Plan B. The satire is directed at the ridiculous ideas for improving the lives of the natives which would be foisted on them by desk-men and army types in faraway Washington. The comedy in the situation results when the "impracticable idealism" of the Washington dreamers faces the "uncommon sense" of the natives.

WINS AWARDS—SUCCESSFUL FILM

The two most highly prized awards on Broadway are the Critics Circle Award, given by the New York critics, and the Pulitzer Prize. *The Teahouse of the August Moon* won both awards in the 1953-4 season. In nineteen years, only four other plays had been so honoured.

The movie version of the play was highly successful. The cast included Marlon Brando as Sakini, Paul Ford as Colonel Purdy, Glenn Ford as Captain Fisby, Eddie Albert as Captain McLean and Henry Morgan as Sergeant Gregovich. Lotus Blossom was played by Machiko Kyo. Jack Cummings was the producer and the screen adaptation was written by the playwright, John Patrick. The picture was released in 1956.

STAGING THE PLAY

In producing the play, your task is to achieve a kind of magic, a kind of visual and oral music in which the audience is as delighted with *how* the play looks and sounds as with *what* it sees and hears. In other words, you should seek what Brooks Atkinson calls the marriage of form and content which is so richly satisfying when this play is well produced.

How to achieve this magic? My first suggestion is that you should read about the Japanese theatre, because your production should borrow heavily from it. This is a fascinating subject. The Japanese theatre has two great traditions, the old, formal, ceremonial Noh plays and the picturesque, popular, historical Kabuki drama. Find out all you can about them.

Beyond the Japanese theatre there opens up for your study the whole range of oriental music, painting, literature and philosophy. The more deeply you saturate yourself in the thought and imagery of the East, the more interesting your production will be.

You should also draw on the knowledge and experience of those in your community who have come from the East. You may be so fortunate as to find some who have first-hand knowledge and experience of the traditional Japanese theatre.

The costumes and settings should be charming and characteristic of the Japanese scene. In particular, the teahouse should be a vision of loveliness.

Nothing will help more in the effective staging of the play than a skilful use of the cyclorama—the name given to the blue skycloth or grey back wall of the stage against which lights are thrown. All the scenes in the village will be vividly appealing when set against a sunlit sky by day or the deep blue of an evening sky. Against this cyclorama, the stage pictures should be carefully grouped and composed: the jeep loaded high; the gift-giving ceremony; the love scene between Seiko and Lotus Blossom; the return of the villagers from Big Koza; and most of all, the teahouse with its lovely ceremonial. This series of clearly-etched stage pictures, each looking like a quaint and charming Japanese print, will leave a lasting impression on the mind of the audience.

Voices and music must also create the oriental mood. They must be handled with understanding and a sense of grace, beauty, and proportion. With the proper make-up and careful attention to his speech, Sakini should be an authentic Okinawan. In most productions, the villagers are played by Japanese or by others who can lend truth to the stage in appearance and voice. The Luchuan dialect which is given in the play is described as a phonetic approximation to the language that should be used. The whole question of how it sounds can be left to those of your advisers who are familiar with the language. Oriental music, played by stringed instruments, should be used to heighten both the comedy and pathos of the play. Recordings are available; again you should be advised by those who know the musical traditions of the East.

The actual arrangement of the scenes corresponds to a considerable degree to that employed in *I Remember Mama*. Sakini, the narrator and interpreter, plays in front of the bamboo curtain, speaking directly to the audience. The down right area of the stage, behind the first bamboo curtain, is identified with Colonel Purdy and corresponds to the down right turntable of *I Remember Mama*. The down left area is identified with Captain Fisby throughout. The background is seen through the two centre panels. Both down right and down left areas can be cleared for big settings such as the teahouse.

If you are reading the play in class, it would be well to keep this arrangement: have Purdy at the right, Fisby at the left, and the village scenes up stage; Sakini can move freely across the cleared area between the first and second seats to talk to his audience.

More than any other play in the book, this one needs the unfamiliar oriental background if we are to receive the deepest pleasure from it. But the play is so alive, so touching, so humorous—with three or four laughs on each page if you read it well—that I know you will enjoy it immensely even in a class reading.

CAST

The Teahouse of the August Moon opened at the Martin Beck Theatre in New York City on October 15, 1953. It was produced by Maurice Evans in association with George Schaefer and was directed by Robert Lewis. The production was designed by Peter Larkin with costumes by Noel Taylor. The cast, in order of appearance, was as follows:

SAKINI	David Wayne
SERGEANT GREGOVICH	Harry Jackson
COL. WAINWRIGHT PURDY III	Paul Ford
CAPTAIN FISBY	John Forsythe
OLD WOMAN	Naoe Kondo
OLD WOMAN'S DAUGHTER	Mara Kim
THE DAUGHTER'S CHILDREN	Moy Moy Thom, Joyce Chen and Kenneth Wong
LADY ASTOR	Saki
ANCIENT MAN	Kame Ishikawa
MR. HOKAIDA	Chuck Morgan
MR. OMURA	Kuraji Seida
MR. SUMATA	Kaie Deei
MR. SUMATA'S FATHER	Kikuo Hiromura
MR. SEIKO	Haim Winant
MISS HIGA JIGA	Shizu Moriya
MR. KEORA	Yuki Shimoda
MR. OSHIRA	William Hansen
VILLAGERS	Jerry Fujikawa, Frank Ogawa, Richard Akagi, Laurence Kim and Norman Chi
LADIES' LEAGUE FOR DEMOCRATIC ACTION	Vivian Thom, Naoe Kondo, Mary Ann Reeve and Mara Kim
LOTUS BLOSSOM	Mariko Niki
CAPTAIN MCLEAN	Larry Gates

ACT I

ACT II

ACT III

THE TEAHOUSE OF THE AUGUST MOON

ACT I

SCENE ONE

SCENE: *Okinawa. Colonel Purdy's office, G.H.Q.*

Directly behind the house curtain is a second curtain consisting of four panels of split bamboo. Each of these sections can be raised and lowered individually.

AT RISE: *As the house lights dim, the Oriental strains from a stringed instrument can be heard playing softly in the background. A pool of light picks up* SAKINI *standing framed against the bamboo backing. He wears a pair of tattered shorts and a native shirt. His shoes, the gift of a G.I., are several sizes too large. His socks are also too large and hang in wrinkles over his ankles. He is an Okinawan who might be any age between thirty and sixty. In repose his face betrays age, but the illusion is shattered quickly by his smile of childlike candour.*

With hands together in prayer-like supplication, he walks down to the footlights and bows to the audience centre in

---

186

solemn ritual. Then he bows from the waist—to the left and to the right.

Straightening up, he examines the audience seated before him with open curiosity. The music ceases. As it ceases, SAKINI *begins to work his jaws vigorously.*

SAKINI.   Tootie-fruitie.

> (*He takes the gum from his mouth and, wrapping it carefully in a piece of paper, puts it in a matchbox and restores it to a pocket in his shirt.*)

Most generous gift of American sergeant.

> (*He resumes his original posture of dignity.*)

Lovely ladies, kind gentlemen:
Please to introduce myself.
Sakini by name.
Interpreter by profession.
Education by ancient dictionary.
Okinawan by whim of gods.
History of Okinawa reveal distinguished record of conquerors.
We have honour to be subjugated in fourteenth century by
    Chinese pirates.
In sixteenth century by English missionaries.
In eighteenth century by Japanese war lords.
And in twentieth century by American Marines.
Okinawa very fortunate.
Culture brought to us. . . . Not have to leave home for it.
Learn many things.
Most important that rest of world not like Okinawa.
World filled with delightful variation.
Illustration.
In Okinawa . . . no locks on doors.
Bad manners not to trust neighbours.
In America . . . lock and key big industry.
Conclusion?
Bad manners good business.

In Okinawa . . . wash self in public bath with nude lady quite
   proper.
Picture of nude lady in private home . . . quite improper.
In America . . . statue of nude lady in park win prize.
But nude lady in flesh in park win penalty.
Conclusion?
Pornography question of geography.
But Okinawans most eager to be educated by conquerors.
Deep desire to improve friction.
Not easy to learn.
Sometimes painful.
But pain makes man think.
Thought makes man wise.
Wisdom makes life endurable.
So . . .

> (*He crosses back to the left of the first of the panels.*)

We tell little story to demonstrate splendid example of bene-
volent assimilation of democracy by Okinawa.

> (*He claps his hands, signalling the stagehand to raise
> the first of the four panels. Flush against the curtain
> is revealed a sign nailed onto a denuded palm stump.
> It points toward the other side of the stage and reads:*
> COL. WAINRIGHT PURDY III.)

Boss by name of Colonel Purdy—Three. Number three after
name indicate he is a son of a son of a son.

> (*He steps to the next panel and claps again. The
> screen rolls up revealing a laundry line tied to a
> second denuded stump. As these panels are raised
> the background is revealed in sections. It includes
> a jeep parked against a pile of empty gasoline
> drums, trees ripped of foliage by recent gunfire—
> all creating an impression of general destruction.
> There are several articles of wearing apparel hang-
> ing on the laundry line, foremost of which is a pair
> of khaki pants size forty.*)

Colonel Purdy, Three, displays splendid example of cleanliness for native population to follow. But native population cannot follow. Native not *have* two pairs of pants.

> (*He then claps for the next screen to rise, revealing more of the laundry. To the extreme right is seen the outside of Colonel Purdy's Quonset office. Nailed on the post holding the other end of the line is a sign reading:* OFFICERS' LAUNDRY ONLY.)

Colonel Purdy put up many signs. This exceedingly civilized. Make it very easy for uncivilized to know what *not* to do. Here laundry of officer not to fraternize with laundry of enlisted man.

> (SAKINI *now signals for the last panel to be raised, revealing the inside of the hut. Colonel Purdy's vacant desk is beside the door. A sign denotes his proprietorship. Another sign admonishes the visitor to* THINK! *The office is small and sparse. A bulletin board for "Daily Orders" hangs on the upstage wall. Against this wall is the desk of Sergeant Gregovich. Behind a sign denoting his rating sits the* SERGEANT. *His posture is frozen—as if awaiting a signal to come to life.* SAKINI *crosses down centre to explain to his audience.*)

This gentleman honourable Sergeant Gregovich—assistant to Colonel Purdy. Not son of a son of a son.

> (*He turns toward the* SERGEANT.)

Play has begun, Sergeant.

> (GREGOVICH *now comes to life. He begins to chew his gum vigorously and to look about the office. He rises and crosses down to Colonel Purdy's desk. He gets down on his hands and knees in front of the desk and reaches under it.*)

Oh, you know what he is doing? Explanation. Colonel Purdy great student of history. Every month wife of Colonel Purdy send him magazine called *Adventure Magazine*. Cover has picture of pirate with black patch over eye. Everybody try to steal magazine. Colonel hide under desk so he can read first.

(GREGOVICH *rises triumphantly with the magazine.*)

But Sergeant always find. Smart mouse.

(GREGOVICH *returns to his desk and buries himself behind the pages of the magazine. At this point* COLONEL PURDY *himself enters from the left. As his laundry has indicated, he is a man of proportions. The worries of the world in general and the Army of Occupation in particular weigh heavily on his shoulders. He stops to glance at the nearest official sign. He takes out a small notebook to make an entry. Sakini's presence is not recognized until indicated.*)

This gentleman exalted boss—Colonel Purdy, Three. Subject of sovereign American city of Pottawattamie, Michigan.

(COLONEL PURDY *hiccups and taps his chest.*)

Also subject to indignity of indigestion. Colonel Purdy explain this by saying—

PURDY (*clears his throat and says to himself*). An occupational disorder of the Army of Occupation.

(*He taps his chest again and puts the notebook away.*)

SAKINI. Colonel Purdy very wise man. Always hit nail on head. Every morning, look at sky—

(COLONEL PURDY *puts his hands on his hips and glances skyward.*)

And make prophecy.

PURDY. It's not going to rain today.

SAKINI. And you know what? Not rain. Of course, not rain here this time of year in whole history of Okinawa. But Colonel not make mistake.

(COLONEL PURDY *goes down the laundry line and stops
to button the top of a pair of shorts.*)

Colonel Purdy gentleman of propriety.

(PURDY *goes back to count articles of clothing.*)

And precision. Always count laundry.

PURDY (*counts aloud*).   Un—deux—trois.

SAKINI.   Explanation. Army teach Colonel French for in-
vasion of Europe. Then send him to Okinawa instead.

PURDY.   . . . quatre—cinq—six—sept.   (*He beams with
satisfaction.*)

SAKINI.   Very good. Colonel count in French and not notice one pair shorts missing in Okinawa.

PURDY.   (*His expression quickly changes.*)   What?

(*He goes down the line and counts again in English.*)

One, two, three, four, five, six, seven!

(*He inhales deeply for an explosion.*)

SAKINI (*rushes down to the footlights*).   Oh—ladies please
close ears unless want to hear unladylike oath.

(*He puts his hands over his own ears.*)

PURDY (*explodes*).   Damitohell! Damitohell! Damitohell!

SAKINI.   Now Colonel yell loud for Sakini. But Sakini
hide. Pretend to be asleep.

(*He promptly curls up on the ground beside the office,
with his back to the* COLONEL.)

PURDY.   Sakini!

(SAKINI *snores.* PURDY *strides over to tower above
him.*)

Sakini!

SAKINI (*rises quickly*).   Oh—oh. Good morning, boss.
You sure surprise me.

PURDY.   *Where* is the boy that does my laundry?

SAKINI.   Bring laundry back and go home to sleep, boss.

PURDY.   I want you to find out why my laundry comes back every week with one piece missing!

SAKINI.   Gets lost, boss.

PURDY.   I *know* it gets lost. What I want to find out is *how* it gets lost.

SAKINI.   Very simple. Boy takes laundry to top of mountain stream and throws in water. Then runs down hill fast as dickens to catch laundry at bottom. Sometimes not run fast enough.

PURDY (*heaves a martyr's sigh*).   No wonder you people were subjugated by the Japanese. If you're not sleeping you're running away from work. Where is your "get-up-and-go"?

SAKINI.   Guess "get-up-and-go" went.

(SAKINI *starts to sit on the ground.*)

PURDY.   Well, get up and go over to the mess and see if Captain Fisby has arrived. If he has, tell him to report to me at once. Hurry!

(*As* SAKINI *starts across the stage* PURDY *looks with annoyance at the G.I. socks that hang down over Sakini's ankles.*)

Sakini!

SAKINI (*stops*).   Yes, boss?

PURDY.   You're a civilian employee in the pay of the United States Army. And should dress accordingly. *Pull Your Socks Up!*

SAKINI.   Yes, boss.

(*He leans over and pulls up his socks—not a great improvement.*)

Anything else, boss?

PURDY.   That will be all.

(SAKINI *ambles across the stage so slowly that the* COLONEL *explodes with exasperation.*)

Is that as *fast* as you can walk!

SAKINI.   Oh, no, boss. But if walk any faster—socks fall down.

> (*As* SAKINI *exits,* COLONEL PURDY *closes his eyes and counts to ten in vehement French.* PURDY *remains arrested in this position.* SAKINI *re-enters downstage. He signals the closing of the panels left, shutting out the* COLONEL.)

SAKINI.   Introduction now over. Kindly direct attention to office.

> (*He leans out toward the footlights and calls across stage.*)

Oh, Honourable Sergeant—really now to continue.

> (SERGEANT GREGOVICH *again comes to life. He glances out the office door and quickly hides the* Adventure Magazine. *He stands at attention as* COLONEL PURDY *enters.* SAKINI *exits into the wings.*)

GREGOVICH.   Good morning, sir.

PURDY.   At ease.

> (COLONEL PURDY *sits down behind his desk and begins searching through the papers on it.*)

I'm thinking of getting rid of that interpreter. He doesn't set a good example.

GREGOVICH.   We've got to have someone around that speaks the language, sir.

PURDY.   You're quite right, Sergeant. You're quite right. It isn't often I make a mistake, but when I do—

GREGOVICH.   It's a beaut?

PURDY (*stiffly*).   I wasn't going to say that. I was going to say—I admit it.

GREGOVICH.   Sorry, sir.

PURDY.   We've got a new officer reporting this morning. He's been transferred to us from "Psychological Warfare". (*Benevolently.*) I don't suppose you happen to know who *they* are?

GREGOVICH. Aren't they something at the rear of the Rear Echelon?

PURDY. They're just the cream of the Army's geniuses. They're just the brains behind the fighting heart. Every man jack of them has a mind like a steel trap. And we are lucky to be getting one of their officers.

GREGOVICH. I'll watch my step, sir.

PURDY. While we're waiting for Captain Fisby, I want you to make a note of some new signs I want painted.

GREGOVICH (*takes up a pad*). The painter hasn't finished the ones you ordered yesterday, sir.

PURDY. There's only one answer to that. Put on another sign painter. Now. I noticed the men were dancing with each other in the canteen the other night.

GREGOVICH. Yes, sir. (*He writes on his pad.*) "No dancing allowed."

PURDY (*annoyed*). I didn't say that, Gregovich! I don't object to the men dancing. I want them to enjoy themselves. But it doesn't set a good example for the natives to see non-coms dancing with enlisted men. So have a sign posted saying, "Sergeants Are Forbidden to Dance with Privates."

GREGOVICH. Yes, sir.

PURDY. Have another sign put up beside that clear pool of water just below the falls—"For Officers Only."

GREGOVICH. Where will the men bathe, sir?

PURDY. There is another pool just below it they can use.

GREGOVICH. If you'll pardon me, sir—they're not going to like that. They'll be bathing in water the officers have already bathed in.

PURDY. That's a valid objection, Gregovich. We don't want to do anything unreasonable. (*He concentrates for a moment.*) How far is the second pool below the first?

GREGOVICH. About three hundred yards.

PURDY (*satisfied*). Then it's quite all right. Water purifies itself every two hundred feet.

GREGOVICH.   Do you think that will satisfy the men, sir?

PURDY.   I don't see why it shouldn't. It satisfies science. Well, you might as well take those memos to the sign painter now.

GREGOVICH.   Yes, sir.

> (*He goes out. As soon as he is gone,* COLONEL PURDY *moves round to the front of his desk and feels under it for his* Adventure Magazine. *When he fails to find it, he kneels down on all fours to peer under the desk.* SAKINI *enters and looks around. He steps over and taps the nearest part of Colonel Purdy— his ample rear end.*)

SAKINI.   Sakini here, boss.

PURDY (*glances around indignantly*).   Don't *ever* put your finger on an officer!

SAKINI.   Not right, boss?

PURDY.   No! If you want to announce your presence— knock!

> (*He peers under the desk again.*)

Can't you natives learn anything about custom?

> (SAKINI *stands unhappily a moment, then leans forward and knocks gently on the* COLONEL. PURDY *rises in wrath.*)

What do you think you're doing?

SAKINI.   Not know, boss. Do what you ask.

PURDY (*moves behind his desk*).   *Everything* in this God-forsaken country conspires to annoy me.

> (*He turns to* SAKINI.)

Well, where is Captain Fisby?

SAKINI (*points out the door*).   He come now. I run ahead.

> (*He points to his ankles.*)

Socks fall down.

> (*He then steps back to allow* CAPTAIN FISBY *to enter.*

CAPTAIN FISBY *is in his late twenties, nice-looking and rather on the earnest side. He is nervous and eager to make a good impression. He salutes smartly.*)

CAPTAIN FISBY. Captain Fisby reporting, sir.

PURDY (*returns the salute*). Welcome to Team 147, Captain.

(*He puts out his hand.*)

FISBY (*shakes hands*). Thank you, sir.

PURDY. I can't tell you how glad I am to have you, Captain. Frankly, we're so desperate for officer personnel I'd be glad to see you even if you had two heads.

(SAKINI *breaks into gales of laughter.* PURDY *turns to him icily.*)

That will be all, Sakini. You can wait outside.

SAKINI (*bows*). I sit by door. Not sleep!

(*He exits.*)

PURDY. Sit down, Captain, sit down.

(FISBY *sits facing* PURDY.)

Have you unpacked?

FISBY (*proudly*). Yes sir. I got in last night and unpacked at once.

PURDY. Well, that's too bad, because you'll have to pack again. I'm sending you to Tobiki at once. We need a man of your calibre up there right away.

(*He laughs with forced heartiness.*)

FISBY (*forces a laugh in return*). Thank you.

PURDY. I'm informed, Captain, that you requested this transfer from "Psychological Warfare" to *my* outfit. May I say that I am honoured.

FISBY. Well—in all fairness, sir—I think I should tell you . . . the information is only partly true.

PURDY (*pauses*). You *didn't* request this transfer to me?

FISBY.   I was *requested* to request it, sir.

PURDY.   Oh.

  (*He blinks to aid his digestion of this information.*)
May I ask why?

FISBY.   Well, my propaganda to undermine enemy morale always seemed to undermine the staff's morale instead, sir.

PURDY.   *How* did you get into "Psychological Warfare" in the *first* place?

FISBY.   I had been requested to request a transfer.

PURDY.   From what?

FISBY.   Paymaster General's office.

PURDY.   What was your duty there?

FISBY.   I was in charge of the payroll computation machine until—until— (*He flounders unhappily.*)

PURDY.   Until *what*?

FISBY.   Well, sir, machines have always been my mortal enemies. I don't think they're inanimate at all. I think they're full of malice and ill will. They—

PURDY.   I *asked* you what happened, Captain.

FISBY.   Well, this computation machine made a mistake of a quarter of a million dollars on the payroll. Unfortunately, the men were paid *before* the mistake was discovered.

PURDY.   What did they do to you?

FISBY.   For a while I was given a job licking envelopes.

PURDY.   Then you asked for a transfer?

FISBY.   No, sir, I developed an allergy to glue.

PURDY.   How many outfits in this man's army have you been in, Captain?

FISBY.   How many are there, sir?

PURDY.   Never mind. I admit disappointment but not defeat. I'd thought you were given to me in recognition of my work here. Frankly, I expect to be made a general soon, and I want that star for my wife's crown. Naturally, that's very hush-hush.

FISBY (*nods*).   Naturally. Maybe I just wasn't cut out to be a soldier.

PURDY.   Captain, none of us was cut out to be a soldier. But we do the job. We adjust. We adapt. We roll with the punch and bring victory home in our teeth. Do you know what *I* was before the war?

FISBY (*hesitates unhappily*).   A football coach?

PURDY.   I was the Purdy Paper Box Company of Pottawattamie. What did I know about foreigners? But my job is to teach these natives the meaning of democracy, and they're going to learn democracy if I have to shoot every one of them.

FISBY.   I'm sure your wife wouldn't want her star that way, sir.

PURDY.   What did you do before the war?

FISBY.   I was an associate professor at Muncie.

PURDY.   What did you teach?

FISBY.   The humanities.

PURDY.   Captain, you are finally getting a job you're qualified by training to handle—teaching these natives how to act human.

FISBY.   The humanities isn't quite that, sir.

PURDY.   If you can teach one thing you can teach another. Your job at Tobiki will be to teach the natives democracy and make them self-supporting. Establish some sort of industry up there.

FISBY.   Is there a general plan?

PURDY.   There is a specific plan.

(*He extends a document the size of a telephone book.*)

Washington has drawn up full instructions pertaining to the welfare and recovery of these native villages. *This* is Plan B. Consider it your *Bible*, Captain.

FISBY.   I'll study it carefully, sir. There might be some questions I'd like to ask you.

PURDY (*points to Plan B*).   Washington has anticipated all your questions.

FISBY. But I was thinking—

PURDY. You don't even have to think, Captain. This document relieves you of that responsibility.

FISBY. But in dealing with the natives, sir—

PURDY (*interrupts*). It's all covered in Section Four: "Orienting the Oriental." How is your Luchuan?

FISBY. I don't know, sir. What is it?

PURDY. It's the native dialect. Well, I can see you'll need an interpreter.

(*His eyes light up and he slaps his desk.*)

I have just the man for you!

(*He turns and calls out the door.*)

Sakini!

FISBY. I could study the dialect, sir.

PURDY. No need. We won the war. I'll give you my own interpreter.

FISBY. Oh, I wouldn't want to deprive you of—

PURDY. I insist.

(SAKINI *enters. He bows—and then remembers. He leans forward and politely knocks on the desk.*)

SAKINI. Sakini present. Socks up. Not sleeping.

PURDY. Sakini, this is Captain Fisby.

FISBY. Hello, Sakini.

SAKINI (*bows, then turns to* PURDY). We meet already.

(*He smiles in comradeship.*)

You forget, boss?

PURDY (*covers his face, counts to ten, then looks up*). I am assigning you to Captain Fisby. He's going to take charge of a village at the top of Okinawa—a village called Tobiki.

SAKINI. Oh! Tobiki very nice place, boss. But not at top of Okinawa. At bottom.

PURDY. Don't tell me where the villages under my command are located. I happen to have looked at the map.

SAKINI.   So sorry, boss. But I happen to get born in Tobiki.
Is at bottom.

PURDY (*whips a map out of his desk*).   Then it's time you
learned where you were born. I also happen to give a course
in map reading.

SAKINI.   So sorry, boss. But map upside down.

FISBY (*looks at map*).   He's right.

PURDY (*looks at map—turns it around*).   Why in hell
doesn't the Army learn how to draw a map properly!

(*Turns to* SAKINI.)

That will be all, Sakini. Find Sergeant Gregovich and have
him assign a jeep to Captain Fisby. Then load supplies and
the captain's gear in the jeep. You will be leaving at once.
I'll send rice rations later.

SAKINI (*takes the Colonel's hand and pumps it*).   Oh, thank
you, boss. You very kind to send me home. I mention you
in prayer to gods.

(*He turns to* FISBY.)

I wait at jeep for you, Captain.

(*He starts to run, then slows down quickly.*)

Very happy, sir. Socks up.

(*He goes out.* PURDY *turns wearily to* FISBY.)

PURDY.   I sometimes think we Occupation Teams have it
tougher than combat troops.

(*He quickly holds up a protesting hand.*)

Granted they have it rough for a while. But we have the killing daily grind, with no glory in it.

FISBY.   Yes, sir, I know what you mean. Life itself is a
battlefield with its own obscure heroes.

PURDY (*looks at* FISBY *with surprise*).   I consider that
poetry, Captain.

FISBY.   I'm afraid it's just prose, sir. And it isn't mine, it's
Victor Hugo's.

PURDY (*corrected*).   Oh, yes. Victor Hugo! How I loved *Tale of Two Cities*.

FISBY.   Isn't that Dickens, sir?

PURDY.   I guess I was thinking of the movie. Well! To get back to Tobiki. Your first job when you get there will be to establish a municipal government and build a school.

FISBY.   A school?

PURDY.   It's all in Plan B.   I'll see that the cement and lumber are sent down to you. Plan B calls for the schoolhouse to be pentagon-shaped.

FISBY.   If you say so, sir.

PURDY.   When the school is built, you will organize a Ladies' League for Democratic Action. You will deliver a series of lectures on democracy as outlined in the outline. Captain, this is a chance for you to make a name for yourself.

FISBY.   I will, sir. You see, I feel that I've personally delayed victory at least a year, and I have to vindicate myself.

PURDY.   That's the kind of talk I like to hear from my officers. Well, I won't detain you then.

(*He rises.*)

My only order to you is: Put that village on the map.

FISBY.   Yes, sir.

PURDY.   Send me a bimonthly Progress Report—in triplicate.

FISBY.   Yes, sir.

PURDY.   Don't duplicate your work.

FISBY.   No, sir.

PURDY.   Fire those natives with the Spirit of Occupation.

FISBY.   Yes, sir.

PURDY.   And remember—that the eyes of Washington are on our Occupation Teams. And the eyes of the world are on Washington.

FISBY.   I'll keep the eyes in mind, sir.

PURDY.   Good-bye, Captain.

(FISBY *salutes smartly and goes out.* PURDY *stands for a moment, moved by the vastness of the canvas. Then he turns to his desk.*)

Where the hell is my *Adventure Magazine!*

THE SCENE BLACKS OUT QUICKLY

SCENE TWO

SCENE: *Outside Captain Fisby's quarters, G.H.Q.*

TIME: *Few minutes later.*

AT RISE: CAPTAIN FISBY *and* SAKINI *enter from left and cross before the panels, all of which are now down.*

SAKINI.   Everything all ready, boss. We go to Tobiki now?

FISBY.   I guess so. Well, wish me luck, Sakini. I'm going out to spread the gospel of Plan B.

SAKINI.   You already lucky, boss. You got me.

FISBY (*smiles*).   Thanks . . . do you know the road?

SAKINI.   No road, boss—just path for wagon cart and goat.

FISBY.   Will a jeep make it?

SAKINI.   We find out, boss.

FISBY.   Naturally. How long will it take us?

SAKINI.   Oh—not know until we arrive, boss.

FISBY.   Naturally. Well, we might as well get started. I'll drive and you give directions.

SAKINI.   Oh, very happy to go home.

FISBY.   Where is the jeep?

SAKINI.   Right here, boss.

(*He turns and claps his hands. The panels go up. The laundry line has been removed and the jeep pulled down centre. The jeep is piled with Fisby's belongings. Perched high on the top of this pyramid sits a very old and very wrinkled* NATIVE WOMAN.*

SAKINI *pays no attention to her as he goes around the jeep test-kicking the tires. And the* OLD WOMAN *sits disinterested and aloof from what goes on below her.*)

FISBY. Hey, wait a minute! What's she doing up there?

(*He points to her. The* OLD WOMAN *sits with hands folded serenely, looking straight ahead.*)

SAKINI. She nice old lady hear we go to Tobiki village. She think she go along to visit grandson.

FISBY. Oh, she does. Well, you explain that I'm very sorry but she'll have to take a bus.

SAKINI. No buses to Tobiki. People very poor—can only travel on generosity.

FISBY. I'm sorry, but it's against regulations.

SAKINI. She not fall off, boss. She tied on.

FISBY. Well, untie her and get her down. She'll just have to find some other way to visit her grandson.

SAKINI. Her grandson mayor of Tobiki village. You make him lose face if you kick old grandmother off jeep.

FISBY. She's the mayor's grandmother?

SAKINI. Oh yes, boss.

FISBY. Well, since she's already tied on, I guess we can take her.

(*He looks at the bundles.*)

Are all those *mine*?

SAKINI. Oh, no. Most of bundles belong to old lady. She think she visit three or four months so she bring own bed and cooking pots.

FISBY. Well, tell her to yell out if she sees any low branches coming.

(*He starts to get in.*)

Let's get started.

SAKINI. Oh, can't go yet, boss.

FISBY. Why not?

SAKINI.   Old lady's daughter not here.

FISBY (*glances at watch*).   We can't wait for a lot of good-byes, Sakini!

SAKINI (*looking behind* FISBY).   Oh, she come now—right on dot you bet.

> (CAPTAIN FISBY *turns to witness a squat young* NATIVE WOMAN *come on pushing a wheelbarrow loaded with bundles. She stops long enough to bow low to* FISBY—*then begins to tie bundles onto the jeep.*)

FISBY.   Sakini, can't the old lady leave some of that stuff behind?

SAKINI.   Not her things, boss. Belong to daughter.

FISBY.   Wait a minute. Is the daughter planning on going with us, too?

SAKINI.   Old lady very old. Who take care of her on trip?

FISBY.   Well, I—

> (*The* DAUGHTER *takes the wheelbarrow and hurries off.*)

Hey—you come back! Sakini—tell her to come back. We can't carry any more bundles.

SAKINI (*calmly*).   Oh, she not go to get bundles, boss. She go to get children.

FISBY.   Come here, Sakini. Now look—this sort of thing is always happening to me and I have to put a stop to it some place. This time I'm determined to succeed. It's not that I don't *want* to take them. But you can see for yourself, *there's no room left for kids!*

SAKINI.   But daughter not go without children and old lady not go without daughter. And if old lady not go, mayor of Tobiki be mad at you.

> (*Turns to see the* DAUGHTER *hurry back with three children in tow. They all bow politely to* FISBY. *Their mother then piles them on the hood of the jeep.*)

FISBY.   For Pete's sake, Sakini, how does she expect me to see how to drive!

SAKINI.   Old lady got very good eyesight. She sit on top and tell us when to turn.

(*At this point one of the* CHILDREN *climbs off the hood and points offstage.*)

CHILD.   A! Wasureta!

DAUGHTER.   Wasureta? Nanisa?

CHILD.   Fija dayo.

(*The* CHILD *dashes offstage.*)

FISBY.   Now, where's *he* going?

SAKINI (*to* DAUGHTER).   Doshtano?

DAUGHTER.   Fija turete kurendes!

SAKINI (*to* FISBY).   He go to get goat.

FISBY.   A goat!

SAKINI.   Can't go and leave poor goat behind.

DAUGHTER (*waves gaily to the* OLD WOMAN *on top of the jeep*).   Okasan daijobu!

(*She climbs the pyramid of bundles to settle beside her.*)

FISBY.   Well, right here is where we start seeing who's going to lose face. No goat is going to travel on this jeep.

SAKINI.   You not like goats, boss?

FISBY.   It has nothing to do with whether I like goats or not. I'm positive the colonel wouldn't like it.

SAKINI.   But children not go without goat, mother not go without children, old lady not go without daughter—

FISBY (*repeats with* SAKINI).   —and if old lady not go, the mayor of Tobiki be mad at you!

(FISBY *sees the goat being led on by the* SMALL BOY.)

Oh, no!

NOTE: The Luchuan dialect used throughout the play is merely a phonetic approximation.

SAKINI.   Everybody here, boss. Goat not got children. Goat unmarried lady goat.

FISBY.   All right, all right. Put it on the hood with the kids.

(*The goat is placed on the hood and held by the* CHILDREN.)

We've got to get started or we'll never get off the ground.

SAKINI.   All ready to go, boss. You get in now. Nobody else going.

(*But before* FISBY *can climb in an* OLD MAN *comes hurrying in and, without looking to the right or left, climbs on the back of the jeep and settles down.*)

FISBY.   Now who the hell is he?

SAKINI (*looks at* OLD MAN).   Now who the hell is he?

(*Back to* FISBY.)

Not know, boss, never see before.

FISBY.   Is he a relation of theirs?

SAKINI (*to the woman on top of the jeep*).   Kore dare?

MOTHER.   Mitakoto nai hito desu.

SAKINI.   She say she never see him before, boss.

FISBY.   Well, ask him what he's doing here!

SAKINI (*goes to the* OLD MAN).   Ojisan, doshtano?

OLD MAN.   Washimo notte ikuyo.

SAKINI.   He say he see people going somewhere on trip and he think maybe he like to go somewhere, too.

FISBY.   Tell him to get off and get off quick!

SAKINI.   Dame dayo, ojisan, orina, orina!

OLD MAN (*angrily*).   Fija noserunnera washimo noruyo!

SAKINI.   He say why not take him? You take goat. He say maybe you think he not as good as goat?

FISBY.   Look, Sakini, explain to him that the eyes of the world are on Washington and the eyes of Washington are on me. I can't be responsible for——

(*But before this can be translated,* COLONEL PURDY *stalks on and comes to an abrupt halt.*)

PURDY. Captain Fisby!

FISBY. Yes, sir.

PURDY. What in the name of Occupation do you think you're doing!

FISBY. It's hard to explain, sir. . . . I, ah . . . ah . . .

>(*As he founders, the* OLD LADY *on top of the bundles comes to life. She looks down and screams shrilly.*)

OLD LADY. Yakamashii oyajijana, hayo *iko, iko!*

PURDY. What is *she* saying?

SAKINI. She say . . . tell fat old man to shut up so we can get started!

>(*As* COLONEL PURDY's *jaw drops, the panels drop also.*)

BLACKOUT

SCENE THREE

SCENE: *Tobiki village.*

TIME: *Ten days later.*

AT RISE: *All the bamboo panels are down.* SAKINI *walks in front of them to the centre of the stage from the wings.*

SAKINI (*bows*).

Distance from Headquarters to Tobiki village by map . . . two inches.

By horse . . . three days.

By foot . . . four days.

By jeep . . . ten days.

Explanation:

Captain want to go to Tobiki.

Children want to go ocean. Never see ocean.

We see ocean.

Captain want to go to Tobiki.

Old lady's daughter want to visit Awasi.

We go Awasi.

Old lady make second mistake.

Captain demand we go Tobiki.

Ancient man have cousin in Yatoda.

We go Yatoda.

Damn fool old lady not know one road from another.

Now we arrive Tobiki.

Tobiki welcome rice and democracy.

> (*He claps his hands for the panels to be raised, then walks into the scene. The destitute village of Tobiki is revealed with its sagging huts and its ragged villagers grouped in the square just outside of Captain Fisby's office. This is a small bamboo structure with a thatched roof. It has a makeshift desk and field telephone. There is a cot crowded against the upper wall.* FISBY, *his glasses on, sits studying Plan B. He puts the document down, and, taking off his glasses, calls to* SAKINI.)

FISBY.   Sakini!

SAKINI.   Right here, boss. Not asleep, boss.

FISBY.   Good. According to Plan B, my first job here is to hold a public meeting.

SAKINI.   Public waiting in public square . . . eager to meet new boss, boss.

FISBY.   Good. Now, Plan B calls for a lecture on the ABC's of democracy.

> (*He turns to* SAKINI.)

Make sure they understand that I come as a friend of the people. That we intend to lift the yoke of oppression from their shoulders.

SAKINI. · Oh, they like that, boss. This their favourite speech.

FISBY.   What do you mean, their favourite speech?

SAKINI.   Oh, Japanese say same things when they come, boss. Then take everything.

FISBY.   Well, we're not here to *take* anything.

SAKINI.   They got nothing left to take away, boss.

FISBY (*annoyed*).   Well, if they *did* have, we wouldn't take it. We're here to *give* them something.

SAKINI.   Oh, not get angry, boss. We not mind. After eight centuries we get used to it. When friends come now, we hide things quick as the dickens.

FISBY (*rises, a little upset*).   Well, I guess it's up to me to convince them we really are friends. Let's meet the villagers.

> (*He picks up his papers.*)

And let them meet Plan B.

> (*As they step out the door to the office, the villagers rise and bow respectfully in unison.* FISBY *surveys them.*)

SAKINI (*introducing* FISBY).   Amerikano Taisho-san, Captain Fisby.

FISBY (*bows in return*).   Well, we might as well get started, Sakini.

> (*He finds a box and stands on it. He glances into Plan B and clears his throat.*)

Citizens of Tobiki village. I—

SAKINI (*interrupts*).   Sorry, boss. Can't begin lecture yet.

FISBY.   Why not?

SAKINI.   Not good manners. People bring you gifts. You must accept gifts first.

FISBY.   But I'm here to bring gifts from my government to them.

SAKINI.   Very rude to make people feel poor, boss.

FISBY.   I don't want to make anyone feel poor, but—

SAKINI.   You make them lose face if you refuse, boss. They not accept democracy from you.

FISBY.   All right. All right, then. Say to them that I'll

accept their gifts in the name of the United States Occupation Forces.

SAKINI (*turns to the* VILLAGERS).   Soreja moratte okuyo!

> (MR. HOKAIDA, *an enormous villager in tattered peasant clothes, steps forward.*)

MR. HOKAIDA (*bows diffidently and offers his present to* FISBY).   Amerika-san, korewo dozo.

SAKINI.   This Mr. Hokaida, boss. He give you fine present.

FISBY.   Thank you. Thank you very much.

> (*He takes it and turns to* SAKINI *puzzled.*)

What is it?

SAKINI.   You not know?

FISBY.   No.

SAKINI.   Oh, where you been all your life, boss?

FISBY.   Living without one of these, I guess.

SAKINI.   Is very splendid cricket cage, boss.

FISBY.   What's it used for?

SAKINI.   Keep cricket in.

FISBY.   Why?

SAKINI.   So Fortune smile on you. Cricket very good luck.

FISBY.   But there's no cricket in it.

SAKINI.   Bad luck to give cricket. You must catch your own fortune. No one can get it for you.

FISBY (*considers this*).   Thank him and tell him I'll keep my eye out for a cricket.

SAKINI.   Ya, arigato.

> (MR. HOKAIDA *bows away as an* ANCIENT NATIVE *steps forward and bows.*)

This Mr. Omura. He bring you gift of chopsticks.

MR. OMURA.   Korede mainichi gochiso wo, dozo.

SAKINI.   He say: May only food of gods touch your lips.

> (*As* FISBY *bows,* MR. SUMATA, *a nervous citizen in a torn straw hat, pushes his way toward* SAKINI.)

MR. SUMATA.   Sugu modotte kuruyo!

SAKINI. Doshtandes?

MR. SUMATA. Ima sugu presento motte kuruyo.

(*He turns and runs hurriedly off stage right.*)

FISBY. What was that?

SAKINI. That Mr. Sumata. He have present at home for you. He say not go away until he get.

(*A rather handsome young Tobikian,* MR. SEIKO, *now steps forward and extends a pair of wooden sandals.*)

MR. SEIKO. Dozo korewo chakini.

SAKINI. This Mr. Seiko. He bring you geta.

FISBY. Geta?

SAKINI. Wooden sandals. Very comfortable for tired feet. He say: May you walk in prosperity.

FISBY. Tell him I shall walk in the—the cool—meadow —of—of pleasant memories. Is that all right?

SAKINI. Oh, that's very pretty, boss.

(*He turns to* MR. SEIKO.)

Ya, arigato, Seiko-san.

MR. SEIKO (*beams, bows, and backs away*). Iya, kosi no itari desu.

SAKINI. He say you do him honour.

(*Here a chunky, flat-faced, aggressive* YOUNG WOMAN *with heavy glasses pushes forward with her present.*)

Oh, this Miss Higa Jiga—unmarried lady. She bring you three eggs.

FISBY. Tell her I shall eat them for breakfast.

(*He bows to her.*)

SAKINI. Captain-san, daisuki desu.

MISS HIGA JIGA. Kame no tamago desu.

(*She bows away.*)

SAKINI. She say she hope you enjoy turtle eggs.

FISBY (*grins and bows to her*). She'll never know.

SAKINI.   You very big success. They sure like you already.

(*Another* VILLAGER *steps forward and offers a gift.*)

This Mr. Keora. He bring you another cricket cage. Minus cricket.

FISBY.   Say to him—that my prospects of good fortune are doubled.

(*He looks rather pleased with himself.*)

SAKINI.   Kagowa futatsu de, un wa bai!

MR. KEORA.   Hoho! Naka naka shiteki desna!

(*He bows away.*)

SAKINI.   He say you are inspired poet.

FISBY (*modestly*).   It's all in getting the hang of it.

SAKINI (*introducing the next citizen, a very* OLD MAN *leaning on a stick*).   This old man Mr. Oshira. He bring you fine lacquered cup he make himself.

FISBY.   Tell him I'm forever in his debt for such a beautiful gift.

OSHIRA.   You are most welcome, Captain.

FISBY (*turns to him in surprise*).   You speak English!

SAKINI.   Mr. Oshira teach me English when I am little boy in Tobiki.

OSHIRA.   In my youth I work in Manila. How is Mr. McKinley?

FISBY (*puzzled for a moment*).   Who? Oh—President McKinley. I'm afraid someone shot him.

OSHIRA.   I am sad.

FISBY.   It was a long time ago.

OSHIRA.   Yes, a long time.

(*He indicates the cup.*)

May August moon fill your cup.

FISBY.   May I ask, why an August moon?

OSHIRA.   All moons good, but August moon little older, little wiser.

FISBY.   Did Sakini say you made this cup yourself?

OSHIRA. Oh, yes. I learned from my father before me who learned from his father before him. Is our heritage.

SAKINI. Look, boss, this cup thin as paper, carved from one block of wood. Then painted many times with red lacquer.

FISBY. And did you paint the gold fish inside?

OSHIRA (*nods*). It is imperfect.

SAKINI. When Mr. Oshira little boy, he work ten years to learn how to paint gold fish exactly like his papa paint.

FISBY. It's just beautiful! Can you still make things like this?

OSHIRA. One does not forget.

FISBY. Sakini, here's an industry we can start right away. This is a lost art.

(*Turns to* OSHIRA.)

Is there any way we could mass-produce these?

OSHIRA. Mass-produce?

FISBY. You know—set up machines and turn them out by the gross.

OSHIRA (*shakes his head*). I take pride in making one cup at time, Captain. How can I take pride in work of machine?

FISBY. How many of these could you turn out in a day?

OSHIRA. If I work hard, maybe one or two a week.

FISBY (*disappointed*). Well, it's a start. Make as many as you can. We'll send them up to the American Post Exchange and sell them as fast as you can turn them out.

OSHIRA. I shall do my best. The swiftness of my youth has deserted me, sir.

(*He bows and moves back.*)

But I shall make fewer mistakes.

FISBY (*excitedly*). Sakini, tell Mr. Omura to make up a batch of chopsticks. Have everybody get to work making cricket cages, wooden sandals and—

(*Pointing.*)

—these straw hats. We'll put this village in the souvenir business.

SAKINI. We all make money, boss?

FISBY. If they can turn out enough of these things, I guarantee the recovery of Tobiki village. Tell them.

SAKINI. Kore dondon tskuru yoni . . .

(*There is a general exchange of chatter and approval.*) They say they make everything, fast as the dickens, boss.

FISBY. Good. We're in business. Now ask them if they'd mind postponing the rest of the gifts until later. I'd like to tell them what *we're* planning for *them*.

SAKINI. Sa, sono hanashi shiyo.

CITIZENS. No agerumono naiyo! Hanashi wo kiko.

SAKINI. They say sure. They got no more presents anyhow.

FISBY. Good. First I want to tell them about the school we're going to build for their children. All set to translate?

SAKINI. All set.

FISBY. All right.

(*He consults Plan B.*)

Plan B says the direct approach is most effective. This is it.

(*He steps back up on a box and looks forcefully at his listeners. Then he points a dramatic finger at them.*)

Do you want to be ignorant?

SAKINI (*also points a finger*). Issho bakaja dame daro?

(*The* CITIZENS *make a noise that sounds like "Hai."*)

FISBY. What did they say?

SAKINI. They say "Yes."

FISBY. What do you mean, "yes"? They *want* to be ignorant?

SAKINI. No, boss. But in Luchuan "yes" means "no." They say "yes," they *not* want to be ignorant.

FISBY. Oh.

(*He turns back to his rapt audience and assumes his forensic posture.*)

Do you want your *children* to be ignorant?

SAKINI   Issho kodomotachi mo bakaja dame daro?

(*The* VILLAGERS *respond quickly with a noise that sounds like "Iie".*)

FISBY.   What did they say then?

SAKINI.   They say "No."

FISBY.   "No" they do, or "No" they don't?

SAKINI.   Yes, they not want no ignorant children.

FISBY.   Good.

(*He turns back to the* VILLAGERS.)

Then this is what my government is planning to do for you. First there will be daily issues of rice for everyone.

SAKINI.   Mazu kome no hykyu!

(*The* VILLAGERS *cheer.*)

FISBY.   We will build a fine new school here for your children.

(*Then recalling Colonel Purdy's dictum.*)

Pentagon-shaped.

SAKINI.   Gakko taterundayo katachi wa—

(*He flounders.*)

Ah—Pentagon.

(*The* CITIZENS *look at each other, puzzled.*)

MISS HIGA JIGA.   Nandesutte?

SAKINI.   Pentagon.

MISS HIGA JIGA.   Sore wa nandesuka?

SAKINI.   They say what is Pentagon? Never hear before.

FISBY.   Never heard of the *Pentagon*!

SAKINI.   No, boss.

FISBY.   Well, they certainly do need a school here. The Pentagon is—is—

(*He looks down at their eager faces.*)
Well, it really means five-sided.

SAKINI. Kabega itsutsusa, ii, ni, san, yon, go.

(*Holds up five fingers. There is a burst of laughter from the* CITIZENS.)

MISS HIGA JIGA (*giggling*). Ara, gokakuno kodomo nante arimasenyo.

SAKINI. They say no children in Tobiki got five sides.

FISBY. The *school* will be five-sided—like a building in Washington.

SAKINI (*explains*). Chigauyo, chigauyo, onaji mono arundes yo, Washington ni.

(*There is a decided reaction of approval.* SAKINI *turns back to* FISBY.)

They very impressed.

FISBY (*continuing*). Everyone will learn about democracy.

SAKINI. Mazu minshu shugi bera-bera bera-bera.

MISS HIGA JIGA. Minshu shugi bera-bera bera-bera?

SAKINI. They say: Explain what is democracy. They know what rice is.

FISBY. Oh. (*He scratches his head.*) Well, it's a system of self-determination. It's—it's the right to make the wrong choice.

SAKINI. Machigattemo iindayo.

(*They look up blankly, silently.*)

FISBY. I don't think we're getting the point over. Explain that if I don't like the way Uncle Sam treats me, I can write the President himself and tell him so.

SAKINI. Daitoryo ni tegami kaitemo iinosa.

(*The* VILLAGERS *all laugh heartily.*)

MISS HIGA JIGA. Masaka soonakoto!

SAKINI (*triumphantly*). They say: But do you *send* the letters?

FISBY.   Let's get on with the lecture.

(*He turns back to the citizens and reads from Plan B.*)

Tell them hereafter all men will be free and equal. . . .

SAKINI.   Subete, jiyuu, to byodo, de ar, de ar.

FISBY (*increases his tempo and volume*).   Without discrimination . . .

SAKINI (*taking* FISBY's *tone*).   Sabetsu taigoo haishi de ar.

FISBY.   The will of the majority will rule!

SAKINI.   Subete minna de kime, de ar!

FISBY (*finishing with a flourish*).   And Tobiki village will take its place in the brotherhood of democratic peoples the world over!

SAKINI (*rising to new demagogic heights*).   Koshite, Tobiki, jiyuu, Okinawa, byodo sabetsu, taigu—haishi, jiyuu, byodo de ar, de ar.

(*A great burst of applause greets* SAKINI's *performance. He turns to* FISBY.)

We going over big, boss.

FISBY (*agrees with a nod*).   Now to get this village organized. Is the mayor here?

SAKINI (*points*).   Mr. Omura is mayor, boss.

(MR. OMURA *steps forward.*)

He only one in Tobiki with white coat.

FISBY (*glances at the worn, ragged coat*).   It looks to me as if you'll have to get a new coat or a new mayor soon.

SAKINI.   Better keep mayor, boss. Impossible to get white coat.

FISBY.   Well, since we've got a mayor, we only have to find a Chief of Agriculture and a Chief of Police. That's going to present a problem.

SAKINI.   No problem, boss. You just look over gifts and see who give you best gift. Then you give him best job.

FISBY.   Sakini, that is *not* the democratic way. The people themselves must choose the man best qualified. Tell them they are to elect their own Chief of Agriculture.

SAKINI. Sah! Senkyo desu. Mazu Chief of Agriculture.

WOMEN VILLAGERS (*push* MR. SEIKO *forward shouting*). Seiko-san, Seiko-san ga ii, Seiko-san!

SAKINI. They say elect Mr. Seiko. He best qualified for agriculture.

FISBY. He's an experienced farmer?

SAKINI. No, boss. He's artist. He draw lovely picture of golden wheat stalk with pretty green butterfly.

FISBY. Drawing pictures of wheat doesn't make him a wheat expert.

SAKINI. Wheat not grow here anyhow, boss. Only sweet potatoes.

FISBY. All right, all right! If he's their choice.

SEIKO. Ano! Watashimo shiroi koto wo.

SAKINI. He say do he get white coat like the mayor?

FISBY. Tell him I'll get him a helmet that says "Chief of Agriculture" on it.

SAKINI. Yoshi, yoshi, kammuri ageruyo.

(SEIKO *bows and backs away.*)

FISBY. Next we want to elect a Chief of Police.

SAKINI. Kondowa Chief of Police!

VILLAGERS (*clamour and push the fat* MR. HOKAIDA *forward*). Hokaida-san. Soda, soda. Hokaida-san.

FISBY. What are *his* qualifications for office?

SAKINI. People afraid of him. He champion wrestler.

(MR. HOKAIDA *flexes his muscles.*)

FISBY. Well, no one can say this isn't self-determination.

MR. HOKAIDA. Washime ano kammuri wo.

SAKINI. He say do he get helmet too?

FISBY (*nods*). I'll requisition another helmet.

SAKINI. Agemasuyo.

MR. HOKAIDA (*bows smiling*). Ya, doomo.

FISBY. Now for the ladies. We intend to organize a

Ladies' League for Democratic Action. We'll want to elect a League President.

SAKINI. Oh, ladies never vote before—they like that.

(*He turns to the* LADIES.)

Kondowa Ladies' League for Democratic Action!

(*This announcement is greeted by excited chatter. The* LADIES *push* MISS HIGA JIGA *forward.*)

LADIES. Higa-Jiga-san—Higa-Jiga-san!

SAKINI. They say they elect Miss Higa Jiga. They think she make classy president.

MISS HIGA JIGA (*points to her head*). Ano, watashi nimo ano booshio . . .

FISBY (*laughs*). All right, I'll see that she gets a helmet, too. Now ask them if they have any question they'd like to ask *me*.

SAKINI. Sa, nanka kikitai koto ga attara.

OLD WOMAN. Sakini-san, ima nanji kaina?

SAKINI. They say they like to know what time is it?

FISBY (*puzzled*). Time? (*Glances at his watch.*) Quarter of five, why?

SAKINI. They say they got to hurry then. They not like to miss sunset. This is time of day they sit in pine grove, sip tea and watch sun go down.

FISBY. All right, thank them and tell them they can go have tea in the pine grove.

SAKINI. Ya, minna kaette mo iiyo.

(*They bow and, chattering happily among themselves, go off right.* FISBY *gathers up his gifts.*)

FISBY. How do you think we did, Sakini?

SAKINI. They co-operate, boss. Future look very rosy.

FISBY. Where do you think I can find a cricket?

SAKINI. One come along. May have one in house now and not know it.

FISBY.   Well, I'll take these things in and get started on my Progress Report.

> (*He goes to the office hut.*)

SAKINI.   I take a little snooze then. Public speaking very exhausting.

FISBY (*as he goes inside*).   *I* think I handled it pretty well.

> (*He sits down at his desk. He examines his gifts and then, putting on his glasses, begins to study Plan B again. After a moment,* MR. SUMATA *enters from the right. He carries a couple of battered suitcases. He is followed by* LOTUS BLOSSOM, *a petite and lovely geisha girl in traditional costume. When they are about centre stage, young* MR. SEIKO *runs up after the geisha girl. She turns to him.*)

SEIKO.   Ano, chotto . . .

LOTUS BLOSSOM.   Ara! Nani?

SUMATA (*steps in front of* SEIKO *and points an angry finger under his nose*).   Dame, dame, atchi ike.

> (SEIKO *bows head and retreats.* MR. SUMATA *then turns to* SAKINI.)

Amerika-san doko?

SAKINI (*indicates the office*).   Asco.

SUMATA (*indicates geisha girl*).   Kore tsurete kitandayo.

SAKINI.   Oh? Do-sunno?

SUMATA.   Kore Taisho-san ni agetainja.

> (*He bows and goes off quickly, almost running. The* GEISHA *remains with* SAKINI. SAKINI *smiles and steps inside the office. He stands behind* FISBY.)

SAKINI.   You busy, boss?

FISBY (*without turning around to him*).   Yes, but what is it?

SAKINI.   Mr. Sumata leave present for you, boss.

FISBY.   Put it on the shelf where it'll be out of the way.

SAKINI (*glances back outside*). Not able to do, boss. Present get mad.

FISBY (*turns around*). What's this about, Sakini?

SAKINI (*motions to the* GEISHA, *who steps inside smiling. She bows*). Here you are, boss.

FISBY (*rising*). Who is *she*?

SAKINI. Souvenir.

FISBY. What are you talking about?

SAKINI. Present from Mr. Sumata.

FISBY. Wait a minute. Is he kidding? I can't accept a human present.

SAKINI. Oh, human present very lovely. Introducing Lotus Blossom, geisha girl first class.

(*He turns to* LOTUS BLOSSOM.)

Amerika-san no Captain Fisby.

LOTUS BLOSSOM (*smiling happily*). Ara, ii otokomaene! Watashi sukidawa.

SAKINI. She say she very happy to belong to handsome captain. She say she serve you well.

FISBY. She's not going to serve me at all. You get that Mr. Sumata and tell him I'm returning his present.

SAKINI. Impossible to do, boss. Mr. Sumata leave present and go up mountains to visit cousin. He say good-bye and wish you much success in Tobiki.

LOTUS BLOSSOM (*sweetly*). Watashi kokoni sumun desho?

SAKINI. She say, where do you want her to stay, boss?

FISBY. You tell her I don't care where she stays. She can't stay here.

SAKINI (*shocked*). Where she go, then? She got no home. Mr. Sumata already gone away.

FISBY. Well, find her a place for the time being.

SAKINI (*grins*). Plenty of room in my house, boss. Just me and my grandpapa.

FISBY. No, I can't do that. Sit her over on that box until I can think where to put her.

SAKINI. You can put her in business, boss.

FISBY. You keep a civil tongue in your head, Sakini.

LOTUS BLOSSOM (*comes over to* FISBY, *whom she has been watching with great interest*).Okimono to ozohri motte kimasune.

SAKINI. She like to put on your sandals and kimono for you. She trained to please you, boss.

FISBY. I know what she's trained to do. And I don't need any translation.

(*He sits down at his desk again.*)

Sakini . . . take my supplies out of the shack and bring them over here. We'll set her up there where I can keep an eye on her.

SAKINI. Not very democratic, boss. You make her lose face if she not make you comfortable, boss. She think she bad geisha girl.

FISBY. You tell her . . . I've got some face to save, too . . . so she can just forget this Oriental hanky-panky.

SAKINI. Anta irantesa!

LOTUS BLOSSOM (*waves him away*). Ara, nani ittennoyo. Imasara ikettatte ikarenai desho.

FISBY. Well, what did she say?

SAKINI. She say for me to go on home to grandpapa . . . she first-class geisha girl . . . she know her business. Good night, boss.

(FISBY *stands eyeing* LOTUS BLOSSOM *as* SAKINI *goes out. The lights go down quickly. During the brief blackout, the two centre panels are lowered, shutting out the village street. The office of Colonel Purdy is swung into place in the last panel right. The lights come up on* PURDY *twisting the bell on his field telephone.*)

PURDY. What do you mean . . . there's no answer? Well, keep trying. I'm not the kind of a man to take "no answer" for an answer.

(*The lights come up on the opposite side of the stage in Fisby's office.* FISBY *is holding onto his jacket buttons.* LOTUS BLOSSOM *stands in front of him holding out his robe. She is gently persistent and puzzled at his reticence.*)

FISBY. It's *not* a kimono . . . it's a bathrobe. And I don't *want* to put it on.

LOTUS BLOSSOM (*reaches to unbutton his jacket*). Sa! Shizukani shimasho ne.

FISBY. No, it's against regulations.

(*Phone rings. He takes the robe away from* LOTUS BLOSSOM *and sits on it. Then he picks up the phone.*) *Hello!*

PURDY (*jumps*). You don't have to shout. I can hear you. This is Colonel Purdy.

FISBY (*leaps to his feet and pushes* LOTUS BLOSSOM *behind as if to hide her*). Yes, sir.

PURDY. Just thought I'd check up on you. How are things going?

(LOTUS BLOSSOM *begins to fan her master.*)

FISBY. Well, everything seems to be under control at the moment.

(*He sits down and takes out a cigarette.* LOTUS BLOSSOM *promptly lights it for him.*)

PURDY. Anything *I* can do for you?

FISBY (*pauses*). I can't think of anything, sir.

PURDY. I realize it's bound to get lonely for you down there . . . so you know what I'm going to do, my boy?

FISBY. (LOTUS BLOSSOM *gets the geta and kneels before him.* FISBY *watches her apprehensively and asks . . .*) What are you going to do?

PURDY. I'll tell you. I'm going to send you some of my old *Adventure Magazines*.

FISBY (*as* LOTUS BLOSSOM *starts to take off his shoes*). No, *no*. I don't want them.

(*Into the phone.*)

I mean . . . yes . . . thank you.

(*He rises and twists about trying to pull his foot away from* LOTUS BLOSSOM.)

I'd like something to read.

PURDY.   How are you getting along with the natives?

FISBY (*his leg over the chair*).   The problem here, sir, is a very old one. It seems to be a question of who's going to lose face.

PURDY.   I understand. As Mrs. Purdy says, "East is East and West is West, and there can be no Twain." But you're making progress?

FISBY.   Nothing I'd like to put on paper, sir.

(LOTUS BLOSSOM *gets his shoes off and slips the sandals on.*)

PURDY.   Well, when things get moving down there, send in a detailed Progress Report.

FISBY.   If that's what you want, sir.

(LOTUS BLOSSOM *recovers the robe. She reaches out to unbutton his jacket.*)

PURDY.   You'll find these people lack the capacity for sustained endeavour. Don't hesitate to build a fire under them.

FISBY (*struggling to keep his jacket on*).   That won't be necessary, sir.

PURDY.   Don't forget . . . the eyes of Washington are on you, Fisby.

FISBY (*as* LOTUS BLOSSOM *tries to pull his jacket over his head*).   I hope not, sir.

PURDY (*ponders*).   Fisby, it just occurred to me. Have you given any thought to physical education?

FISBY.   If I may say so, sir . . .

(LOTUS BLOSSOM *gets one arm out.*)

I consider the suggestion . . .

(*He hugs the other sleeve.*)

a masterpiece of timeliness.

(*He gets down on one knee.*)

PURDY.   Thank you, my boy.

(*Pauses.*)

Could you use a deck of cards?

Hello? Hello, Fisby . . . you're getting weak.

(*As* FISBY *looks back at the telephone and nods in complete agreement, the two scenes black out simultaneously. The panels fall. A spot picks up* SAKINI *as he steps from the wings.*)

SAKINI.

Discreet place to stop now and sip soothing cup of jasmine tea.

Conclusion?

Not yet.

Continuation shortly.

Lotus Blossom not lose face!

(*He bows.*)

THE CURTAIN FALLS

ACT II

SCENE ONE

SCENE: *Tobiki village.*

TIME: *A few days later.*

AT RISE: *All the panels are down.* SAKINI *enters from the wings and crosses down to the footlights centre. He bows to the audience.*

SAKINI.

Lovely ladies, kind gentlemen:

Most travelled person in history of world is summer sun.

Each day must visit each man no matter where he live on globe.

Always welcome visitor.

Not bring gossip.

Not stay too long.

Not depart leaving bad taste of rude comment.

But summer sun never tell topside of world what bottomside like.

So bottomside must speak for self.

We continue with little story of Tobiki.

Centre of industry.

Seat of democracy.

> (*He beams.*)

Home of geisha girl.

> (*He goes to the right proscenium arch as all the panels are raised, revealing the empty street outside of Fisby's office.* FISBY *enters, starts across stage,* SAKINI *falling in step behind him.*)

Was wondering what happened to you, boss?

FISBY (*stops*). I went down to inspect the sweet-potato fields. Sakini, no one was there. The potatoes were piled up, but no one was working.

SAKINI. Very hot day, boss.

FISBY. But I can't find my Chief of Agriculture. Or the Mayor, or the Chief of Police. Where is everybody?

SAKINI. Lotus Blossom leave belongings over at Awasi—got no way to bring things here. So—everybody take wheelbarrow to help move Lotus Blossom to Tobiki.

FISBY. And has she got so many things that it takes my entire staff to move her to this village?

SAKINI. No, boss, but Chief of Police not trust Chief of Agriculture, and Mayor not trust Mr. Oshira, so all go.

FISBY. Mr. Oshira? That old man!

SAKINI. He's old, boss, but not dead.

FISBY. A fine way for officials to behave! You tell them I want to see them the moment they come back.

(*He starts for his office.*)

A fine thing!

SAKINI. Nothing to worry about, boss. They not beat your time. You own Lotus Blossom.

FISBY. I do *not* own her. It's not a question of—of—

(*He sits down at his desk.*)

Well, this sort of nonsense isn't going to stop my work.

(*He shifts the papers on his desk.*)

I intend to get started on that schoolhouse today. We've got the materials, so all we need now is some good carpenters.

(*He turns to* SAKINI, *who has followed him inside.*)

Who is the best carpenter in the village?

SAKINI. Mr. Sumata.

FISBY. Fine. Get hold of him. Wait a minute! Isn't he the joker who gave me Lotus Blossom?

SAKINI. Mr. Sumata has finger in lots of pies, boss.

FISBY. Well, since he's vanished, who is the next best carpenter?

SAKINI. Father of Mr. Sumata.

FISBY. Where is he?

SAKINI. Go on vacation with Mr. Sumata.

FISBY (*beginning to get annoyed*).   Well, who is the *third* best carpenter, then?

SAKINI.   No more, boss. Only Sumata and son. They have what you call monopoly.

FISBY.   There's something fishy about their disappearing.

(MISS HIGA JIGA, *wearing a red helmet with flowers, followed by several other* LADIES, *comes storming across the stage to the office door.* SAKINI *hears them and goes to the door.*)

MISS HIGA JIGA (*angrily*).   Watashitachi sabetsu taigu desyo!

FISBY (*goes to the door also*).   What's the matter with her?

SAKINI.   Miss Higa Jiga say do you know what we got in this village, boss? Discrimination.

FISBY (*wearily*).   Where?

(SAKINI *turns to* MISS HIGA JIGA.)

MISS HIGA JIGA (*indignantly*).   Watashitachi hykyu matte itara Lotus Blossom ga kite clarku ga anata desuka ma dozo kochirae watashitachi nijikan mo machi mashita yo.

SAKINI.   She say that Ladies' League for Democratic Action wait in line for rice rations. Along comes Lotus Blossom and ration clerks say, "Oh, how do you do. Oh, please don't stand in line. You come inside and have cup of tea." Then clerks shut up warehouse and leave Ladies' League waiting in sun two hours.

FISBY.   It's things like this that undermine the democratic ideal. You tell Miss Higa Jiga I intend to do something about it.

(*He storms into his office.*)

SAKINI (*turns to* MISS HIGA JIGA).   Nantoka shimasuyo.

FISBY.   I can see right now we're going to have to get rid of the disrupting factor in our recovery.

(*He picks up the field telephone and twists the handle.*)

Get me Major McEvoy at Awasi.

SAKINI (*follows* FISBY *inside*). What are you going to do, boss?

FISBY. This village isn't big enough for Plan B and a geisha girl.

SAKINI. Oh, boss, Tobiki never have geisha girl before. We like very much.

FISBY. She has to go.

(*Then into the telephone.*)

Major McEvoy? Captain Fisby at Tobiki. I have a request from one of my people to transfer to your village. Yes, it's a female citizen. Profession? Well . . .

(*He looks at* SAKINI.)

SAKINI. Oh, please not send her away, boss. Not democratic.

FISBY. As a matter of fact her name *is* Lotus Blossom. *How* did *you* know? What do you mean, what am I trying to put over on you? Oh, you did?

(*He hangs up. Then he glares at* SAKINI.)

SAKINI (*with great innocence*). He knows Lotus Blossom, boss?

FISBY. Very well. She was at Awasi and damn near wrecked his whole plan for recovery. She's been booted out of every village by every commander on the island.

SAKINI. Oh, poor little Lotus Blossom.

FISBY. Poor little Lotus Blossom my eye. She upsets every village she's in.

SAKINI. Not her fault she beautiful, boss.

FISBY. No wonder that Mr. Sumata disappeared. The major paid him a hundred yen to get her out of his village.

SAKINI (*eagerly*). You keep her now, boss?

FISBY. I have to.

(*He points a finger at* SAKINI.)

Well, she's not going to get away with causing dissension in *my* village!

(MISS HIGA JIGA, *weary of waiting outside, storms in.*)

MISS HIGA JIGA.   Doshte itadakemasno Daitoryo ni tegami wo kakimasawayo.

FISBY (*pleads*).   Tell her to go away.

SAKINI.   She say she waiting for some democratic action. She say if she don't get it, she thinks she write this Uncle Sam you talk about.

FISBY.   Now, look. I don't want complaints going into Headquarters. Tell her discrimination is being eliminated.

SAKINI.   Sabetsu yamemasyo.

MISS HIGA JIGA.   Yamenakutemo iinoyo, watashitachi nimo wakete itadakeba.

SAKINI.   Miss Higa Jiga say please not eliminate discrimination. She say just give her some too.

FISBY.   And just what does she mean by that?

SAKINI.   She say Lotus Blossom unfair competition.

FISBY.   Granted.

SAKINI.   She say you promise everybody going to be equal.

FISBY.   I intend to keep my word.

SAKINI.   Well, she say she can't be equal unless she has everything Lotus Blossom has.

FISBY.   What Lotus Blossom's got, the Government doesn't issue.

SAKINI (*taking a piece of paper which* MISS HIGA JIGA *waves*).   She make list, boss. Shall I read, boss?

FISBY.   Go ahead.

SAKINI.   She wants you to get her and ladies in League following items:

A. Red stuff to put on lips like geisha.

B. Stuff that smell pretty—

FISBY.   Now, *just* wait a minute. What would H.Q. think if I requisitioned lipstick!

SAKINI (*hands list back to* MISS HIGA JIGA).   Dame desuyo.

MISS HIGA JIGA.   Jaa Daitoryo ni tegami wo dashimaswa.

SAKINI. She say she sorry, but now she guess she just have to write this letter to Uncle Samuel after all.

FISBY (*throws up his hands*). All right. *All right!* Tell her I'll call up post exchange at Awasi and see if they have any shaving powder and toilet water.

SAKINI. Ya, katte agemasuyo.

MISS HIGA JIGA (*beams*). Ano wasure naidene bobby pin.

SAKINI. She say, not forget bobby pins for hair.

FISBY. I think I might have been happier in the submarine command.

MISS HIGA JIGA (*stops as she is about to go*). Mohitotsu onegai watashitachi mo mina geisha ni.

SAKINI. She say one more thing. Can you get Lotus Blossom to teach Ladies' League all to be geisha girls?

FISBY (*leaps to his feet*). Teach the innocent women of this village to be—*No!*

> (MISS HIGA JIGA *shrugs and goes outside. As* FISBY *sinks back at his desk,* MISS HIGA JIGA *talks excitedly to the* WOMEN *gathered outside. They run off giggling.* FISBY *sits at his desk and picks up Plan B.*)

Plan B!

> (*He thumbs through its pages.*)

Let's just see if Washington anticipated *this.*

> (*He buries his chin in his hands.* SAKINI *sits quietly watching him. Outside in the village street,* LOTUS BLOSSOM *enters and starts daintily toward the office. She has only gotten halfway when* SEIKO *overtakes her.*)

SEIKO (*panting*). Ano, chotto.

LOTUS BLOSSOM (*stops and looks at him archly*). Nani?

SEIKO (*takes a chrysanthemum bud from his waist*). Ano korewo dozo.

LOTUS BLOSSOM (*takes it indifferently*). Ara, so arigato.

SEIKO (*strikes his heart passionately*). Boku no, kono, hato, o.

LOTUS BLOSSOM (*flicks her finger*). Anato no hahto? Ara shinzo ne.

SEIKO (*disembowels himself with an imaginary knife*). Harakitte shinimas.

LOTUS BLOSSOM (*yawns*). Imagoro sonnano hayaranai noyo.

SEIKO (*points toward Fisby's office*). Soka Amerika-san ga iinoka?

LOTUS BLOSSOM (*haughtily*). Nandeste! Sonnakoto yoke-ina osowa.

SEIKO (*laughs derisively*). Nanda rashamon janaika.

LOTUS BLOSSOM (*backs him up with an angry finger*). Watashimo kotoni kansho shinaideyo.

SEIKO (*bows his head*). Gomen nasai iisugi deshta.

LOTUS BLOSSOM (*points away*). Atchi, itte.

> (SEIKO *sighs, turns and plods off towards the sweet-potato fields, crushed and dejected.* LOTUS BLOSSOM *tidies her hair and continues to the office. She calls in coyly*)

Fuisbee-san!

SAKINI (*rises and looks out the door*). Oh, what do you think, boss? Lotus Blossom back. She come to see you.

FISBY. And high time.

> (*He turns to face the door as* LOTUS BLOSSOM *enters and bows.*)

Where have *you* been all day? Never mind, I know—upsetting the agricultural horse cart.

LOTUS BLOSSOM. Fu-san no kao nikkori nasaruto totemo kawaii wa.

SAKINI. She say sun burst through the clouds now that you smile on her.

FISBY. I'm not smiling.

(She hands him Seiko's chrysanthemum bud.)

SAKINI.   Oh, boss, you know what she give you?

FISBY.   The works.

SAKINI.   When lady give gentleman chrysanthemum bud, in Okinawa that means her heart is ready to unfold.

FISBY.   Well, this is one bud that's not going to flower.

LOTUS BLOSSOM *(offering a box she has brought)*.   Kore otsukemono yo. Dozo.

SAKINI.   She say, you like to eat some tsukemono? Tsukemono nice thing to eat between meals.

FISBY.   No.

LOTUS BLOSSOM *(takes geta and kneels beside him)*.   Dozo ohaki osobase.

FISBY.   Tell her to *leave my feet* alone.

LOTUS BLOSSOM *(studies FISBY)*.   Kasa kaburu. Nisshabyo nanoyo.

SAKINI.   She worried about you, boss. She say, when you go in hot sun, should wear *kasa*—that straw hat—on head.

FISBY.   Tell her never mind about my feet or my head. I want her to stop interfering with the recovery program. To stop causing rebellion and making the men—ah—ah—discontented.

SAKINI *(turns to LOTUS BLOSSOM)*.   Jama shicha dame dayo.

LOTUS BLOSSOM *(smiles)*.   Fu-san ocha ikaga?

SAKINI.   She say: You want some tea?

FISBY *(throwing himself down on his cot)*.   No.

LOTUS BLOSSOM.   Shami demo hikimashoka?

SAKINI.   She say: You want some music?

FISBY.   No.

LOTUS BLOSSOM *(giggles)*.   Ara Fu-san-tara yaiteruno.

SAKINI.   She say: You jealous, boss?

FISBY *(mirthlessly)*.   Ha!

LOTUS BLOSSOM.   Honto ni doshita no?

SAKINI.   She say: You want to tell her your troubles, boss?

FISBY.   Why should I tell her my troubles?

SAKINI.   She geisha girl, that's her *business*, boss.

FISBY.   Some business.

LOTUS BLOSSOM.   Shoga naiwane. Mah soshite irasshai yo.

SAKINI.   She say she hear about lack of co-operation here. She feel very bad. She say she want to help because you best boss she ever had. You not make her work and you not take money from her.

FISBY (*sits up on his cot*).   Did the other men who owned her . . . hire her out and then take money from her?

SAKINI.   Oh, sure.

FISBY.   Well, where I come from we have a name for men who—who—do *that* sort of thing.

SAKINI.   You have geisha business in America, too?

FISBY (*rises*).   No! Sakini, you give her to understand I have no intention of putting her to—to work.

SAKINI.   Why not, boss? She pay all her dues to Geisha Guild. She member in good standing.

FISBY.   You mean they've got a union for this sort of thing?

SAKINI.   Geisha girl have to be protected, boss. Must keep up rates.

FISBY.   This is the most immoral thing I've ever heard of. Haven't you people any sense of shame?

SAKINI.   We bad not to be ashamed, boss?

FISBY.   Obviously, there is a fundamental difference between us that can't be reconciled. I don't say that where I come from there's no such thing as prostitution. But, by God, we don't have unions, set rates and collect dues!

SAKINI.   But geisha girl not prostitute, boss.

FISBY.   At least we have the decency—

        (*He stops.*)

What do you mean, geisha girls aren't prostitutes? Everybody knows what they do.

SAKINI.   Then everybody wrong, boss.

FISBY. Well, what do they get paid for, then?

SAKINI. Hard to explain fundamental difference. Poor man like to feel rich. Rich man like to feel wise. Sad man like to feel happy. All go to geisha house and tell troubles to geisha girl. She listen politely and say, "Oh, that's too bad." She very pretty. She make tea, she sing, she dance, and pretty soon troubles go away. Is not worth something, boss?

FISBY. And that's *all* they do?

SAKINI. Very ancient and honourable profession.

FISBY. Look, Sakini, I apologize. I guess I jumped the gun. And I'm glad you explained. It sort of puts a new light on things.

(*He turns to* LOTUS BLOSSOM *and grins.*)

LOTUS BLOSSOM. Ara, kyuni nikkorisite, mada okotteru no.

SAKINI. She say: Why are you smiling at her all of a sudden? You mad or something?

FISBY. Tell her that I'm a dope. That I have a coconut for a head.

SAKINI. No use, boss. She not believe.

FISBY. Then will you ask her if she'd be kind enough to give geisha lessons to the Ladies' League for Democratic Action?

SAKINI. Odori ya shami Ladies' League ni oshiete?

LOTUS BLOSSOM. Er iiwa, demo kumiaiaga kowaiwane.

SAKINI. She say Geisha Guild closed shop, but she teach if you not report her.

(*At this point the men of the village come across the square and stop before the office.* LOTUS BLOSSOM *goes to the door. Immediately there are ohs and ahs from the men.*)

FISBY. What is that?

SAKINI. Sound like Okinawan wolf call, boss.

FISBY. Well, let's find out.

(*He goes outside to face the group, followed by* SAK-
INI.)

Ask what's the matter.

SAKINI. Doshtano?

MR. KEORA. Minna gakko nanka yori chaya ga ii soda.

SAKINI. They say they just held meeting in democratic
fashion and majority agree on resolution. They want you to
build them cha ya.

FISBY. A what?

SAKINI. Cha ya. That's teahouse, boss.

FISBY. A teahouse?

SAKINI. Yes, boss. They say now that this village have
geisha girl just like big city, they should have teahouse like
big city, too.

FISBY. But I can't build them a teahouse . . . I have no
authority to do that.

SAKINI. But you tell them will of majority is law. You
going to break law?

FISBY. They're going to get a school . . . that's enough.

SAKINI. But majority too old to go to school . . . they want
teahouse.

FISBY. There is no provision in Plan B for a teahouse.

LOTUS BLOSSOM. Ano . . . ochaya sae tatereba mondai
naija nai no.

SAKINI. Lotus Blossom say teahouse in Tobiki make recovery program work. Everybody make geta and cricket
cages like crazy so they can spend money at teahouse.

FISBY. I haven't got any materials to build a teahouse.

SAKINI. Zairyo ga naiyo.

LOTUS BLOSSOM. Ara, kinoo renga ya zaimoku takusan
kite orimashitayo.

SAKINI. She say Army truck come yesterday and leave
beautiful brick and lovely paint.

FISBY. For the new *schoolhouse*. Tell them . . . it just
can't be done.

SAKINI.   Dame, dame, dame desuyo!

(FISBY *looks down into the disappointed faces of the*
VILLAGERS.)

VILLAGERS.   Achara-san, iijiwaru dane.

SAKINI.   They say you very mean to them after *all* the
nice presents they give you.

FISBY.   I'm sorry.

SAKINI.   They say very sorry too, boss. You know why?

FISBY.   I think I do.

SAKINI.   No, boss. When you leave here . . . Tobiki be
forgotten village. Not have park, not have statue . . . not
even lovely jail. Tobiki like to be proud. Teahouse give them
face.

FISBY.   It's going to be a fine schoolhouse. Five sides.

OSHIRA.   May I speak, Captain-san?

FISBY.   Of course, Mr. Oshira.

OSHIRA.   There are lovely teahouses in the big cities. But
the men of Tobiki have never been inside them. We are too
poor and our clothes are too ragged. All of my life I have
dreamed of visiting a teahouse where paper lanterns cast a
light in the lotus pond and bamboo bells hanging in the pines
tinkle as the breezes brush them. But this picture is only in
my heart . . . I may never see it. I am an old man, sir. I shall
die soon. It is evil for the soul to depart this world laden with
envy or regret. Give us our teahouse, sir. Free my soul for
death.

FISBY (*unhappily*).   But . . . we haven't got any carpenters.

SAKINI (*calls over the heads of the group*).   Oi! Daiku-
san! Daiku-san!

(MR. SUMATA and HIS FATHER *come trotting across
the stage carrying their carpenter boxes.* SAKINI
turns to FISBY.)

Oh, what you think? Mr. Sumata and his papa just come
down from mountains!

FISBY (*gives* SAKINI *a penetrating but defeated look*). All right. All right! I haven't got a chance. I guess Uncle Sam is going into the teahouse business.

(*He turns and goes back into his office, followed by* LOTUS BLOSSOM. *He picks up Plan B.* SAKINI *announces the decision from the steps.*)

SAKINI. Cha ya, tatete iiyo!

(*There is an outburst of cheers from the* VILLAGERS. *It sounds very much like* "Fisby-san, Banzai, Uncle Sam, Banzai!" *Inside* FISBY *begins tearing up Plan B.* LOTUS BLOSSOM *kneels before him, geta in hand.* FISBY *extends his feet and smiles down at her. The cheering ouside continues. As the panels descend*—

THE SCENE BLACKS OUT QUICKLY

SCENE TWO

SCENE: *Colonel Purdy's office, G.H.Q.*

TIME: *Few weeks later.*

AT RISE: *The right panel is lifted. A light picks up* COLONEL PURDY. *He sits at his desk fuming over a report. The rest of the stage remains dark. He calls* GREGOVICH *on his office inter-com.*

PURDY. Gregovich!
GREGOVICH'S VOICE. Yes, sir?
PURDY. Get me Captain Fisby at Tobiki.
GREGOVICH. Yes, sir.

(*The extreme left panel rises leaving the intervening panels lowered.* FISBY *sits with his feet propped up on his desk. He is wearing his bathrobe "kimono."* LOTUS BLOSSOM *stands at his side fanning him. Over*

*the scene, the sound of hammering and sawing can
be heard. Over this the phone can be heard to ring.*
FISBY *lifts the receiver.*)

FISBY. Captain Fisby.

PURDY. Colonel Purdy.

FISBY (*over noise*). Who?

PURDY. Colonel Purdy!

FISBY. I can't hear you. Hold on a minute.

(*He turns to* LOTUS BLOSSOM.)

See if you can stop that hammering on the teahouse for a
minute.

(*He goes through the motions.* LOTUS BLOSSOM *nods
understandingly and goes out.*)

PURDY. What's going on down there, Fisby?

FISBY (*as the noises cease*). Now, who is it?

PURDY. Colonel Purdy.

FISBY (*wraps his robe about his legs quickly*). Oh, good
afternoon, Colonel.

PURDY. I want to talk to you about your Progress Report.

FISBY. I sent it in.

PURDY. I have it. I have it right in front of me. I've read
it twice. Now, suppose *you* tell *me* what it says.

FISBY. What would you like to have me explain, sir?

PURDY. I'd like you to explain why there's nothing in here
about the schoolhouse. Didn't you get the lumber?

FISBY (*uneasily*). Yes, sir . . . it's being used right now.
But we'll need some more, I'm afraid.

PURDY. I sent ample according to specifications. How big
a structure are you building?

FISBY. Well . . . we ought to consider expansion. Popu-
lations increase.

PURDY. We don't need to consider expansion. Our troops
will be out of here by the next generation. Which brings me
to another point.

(*He refers to the report.*)

What's this about six kids being born last week?

FISBY.   Well, there wasn't much else to fill the Progress Report, sir.

PURDY.   Then you've failed at your indoctrination. Don't you know yet that births are entered under "Population Increases"? They are not considered progress.

FISBY.   But they weren't children, sir. They were kids . . . goats.

PURDY.   There must be something wrong with this connection. It sounded just as if you said "goats".

FISBY.   I did, sir. Kids . . . goats. You see, we're trying to increase the livestock herd down here. I thought . . .

PURDY.   Goats! I don't care what you thought. Look here, Fisby. Suppose some Congressman flew in to inspect our team. How would I explain such a report?

FISBY.   Well, goats will breed, sir. Congress can't stop that. And I've been concerned with . . .

PURDY.   The population of civilians alone concerns us. I want to know exactly what progress you've made as outlined in Plan B.

FISBY.   Well . . . I'm getting along fine with the people.

PURDY.   In other words, nothing. Listen to me. Do you realize what Major McEvoy has accomplished in his village?

FISBY.   No, sir.

PURDY.   Well, I'll tell you. His fourth-graders know the alphabet through "M" and his whole village can sing "God Bless America" in English.

FISBY.   Yes, sir. That's real progress, sir. I wish I could say the same.

PURDY.   See that you do. I don't want any rotten apples in my barrel. Now . . . I want to know exactly what you have accomplished in the five weeks you've been down there.

FISBY.   Well, sir . . . I've started an industry. I'm sending our first shipment out for sale this week.

PURDY. What are you making?

FISBY (*looks down at his feet*). Oh, getas and . . .

PURDY. Wait a minute . . . what in God's name is a *geta*?

FISBY. Not "a" geta . . . *getas* . . . you have to have two.

PURDY. Are you breeding some *other* kind of animal?

FISBY. You wear them on your feet, sir. Excellent for strengthening the metatarsal muscles. Then . . . I have a group busy building cricket cages. . . .

PURDY. Captain Fisby!

FISBY. Yes, sir.

PURDY. What kind of cages did you say?

FISBY. Cricket. Like in cricket on the hearth. I think we'll find a great market for them. Of course, we don't supply the crickets.

PURDY. Naturally not. Captain Fisby . . . have you been taking your salt pills?

FISBY. Yes, sir . . . I take them at cha ya . . . with my tea

PURDY. Have you been going out in the sun without your helmet?

FISBY. I wear a kasa, sir . . . it's more practical . . . wind can blow through the straw.

PURDY. I see. I see. That will be all, Captain.

(*He hangs up quickly.*)

FISBY. Hello . . . hello . . .

(*He hangs up and sits looking at the phone rather puzzled. The lights go down in his office and the panel descends.* COLONEL PURDY *also sits looking at the phone in his office. He calls* SERGEANT GREGOVICH *on the inter-com.*)

PURDY. Sergeant! What is the name of that psychiatrist over at Awasi?

GREGOVICH. Captain McLean?

PURDY. Get him on the phone. My man at Tobiki has gone completely off his rocker!

THE SCENE BLACKS OUT QUICKLY

SCENE: *Captain Fisby's office, Tobiki.*

TIME: *A few days later.*

AT RISE: *The office is empty as the panel rises. After a moment* CAPTAIN MCLEAN *enters. He is an intense, rather wild-eyed man in his middle forties. He glances about furtively, then begins to examine the papers on Fisby's desk. He makes several notes in a notebook. He picks up Fisby's cricket cage and is examining it intently when* FISBY *enters behind him. He halts upon seeing* MCLEAN. FISBY *is wearing his blue bathrobe, his geta and a native straw hat.*

FISBY. Well, who are you?

MCLEAN (*gasps in surprise*). Oh, you startled me.

FISBY. Can I do anything for you? I'm Captain Fisby.

MCLEAN. I'm Captain McLean. There was no one here . . . so I came in.

FISBY. (*He looks at his insignia.*) Oh, medical corps. What brings you to Tobiki?

MCLEAN. Well, I'm—I'm on leave. Thought I'd spend it making some—some—ethnological studies.

    (*He adds quickly*)

Of the natives.

FISBY. Well, you couldn't have come to a more interesting spot. Sit down, Captain.

MCLEAN (*sits*). Thank you. Would you have any objection to my spending a week or so making my studies, Captain?

FISBY. Not at all. Make yourself at home. I'll take that if it's in your way.

    (*He reaches out to relieve* MCLEAN *of the cricket cage he still holds.*)

MCLEAN (*glances at the cage in his hand and laughs awkwardly*). Oh, yes. I was just examining it.

FISBY (*pleased at his authority on the subject*).   It's a cricket cage.

MCLEAN (*pauses*).   You . . . like crickets?

FISBY.   I haven't found one yet.   But at least I've got the cage.   I've got two . . . if you want one.

MCLEAN.   Thank you, no.   Thank you very much.

(*He looks at* FISBY'*s attire.*)

What happened to your uniform, Captain?

FISBY.   It's around.   I find getas and a kimono much more comfortable in this climate.

MCLEAN.   But isn't that a bathrobe?

FISBY (*shrugs*).   It passes for a kimono.   Would you like to take off your shoes, Captain?

MCLEAN.   Thank you . . . no.   I'll keep them on if you don't mind.

FISBY.   Can I offer you some tsukemono?   You eat these during the day between meals.

(*He extends a platter.*)

Tsukemono means fragrant things.

MCLEAN.   I just had a chocolate bar, thank you.

(*He rises and looks out the door.*)

May I ask what you're building down the road?

FISBY (*proudly*).   That's my cha ya.

(*He pops a few tsukemonos into his mouth.*)

It's really going to be something to write home about.

MCLEAN.   Cha ya?

FISBY.   Well, it just so happens, Captain, that I own a geisha girl.   That might sound strange to you, but you get used to these things after a while.   And if you have a geisha, you've got to have a cha ya.   Sure you don't want some tsukemono?

MCLEAN.   I really couldn't eat a thing.

(*He glances out the door again.*)

May I ask what the men are doing down there wading in that irrigation ditch?

FISBY.   They're not wading, they're building a lotus pond. You can't have a cha ya without a lotus pond.

MCLEAN (*sits opposite* FISBY).   How have you felt lately, Fisby?

FISBY.   McLean, I'll tell you something. I've never been happier. I feel reckless and free. And it all happened the moment I decided not to build that damned pentagon-shaped school.

MCLEAN.   That what?

FISBY.   The good colonel ordered me to build a pentagon-shaped schoolhouse down here. But the people wanted a teahouse. Believe it or not, someone gave me a geisha girl. So I'm giving this village what it wants. That must all sound pretty crazy to you, Mac.

MCLEAN.   Well, yes and no.

FISBY.   These are wonderful people with a strange sense of beauty. And hard-working . . . when there's a purpose. You should have seen them start out day before yesterday, great bundles of things they'd made piled high on their heads. Getas, cricket cages, lacquer ware—things to sell as souvenirs up north. Don't let anyone tell you these people are lazy.

MCLEAN.   Oh. I see. I see.

FISBY.   No, you don't. But you'll have a chance to study them.

MCLEAN.   So you're building them a teahouse.

FISBY.   Next thing I'm going to do for them is find out if this land here will grow anything beside sweet potatoes. I'm going to send for fertilizers and DDT and—

MCLEAN (*leaps to his feet*).   Chemicals!

FISBY.   Sure, why not?

MCLEAN.   Do you want to poison these people?

FISBY.   No, but—

MCLEAN.   Now you've touched on a subject that is very close to me. For years I've planned to retire and buy a farm— raise specialties for big restaurants. So let me tell you this.

Chemicals will kill all your earthworms, and earthworms aerate your soil.

FISBY. They do?

MCLEAN. Do you know an earthworm leaves castings eight times its own weight every day?

FISBY. That much!

MCLEAN. Organic gardening is the only thing. Nature's way—compost, manure, but no chemicals.

FISBY. Hey! You know a lot about this.

MCLEAN (*modestly*). I should. I've subscribed to all the farm journals for years.

FISBY. Say, you could help these people out while you're here—if you would. Do you think you could take over supervision—establish a sort of experimental station for them?

MCLEAN. Well, I—no—no—I haven't time.

FISBY. Take time. This is a chance for you to put some of your theories into practice.

MCLEAN (*haughtily*). They are not theories. They are proven facts.

FISBY. I'll give you a couple of men to help, and all you'd have to do is tell us how.

MCLEAN (*hesitates*). Is your soil acid or alkaline?

FISBY. Gosh, I don't know.

MCLEAN. Well, that's the very *first* thing you have to find out. Do you have bees?

FISBY. I haven't seen any.

MCLEAN (*shakes his head sadly*). People always underestimate the importance of bees for pollinating.

FISBY (*slaps him on the back*). Mac, you're just the man we've needed down here. You're a genius!

MCLEAN. I'll want plenty of manure.

FISBY. You'll get it.

MCLEAN. And I'll want to plan this program scientifically. I wish I had some of my books . . . and my seed catalogues.

(*He measures from the floor.*)

I've got a stack of catalogues that high.

FISBY.   Why don't you make a list, and I'll get the boys over at the airstrip to fly us in seeds from the States.

MCLEAN (*The gardener fever possesses the doctor as he begins to make his list.*)   Every spring I've made lists of seeds and never had any soil to put them in. And now . . . I could actually germinate.

(*He writes.*)

Corn—Golden Bantam.

(*Then adds enthusiastically*)

And Country Gentleman! Hybrid.

FISBY.   Why don't I just leave you with your list while I check on the lotus pond?

(MCLEAN *doesn't hear him.*)

Well, I'll be back for tea. We have tea in the pine grove and watch the sun go down.

(*He goes out.*)

MCLEAN (*continues with his list reading aloud*).

Cucumbers—Extra Early Green Prolific.

(*His enthusiasm mounts.*)

Radishes—Crimson Giant!

(*The telephone begins to ring; he ignores it as he writes.*)

Tomatoes—Ponderosa Earliana.

(*The telephone rings insistently.*)

Watermelon!

(*He closes his eyes ecstatically.*)

(*The panel rises on the opposite side of the stage revealing Colonel Purdy's office. The intervening panel remains down.* COLONEL PURDY *sits at his desk jiggling his telephone hook.*)

PURDY. What's the matter with this connection! Ring again!

MCLEAN (*ignores the ringing*). Watermelon—All-American Gold Medal!

> (*He writes it down as the phone rings. He looks up impatiently and lifts the receiver.*)

Hello!

PURDY (*confidentially*). Who is this?

MCLEAN. This is Captain McLean.

PURDY. This is Colonel Purdy. Can you talk?

MCLEAN. Why not?

PURDY. I was anxious to hear your report on you-know-who.

MCLEAN. On *who*?

PURDY. *Captain Fisby*! The man I sent you down to examine.

MCLEAN. Oh. (*He weighs his problem quickly.*) Oh. Well . . . I'll have to stay down here several weeks for some . . .

PURDY. Several weeks!

MCLEAN. Rome wasn't built in a day.

PURDY. What?

MCLEAN. I said, Rome wasn't built in a day.

PURDY (*digests this*). Well . . . you're the doctor.

MCLEAN. I'll send in a report . . . from time to time. I can tell you now I expect to work miracles down here.

PURDY. Splendid . . . splendid. Is there anything I can send? Some old *Adventure Magazines* or anything?

MCLEAN. There are a couple of books I'd like, but I don't think you could get them.

PURDY (*picks up pencil*). You name them.

MCLEAN. Well . . . one is *Principles of Pea Production*, and the other is *Do's and Don'ts of Cabbage Culture*.

> (PURDY *starts to write . . . then stops.*)

And do you think you could lay your hands on a soil test kit?

PURDY (*looks at earphone*).   A what?

MCLEAN (*enunciating*).   *A soil test kit.* I want to see if the soil is sour down here.

PURDY.   Sour, did you say?

MCLEAN.   Yes . . . if your soil is sour your seeds won't germinate. And I sure wish I had some bees.

PURDY.   There *is* something wrong with this connection!

MCLEAN.   I'm going to take time out here to build up the soil with manure.

PURDY (*unbelieving*).   Did you say manure?

MCLEAN.   I've lost faith in chemicals. You kill all your worms. I can tell you, when you kill a worm, Colonel . . . you're killing a friend.

(*There is a long pause.*)

Hello . . . hello.

PURDY (*puts down the phone and turns to the squawk box*). Gregovich, where is Plan B!

GREGOVICH'S VOICE.   What did you want, sir?

PURDY.   I want to see who I send to analyse an analyst.

THE PANELS FALL QUICKLY ON EACH SIDE OF THE STAGE

SCENE FOUR

SCENE: *Village square, Tobiki.*

TIME: *Few weeks later.*

AT RISE: *The panels rise to reveal the village square and Fisby's office. Natives are seated in the square, great bundles beside them. Others arrive and sink into positions of dejection.* FISBY *works at his desk.* SAKINI *enters and looks at the* VILLAGERS.

SAKINI (*to* MR. KEORA).   Doshtano?

KEORA.   Hitotsu mo unremasenna.

SAKINI. Oh, oh . . . too bad.

(SAKINI *crosses and enters Fisby's office.*)

Boss!

FISBY. Yes?

SAKINI. Mr. Keora and everybody back from Big Koza.

FISBY. Good. Let's see how they made out.

(*He steps outside followed by* SAKINI. *He stops as he sees his* VILLAGERS *sitting dejectedly before their large bundles. He turns to* SAKINI.)

What's the matter?

SAKINI. Mr. Keora very tired. Walk two days with bundle on back to sell straw hats to American soldiers at Big Koza. Nobody buy, so walk back. Too many damn hats now, boss.

FISBY. He couldn't sell *any*?

(SAKINI *shakes his head.*)

Why not?

SAKINI (*shrugs*). Soldiers not want. Soldiers say . . . what you think we are . . . hayseed? So come home.

FISBY (*sees old* MR. OSHIRA *and crosses to him.* OSIIIRA *rises*). Mr. Oshira . . . did you take your lacquer ware to Yatoda?

OSHIRA. Oh, yes . . . but come back . . . not go again.

FISBY. But I don't understand. . . . The Navy always spends money.

OSHIRA. Sailors say, "Oh, pretty good . . . how much you want?" I say, "Twenty-five yen." They say, "Oh, too much . . . can get better in five-and-ten-cent store. Give you one nickel."

FISBY. Did you explain how many years it took you to learn how to turn out such work?

OSHIRA (*nods*). They say, "What you want us to do, cry?"

FISBY (*angrily*). Damn stupid morons!

(*He turns back to* OSHIRA.)

Did you tell them that each cup was handmade?

OSHIRA.   They say . . . not care. They say . . . at home have big machines that turn out ten cups every minute. They say . . . take nickel or jump in lake.

FISBY (*unhappily*).   So you had to carry them all the way back?

SAKINI.   Poor Mr. Oshira. No one want his lacquer ware.

FISBY.   Well, he's wrong. He's a great artist and I'll buy everything he's made myself.

SAKINI.   But you not able to buy everything from everybody in Tobiki, boss.

FISBY (*sits down on steps*).   Tell them that they should all be proud of their work. And that I'm proud of all of them.

SAKINI.   Gokro, gokro san.

FISBY.   I'll think of something . . . I'll hit on an idea to bring money to this village yet.

SAKINI.   Boss . . . you stop work on teahouse now?

FISBY.   No! You'll get a teahouse if I give you nothing else.

SAKINI.   They sure wish they could make some money to spend at teahouse, boss. Not like to go like beggars.

FISBY.   Give me a little time, Sakini.

> (*As they sit around, each deep in his personal problems,* MCLEAN *enters. His uniform is gone. He is wearing his bathrobe, a straw hat and geta.*)

MCLEAN.   Fisby! You're just the man I want to see. Can I have a couple of boys to help me? The damn Japanese beetles are eating up my Chinese peas.

FISBY (*dispiritedly*).   Sure . . . I'll get a couple for you.

MCLEAN (*looks around*).   What's the matter?

FISBY.   There's no market for our products.

MCLEAN.   Oh . . . that's too bad. What are you going to do?

> (*He sits down.*)

FISBY.   Try to think of something.

OSHIRA. The world has left us behind.

(*The* VILLAGERS *begin to rise and pick up their handiwork.*)

SEIKO. Amerika-san no seija naiyo. Sa, Sa, kaette yakezake da!

SAKINI. They say . . . tell you not your fault no one wants to buy, boss. They say guess they go home now and get drunk.

FISBY. Tell them I don't blame them. If I had anything to drink . . . I'd do the same.

(*As they start to file out, both* MCLEAN *and* FISBY *have a delayed reaction. They leap to their feet together.*)

Wait a minute!

(*The* VILLAGERS *stop.*)

What are they going to get drunk on?

SAKINI. They got nothing but brandy.

MCLEAN. Nothing but *brandy*!

FISBY. How did they manage to get brandy?

SAKINI. We make very fine brandy here, from sweet potatoes. Been making for generations.

FISBY. You make a brandy *yourselves*?

SAKINI. Oh, yes. We make for weddings and funerals.

FISBY (*looks at* MCLEAN). What does it taste like?

SAKINI. You want some, boss?

(*He turns to* HOKAIDA.)

Imozake, skoshi!

FISBY. Sakini, if this stuff is any good at all, we're in business. This is one thing I *know* our men will buy.

SAKINI. Oh . . . I think we not like to sell brandy. Only make for ceremony.

MCLEAN. It may not be any good anyhow. There are some things even the troops won't drink.

HOKAIDA (*returns with an earthen jug*). Hai, imozake.

(*He hands the jug to* FISBY.)

SAKINI.   There you are, boss. You like taste now?

FISBY.   I'd like to smell it first.

(*He gives it a sniff and jerks his head back.*)

MCLEAN.   Obviously, it has a kick.

FISBY.   How old is this brandy, Sakini?

SAKINI (*turns to* HOKAIDA).   Kore itsuno?

HOKAIDA (*holds up seven fingers*).   Issukan mae dayo.

FISBY.   Seven years old?

SAKINI.   Oh, no, boss. He make last week.

FISBY.   It couldn't smell like that in only a week.

SAKINI.   Is village secret. You try now?

FISBY (*hands it to* MCLEAN).   You try it, Mac. You're a medical man.

MCLEAN (*backs away*).   You first.

FISBY.   I insist. You're my guest.

MCLEAN.   I waive the honour.

FISBY (*turns to* SAKINI).   Has anyone ever gone blind or died from this?

MCLEAN.   He said they make it for funerals.

SAKINI.   Oh, no, boss. We not blind. We not dead.

FISBY.   There, you see.

MCLEAN.   They've worked up an immunity over the years.

FISBY.   Well, I don't want to kill any of my countrymen. Couldn't you make some sort of test, Doc?

(*As* MCLEAN *considers this, the bleat of a goat is heard offstage.* FISBY *and* MCLEAN *exchange looks and nod.*)

Sakini, get Lady Astor.

(*To* MCLEAN.)

That's Miss Higa Jiga's goat. She asked me to give it a classy name.

(SAKINI *goes to get* LADY ASTOR.)

MCLEAN. I'm not sure what we'll prove. Goats have hardy stomachs.

SAKINI (*returns leading a goat*) Boss, you make guinea pig of goat?

FISBY. If this passes the goat-test, it's all right. No Marine would ever admit he had a weaker stomach than a goat.

MCLEAN. May I borrow this a moment?

> (*He takes* MR. HOKAIDA's *red helmet and pours into it from the jug.*)

SAKINI. Lady Astor very lucky goat.

FISBY. You hold her, Sakini. Proceed, Doctor . . . in the name of science.

> (*The goat sniffs the contents of the helmet.*)

We're either going to have an industry or goat meat for dinner.

> (LADY ASTOR *begins to drink the concoction. They watch her lap up the liquor and lick her lips with relish.*)

MCLEAN (*stands back*). It doesn't seem to affect her.

> (*Draws his fingers back and forth in front of the goat's eyes.*)

Reflexes all right.

FISBY. Let's watch her a minute. The future of Tobiki and the health of the Army are at stake here.

> (FISBY *and* MCLEAN *and the* VILLAGERS *stand watching the goat.* LADY ASTOR *is quite content.* FISBY *rises.*)

Well, here goes.

> (*He takes the jug and samples the contents himself.* MCLEAN *watches him. Then he, too, tests from the jug. They look at each other and grin.*)

Whee!

> (*He dashes for his office.*)

SAKINI (*follows*). What are you going to do, boss?

FISBY.   I am about to form the Co-operative Brewing Company of Tobiki.

> (FISBY *is followed by* SAKINI, MCLEAN, *and some of the* VILLAGERS. *He picks up the phone.*)

Get me the Officers' Club at Awasi.

SAKINI.   We going to make brandy, boss?

FISBY.   I'll tell you in a minute.

> (*He turns back to the telephone.*)

Hello . . . Officers' Club, Awasi? This is Captain Fisby at Tobiki. Oh, hello, Major, how are you? Major, when I was with your unit, you could never keep a supply of liquor in the club, and I stumbled onto something and wondered if you'd be interested. Tobiki, as you know, is the heart of the brandy industry and—

> (*He takes the phone away from his ear as the word brandy is shouted back at him.*)

Yes . . . brandy. . . .

> (*He turns to* MCLEAN.)

Doc, look up the word "sweet potato" and see if it has another fancier name.

> (*He turns back to the phone.*)

Yes . . . I'm here . . . yes . . . I could get you some if you could pay their price and keep the source secret. Oh, yes, it's been made here for generations. Why, you never tasted anything like it.

MCLEAN.   The Haitian word for sweet potato is *b-a-t-a-t-a*.

> (*He spells it out.*)

FISBY (*into the phone*).   You've heard of Seven Star Batata, haven't you? Well, Tobiki is where it's made.

> (*He turns to* MCLEAN.)

The Seven Star did it.

SAKINI.   Brandy much better if eight or ten days old, boss.

FISBY. We also have Eight Star and Ten Star. Well, naturally the Ten Star comes a little higher. It sells for—

(*He looks at* SAKINI *desperately.* SAKINI *holds up ten fingers.*)

A hundred occupation yen a gallon.

SAKINI. I meant *ten* yen, boss.

FISBY. Delivered. All right, we'll send up five gallons in about a week. It'll be delivered by our Department of Agriculture. You're welcome.

(*He hangs up and turns to* SAKINI.)

Sakini, if every family in Tobiki starts making brandy, how much can we turn out in a week?

SAKINI. Oh, maybe . . . forty . . . fifty gallons.

FISBY. Better aim for eighty.

(*He lifts the receiver again.*)

I'd like to get the naval base at Big Koza, Officers' Club, Commander Myers.

SAKINI. Maybe if everybody build private stills, Tobiki can turn out hundred gallon.

FISBY. I'll know better after I talk to the Navy.

(*He speaks into the phone.*)

Commander Myers? Captain Fisby at Tobiki. Commander, we've got a surplus of brandy down here and I was wondering . . .

(*Again he takes the phone away from his ear as the word brandy is blasted back.*)

Yes. Brandy. Ten Star Batata. Well, Lady Astor won't drink anything else. Oh . . . we could supply you with as much as you want at a hundred yen a gallon. Fifteen gallons? Right! It will be delivered Horse Cart Special in ten days.

(*He hangs up and turns to the others crowding into his office.*)

Sakini, tell them to all start making brandy, and in a week or

two everyone in this village is going to have more money
than he ever dreamed of.

SAKINI.   Ah, dondon kaseide sake tsukreba minna kanega
mokaruyo!

MR. KEORA.   Minna shiroi koto katte moii darone?

SAKINI.   They say . . . if they work like the dickens, can
they all have white coats like the mayor?

FISBY.   Yes. I'll get the cloth somewhere. That's a
promise.

(*The telephone rings.*)

Wait a minute. Hello? Well, word gets around fast.

(*He picks up his order blank.*)

Twenty gallons? PX, GHQ, C.O.D. O.K.

(*He hangs up.*)

Get to work, boys!

(*As they turn to leave,* FISBY *suddenly leaps to his
feet.*)

Wait!

(*They stand frozen as he crouches and starts toward
them. He slaps his hand on the floor and then rises
triumphantly.*)

I got my cricket!

(*The* VILLAGERS *cheer for* FISBY.)

THE PANELS FALL QUICKLY

ACT III

SCENE ONE

SCENE: *Teahouse of the August Moon.*

TIME: *Several weeks later.*

AT RISE: *All the panels are down.* SAKINI *steps from the wings to address the audience.*

SAKINI (*bows*).

Ability of Americans for mass production equalled only by
American capacity for consumption.

Fortune often comes in back door while we look out front
window.

Prosperity not only smile on Tobiki.

Prosperity giggle like silly girl.

Very strange.

Things we do best . . . not wanted.

Things we think least of . . . wanted most.

No conclusion.

Tobiki now village of beautiful houses.

But loveliest of all is Teahouse of August Moon.

> (*He goes off extreme left, signalling for the panels to rise. Offstage the music of string instruments can be heard playing softly. The panels go up. The ugly thatched huts are gone. In the centre of the stage, exquisite in its simplicity, stands the teahouse. Small bells tinkle from its pagoda roof. Soft lights glow through the coloured paper panels. Dwarf pines edge the walk leading to a small bridge. An August moon hangs in the autumn sky. The silhouette of* LOTUS BLOSSOM *is framed in the centre panel by the soft back lighting. She slides the panel open and steps into the almost bare centre room of the teahouse. She crosses and lights the lanterns hanging from the eave extensions. As she goes through this*

ceremony, the GUESTS *wander in. Before they enter the teahouse, they remove their shoes and rinse their fingers in the ceremonial bamboo basin. Then they enter and seat themselves on green floor mats. The* WOMEN *are dressed in silk kimonos of varying hues and the majority of the men wear spotless white suits.* LOTUS BLOSSOM *bows to them and returns through the sliding door again.* FISBY *and* MCLEAN, *followed by* SAKINI, *enter.* SAKINI *wears a white suit and the* AMERICANS *wear their bathrobes and geta. They are greeted enthusiastically by the* GUESTS.)

SAKINI. I tell Lotus Blossom you here, boss.

(*He disappears through the sliding panel in the centre of the teahouse.*)

FISBY (*as they walk around inspecting the grounds*). It's really something, isn't it?

MCLEAN. Where'd they get the cloth?

FISBY. They made them.

MCLEAN. Where'd they get the cloth?

FISBY. I got it from the naval base at Awasi for ten gallons of brandy. It's target cloth.

MCLEAN. Those kimonos aren't target cloth.

FISBY. Parachute silk. Six gallons' worth.

(LOTUS BLOSSOM *enters, followed by* SAKINI. *She hurries down to* FISBY *and bows. She extends a yellow chrysanthemum to him.*)

SAKINI. Chrysanthemum bud in full bloom, boss.

LOTUS BLOSSOM. (*She bows as* FISBY *accepts the gift.*) Hop-pee.

(*Her eyes almost disappear in a great smile of pride.*)

FISBY. What did she say?

SAKINI. I try like the dickens to teach her to say "happy birthday," but she can't say "birthday," boss.

LOTUS BLOSSOM. Hop-pee.

FISBY. Well . . . I'm floored!

(*He bows to her.*)

Thank you, Lotus Blossom.

(*To* SAKINI.)

How did you know?

MCLEAN. I gave you away.

SAKINI. Everybody in village like to show appreciation, boss.

FISBY. I should have a kimono made. When you said "formal," I thought this would do.

LOTUS BLOSSOM. Hop-pee. Hop-pee.

FISBY. And a hop-pee hop-pee to you.

GUESTS (*murmur in the background*). Hayaku oiwai haji-meyo, soda, soda.

SAKINI. Everybody impatient to get on with the party, boss.

LOTUS BLOSSOM. Hop-pee.

(*She indicates the centre mat.*)

SAKINI. You sit down now, boss. Lotus Blossom going to dance in your honour.

FISBY. You hear that. . . . She's going to dance.

(*Quickly sits down.*)

Sit down, you farmer. . . . This is in my honour.

MCLEAN. My, my! How am I going to stall Purdy so I can stay down here?

FISBY. I'll have a relapse for you.

(*They turn to watch* LOTUS BLOSSOM *as she takes her position and the first notes are struck by the musicians present.* LOTUS BLOSSOM *performs for them a traditional dance of infinite grace and delicacy. She finishes, concluding her performance in front of* FISBY, *who rises and bows to her.*)

What a lovely little thing you are! This belongs to you.

(*He returns the chrysanthemum with a flourish.* LOTUS BLOSSOM *accepts it and seats herself quickly on a mat and hides her head.*)

SAKINI. Oh, boss . . . you know what you do!

FISBY. It called for flowers.

SAKINI. That mean you give your heart to her.

FISBY (*lightly*). Well, I do. We all do.

(*Turns to* MCLEAN.)

Wasn't that beautiful, Mac!

MCLEAN. She can dance in my cha ya any day.

SAKINI. You sit beside Lotus Blossom now, boss. You guest of honour and referee.

FISBY (*starts to sit down*). *Referee!* I thought this was a birthday party.

SAKINI. Lotus Blossom now putting on wrestling match for you, boss.

FISBY. *Wrestling* match?

LOTUS BLOSSOM (*stands and claps hands*). Sa, osumo hajime mashoyo.

(*Immediately two men bring in four poles which they set up downstage centre to mark a square. Each pole has coloured cloth hanging from it.*)

MCLEAN. Who is wrestling?

(*He sits next to* FISBY.)

SAKINI. Wrestling match between Chief of Agriculture and Chief of Police.

FISBY (*to* LOTUS BLOSSOM). Hokaida and Seiko?

(*She nods.*)

SAKINI. Grudge fight, boss.

FISBY. Really?

SAKINI. Whoever win match get to haul sweet potatoes for Lotus Blossom.

FISBY. (*Watching the poles being set up, he indicates them to* LOTUS BLOSSOM.) Why have they wrapped coloured cloth around the poles?

LOTUS BLOSSOM. Kuro wa fuyu, Ao wa haru, Akaga natsu de, Shirowa akiyo. Wakkatta?

SAKINI. She explain, boss, the black cloth remind us of winter, green cloth remind us of spring, red is the summer and white the autumn.

LOTUS BLOSSOM (*claps her hands*). Osumo, osumo!

(MR. HOKAIDA, *bare except for a pair of black shorts, enters and crosses to one corner of the ring, where he squats on his heels. An outburst of approval greets his entrance. He smiles with fatuous pleasure, and makes a desperate effort to hold in his fat stomach.*)

MCLEAN. Do his black shorts mean anything?

SAKINI. Just easy to clean.

(LOTUS BLOSSOM *claps her dainty hands again.* MR. SEIKO *enters, lean and wiry, also wearing black shorts and a sweat shirt reading* U.S.S. Princeton.)

FISBY. Where did he get that?

SAKINI. Sailor at naval base. Some class, eh?

(MR. SEIKO *peels off the shirt to great applause and squats in the opposite corner. He glares across at* HOKAIDA, *who thrusts his jaw forward.*)

They waiting on you to give signal now, boss.

FISBY. Waiting on *me*?

SAKINI. Oh, yes . . . you are Honourable Referee.

LOTUS BLOSSOM (*hands her fan to* FISBY). Korede aizu shite kudasai.

FISBY. What do I do with this?

SAKINI. Now you cover face with fan.

FISBY. Why?

SAKINI. That mean you not take sides. Now you go to centre of ring and drop fan from face.

MCLEAN.   And get the hell out in a hurry.

FISBY.   How many falls?

SAKINI.   No falls, boss. First one to throw other out of ring—winner.

> (FISBY *covers his face with the fan and walks down centre. The two wrestlers crouch, poised to leap, their eyes on the fan.* FISBY *whips the fan away from his face and dashes back out of range. The protagonists circle each other slowly. Suddenly all hell breaks loose. The teahouse guests cheer their favourite. The fat* MR. HOKAIDA *picks up* MR. SEIKO *and subjects him to a series of head spins and thumpings. But he exhausts himself; and it is* SEIKO *who ends by tossing* HOKAIDA *out of the ring. A cheer rises from the guests.* FISBY *sighs with relief.*)

Now the judges must decide who wins.

FISBY.   Decide! Is there any doubt?

> (*The three judges confer. They then turn to* MR. HOKAIDA *and bow.*)

SAKINI.   Mr. Hokaida! The winner . . .

> (*This startling announcement is greeted with approval.* SEIKO *beats his head and wails.*)

FISBY.   How *could* he be the winner! He was thrown out of the ring.

SAKINI.   Maybe so, but judges all cousins of Mr. Hokaida.

FISBY.   But the judges are wrong.

SAKINI (*confidentially*).   We know who really win . . . but this way nobody lose face.

> (SEIKO *and* HOKAIDA *exit.*)

LOTUS BLOSSOM.   Sa kondo wa Fu-san no ban yo.

SAKINI.   Lotus Blossom say guests now wish *you* to perform.

FISBY.   Perform what?

SAKINI.   They like now for you and doctor to sing song or something.

FISBY.   Sing!

SAKINI.   Must do, boss. Bad manners to refuse.

FISBY (*repeats in alarm*).   Sing!

(*He turns to* MCLEAN.)

Get on your feet, Mac, we've got to sing something.

MCLEAN.   What?

FISBY.   We could sing the national anthem.

MCLEAN.   No, we couldn't—I don't know the words.

FISBY.   How about "Deep in the Heart of Texas"?

MCLEAN.   Why not? There're no Texans here.

(*They step forward.*)

FISBY.   Mac, let's have some fun.

(*He turns to* SAKINI.)

Sakini, you tell them they must all help us. They must clap and sing "Deep in the Heart of Texas" every time *we* do.

SAKINI (*beaming*).   Tewo tataite Deep in the Heart of Texas.

(*Demonstrates clapping.*)

Koshte, Deep in the Heart of Texas.

(*The* VILLAGERS *chatter and agree with enthusiasm.* FISBY *and* MCLEAN *stand close together and begin singing. Each time they come to the designated phrase,* SAKINI *gives a signal and the* VILLAGERS *join in lustily. Lost in their eager concentration, no one observes the entrance of* COLONEL PURDY. *He looks from the "kimono"-clad figures of* FISBY *and* MC-LEAN *to the assemblage. As he shouts at* FISBY, *his voice is drowned out by the chorus of "Deep in the Heart of Texas." The song continues.* PURDY *signals off stage.* GREGOVICH *enters and is instructed by* COLONEL PURDY *to end the objectionable noises.*)

GREGOVICH.   Captain Fisby!

> (*Again the voice coincides with the shouts of "Deep in the Heart of Texas" and is lost.* COLONEL PURDY *stalks downstage centre, followed by* GREGOVICH.)

PURDY.   Captain Fisby! What in the name of Occupation is going on here?

> (FISBY *gasps and backs away. Suddenly aware of his bathrobe, he stoops down to cover his bare legs.* MCLEAN *surrenders completely to panic. He runs to hide behind guests. The* GUESTS, *alarmed by the sudden intrusion, scatter in all directions. In the midst of this bedlam—*

THE PANELS ARE LOWERED

SCENE TWO

SCENE: *Office of Captain Fisby, Tobiki.*

TIME: *Next morning.*

AT RISE: *The four bamboo panels are down.* SAKINI *enters from the wings right and crosses down to the footlights.*

SAKINI (*bows*).

When present is blackest,
Future can only be brighter.
Okinawa invaded many times.
Not sink in ocean yet.
Survive Chinese.
Survive Japanese.
Survive missionaries and Americans.
Invaded by typhoon.
Invaded by locust.
Invaded by cockroach and sweet-potato moth.
Tobiki now invaded by Honourable Colonel.
Not sink in ocean.

(*He goes to the left side of the stage and raises the panels in front of Fisby's office. He then exits.* COLONEL PURDY *is seated at Fisby's desk going through his papers.* FISBY *stands behind him nervously watching.* MCLEAN *sits on the cot biting his nails. He rises.*)

PURDY (*without looking up*). Sit down!

(MCLEAN *sits down again.* PURDY *turns to* FISBY *and glares at him.*)

Where are your bimonthly Progress Reports?

FISBY. I—I think they should be right here under the cricket cage, sir.

PURDY (*takes some papers from under the cage and glances at them*). These are all completely blank.

(*He turns to* FISBY.)

Fisby, you can't convince me that you've been down here for two months doing absolutely nothing.

FISBY. Oh, no, sir, I mean yes, sir, I have not been doing "nothing."

PURDY. You're beginning to sound like a native.

MCLEAN (*rises*). The tendency is always to descend to the level of the environment, sir. It's a primary postulate of psychology.

PURDY (*turns on him*). Well, it's a primary regulation of the Army to make out reports!

(*Back to* FISBY.)

Now, I want to know exactly what you've accomplished here from the moment you arrived.

FISBY. Well, let me think. . . .

MCLEAN. Could I—

PURDY. Sit down! (*He turns to* FISBY.) How many lectures have you delivered to the village children on democratic theory?

FISBY. Well, let me see.

PURDY. Four—five?

FISBY (*thinks*). Not that many, sir.

PURDY. Three?

MCLEAN (*hopefully*). Two?

FISBY. N-no.

PURDY. You only delivered *one* lecture?

FISBY. None, sir.

PURDY. Don't tell me you haven't delivered a single lecture!

FISBY. Yes, sir, I haven't delivered no lecture. I mean . . . any lecture.

PURDY. Did you organize a Ladies' League for Democratic Action?

FISBY (*beaming*). Yes, sir. I sure did. I did that all right.

PURDY. And how many lectures on democratic theory have you given *them*?

FISBY (*deflated again*). None, sir.

PURDY. You can't mean none. You must mean one or two.

FISBY. No, sir, none.

PURDY. I refuse to believe it.

FISBY. I'm glad, sir.

MCLEAN (*rises in desperation*). Sir, I *must* go.

PURDY. Where!

MCLEAN. My *seedlings* are wilting. I have to transplant them.

PURDY. Captain, you will pack your gear and transplant yourself to your unit at once.

MCLEAN. Yes, sir.

(*He turns to* FISBY.)

They'll die. It's murder.

(*He goes to the door and turns sadly to* FISBY *again.*)

Please take care of my beans.

(*He exits.*)

PURDY (*turns back to* FISBY). Now! Is the schoolhouse finished?

FISBY (*sighs*). No, sir.

PURDY. *Why* isn't it finished?

FISBY. It isn't finished, sir, because it isn't started.

PURDY. I have a splitting headache, Fisby. I ask you not to provoke me needlessly. Now, where is the schoolhouse?

FISBY. I never built it.

PURDY. Don't stand there and tell me you never built it. I sent the lumber down two months ago.

FISBY (*impressed*). Is it *that* long, sir?

PURDY. What did you do with the lumber I sent?

FISBY. Well, I built a teahouse.

PURDY (*stares at him*). I don't suppose you have any aspirin here?

FISBY. No, sir, I haven't.

PURDY. Now, sit down, Fisby. I want to be fair.

(FISBY *sits down.*)

I'm a patient man. When I run into something that defies reason, I like to find the reason.

(*Explodes.*)

What in the name of Occupation do you mean by saying you built a *teahouse* instead of a *schoolhouse*!

FISBY. It's a little hard to explain, sir. Everybody in the village wanted one . . . and Lotus Blossom needed it for her work.

PURDY. And just what is your relationship with this woman?

FISBY. Well, she was a present. So to speak. She's a geisha girl—after a fashion.

PURDY. You built this teahouse—this place for her to ply her trade—with lumber belonging to the Army of Occupation of the United States Government?

FISBY. Well, it just seemed like lumber at the time.

PURDY.   Fisby, are you operating a house of prostitution here on Government rice?

FISBY.   No, sir! Geishas aren't what you think.

PURDY.   Don't tell me what to think. Army Intelligence warned me I'd find something mighty peculiar going on in Tobiki.

FISBY.   What's Army Intelligence got to do with it, sir?

PURDY.   You're not very cunning, Fisby. With all the Occupation money on the island finding its way to this village, did you think it wouldn't come to the attention of Intelligence?

FISBY.   Oh.

PURDY.   Why did you do it, Fisby, why!

FISBY.   Well, Lotus Blossom had to have a place to teach the Ladies' League how to become geishas and—

PURDY.   Fisby! You mean to say you've turned all the decent women of this village into professional . . .

(He slumps into the chair.)

How could you sink to such depths, man!

FISBY.   I was only giving in to what the majority wanted, sir.

PURDY.   I don't doubt that statement—not at all. It is a sad thing that it took a war to convince me that most of the human race is degenerate. Thank God I come from a country where the air is clean, where the wind is fresh, where—

FISBY *(interrupts)*.   For heaven's sake, sir, would you please listen to me instead of yourself! There is not a thing goes on in that teahouse that your mother couldn't watch.

PURDY *(leaps to his feet and points a warning finger)*.   You be careful how you use my mother's name, Fisby.

FISBY.   Well, *my* mother, then. I swear there's nothing immoral about our teahouse.

PURDY.   Then answer me this. What is bringing all that Occupation money to this particular village? There is only one thing that attracts that kind of money.

FISBY.   Well, evidently there are two things.

PURDY.   And if it isn't honour that you sell here, what is it?

FISBY (*sighs unhappily*).   We . . . make things.

PURDY.   What?

FISBY.   Mats . . . and hats . . . and cricket cages.

PURDY.   One hundred and fifty thousand yen finds its way to this village every month. You can't convince me that the American soldier is spending that much on "cricket cages."

FISBY.   Well, naturally . . . not all of it.

(*The telephone rings.* FISBY *looks at it apprehensively.*)

PURDY.   Answer it.

FISBY (*pauses*).   It's nothing important, sir.

PURDY.   It might be for me. Answer it.

FISBY (*airily*).   Oh, it rings all day, sir. Pay no attention.

PURDY.   Then *I'll* answer it!

(*He picks up the telephone.* FISBY *covers his face.*)

Hello? *What* do you want? Who is this? Well, Commander Myers, I think you have the wrong connection. This is not a brewery. Yes . . . yes . . . yes!

(*He turns to look at* FISBY.)

Oh . . . I see. I see. I see.

(*He hangs up. He turns to* FISBY, *who smiles weakly.*)

FISBY.   It was the only thing we could make that anyone wanted to buy, sir.

PURDY.   Brandy! (*Sadly*) I don't know which is worse. Putting your country in the white slave trade or the wholesale liquor business. Congress will have to decide.

FISBY.   We've the most prosperous village on the island, sir.

PURDY.   This ends my Army career. I promised Mrs. Purdy I'd come out a general. You've broken a fine woman's heart, Fisby.

FISBY.   You said to make the village self-supporting, sir.

PURDY.   I didn't tell you to encourage lewdness and drunkenness. You've sullied the reputation of your nation and all the tears—

PURDY. All right, sir, shall I kill myself?

PURDY. Oh, don't minimize this. You don't know the enemy's genius for propaganda.

FISBY. Does anyone have to know, sir? We're doing all right.

PURDY (*explodes*). Yes, they have to know! I requested an investigation myself. I've notified the Inspector General. Now I'll have to radio the whole story to Washington.

FISBY. Oh.

PURDY (*calmer*). Well, what have you done with all this money you've made so dishonestly?

FISBY. Banked it in Seattle.

PURDY. Oh, that's despicable—making a personal fortune off the labour of these ignorant people.

FISBY. I haven't touched a cent for myself, sir. It's been deposited in the name of the Tobiki Co-operative. The whole village are equal partners. Share and share alike.

PURDY (*leaps up*). That's *Communism*!

FISBY. Is it?

PURDY (*sinks down again*). I'll be lucky to get out of this war a private.

(*He is a beaten man.*)

Well, there is only one thing for me to do.

FISBY. What is that, sir?

PURDY. First, you are to consider yourself under technical arrest. You will proceed to H.Q. at once to await court-martial.

FISBY. Yes, sir.

PURDY (*steps to the door*). Gregovich!

(*He turns back to* FISBY.)

I must go on to Awasi this afternoon on an inspection tour. But before I leave, I intend to wipe this stain from our country's honour.

(SERGEANT GREGOVICH *enters and salutes.*)

GREGOVICH. You called, sir?

PURDY. I did. We have some business to attend to here before going on to Awasi.

GREGOVICH. Yes, sir. I'm glad to hear it.

(*He turns to* FISBY.)

May I congratulate you on what you've done to this village, sir. It's a dream.

FISBY. Thank you, Sergeant.

PURDY. It is an alcoholic dream. It is one vast distillery. I want you to take a detail and some axes and smash every still in this village.

GREGOVICH. Destroy them?

PURDY. Beyond repair. I want you to take another detail and rip down that teahouse.

GREGOVICH. But, Colonel—

PURDY. Pile the lumber beside the warehouse. That is an order. Do you understand?

GREGOVICH. Yes, sir!

(*As he turns to follow orders,* FISBY *sinks into his chair and the scene blacks out quickly.*)

CURTAIN

SCENE THREE

SCENE: *Teahouse of the August Moon.*

TIME: *A few hours later.*

AT RISE: *All the panels are down. Behind the screens can be heard the destruction of the stills and the dismantling of the teahouse.* SAKINI *comes out from the wings and crosses down to the footlights. He flinches at the sound of an ax falling on wood.*

SAKINI (*sadly*). Oh, no comment.

(*He walks back into the wings as all the panels are raised simultaneously. Only the frame of the teahouse has been spared. The paper panels have disappeared, the pagoda roof is gone with its tinkling bells. There are no coloured lanterns and no dwarf pines to grace the path. The bare supports stand stark and ugly. Resting at the edge of the frame is a wheelbarrow.* LOTUS BLOSSOM *is collecting the last of her possessions. She takes a brass brazier down to place in the wheelbarrow. Then she stands with her back to the audience surveying all that remains of the teahouse.* FISBY *comes on, and, seeing* LOTUS BLOSSOM, *hesitates. Then he crosses to stand beside her. He takes her hand, and the two of them stand looking at the ruins.* LOTUS BLOSSOM *walks to the centre of the teahouse and sits on the bare floor.* FISBY *comes up and sits on the floor facing her. She goes through the ceremony of pouring him an imaginary cup of tea.* FISBY *accepts with mock formality. As he takes the cup and pretends to drink it,* LOTUS BLOSSOM *covers her face with her hands.* FISBY *sits watching her mutely.*)

SAKINI (*entering*). Jeep all loaded, boss.

FISBY. I'll be along in a minute.

SAKINI. Oh, pretty soon have nice schoolhouse here.

FISBY (*bitterly*). Pentagon-shaped.

SAKINI. Not be too bad. You take Lotus Blossom with you?

FISBY. No.

SAKINI. What happen to her then?

FISBY. What would have happened to her if we'd never come along?

SAKINI. Not know. Maybe some day she meet nice man and give up Geisha Guild.

FISBY. Ask her if there is anything I can do for her before I go.

SAKINI (*comes up to stand behind them*). Nanika iitai?

LOTUS BLOSSOM (*softly*). Fu-san, watashito kekkon shite chodai.

SAKINI (*scolding*). Sonna bakana koto.

LOTUS BLOSSOM (*persistent*). Iikara hayaku itte!

FISBY. What does she want?

SAKINI. Oh, that crazy Lotus Blossom. She want you to marry her.

FISBY. Why should she want to marry me?

SAKINI. She think you the nicest man she ever see, boss.

FISBY. Tell her that I am clumsy, that I seem to have a gift for destruction. That I'd disillusion her as I have disillusioned her people.

SAKINI. Kokai suruyo.

LOTUS BLOSSOM. Ikitai noyo. Amerika ni. Ikitai noyo.

SAKINI. She say she like to go to America. There everybody happy. Sit around and drink tea while machines do work.

FISBY. She wouldn't like it, Sakini. I should hate to see her wearing sweaters and sport shoes and looking like an American looking like an Oriental.

SAKINI. But she want to be an American, boss. She never see an American she not like, boss.

FISBY. Some of them wouldn't like her, Sakini. In the small town where I live, there'd be some who would make her unhappy.

SAKINI. Why, boss?

FISBY. She'd be different.

SAKINI. Dame dayo.

LOTUS BLOSSOM (*takes* FISBY's *hand*). Sonna koto naiwa, Amerikatte minshu shugi desumono ne.

SAKINI. She say not believe that. In America everybody

love everybody. Everybody help everybody; that's democracy.

FISBY.   No. That's faith. Explain to her that democracy is only a method—an ideal system for people to get together. But that unfortunately . . . the people who get together . . . are not always ideal.

SAKINI.   That's very hard to explain, boss. She girl in love. She just want to hear pretty things.

FISBY.   Then tell her that I love what she is, and that it would be wrong to change that. To impose my way of life on her.

SAKINI.   Tassha dene!

FISBY.   Tell her that I shall never forget her. Nor this village. Tell her that in the autumn of my life—on the other side of the world—when an August moon rises from the east, I will remember what was beautiful in my youth, and what I was wise enough to leave beautiful.

SAKINI.   Issho wasurenai kara ne. Mangetsu no yoru niwa anata o omoidashimasu.

LOTUS BLOSSOM (*remains silent a moment*).   Watashi mo Fu-san no koto issho wasurenaiwa. Fu-san no koto uta ni shite. Okinawaju ni hirome masu.

SAKINI.   She say she always remember you, boss. She say she guess maybe she be what she is—first-class geisha girl. She want you to know she make up long song-story about you to sing in teahouse. And maybe hundred years from now, you be famous all over Okinawa.

FISBY (*rises*).   I'd like that.

LOTUS BLOSSOM (*rises*).   Iinoyo. Fu-san damedemo Seiko-san ga irun dakara.

SAKINI.   She say, since you not marry her, maybe you suggest somebody here.

(FISBY *laughs.*)

She say that Mr. Seiko been looking at her like sick goat. She say what you think of him?

FISBY.   Well, he took an awful beating just so he could carry her sweet potatoes.

LOTUS BLOSSOM.   Fu-san, Seiko-san iito omouno?

SAKINI.   She say you think she ought to marry him?

FISBY.   I think she ought to decide for herself.

(*And* MR. SEIKO *enters. He is dressed in his white suit and his hair is slicked down tight. He crosses to* LOTUS BLOSSOM. *They all turn to look at him.*)

SEIKO (*bows to* LOTUS BLOSSOM).   A, boku, oshimasho.

SAKINI (*to* FISBY).   Mr. Seiko tell Lotus Blossom he sure like to push her wheelbarrow for her.

LOTUS BLOSSOM.   Iikara sakini itte chodai.

SAKINI.   She say, oh, all right, but not to think that means she's his property.

MR. SEIKO (*beams like a schoolboy and, picking up the handles of the wheelbarrow, he trots off stage with* LOTUS BLOSSOM's *possessions. She turns to* FISBY *and hands him her fan.*)

LOTUS BLOSSOM.   Korede aizu shite chodai. Soremade watashi dokonimo ikimasen kara.

SAKINI.   She say she go now, but you still her boss. She not go until you give signal.

(FISBY *takes the fan and puts it before his eyes. Without waiting for him to drop it,* LOTUS BLOSSOM *runs off right. When he lowers the fan, he knows she's gone. He sits down on the platform that had been the teahouse veranda.*)

You go now, boss?

FISBY.   Shortly.

SAKINI.   Since you not take Lotus Blossom, maybe you take me, boss?

FISBY.   Major McEvoy is coming down to take charge. You'll work with him.

SAKINI.   Would rather work with you.

FISBY.   You'll like Major McEvoy.

SAKINI.   I'll work for you for half price, boss.

FISBY.   Major McEvoy will need your help in getting this village on its feet again.

SAKINI.   You very hard man to bargain with, boss. If you want, I work for rice rations only.

FISBY.   No.

SAKINI.   You mean you going to make me work for *nothing*, boss?

FISBY.   I mean *yes*, you're *not* going to work for me at all. And you belong here.

SAKINI.   You know what I think happen when Americans leave Okinawa?

FISBY.   What?

SAKINI (*grins*).   I think maybe we use pentagon-shaped schoolhouse for teahouse.

           (FISBY *laughs. He gives* SAKINI *a slap on the shoulder*.)

FISBY.   Good-bye, Sakini, you're a rare rascal and I'll miss you.

SAKINI.   Good-bye, boss.

           (FISBY *starts off left. He has gone halfway when* SAKINI *calls*.)

Boss—

FISBY (*stops*).   Yes?

SAKINI.   You not failure.

FISBY (*laughs*).   I'll tell you something, Sakini. I used to worry a lot about not being a big success. I must have felt as you people felt at always being conquered. Well, now I'm not so sure who's the conqueror and who the conquered.

SAKINI.   Not understand, boss.

FISBY.   It's just that I've learned from Tobiki the wisdom of gracious acceptance. I don't want to be a world leader. I'm making peace with myself somewhere between my ambitions and my limitations.

SAKINI. That's good?

FISBY. It's a step backward in the right direction.

(*He throws* SAKINI *a salute.*)

Take care.

(*He walks off and* SAKINI *watches him go. Then, with a sigh,* SAKINI *turns to survey the skeleton of the teahouse. The silence is broken by the stormy entrance of* COLONEL PURDY.)

PURDY. Sakini! Where is Captain Fisby?

SAKINI (*points*). Just leaving, boss.

PURDY (*shouts*). Fisby! Fisby!

(*Gestures frantically.*)

Come back here at once!

(*He goes to the platform and sinks down gasping.*)

I'm not in shape—too much paper work.

(FISBY *returns from the left.*)

Where in hell have you been, Fisby? I've been looking all over for you.

FISBY. I'm ready to leave, sir.

PURDY. You can't leave. You've got to stay here. You've got to help me, Fisby.

FISBY. Help doing what, sir?

PURDY. Pulling this village back together again. All hell has broken loose, Fisby.

(*He sits down to wipe his brow.*)

Where is Gregovich?

FISBY. Breaking up the last of the stills, sir.

PURDY. Oh, *no*! (*He holds his head.*)

FISBY. What's happened, sir?

PURDY. I radioed the report to Washington. Some fool senator misunderstood. He's using this village as an example of American "get-up-and-go" in the recovery program. The

Pentagon is boasting. Congress is crowing. We're all over the papers.

FISBY.   But that's wonderful, sir.

PURDY.   No, it's not wonderful. A Congressional Committee is flying over to study our methods. They are bringing in photographers for a magazine spread. Today, Fisby, today!

FISBY.   Oh, that's bad, sir.

PURDY (*wails*).   Gregovich!

FISBY.   Isn't there any way to stall them off, sir? Quarantine the place or something?

PURDY.   You can't quarantine a congressman. They have immunity or something.

(*He takes* FISBY *by the jacket.*)

Fisby, help me. I don't ask it for my sake. I ask it for Mrs. Purdy. I could be a brigadier yet.

(*Before* FISBY *can answer,* GREGOVICH *comes in from the left and salutes.*)

GREGOVICH.   You called, sir?

PURDY (*hurries over to him*).   Gregovich! Gregovich! You haven't destroyed all the stills, have you, Gregovich? No, of course you haven't.

GREGOVICH.   Yes, sir, I have. I carried out orders to the letter.

PURDY (*turns away shouting*).   Why can't someone disobey orders once in a while! What has happened to the American spirit of rebellion!

(GREGOVICH *hiccups, smiles sillily and folds up on the floor.* FISBY *and* PURDY *race over to kneel beside him.*)

Sunstroke?

FISBY.   Potato brandy.

PURDY.   Sergeant, wake up. Do you hear me? That's an order.

FISBY.   I'm afraid he's passed out, sir.

PURDY. It's desertion. I need every man. Gregovich, get to your feet!

(*With* FISBY's *help he gets* GREGOVICH *to his feet.*)

GREGOVICH. Sorry, sir.

PURDY. I want to ask you some questions. Stop weaving.

GREGOVICH. *You're* weaving, sir. *I'm* perfectly still.

PURDY. You smell like a brewery.

GREGOVICH. I fell in a vat.

PURDY. You got drunk.

GREGOVICH. No, sir. I fell in a vat. Naturally, I had to open my mouth to yell for help.

PURDY. Go to the office and sober up at once.

GREGOVICH. Yes, sir.

(*He salutes with a happy smile, jogs off.*)

PURDY. I'm a sinking ship . . . scuttled by my own men.

(*He sinks.* SAKINI, *who has been sitting with arms folded and a fatuous grin on his face, speaks up.*)

SAKINI. Colonel Purdy?

PURDY. Don't bother me.

SAKINI. Stills not all destroyed.

PURDY. I haven't got time to . . . What did you say?

SAKINI. We not born yesterday. Get sergeant drunk . . . and give him water barrels to break.

PURDY. Sakini, my friend, you're not just saying that to make me feel better?

SAKINI. Oh, stills all good as ever. Production not cease yet.

FISBY (*fondly*). You really are a rogue, Sakini.

PURDY. No . . . He's really an American. He has get-up-and-go.

FISBY. Sakini, if everybody in the village worked together . . . how long would it take to rebuild the teahouse?

PURDY. We don't ask the impossible.

SAKINI. Oh, maybe three minutes . . . maybe five.

PURDY. That's impossible.

SAKINI. We not destroy. Just take away and hide. You watch now, boss.

> (*He turns and calls.*)

Oi, mo iiyo, mo iiyo.

> (*From the wings, right and left, the* VILLAGERS *step out.*)

Oi, haba, haba.

> (*The* VILLAGERS *respond with happy cries and dash off.*)

Country that has been invaded many times soon master art of hiding things.

PURDY. You think we can pull it off, Sakini?

SAKINI. You watch now.

> (*And even as he speaks, the sections of the teahouse are carried in and the swift work of putting them together progresses before our eyes. Music is heard in the background. The pagoda roof with its tinkling bells is lowered. The dwarf pines and the arched bridge are brought back. The coloured panels are slipped into place and the lanterns are hung.* LOTUS BLOSSOM *comes on with flowers which she arranges.* SAKINI *snaps his fingers and the August moon is magically turned on in the sky. When the final lantern is hung,* MCLEAN *comes in. He stops. His mouth falls open.*)

PURDY. Close your mouth, Captain—haven't you ever seen a cha ya before?

> (*He turns back to* FISBY.)

Fisby, this is a land of adventure . . . a land of jade and spices . . . of Chinese junks and river pirates. . . . Makes a man's blood pound.

FISBY. Colonel . . . I consider what you just said pure . . . (*He pauses.*) . . . poetry.

PURDY. Thank you . . . thank you, boy.

(*He sighs ecstatically.*)

It's the mystery of the Orient.

FISBY. It's beautiful. Simply beautiful.

PURDY. There's only one thing wrong. It needs a sign to tell people what it is. And I think we ought to put a sign up over there naming this Grace Purdy Avenue. And another sign . . .

FISBY. Colonel Purdy. Won't you have a cup of tea?

(*He takes his arm. As he propels him toward the tea-house, he speaks over his shoulder to* SAKINI.)

Twenty Star for the colonel, Sakini.

(*As the bamboo panels begin to descend on the tea-house,* SAKINI *steps down to the audience.*)

SAKINI.

Little story now concluded.

History of world unfinished.

Lovely ladies . . . kind gentlemen—

Go home to ponder.

What was true at the beginning remains true.

Pain makes man think.

Thought makes man wise.

Wisdom makes life endurable.

Our play has ended.

May August moon bring gentle sleep.

(*He bows.*)

THE CURTAIN FALLS

THE PEOPLE IN THE PLAY

The characterization in *The Teahouse of the August Moon* has something of the simplicity, the naïve quality of a fairy tale. The people are inclined to be all good or all bad—stupid, silly and ugly, or wise and lovely. They are not drawn with subtlety; they are types. The actor must endow them with his own life and character.

Many fables are told in broad, comic vein. This is the case with *Teahouse*. Its comic figures are intensely amusing. In Colonel Purdy, playwright John Patrick pokes fun at the stuffed shirts of the Army. Purdy is the pompous, fatuous, ridiculous colonel type, mouthing platitudes and with a grotesque penchant for the obvious. His love of adventure magazines indicates his reading level. The author explores a rich vein of humour in making laundry his specialty. Almost touching, if they were not so wildly funny, are his child-like ambitions, his dreams of greatness, and his praise of Grace Purdy, "that fine woman".

Gregovich is a stock army type—the brawny dumb sergeant with a kind of animal cunning.

Fisby and McLean start out as types: Fisby the army misfit—McLean the loony psychologist with a gardening complex. But while much hilarious comedy derives from this initial drawing of these two men, and from their relations with Colonel Purdy, the playwright intends them to be more than stock types. Fisby is a misfit because of his better qualities. It is only in the heartlessly efficient army that he is out of place. Indeed, as a professor of the humanities, he is out of step with the whole trend of American life, with its aggressive materialism and its "mass man" standards.

Fisby muddles his way toward a new sense of values and a new understanding of the East and what it can contribute to the West. What he learns is what the author wants us to learn; he becomes increasingly a "straight" or serious character. Lotus Blossom's love for him and his sad realization that she would not belong in America give genuine pathos to the play in its closing moments.

Thus, Fisby and McLean start as farcical, broadly comic figures and become persons who live for us on the plane of comedy and truth. Purdy and Gregovich, on the other hand, are past help and past cure. They remain farcical types to the end. They represent the America that is too insensitive and smug to be aware of its own inadequacies.

In contrast to the foolish if well-meaning Americans, the natives come off very well; perhaps too well for us to accept them completely in our rational and objective moments. But remember that this is a fable! It is also a play which aims to entertain. As such it may make its points by slanting and by over-emphasizing certain aspects of the story and character-ization.

Four of the villagers stand out. First there is that ageless, affable rogue, Sakini, with his "smile of child-like candour". He is shrewd. He sees through the pretences of the supposedly superior race. Sly and amusing, he is a memorable figure in the great tradition of lovable, sly, servant rogues in the master-pieces of Sheridan, Molière and Shakespeare.

Then there is the gentle, wise, old artist, Mr. Oshira, who does not want to die without having known the joys of a tea-house. And the amusing, democratically-minded spinster—like a Japanese version of one of Gilbert and Sullivan's terrifying females—Miss Higa Jiga. And most important of all, a real heroine to grace our fairy tale, the fragile, charming, lovely Lotus Blossom.

CHALLENGING QUESTIONS

Like most fables, *The Teahouse of the August Moon* has a moral. In fact it has several morals, several lessons for us to learn. As you read it you will meet many challenging ideas which you can discuss with your friends and class-mates.

You will find a searching criticism of our democracy in our next play, *An Enemy of the People*. But the *Teahouse*, charm-ing and delightful as it is, nevertheless raises questions for which, as a citizen of a better Canada in the future, you will want to find the answers.

Is our Western civilization really superior to the older civiliza-tions of the East? Have we something to learn from the East about the virtues of wisdom, serenity, gentleness, patience, humour, courtesy, grace and contemplation?

Is our democracy as lofty and as perfect an ideal as we have believed it to be? If the majority of the people in a nation are common, thoughtless, vulgar, intolerant, lacking in culture or insensitive to higher values, should their will control and direct our civilization?

The end of the play leaves me with a sense of sadness. If we agree that a selfish and too complacent West has learned something from a wiser and gentler East, what has that East learned in return from the West? That brandy is a valuable export to us? The need for a certain amused tolerance?

We who have boasted of our Western way of life for so long —we who have been the rulers of the world—are really only a minority. The time has come when, if we are to survive, we must learn to get along with, and to help, the teeming millions who form the great majority of the peoples of the world in older, wiser, but "undeveloped" lands.

OUR TWO AUTHORS

Vern Sneider, author of *The Teahouse of the August Moon*, was born and lives in Monroe, Michigan. During World War II he saw service both in the Navy and in the Army. He was an intelligence officer in the Army and was later transferred to Military Government and sent to Okinawa. Here he had the experiences on which he based his successful novel. He was in charge of Tobaru Village, which he calls Tobiki Village; it was a native refugee camp. He dedicates *The Teahouse of the August Moon* to the people of the village.

Teahouse, which was published in 1951, won the Friends of American Writers award in 1952. Since then Mr. Sneider has written a novel, *A Pail of Oysters*, and *Long Way From Home and Other Stories*.

John Patrick was born in Louisville, Kentucky. He had an unhappy childhood, separated from his parents, and was sent to one southern boarding-school after another. He attended college in New Orleans, Harvard Summer School and Columbia University. His literary career began as a script writer for the National Broadcasting Company and as a film writer in Hollywood. Included among the films he has written are two that you may know—*The President's Lady* and *Three Coins in the Fountain*. His first play, *Hell Freezes Over*, was produced on Broadway in

1935; his second, *The Willow and I*, in 1942. Before the opening night of *The Willow and I*, however, he enlisted in the American Field Service. He served in Africa, Syria, India and Burma. Thus, like Vern Sneider, he had first-hand knowledge of the problems of the occupation forces in the East.

His first successful play was *The Hasty Heart*, which was produced in 1944. He wrote it in longhand in twelve days aboard a transport in the Pacific coming home on furlough. It is a play you will enjoy reading. His next three plays were not successful, but the *Teahouse* was a great triumph. The month after its opening it was bringing Patrick $2,100 a week, and continued to do so while it played to capacity houses during its long run. Countless productions by touring companies, amateur and foreign troupes have made it one of the most profitable plays of the modern theatre.

Patrick is unmarried, as was John van Druten. He spends much of his time on a farm; in this respect also he resembles the author of *I Remember Mama*, who lived on a farm in California. Patrick's farm is in Rockland County in New York. It consists of sixty-five acres of woodlands and fields. You will be interested to hear his comment on how farming and the writer's life fit together. "When I get up in the morning I make some notes. If things go well I go to work at the typewriter. If not, I get out the tractor and yank out some more trees round the plowed field. I make notes while I do that and pretty soon I go back to the typewriter."

AN ENEMY OF THE PEOPLE

HENRIK IBSEN

adapted by
ARTHUR MILLER

IBSEN FOR OUR TIME

Once you begin our fourth play you may find it difficult to put it down. It is a powerful, exciting drama, written with burning conviction.

Searching for a play from across the sea to include in our anthology we naturally thought of Ibsen, the greatest of modern playwrights. But three-quarters of a century have passed since he wrote his challenging social dramas, and many teenagers find his plays somewhat difficult to read, chiefly because their language is not of our time.

So we turned to this adaptation of his famous play, *An Enemy of the People*. It is written by Arthur Miller, one of our foremost contemporary dramatists.

Here is Arthur Miller's own preface, telling you why he decided to adapt this Ibsen play, outlining the changes he made, and describing the principles and techniques which he applied in his "translation".

ARTHUR MILLER'S PREFACE

1

At the outset it ought to be said that the word "adaptation" is very distasteful to me. It seems to mean that one writer has ventured into another's chicken-coop, or worse, into the sacred chamber of another's personal creations and rearranged things without permission. Most of the time an adaptation is a playwright's excuse for not writing his own plays, and since I am not yet with my back against that particular wall, I think it wise to set down what I have tried to do with *An Enemy of the People*, and why I did it.

There is one quality in Ibsen that no serious writer can afford to overlook. It lies at the very centre of his force, and I found in it—as I hope others will—a profound source of strength. It is his insistence, his utter conviction, that he is going to say what he has to say, and that the audience, by God, is going to listen. It is the very same quality that makes a star actor, a great public speaker, and a lunatic. Every Ibsen play begins with the unwritten words: "Now listen here!" And these words have shown me a path through the wall of "entertainment", a path that leads beyond the formulas and dried-up precepts, the pretence and fraud, of the business of the stage. Whatever else Ibsen has to teach, this is his first and greatest contribution.

In recent years Ibsen has fallen into a kind of respectful obscurity that is not only undeserved but really quite disrespectful of culture—and a disservice to the theatre besides. I decided to work on *An Enemy of the People* because I had a private wish to demonstrate that Ibsen is really pertinent today, that he is not "old-fashioned", and, implicitly, that those who condemn him are themselves misleading our theatre and our playwrights into a blind alley of senseless sensibility, triviality, and the inevitable waste of our dramatic talents; for it has become the fashion for plays to reduce the "thickness" of life to a fragile facsimile, to avoid portraying the complexities of life, the contradictions of character, the fascinating interplay of cause and effect that have long been part of the novel. And I wished also to buttress the idea that the dramatic writer has, and must again demonstrate, the right to entertain with his brains as well as his heart. It is necessary that the public understand again that the stage is *the* place for ideas, for philosophies, for the most intense discussion of man's fate. One of the masters of such a discussion is Henrik Ibsen, and I have presumed to point this out once again.

2

I have attempted to make *An Enemy of the People* as alive to Americans as it undoubtedly was to Norwegians, while keeping it intact. I had no interest in exhuming anything, in asking people to sit respectfully before the work of a celebrated but neglected writer. There are museums for such activities; the theatre has no truck with them, and ought not to have.

And I believed this play could be alive for us because its central theme is, in my opinion, the central theme of our social life today. Simply, it is the question of whether the democratic guarantees protecting political minorities ought to be set aside in time of crisis. More personally, it is the question of whether one's vision of the truth ought to be a source of guilt at a time when the mass of men condemn it as a dangerous and devilish lie. It is an enduring theme— in fact, possibly the most enduring of all Ibsen's themes— because there never was, nor will there ever be, an organized society able to countenance calmly the individual who insists that he is right while the vast majority is absolutely wrong.

The play is the story of a scientist who discovers an evil and, innocently believing that he has done a service to humanity, expects that he will at least be thanked. However, the town has a vested interest in the perpetuation of that evil, and his "truth", when confronted with that interest, must be made to conform. The scientist cannot change the truth for any reason disconnected with the evil. He clings to the truth and suffers the social consequences. At rock bottom, the play is concerned with the inviolability of objective truth. Or, put more dynamically, that those who attempt to warp the truth for ulterior purposes must inevitably become warped and corrupted themselves. This theme is valid today, just as it will always be, but some of the examples given by Ibsen to prove it may no longer be.

I am told that Ibsen wrote this play as a result of his being practically stoned off the stage for daring to present *Ghosts*. The plot is supposed to have come from a news item which told of an Hungarian scientist who had discovered poisoned water in the town's water supply and had been pilloried for his discovery. If this was the case, my interpretation of the theme is doubly justified, for it then seems beyond doubt that Ibsen meant above and beyond all else to defend his right to stand "at the outpost of society", alone with the truth, and to speak from there to his fellow men.

However, there are a few speeches, and one scene in particular, which have been taken to mean that Ibsen was a fascist. In the original meeting scene in which Dr. Stockmann sets forth his—and Ibsen's—point of view most completely and angrily, Dr. Stockmann makes a speech in which he turns to biology to prove that there are indeed certain individuals "bred" to a superior apprehension of truths and who have the natural right to lead, if not to govern, the mass.

If the entire play is to be understood as the working-out of this speech, then one has no justification for contending that it is other than racist and fascist—certainly it could not be thought of as a defence of any democratic idea. But, structurally speaking, the theme is not wholly contained in the meeting scene alone. In fact, this speech is in some important respects in contradiction to the actual dramatic working-out of the play. But that Ibsen never really believed that idea in the first place is amply proved by a speech he delivered to a workers' club after the production of *An Enemy of the People*. He said then: "Of course I do not mean the aristocracy of birth, or of the purse, or even the aristocracy of the intellect. I mean the aristocracy of character, of will, of mind—that alone can free us."

I have taken as justification for removing those examples which no longer prove the theme—examples I believe Ibsen would have removed were he alive today—the line in the original manuscript that reads: "There is no established truth that can remain true for more than seventeen, eighteen, at most twenty years." In light of genocide, the holocaust that has swept our world on the wings of the black ideology of racism, it is inconceivable that Ibsen would insist today that certain individuals are by breeding, or race, or "innate" qualities superior to others or possessed of the right to dictate to others. The man who wrote *A Doll's House*, the clarion call for the equality of women, cannot be equated with a fascist. The whole cast of his thinking was such that he could not have lived a day under an authoritarian regime of any kind. He was an individualist sometimes to the point of anarchism, and in such a man there is too explosive a need for self-expression to permit him to conform to any rigid ideology. It is impossible, therefore, to set him beside Hitler.

3

On reading the standard translations of Ibsen's work it quickly became obvious that the false impressions that have been connected with the man would seem to be justified were he to be produced in "translated" form. For one thing, his language in English sounds impossibly pedantic. Combine this with the fact that he wore a beard and half-lenses in his eyeglasses, and that his plays have always been set forth with yards of fringe on every tablecloth and drapery, and it was guaranteed that a new production on the traditional basis would truly bury the man for good.

I set out to transform his language into contemporary English. Working from a pidgin-English, word-for-word rendering of the Norwegian, done by Mr. Lars Nordenson, I was able to gather the meaning of each speech and scene without the obstruction of any kind of English construction.

For instance, Mr. Nordenson, working from the original Norwegian manuscript, set before me speeches such as: "But, dear Thomas, what have you then done to him again?" Or: "The Mayor being your brother, I would not wish to touch it, but you are as convinced as I am that truth goes ahead of all other considerations." Or: "Well, what do you say, Doctor? Don't you think it is high time that we stir a little life into the slackness and sloppiness of half-heartedness and cowardliness?" This last speech now reads: "Well, what do you say to a little hypodermic for these fence-sitting dead-heads?"

It was possible to peer into the original play with as clear an eye as one could who knew no Norwegian. There were no English sentences to correct and rewrite, only the bare literalness of the original. This version of the play, then, is really in the nature of a new translation into spoken English.

But it is more too. The original has a tendency to indulge in transitions between scenes that are themselves uninteresting, and although as little as possible of the original construction has been changed and the play is exactly as it was, scene for scene, I have made each act seem of one piece, instead of separate scenes. And my reason for doing this is simply that the tradition of Ibsen's theatre allowed the opera-like separation of scenes, while ours demands that the audience never be conscious that a "scene" has taken place at all.

Structurally the largest change is in the third act—Ibsen's fifth. In the original the actual dramatic end comes a little past the middle of the act, but it is followed by a wind-up that keeps winding endlessly to the curtain. I think this over-writing was the result of Ibsen's insistence that his meaning be driven home—and from the front door right through to the back, lest the audience fail to understand him. Generally, in this act, I have brought out the meaning of the play in terms of dramatic action, action which was already there and didn't need to be newly invented, but which was separated by tendentious speeches spoken into the blue.

Throughout the play I have tried to peel away its trappings of the moment, its relatively accidental details which ring the dull green tones of Victorianism, and to show that beneath them there still lives the terrible wrath of Henrik Ibsen, who could make a play as men make watches, precisely, intelligently, and telling not merely the minute and the hour but the age.

CAST

MORTEN KIIL	Art Smith
BILLING	Michael Strong
MRS. STOCKMANN	Florence Eldridge
PETER STOCKMANN	Morris Carnovsky
HOVSTAD	Martin Brooks
DR. STOCKMANN	Fredric March
MORTEN	Ralph Robertson
EJLIF	Richard Trask
CAPTAIN HORSTER	Ralph Dunn
PETRA	Anna Minot
ASLAKSEN	Fred Stewart
THE DRUNK	Lou Gilbert

TOWNSPEOPLE: Lulla Adler, Barbara Ames, Paul Fitzpatrick, James Karen, Michael Lewin, Salem Ludwig, Gene Lyons, John Marley, Arnold Schulman, Robert Simon, Rod Steiger

Production directed by Robert Lewis.
Setting and costumes by Aline Bernstein.
Lighting by Charles Elson.
Presented by Lars Nordenson at the Broadhurst
Theatre in New York on December 28, 1950.

SYNOPSIS OF SCENES

THE ACTION TAKES PLACE IN A NORWEGIAN TOWN

ACT ONE

Scene 1: Dr. Stockmann's living-room.
Scene 2: The same, the following morning.

ACT TWO

Scene 1: Editorial office of the *People's Daily Messenger*.
Scene 2: A room in Captain Horster's house.

ACT THREE

Scene: Dr. Stockmann's living-room the following morning.

AN ENEMY OF THE PEOPLE

ACT I

SCENE ONE

It is evening. DR. STOCKMANN'*s living-room is simply but cheerfully furnished. A doorway, upstage right, leads into the entrance hall, which extends from the front door to the dining-room, running unseen behind the living-room. At the left is another door, which leads to the* DOCTOR'*s study and other rooms. In the upstage left corner is a stove. Toward the left foreground is a sofa with a table behind it. In the right foreground are two chairs, a small table between them, on which stand a lamp and a bowl of apples. At the back, to the left, an open doorway leads to the dining-room, part of which is seen. The windows are in the right wall, a bench in front of them.*

As the curtain rises, BILLING *and* MORTEN KIIL *are eating in the dining-room.* BILLING *is junior editor of the* People's Daily Messenger. KIIL *is a slovenly old man who is feeding himself in a great hurry. He gulps his last bite and comes into the living-room, where he puts on his coat and ratty fur hat.* BILLING *comes in to help him.*

BILLING.   You sure eat fast, Mr. Kiil. (BILLING *is an enthusiast to the point of foolishness.*)

KIIL.   Eating don't get you anywhere, boy. Tell my daughter I went home.

AN ENEMY OF THE PEOPLE

Arthur Miller's adaptation of AN ENEMY OF THE PEOPLE by Henrik Ibsen. Copyright 1950, 1951 by Arthur Miller. This adaptation is protected by copyright, and no public or private performance—professional or amateur—may be given without formal authorization. Communications should be addressed to the author's representative, MCA Management, Ltd., 598 Madison Avenue, New York 22. Inquiries about reprinting should be sent to the publishers, The Viking Press, Inc., 625 Madison Avenue, New York 22.

(KIIL *starts across to the front door.* BILLING *returns to his food in the dining-room.* KIIL *halts at the bowl of apples; he takes one, tastes it, likes it, takes another and puts it in his pocket, then continues on toward the door. Again he stops, returns, and takes another apple for his pocket. Then he sees a tobacco can on the table. He covers his action from* BILLING'*s possible glance, opens the can, smells it, pours some into his side pocket. He is just closing the can when* CATHERINE STOCKMANN *enters from the dining-room.*)

MRS. STOCKMANN.   Father! You're not going, are you?

KIIL.   Got business to tend to.

MRS. STOCKMANN.   Oh, you're only going back to your room and you know it. Stay! Mr. Billing's here, and Hovstad's coming. It'll be interesting for you.

KIIL.   Got all kinds of business. The only reason I came over was the butcher told me you bought roast beef today. Very tasty, dear.

MRS. STOCKMANN.   Why don't you wait for Tom? He only went for a little walk.

KIIL (*taking out his pipe*).   You think he'd mind if I filled my pipe?

MRS. STOCKMANN.   No, go ahead. And here—take some apples. You should always have some fruit in your room.

KIIL.   No, no, wouldn't think of it.

(*The doorbell rings.*)

MRS. STOCKMANN.   That must be Hovstad. (*She goes to the door and opens it.*)

(PETER STOCKMANN, *the Mayor, enters. He is a bachelor, nearing sixty. He has always been one of those men who make it their life work to stand in the centre of the ship to keep it from overturning. He probably envies the family life and warmth of this* ‣

house, but when he comes he never wants to admit he came and often sits with his coat on.)

MRS. STOCKMANN.   Peter! Well, this is a surprise!

PETER STOCKMANN.   I was just passing by . . . (*He sees* KIIL *and smiles, amused.*) Mr. Kiil!

KIIL (*sarcastically*).   Your Honour! (*He bites into his apple and exits.*)

MRS. STOCKMANN.   You mustn't mind him, Peter, he's getting terribly old. Would you like a bite to eat?

PETER STOCKMANN.   No, no, thanks. (*He sees* BILLING *now, and* BILLING *nods to him from the dining-room.*)

MRS. STOCKMANN (*embarrassed*).   He just happened to drop in.

PETER STOCKMANN.   That's all right. I can't take hot food in the evening. Not with my stomach.

MRS. STOCKMANN.   Can't I ever get you to eat anything in this house?

PETER STOCKMANN.   Bless you, I stick to my tea and toast. Much healthier and more economical.

MRS. STOCKMANN (*smiling*).   You sound as though Tom and I throw money out the window.

PETER STOCKMANN.   Not you, Catherine. He wouldn't be home, would he?

MRS. STOCKMANN.   He went for a little walk with the boys.

PETER STOCKMANN.   You don't think that's dangerous, right after dinner? (*There is a loud knocking on the front door.*) *That* sounds like my brother.

MRS. STOCKMANN.   I doubt it, so soon. Come in, please.

> (HOVSTAD *enters. He is in his early thirties, a graduate of the peasantry struggling with a terrible conflict. For while he hates authority and wealth, he cannot bring himself to cast off a certain desire to partake of them. Perhaps he is dangerous because he wants more than anything to belong, and in a radical that is a withering wish, not easily to be borne.*)

MRS. STOCKMANN. Mr. Hovstad—

HOVSTAD. Sorry I'm late. I was held up at the printing-shop. (*Surprised.*) Good evening, Your Honour.

PETER STOCKMANN (*rather stiffly*). Hovstad. On business, no doubt.

HOVSTAD. Partly. It's about an article for the paper—

PETER STOCKMANN (*sarcastically*). Ha! I don't doubt it. I understand my brother has become a prolific contributor to —what do you call it?—the *People's Daily Liberator*?

HOVSTAD (*laughing, but holding his ground*). The *People's Daily Messenger*, sir. The Doctor sometimes honours the *Messenger* when he wants to uncover the real truth of some subject.

PETER STOCKMANN. The truth! Oh, yes, I see.

MRS. STOCKMANN (*nervously to* HOVSTAD). Would you like to . . . (*She points to dining-room.*)

PETER STOCKMANN. I don't want you to think I blame the Doctor for using your paper. After all, every performer goes for the audience that applauds him most. It's really not your paper I have anything against, Mr. Hovstad.

HOVSTAD. I really didn't think so, Your Honour.

PETER STOCKMANN. As a matter of fact, I happen to admire the spirit of tolerance in our town. It's magnificent. Just don't forget that we have it because we all believe in the same thing; it brings us together.

HOVSTAD. Kirsten Springs, you mean.

PETER STOCKMANN. The springs, Mr. Hovstad, our wonderful new springs. They've changed the soul of this town. Mark my words, Kirsten Springs are going to put us on the map, and there is no question about it.

MRS. STOCKMANN. That's what Tom says too.

PETER STOCKMANN. Everything is shooting ahead—real estate going up, money changing hands every hour, business humming—

HOVSTAD. And no more unemployment.

PETER STOCKMANN. Right. Give us a really good summer, and sick people will be coming here in carloads. The springs will turn into a regular fad, a new Carlsbad. And for once the well-to-do people won't be the only ones paying taxes in this town.

HOVSTAD. I hear reservations are really starting to come in?

PETER STOCKMANN. Coming in every day. Looks very promising, very promising.

HOVSTAD. That's fine. (*To* MRS. STOCKMANN.) Then the Doctor's article will come in handy.

PETER STOCKMANN. He's written something again?

HOVSTAD. No, it's a piece he wrote at the beginning of the winter, recommending the water. But at the time I let the article lie.

PETER STOCKMANN. Why, some hitch in it?

HOVSTAD. Oh, no, I just thought it would have a bigger effect in the spring, when people start planning for the summer.

PETER STOCKMANN. That's smart, Mr. Hovstad, very smart.

MRS. STOCKMANN. Tom is always so full of ideas about the springs; every day he—

PETER STOCKMANN. Well, he ought to be, he gets his salary from the springs, my dear.

HOVSTAD. Oh, I think it's more than that, don't you? After all Doctor Stockmann *created* Kirsten Springs.

PETER STOCKMANN. You don't say! I've been hearing that lately, but I did think I had a certain modest part—

MRS. STOCKMANN. Oh, Tom always says—

HOVSTAD. I only meant the original idea was—

PETER STOCKMANN. My good brother is never at a loss for ideas. All sorts of ideas. But when it comes to putting them into action you need another kind of man, and I did think that at least people in this house would—

MRS. STOCKMANN. But Peter, dear—we didn't mean to—

Go get yourself a bite, Mr. Hovstad, my husband will be here any minute.

HOVSTAD.   Thank you, maybe just a little something. (*He goes into the dining-room and joins* BILLING *at the table.*)

PETER STOCKMANN (*lowering his voice*).   Isn't it remarkable? Why is it that people without background can never learn tact?

MRS. STOCKMANN.   Why let it bother you? Can't you and Thomas share the honour like good brothers?

PETER STOCKMANN.   The trouble is that certain men are never satisfied to share, Catherine.

MRS. STOCKMANN.   Nonsense. You've always gotten along beautifully with Tom—That must be him now.

> (*She goes to the front door, opens it.* DR. STOCKMANN *is laughing and talking outside. He is in the prime of his life. He might be called the eternal amateur —a lover of things, of people, of sheer living, a man for whom the days are too short, and the future fabulous with discoverable joys. And for all this most people will not like him—he will not compromise for less than God's own share of the world while they have settled for less than Man's.*)

DR. STOCKMANN (*in the entrance hall*).   Hey, Catherine! Here's another guest for you! Here's a hanger for your coat, Captain. Oh, that's right, you don't wear overcoats! Go on in, boys. You kids must be hungry all over again. Come here, Captain Horster, I want you to get a look at this roast. (*He pushes* CAPTAIN HORSTER *along the hallway to the dining-room.* EJLIF *and* MORTEN *also go to the dining-room.*)

MRS. STOCKMANN.   Tom, dear . . . (*She motions toward* PETER *in the living-room.*)

DR. STOCKMANN (*turns around in the doorway to the living-room and sees* PETER).   Oh, Peter . . . (*He walks across and stretches out his hand.*)   Say now, this is really nice.

PETER STOCKMANN.   I'll have to go in a minute.

DR. STOCKMANN.   Oh, nonsense, not with the toddy on the table. You haven't forgotten the toddy, have you, Catherine?

MRS. STOCKMANN.   Of course not, I've got the water boiling. (*She goes into the dining-room.*)

PETER STOCKMANN.   Toddy too?

DR. STOCKMANN.   Sure, just sit down and make yourself at home.

PETER STOCKMANN.   No, thanks, I don't go in for drinking parties.

DR. STOCKMANN.   But this is no party.

PETER STOCKMANN.   What else do you call it? (*He looks toward the dining-room.*) It's extraordinary how you people can consume all this food and live.

DR. STOCKMANN (*rubbing his hands*).   Why? What's finer than to watch young people eat? Peter, those are the fellows who are going to stir up the whole future.

PETER STOCKMANN (*a little alarmed*).   Is that so! What's there to stir up? (*He sits in a chair to the left.*)

DR. STOCKMANN (*walking around*).   Don't worry, they'll let us know when the time comes. Old idiots like you and me, we'll be left behind like—

PETER STOCKMANN.   I've never been called *that* before.

DR. STOCKMANN.   Oh, Peter, don't jump on me every minute! You know your trouble, Peter? Your impressions are blunted. You ought to sit up there in that crooked corner of the north for five years, the way I did, and then come back here. It's like watching the first seven days of creation!

PETER STOCKMANN.   Here!

DR. STOCKMANN.   Things to work and fight for, Peter! Without that you're dead. Catherine, you sure the mailman came today?

MRS. STOCKMANN (*from the dining-room*).   There wasn't any mail today.

DR. STOCKMANN.   And another thing, Peter—a good income; *that's* something you learn to value after you've lived on a starvation diet.

PETER STOCKMANN. When did you starve?

DR. STOCKMANN. Damned near! It was pretty tough going a lot of the time up there. And now, to be able to live like a prince! Tonight, for instance, we had roast beef for dinner, and, by God, there was enough left for supper too. Please have a piece—come here.

PETER STOCKMANN. Oh, no, no—please, certainly not.

DR. STOCKMANN. At least let me show it to you! Come in here—we even have a table-cloth. (*He pulls his brother toward the dining-room.*)

PETER STOCKMANN. I saw it.

DR. STOCKMANN. Live to the hilt! that's my motto. Anyway, Catherine says I'm earning almost as much as we spend.

PETER STOCKMANN (*refusing an apple*). Well, you are improving.

DR. STOCKMANN. Peter, that was a joke! You're supposed to laugh! (*He sits in the other chair to the left.*)

PETER STOCKMANN. Roast beef twice a day is no joke.

DR. STOCKMANN. Why can't I give myself the pleasure of having people around me? It's a necessity for me to see young, lively, happy people, free people burning with a desire to do something. You'll see. When Hovstad comes in we'll talk and—

PETER STOCKMANN. Oh, yes, Hovstad. That reminds me. He told me he was going to print one of your articles.

DR. STOCKMANN. One of my articles?

PETER STOCKMANN. Yes, about the springs—an article you wrote during the winter?

DR. STOCKMANN. Oh, that one! In the first place, I don't want that one printed right now.

PETER STOCKMANN. No? It sounded to me as if it would be very timely.

DR. STOCKMANN. Under normal conditions, maybe so.

(*He gets up and walks across the floor.*)

PETER STOCKMANN (*looking after him*).   Well, what is abnormal about the conditions now?

DR. STOCKMANN (*stopping*).   I can't say for the moment, Peter—at least not tonight. There could be a great deal abnormal about conditions; then again, there could be nothing at all.

PETER STOCKMANN.   Well, you've managed to sound mysterious. Is there anything wrong? Something you're keeping from me? Because I wish once in a while you'd remind yourself that I am chairman of the board for the springs.

DR. STOCKMANN.   And I would like *you* to remember that, Peter. Look, let's not get into each other's hair.

PETER STOCKMANN.   I don't make a habit of getting into people's hair! But I'd like to underline that everything concerning Kirsten Springs must be treated in a businesslike manner, through the proper channels, and dealt with by the legally constituted authorities. I can't allow anything done behind my back in a roundabout way.

DR. STOCKMANN.   When did I ever go behind your back, Peter?

PETER STOCKMANN.   You have an ingrained tendency to go your own way, Thomas, and that simply can't go on in a well-organized society. The individual really must subordinate himself to the over-all, or—(*groping for words, he points to himself*)—to the authorities who are in charge of the general welfare. (*He gets up.*)

DR. STOCKMANN.   Well, that's probably so. But how does that concern me, Peter?

PETER STOCKMANN.   My dear Thomas, this is exactly what you will never learn. But you had better watch out because someday you might pay dearly for it. Now I've said it. Goodbye.

DR. STOCKMANN.   Are you out of your mind? You're absolutely on the wrong track.

PETER STOCKMANN.   I am usually not. Anyway, may I be

excused? (*He nods toward the dining-room.*) Good-bye, Catherine. Good evening, gentlemen. (*He leaves.*)

MRS. STOCKMANN (*entering the living-room*). He left?

DR. STOCKMANN. And burned up!

MRS. STOCKMANN. What did you do to him now?

DR. STOCKMANN. What does he want from me? He can't expect me to give him an accounting of every move I make, every thought I think, until I am ready to do it.

MRS. STOCKMANN. Why? What should you give him an accounting of?

DR. STOCKMANN (*hesitantly*). Just leave that to me, Catherine. Peculiar the mailman didn't come today.

> (HOVSTAD, BILLING *and* CAPTAIN HORSTER *have gotten up from the dining-room table and enter the living-room.* EJLIF *and* MORTEN *come in a little later.* CATHERINE *exits.*)

BILLING (*stretching out his arms*). After a meal like that, by God, I feel like a new man. This house is so—

HOVSTAD (*cutting him off*). The Mayor certainly wasn't in a glowing mood tonight.

DR. STOCKMANN. It's his stomach. He has a wretched digestion.

HOVSTAD. I think two editors from the *People's Daily Messenger* didn't help either.

DR. STOCKMANN. No, it's just that Peter is a lonely man. Poor fellow, all he knows is official business and duties, and then all that damn weak tea that he pours into himself. Catherine, may we have the toddy?

MRS. STOCKMANN (*calling from the dining-room*). I'm just getting it.

DR. STOCKMANN. Sit down here on the couch with me, Captain Horster—a rare guest like you—sit here. Sit down, friends.

HORSTER. This used to be such an ugly house. Suddenly it's beautiful!

(BILLING *and* HOVSTAD *sit down at the right.* MRS. STOCKMANN *brings a tray with a pot, glasses, bottles, etc., on it, and puts it on the table behind the couch.*)

BILLING (*to* HORSTER, *intimately, indicating* STOCKMANN). Great man!

MRS. STOCKMANN. Here you are. Help yourselves.

DR. STOCKMANN (*taking a glass*). We sure will. (*He mixes the toddy.*) And the cigars, Ejlif—you know where the box is. And Morten, get my pipe. (*The boys go out to the left.*) I have a sneaking suspicion that Ejlif is snitching a cigar now and then, but I don't pay any attention. Catherine, you know where I put it? Oh, he's got it. Good boys! (*The boys bring the various things in.*) Help yourselves, fellows. I'll stick to the pipe. This one's gone through plenty of blizzards with me up in the north. Skol! (*He looks around.*) Home! What an invention, heh?

(*The boys sit down on the bench near the windows.*)

MRS. STOCKMANN (*who has sat down and is now knitting*). Are you sailing soon, Captain Horster?

HORSTER. I expect to be ready next week.

MRS. STOCKMANN. And then to America, Captain?

HORSTER. Yes, that's the plan.

BILLING. Oh, then you won't be home for the new election?

HORSTER. Is there going to be another election?

BILLING. Didn't you know?

HORSTER. No, I don't get mixed up in those things.

BILLING. But you are interested in public affairs, aren't you?

HORSTER. Frankly, I don't understand a thing about it.

(*He does, really, although not very much.* CAPTAIN HORSTER *is one of the longest silent roles in dramatic literature, but he is not to be thought of as characterless therefor. It is not a bad thing to have a courageous, quiet man for a friend, even if it has gone out of fashion.*)

MRS. STOCKMANN (*sympathetically*). Neither do I, Captain. Maybe that's why I'm always so glad to see you.

BILLING. Just the same, you ought to vote, Captain.

HORSTER. Even if I don't understand anything about it?

BILLING. Understand! What do you mean by that? Society, Captain, is like a ship—every man should do something to help navigate the ship.

HORSTER. That may be all right on shore, but on board a ship it doesn't work out so well.

(PETRA *in hat and coat and with textbooks and notebooks under her arm comes into the entrance hall. She is Ibsen's clear-eyed hope for the future—and probably ours. She is forthright, determined, and knows the meaning of work, which to her is the creation of good on the earth.*)

PETRA (*from the hall*). Good evening.

DR. STOCKMANN (*warmly*). Good evening, Petra!

BILLING (*to* HORSTER). Great young woman!

(*There are mutual greetings.* PETRA *removes her coat and hat and places the books on a chair in the entrance hall.*)

PETRA (*entering the living-room*). And here you are, lying around like lizards while I'm out slaving.

DR. STOCKMANN. Well, you come and be a lizard too. Come here, Petra, sit with me. I look at her and say to myself, "How did I do it?"

(PETRA *goes over to her father and kisses him.*)

BILLING. Shall I mix a toddy for you?

PETRA (*coming up to the table*). No, thanks, I had better do it myself—you always mix it too strong. Oh, Father, I forgot—I have a letter for you. (*She goes to the chair where her books are.*)

DR. STOCKMANN (*alerted*). Who's it from?

PETRA. I met the mailman on the way to school this morning and he gave me your mail too, and I just didn't have time to run back.

DR. STOCKMANN (*getting up and walking toward her*). And you don't give it to me until now!

PETRA. I really didn't have time to run back, Father.

MRS. STOCKMANN. If she didn't have time . . .

DR. STOCKMANN. Let's see it—come on, child! (*He takes the letter and looks at the envelope.*) Yes, indeed.

MRS. STOCKMANN. Is that the one you've been waiting for?

DR. STOCKMANN. I'll be right back. There wouldn't be a light on in my room, would there?

MRS. STOCKMANN. The lamp is on the desk, burning away.

DR. STOCKMANN. Please excuse me for a moment. (*He goes into his study and quickly returns.* MRS. STOCKMANN *hands him his glasses. He goes out again.*)

PETRA. What is that, Mother?

MRS. STOCKMANN. I don't know. The last couple of days he's been asking again and again about the mailman.

BILLING. Probably an out-of-town patient of his.

PETRA. Poor Father, he's got much too much to do. (*She mixes her drink.*) This ought to taste good.

HOVSTAD. By the way, what happened to that English novel you were going to translate for us?

PETRA. I started it, but I've gotten so busy—

HOVSTAD. Oh, teaching evening school again?

PETRA. Two hours a night.

BILLING. Plus the high school every day?

PETRA (*sitting down on the couch*). Yes, five hours, and every night a pile of lessons to correct!

MRS. STOCKMANN. She never stops going.

HOVSTAD. Maybe that's why I always think of you as kind of breathless and—well, breathless.

PETRA. I love it. I get so wonderfully tired.

BILLING (*to* HORSTER). She looks tired.

MORTEN.   You must be a wicked woman, Petra.

PETRA (*laughing*).   Wicked?

MORTEN.   You work so much. My teacher says that work is a punishment for our sins.

EJLIF.   And you believe that?

MRS. STOCKMANN.   Ejlif! Of course he believes his teacher!

BILLING (*smiling*).   Don't stop him . . .

HOVSTAD.   Don't you like to work, Morten?

MORTEN.   Work? No.

HOVSTAD.   Then what will you ever amount to in this world?

MORTEN.   Me? I'm going to be a Viking.

EJLIF..   You can't! You'd have to be a heathen!

MORTEN.   So I'll be a heathen.

MRS. STOCKMANN.   I think it's getting late, boys.

BILLING.   I agree with you, Morten. I think—

MRS. STOCKMANN (*making signs to* BILLING).   You certainly don't, Mr. Billing.

BILLING.   Yes, by God, I do. I am a real heathen and proud of it. You'll see, pretty soon we're all going to be heathens!

MORTEN.   And then we can do anything we want!

BILLING.   Right! You see, Morten—

MRS. STOCKMANN (*interrupting*).   Don't you have any homework for tomorrow, boys? Better go in and do it.

EJLIF.   Oh, can't we stay in here a while?

MRS. STOCKMANN.   No, neither of you. Now run along.

(*The boys say good night and go off at the left.*)

HOVSTAD.   You really think it hurts them to listen to such talk?

MRS. STOCKMANN.   I don't know, but I don't like it.

(DR. STOCKMANN *enters from his study, an open letter in his hand. He is like a sleep-walker, astonished, engrossed. He walks toward the front door.*)

MRS. STOCKMANN.   Tom!

(He turns, suddenly aware of them.)

DR. STOCKMANN.   Boys, there is going to be news in this town!

BILLING.   News?

MRS. STOCKMANN.   What kind of news?

DR. STOCKMANN.   A terrific discovery, Catherine.

HOVSTAD.   Really?

MRS. STOCKMANN.   That you made?

DR. STOCKMANN.   That I made. *(He walks back and forth.)* Now let the baboons running this town call me a lunatic! Now they'd better watch out. Oh, how the mighty have fallen!

PETRA.   What is it, Father?

DR. STOCKMANN.   Oh, if Peter were only here! Now you'll see how human beings can walk around and make judgments like blind rats.

HOVSTAD.   What in the world's happened, Doctor?

DR. STOCKMANN *(stopping at the table)*.   It's the general opinion isn't it, that our town is a sound and healthy spot?

HOVSTAD.   Of course.

MRS. STOCKMANN.   What happened?

DR. STOCKMANN.   Even a rather unusually healthy spot! Oh, God, a place that can be recommended not only to all people but to sick people!

MRS. STOCKMANN.   But, Tom, what are you—

DR. STOCKMANN.   And we certainly have recommended it. I myself have written and written, in the *People's Messenger*, pamphlets—

HOVSTAD.   Yes, yes, but—

DR. STOCKMANN.   The miraculous springs that cost such a fortune to build, the whole Health Institute, is a pest-hole!

PETRA.   Father! The springs?

MRS. STOCKMANN *(simultaneously)*.   Our springs.

BILLING.   That's unbelievable!

DR. STOCKMANN.   You know the filth up in Windmill Valley? That stuff that has such a stinking smell? It comes down from the tannery up there, and the same damn poisonous mess comes right out into the blessed, miraculous water we're supposed to *cure* people with!

HORSTER.   You mean actually where our beaches are?

DR. STOCKMANN.   Exactly.

HOVSTAD.   How are you so sure about this, Doctor?

DR. STOCKMANN.   I had a suspicion about it a long time ago—last year there were too many sick cases among the visitors, typhoid and gastric disturbances.

MRS. STOCKMANN.   That did happen. I remember Mrs. Svensen's niece—

DR. STOCKMANN.   Yes, dear. At the time we thought that the visitors brought the bug, but later this winter I got a new idea and I started investigating the water.

MRS. STOCKMANN.   So that's what you've been working on!

DR. STOCKMANN.   I sent samples of the water to the University for an exact chemical analysis.

HOVSTAD.   And that's what you have just received?

DR. STOCKMANN (*waving the letter again*).   This is it. It proves the existence of infectious organic matter in the water.

MRS. STOCKMANN.   Well, thank God you discovered it in time.

DR. STOCKMANN.   I think we can say that, Catherine.

MRS. STOCKMANN.   Isn't it wonderful!

HOVSTAD.   And what do you intend to do now, Doctor?

DR. STOCKMANN.   Put the thing right, of course.

HOVSTAD.   Do you think that can be done?

DR. STOCKMANN.   Maybe. If not, the whole Institute is useless. But there's nothing to worry about—I am quite clear on what has to be done.

MRS. STOCKMANN.   But, Tom, why did you keep it so secret?

DR. STOCKMANN.   What did you want me to do? Go out and blab before I really knew? (*He walks around, rubbing his hands.*) You don't realize what this means, Catherine—the whole water system has got to be changed.

MRS. STOCKMANN. The *whole* water system?

DR. STOCKMANN. The whole water system. The intake is too low, it's got to be raised to a much higher spot. The whole construction's got to be ripped out!

PETRA. Well, Father, at last you can prove they should have listened to you!

DR. STOCKMANN. Ha, she remembers!

MRS. STOCKMANN. That's right, you did warn them—

DR. STOCKMANN. Of course I warned them. When they started the damned thing I told them not to build it down there! But who am I, a mere scientist, to tell politicians where to build a health institute! Well, now they're going to get it, both barrels!

BILLING. This is tremendous! (*To* HORSTER.) He's a great man!

DR. STOCKMANN. It's bigger than tremendous. (*He starts toward his study.*) Wait'll they see this! (*He stops.*) Petra, my report is on my desk . . . (PETRA *goes into his study.*) An envelope, Catherine! (*She goes for it.*) Gentlemen, this final proof from the University—(PETRA *comes out with the report, which he takes*)—and my report—(*he flicks the pages*)—five solid, explosive pages . . .

MRS. STOCKMANN (*handing him an envelope*). Is this big enough?

DR. STOCKMANN. Fine. Right to the Board of Directors! (*He inserts the report, seals the envelope, and hands it to* CATHERINE.) Will you give this to the maid—what's her name again?

MRS. STOCKMANN. Randine, dear, Randine.

DR. STOCKMANN. Tell our darling Randine to wipe her nose and run over to the Mayor right now.

(MRS. STOCKMANN *just stands there looking at him.*)

DR. STOCKMANN. What's the matter, dear?

MRS. STOCKMANN. I don't know . . .

PETRA.   What's Uncle Peter going to say about this?

MRS. STOCKMANN.   That's what I'm wondering.

DR. STOCKMANN.   What can he say! He ought to be glad that such an important fact is brought out before we start an epidemic! Hurry, dear!

(CATHERINE *exits at the left.*)

HOVSTAD.   I would like to put a brief item about this discovery in the *Messenger*.

DR. STOCKMANN.   Go ahead. I'd really be grateful for that now.

HOVSTAD.   Because the public ought to know soon.

DR. STOCKMANN.   Right away.

BILLING.   By God, you'll be the leading man in this town, Doctor.

DR. STOCKMANN (*walking around with an air of satisfaction*).   Oh, there was nothing to it. Every detective gets a lucky break once in his life. But just the same I—

BILLING.   Hovstad, don't you think the town ought to pay Dr. Stockmann some tribute?

DR. STOCKMANN.   Oh, no, no . . .

HOVSTAD.   Sure, let's all put in a word for—

BILLING.   I'll talk to Aslaksen about it!

(CATHERINE *enters.*)

DR. STOCKMANN.   No, no, fellows, no fooling around! I won't put up with any commotion. Even if the Board of Directors wants to give me an increase I won't take it—I just won't take it, Catherine.

MRS. STOCKMANN (*dutifully*).   That's right, Tom.

PETRA (*filling her glass*).   Skol, Father!

EVERYBODY.   Skol, Doctor!

HORSTER.   Doctor, I hope this will bring you great honour and pleasure.

DR. STOCKMANN.   Thanks, friends, thanks. There's one blessing above all others. To have earned the respect of one's neighbours is—is—Catherine, I'm going to dance!

(*He grabs his wife and whirls her around. There are shouts and struggles, general commotion. The boys in nightgowns stick their heads through the doorway at the right, wondering what is going on.* MRS. STOCKMANN, *seeing them, breaks away and chases them upstairs as*

THE CURTAIN FALLS

SCENE TWO

DR. STOCKMANN'S *living-room the following morning. As the curtain rises,* MRS. STOCKMANN *comes in from the dining-room, a sealed letter in her hand. She goes to the study door and peeks in.*

MRS. STOCKMANN. Are you there, Tom?

DR. STOCKMANN (*from within*). I just got in. (*He enters the living-room.*) What's up?

MRS. STOCKMANN. From Peter. It just came. (*She hands him the envelope.*)

DR. STOCKMANN. Oh, let's see. (*He opens the letter and reads*) "I am returning herewith the report you submitted . . . " (*He continues to read, mumbling to himself.*)

MRS. STOCKMANN. Well, what does he say? Don't stand there!

DR. STOCKMANN (*putting the letter in his pocket*). He just says he'll come around this afternoon.

MRS. STOCKMANN. Oh. Well, maybe you ought to try to remember to be home then.

DR. STOCKMANN. Oh, I sure will. I'm through with my morning visits anyway.

MRS. STOCKMANN. I'm dying to see how he's going to take it.

DR. STOCKMANN. Why, is there any doubt? He'll probably make it look as if he made the discovery, not I.

MRS. STOCKMANN. But aren't you a little bit afraid of that?

DR. STOCKMANN. Oh, underneath he'll be happy, Catherine. It's just that Peter is so afraid that somebody else is going to do something good for this town.

MRS. STOCKMANN. I wish you'd go out of your way and share the honours with him. Couldn't we say that he put you on the right track or something?

DR. STOCKMANN. Oh, I don't mind—as long as it makes everybody happy.

(MORTEN KIIL *sticks his head through the doorway. He looks around searchingly and chuckles. He will continue chuckling until he leaves the house. He is the archetype of the little twinkle-eyed man who sneaks into so much of Ibsen's work. He will chuckle you right over the precipice. He is the dealer, the man with the rat's finely turned brain. But he is sometimes likable because he is without morals and announces the fact by laughing.*)

KIIL (*slyly*). Is it really true?

MRS. STOCKMANN (*walking toward him*). Father!

DR. STOCKMANN. Well, good morning!

MRS. STOCKMANN. Come on in.

KIIL. It better be true or I'm going.

DR. STOCKMANN. What had better be true?

KIIL. This crazy story about the water system. Is it true?

MRS. STOCKMANN. Of course it's true! How did you find out about it?

KIIL. Petra came flying by on her way to school this morning.

DR. STOCKMANN. Oh, she did?

KIIL. Ya. I thought she was trying to make a fool out of me—

MRS. STOCKMANN. Now why would she do that?

KIIL. Nothing gives more pleasure to young people than to make fools out of old people. But this is true, eh?

DR. STOCKMANN. Of course it's true. Sit down here. It's pretty lucky for the town, eh?

KIIL (*fighting his laughter*). Lucky for the town!

DR. STOCKMANN. I mean, that I made the discovery before it was too late.

KIIL. Tom, I never thought you had the imagination to pull your own brother's leg like this.

DR. STOCKMANN. Pull his leg?

MRS. STOCKMANN. But, Father, he's not—

KIIL. How does it go now, let me get it straight. There's some kind of—like cockroaches in the water-pipes—

DR. STOCKMANN (*laughing*). No, not cockroaches.

KIIL. Well, some kind of little animals.

MRS. STOCKMANN. Bacteria, Father.

KIIL (*who can barely speak through his laughter*). Ah, but a whole mess of them, eh?

DR. STOCKMANN. Oh, there'd be millions and millions.

KIIL. And nobody can see them but you, is that it?

DR. STOCKMANN. Yes, that's—well, of course anybody with a micro—(*He breaks off.*) What are you laughing at?

MRS. STOCKMANN (*smiling at* KIIL). You don't understand, Father. Nobody can actually see bacteria, but that doesn't mean they're not there.

KIIL. Good girl, you stick with him! By God, this is the best thing I ever heard in my life!

DR. STOCKMANN (*smiling*). What do you mean?

KIIL. But tell me, you think you are actually going to get your brother to believe this?

DR. STOCKMANN. Well, we'll see soon enough!

KIIL. You really think he's that crazy?

DR. STOCKMANN. I hope the whole town will be that crazy, Morten.

KIIL. Ya, they probably are, and it'll serve them right too —they think they're so much smarter than us old-timers. Your good brother ordered them to bounce me out of the council, so they chased me out like a dog! Make jackasses out of all of them, Stockmann!

DR. STOCKMANN.   Yes, but, Morten—

KIIL.   Long-eared, short-tailed jackasses! (*He gets up.*) Stockmann, if you can make the Mayor and his elegant friends grab at this bait, I will give a couple of hundred crowns to charity, and right now, right on the spot.

DR. STOCKMANN.   Well, that would be very kind of you, but I'm—

KIIL.   I haven't got much to play around with, but if you can pull the rug out from under him with this cockroach business, I'll give at least fifty crowns to some poor people on Christmas Eve. Maybe this'll teach them to put some brains back in Town Hall!

(HOVSTAD *enters from the hall.*)

HOVSTAD.   Good morning! Oh, pardon me . . .

KIIL (*enjoying this proof immensely*).   Oh, this one is in on it, too?

HOVSTAD.   What's that, sir?

DR. STOCKMANN.   Of course he's in on it.

KIIL.   Couldn't I have guessed that! And it's going to be in the papers, I suppose. You're sure tying down the corners, aren't you? Well, lay it on thick. I've got to go.

DR. STOCKMANN.   Oh, no, stay a while, let me explain it to you!

KIIL.   Oh, I get it, don't worry! Only you can see them, heh? That's the best idea I've ever—damn it, you shouldn't do this for nothing! (*He goes toward the hall.*)

MRS. STOCKMANN (*following him out, laughing*).   But, Father, you don't understand about bacteria.

DR. STOCKMANN (*laughing*).   The old badger doesn't believe a word of it.

HOVSTAD.   What does he think you're doing?

DR. STOCKMANN.   Making an idiot out of my brother— imagine that?

HOVSTAD.   You got a few minutes?

DR. STOCKMANN.   Sure, as long as you like.

HOVSTAD.   Have you heard from the Mayor?

DR. STOCKMANN.   Only that he's coming over later.

HOVSTAD.   I've been thinking about this since last night—

DR. STOCKMANN.   Don't say!

HOVSTAD.   For you as a medical man, a scientist, this is a really rare opportunity. But I've been wondering if you realize that it ties in with a lot of other things.

DR. STOCKMANN.   How do you mean? Sit down. (*They sit at the right.*) What are you driving at?

HOVSTAD.   You said last night that the pollution comes from impurities in the ground—

DR. STOCKMANN.   It comes from the poisonous dump up in Windmill Valley.

· HOVSTAD.   Doctor, I think it comes from an entirely different dump.

DR. STOCKMANN.   What do you mean?

HOVSTAD (*with growing zeal*).   The same dump that is poisoning and polluting our whole social life in this town.

DR. STOCKMANN.   For God's sake, Hovstad, what are you babbling about?

HOVSTAD.   Everything that matters in this town has fallen into the hands of a few bureaucrats.

DR. STOCKMANN.   Well, they're not all bureaucrats—

HOVSTAD.   They're all rich, all with old reputable names, and they've got everything in the palm of their hands.

DR. STOCKMANN.   Yes, but they happen to have ability and knowledge.

HOVSTAD.   Did they show ability and knowledge when they built the water system where they did?

DR. STOCKMANN.   No, of course not, but that happened to be a blunder, and we'll clear it up now.

HOVSTAD.   You really imagine it's going to be as easy as all that?

DR. STOCKMANN.   Easy or not easy, it's got to be done.

HOVSTAD.   Doctor, I've made up my mind to give this whole scandal very special treatment.

DR. STOCKMANN.   Now, wait. You can't call it a scandal yet.

HOVSTAD.   Doctor, when I took over the *People's Messenger* I swore I'd blow that smug cabal of old, stubborn, self-satisfied fogies to bits. This is the story that can do it.

DR. STOCKMANN.   But I still think we owe them a deep debt of gratitude for building the springs.

HOVSTAD.   The Mayor being your brother, I wouldn't ordinarily want to touch it, but I know you'd never let that kind of thing obstruct the truth.

DR. STOCKMANN.   Of course not, but . . .

HOVSTAD.   I want you to understand me. I don't have to tell you I come from a simple family. I know in my bones what the underdog needs—he's got to have a say in the government of society. That's what brings out ability, intelligence, and self-respect in people.

DR. STOCKMANN.   I understand that, but . . .

HOVSTAD.   I think a newspaperman who turns down any chance to give the underdog a lift is taking on a responsibility that I don't want. I know perfectly well that in fancy circles they call it agitation, and they can call it anything they like if it makes them happy, but I have my own conscience—

DR. STOCKMANN (*interrupting*).   I agree with you, Hovstad, but this is just the water supply and—(*There is a knock on the door.*)   Come in!

(MR. ASLAKSEN, *the publisher, enters from the hall. He is simply but neatly dressed. He wears gloves and carries a hat and an umbrella in his hand. He is so utterly drawn it is unnecessary to say anything at all about him.*)

ASLAKSEN.   I beg your pardon, Doctor, if I intrude . . .

HOVSTAD (*standing up*).   Are you looking for me, Aslaksen?

ASLAKSEN.   No, I didn't know you were here. I want to see the Doctor.

DR. STOCKMANN.   What can I do for you?

ASLAKSEN.   Is it true, Doctor, what I hear from Mr. Billing, that you intend to campaign for a better water system?

DR. STOCKMANN.   Yes, for the Institute. But it's not a campaign.

ASLAKSEN.   I just wanted to call and tell you that we are behind you a hundred per cent.

HOVSTAD (*to* DR. STOCKMANN).   There, you see!

DR. STOCKMANN.   Mr. Aslaksen, I thank you with all my heart. But you see—

ASLAKSEN.   We can be important, Doctor. When the little businessman wants to push something through, he turns out to be the majority, you know, and it's always good to have the majority on your side.

DR. STOCKMANN.   That's certainly true, but I don't understand what this is all about. It seems to me it's a simple, straightforward business. The water—

ASLAKSEN.   Of course we intend to behave with moderation, Doctor. I always try to be a moderate and careful man.

DR. STOCKMANN.   You are known for that, Mr. Aslaksen, but—

ASLAKSEN.   The water system is very important to us little businessmen, Doctor. Kirsten Springs are becoming a gold mine for this town, especially for the property owners, and that is why, in my capacity as chairman of the Property Owners Association—

DR. STOCKMANN.   Yes.

ASLAKSEN.   And furthermore, as a representative of the Temperance Society—You probably know, Doctor, that I am active for prohibition.

DR. STOCKMANN.   So I have heard.

ASLAKSEN.   As a result, I come into contact with all kinds of people, and since I am known to be a law-abiding and solid citizen, I have a certain influence in this town—you might even call it a little power.

DR. STOCKMANN. I know that very well, Mr. Aslaksen.

ASLAKSEN. That's why you can see that it would be practically nothing for me to arrange a demonstration.

DR. STOCKMANN. Demonstration! What are you going to demonstrate about?

ASLAKSEN. The citizens of the town complimenting you for bringing this important matter to everybody's attention. Obviously it would have to be done with the utmost moderation so as not to hurt the authorities.

HOVSTAD. This could knock the big-bellies right into the garbage can!

ASLAKSEN. No indiscretion or extreme aggressiveness toward the authorities, Mr. Hovstad! I don't want any wild-eyed radicalism on this thing. I've had enough of that in my time, and no good ever comes of it. But for a good solid citizen to express his calm, frank, and free opinion is something nobody can deny.

DR. STOCKMANN (*shaking the publisher's hand*). My dear Aslaksen, I can't tell you how it heartens me to hear this kind of support. I am happy—I really am—I'm happy. Listen! Wouldn't you like a glass of sherry?

ASLAKSEN. I am a member of the Temperance Society. I—

DR. STOCKMANN. Well, how about a glass of beer?

ASLAKSEN (*considers, then*). I don't think I can go quite that far, Doctor. I never take anything. Well, good day, and I want you to remember that the little man is behind you like a wall.

DR. STOCKMANN. Thank you.

ASLAKSEN. You have the solid majority on your side, because when the little—

DR. STOCKMANN (*trying to stop* ASLAKSEN's *talk*). Thanks for that, Mr. Aslaksen, and good day.

ASLAKSEN. Are you going back to the printing-shop, Mr. Hovstad?

HOVSTAD.   I just have a thing or two to attend to here.

ASLAKSEN.   Very well. (*He leaves.*)

HOVSTAD.   Well, what do you say to a little hypodermic for these fence-sitting deadheads?

DR. STOCKMANN (*surprised*).   Why? I think Aslaksen is a very sincere man.

HOVSTAD.   Isn't it time we pumped some guts into these well-intentioned men of good will? Under all their liberal talk they still idolize authority, and that's got to be rooted out of this town. This blunder of the water system has to be made clear to every voter. Let me print your report.

DR. STOCKMANN.   Not until I talk to my brother.

HOVSTAD.   I'll write an editorial in the meantime, and if the Mayor won't go along with us—

DR. STOCKMANN.   I don't see how you can imagine such a thing!

HOVSTAD.   Believe me, Doctor, it's possible, and then—

DR. STOCKMANN.   Listen, I promise you: he will go along, and then you can print my report, every word of it.

HOVSTAD.   On your word of honour?

DR. STOCKMANN (*giving* HOVSTAD *the manuscript*).   Here it is. Take it. It can't do any harm for you to read it. Return it to me later.

HOVSTAD.   Good day, Doctor.

DR. STOCKMANN.   Good day. You'll see, it's going to be easier than you think, Hovstad!

HOVSTAD.   I hope so, Doctor. Sincerely. Let me know as soon as you hear from His Honour. (*He leaves.*)

DR. STOCKMANN (*goes to dining-room and looks in*). Catherine! Oh, you're home already, Petra!

PETRA (*coming in*).   I just got back from school.

MRS. STOCKMANN (*entering*).   Hasn't he been here yet?

DR. STOCKMANN.   Peter? No, but I just had a long chat with Hovstad. He's really fascinated with my discovery, and you know, it has more implications than I thought at first. Do you know what I have backing me up?

MRS. STOCKMANN.   What in heaven's name have you got backing you up?

DR. STOCKMANN.   The solid majority.

MRS. STOCKMANN.   Is that good?

DR. STOCKMANN.   Good? It's wonderful. You can't imagine the feeling, Catherine, to know that your own town feels like a brother to you. I have never felt so at home in this town since I was a boy. (*A noise is heard.*)

MRS. STOCKMANN.   That must be the front door.

DR. STOCKMANN.   Oh, it's Peter then. Come in.

PETER STOCKMANN (*entering from the hall*).   Good morning!

DR. STOCKMANN.   It's nice to see you, Peter.

MRS. STOCKMANN.   Good morning. How are you today?

PETER STOCKMANN.   Well, so so. (*To* DR. STOCKMANN.) I received your thesis about the condition of the springs yesterday.

DR. STOCKMANN.   I got your note. Did you read it?

PETER STOCKMANN.   I read it.

DR. STOCKMANN.   Well, what do you have to say?

(PETER STOCKMANN *clears his throat and glances at the women.*)

MRS. STOCKMANN.   Come on, Petra. (*She and* PETRA *leave the room at the left.*)

PETER STOCKMANN (*after a moment*).   Thomas, was it really necessary to go into this investigation behind my back?

DR. STOCKMANN.   Yes. Until I was convinced myself, there was no point in—

PETER STOCKMANN.   And now you are convinced?

DR. STOCKMANN.   Well, certainly. Aren't you too, Peter? (*Pause.*) The University chemists corroborated . . .

PETER STOCKMANN.   You intend to present this document to the Board of Directors, officially, as the medical officer of the springs?

. DR. STOCKMANN.   Of course, something's got to be done, and quick.

PETER STOCKMANN.   You always use such strong expressions, Thomas. Among other things, in your report you say that we *guarantee* our guests and visitors a permanent case of poisoning.

DR. STOCKMANN.   But, Peter, how can you describe it any other way? Imagine! Poisoned internally and externally!

PETER STOCKMANN.   So you merrily conclude that we must build a waste-disposal plant—and reconstruct a brand-new water system from the bottom up!

DR. STOCKMANN.   Well, do you know some other way out? I don't.

PETER STOCKMANN.   I took a little walk over to the city engineer this morning and in the course of conversation I sort of jokingly mentioned these changes—as something we might consider for the future, you know.

DR. STOCKMANN.   The future won't be soon enough, Peter.

PETER STOCKMANN.   The engineer just smiled at my extravagance and gave me a few facts. I don't suppose you have taken the trouble to consider what your proposed changes would cost?

DR. STOCKMANN.   No, I never thought of that.

PETER STOCKMANN.   Naturally. Your little project would come to at least three hundred thousand crowns.

DR. STOCKMANN (*astonished*).   That expensive!

PETER STOCKMANN.   Oh, don't look so upset—it's only money. The worst thing is that it would take some two years.

DR. STOCKMANN.   Two years?

PETER STOCKMANN.   At the least. And what do you propose we do about the springs in the meantime? Shut them up, no doubt! Because we would have to, you know. As soon as the rumour gets around that the water is dangerous, we won't have a visitor left. So that's the picture, Thomas. You have it in your power literally to ruin your own town.

DR. STOCKMANN. Now look, Peter! I don't want to ruin anything.

PETER STOCKMANN. Kirsten Springs are the blood supply of this town, Thomas—the only future we've got here. Now will you stop and think?

DR. STOCKMANN. Good God! Well, what do you think we ought to do?

PETER STOCKMANN. Your report has not convinced me that the conditions are as dangerous as you try to make them.

DR. STOCKMANN. Now listen; they are even worse than the report makes them out to be. Remember, summer is coming, and the warm weather!

PETER STOCKMANN. I think you're exaggerating. A capable physician ought to know what precautions to take.

DR. STOCKMANN. And what then?

PETER STOCKMANN. The existing water supply for the springs is a fact, Thomas, and has got to be treated as a fact. If you are reasonable and act with discretion, the directors of the Institute will be inclined to take under consideration any means to make possible improvements, reasonably and without financial sacrifices.

DR. STOCKMANN. Peter, do you imagine that I would ever agree to such trickery?

PETER STOCKMANN. Trickery?

DR. STOCKMANN. Yes, a trick, a fraud, a lie! A treachery, a downright crime, against the public and against the whole community!

PETER STOCKMANN. I said before that I am not convinced that there is any actual danger.

DR. STOCKMANN. Oh, you aren't? Anything else is impossible! My report is an absolute fact. The only trouble is that you and your administration were the ones who insisted that the water supply be built where it is, and now you're afraid to admit the blunder you committed. Damn it! Don't you think I can see through it all?

PETER STOCKMANN. All right, let's suppose that's true.

Maybe I do care a little about my reputation. I still say I do it for the good of the town—without moral authority there can be no government. And that is why, Thomas, it is my duty to prevent your report from reaching the Board. Some time later I will bring up the matter for discussion. In the meantime, not a single word is to reach the public.

DR. STOCKMANN. Oh, my dear Peter, do you imagine you can prevent that!

PETER STOCKMANN. It will be prevented.

DR. STOCKMANN. It can't be. There are too many people who already know about it.

PETER STOCKMANN (*angered*). Who? It can't possibly be those people from the *Daily Messenger* who—

DR. STOCKMANN. Exactly. The liberal, free, and independent press will stand up and do its duty!

PETER STOCKMANN. You are an unbelievably irresponsible man, Thomas! Can't you imagine what consequences that is going to have for you?

DR. STOCKMANN. For me?

PETER STOCKMANN. Yes, for you and your family.

DR. STOCKMANN. What the hell are you saying now?

PETER STOCKMANN. I believe I have the right to think of myself as a helpful brother, Thomas.

DR. STOCKMANN. You have been, and I thank you deeply for it.

PETER STOCKMANN. Don't mention it. I often couldn't help myself. I had hoped that by improving your finances I would be able to keep you from running completely hog wild.

DR. STOCKMANN. You mean it was only for your own sake?

PETER STOCKMANN. Partly, yes. What do you imagine people think of an official whose closest relatives get themselves into trouble time and time again?

DR. STOCKMANN. And that's what I have done?

PETER STOCKMANN. You do it without knowing it. You're like a man with an automatic brain—as soon as an idea breaks into your head, no matter how idiotic it may be, you get up like a sleep-walker and start writing a pamphlet about it.

DR. STOCKMANN. Peter, don't you think it's a citizen's duty to share a new idea with the public?

PETER STOCKMANN. The public doesn't need new ideas—the public is much better off with old ideas.

DR. STOCKMANN. You're not even embarrassed to say that?

PETER STOCKMANN. Now look, I'm going to lay this out once and for all. You're always barking about authority. If a man gives you an order he's persecuting you. Nothing is important enough to respect once you decide to revolt against your superiors. All right then, I give up. I'm not going to try to change you any more. I told you the stakes you are playing for here, and now I am going to give you an order. And I warn you, you had better obey it if you value your career.

DR. STOCKMANN. What kind of an order?

PETER STOCKMANN. You are going to deny these rumours officially.

DR. STOCKMANN. How?

PETER STOCKMANN. You simply say that you went into the examination of the water more thoroughly and you find that you overestimated the danger.

DR. STOCKMANN. I see.

PETER STOCKMANN. And that you have complete confidence that whatever improvements are needed, the management will certainly take care of them.

DR. STOCKMANN (*after a pause*). My convictions come from the condition of the water. My convictions will change when the water changes, and for no other reason.

PETER STOCKMANN. What are you talking about convictions? You're an official, you keep your convictions to yourself!

DR. STOCKMANN. To myself?

PETER STOCKMANN. As an official, I said. God knows,

as a private person that's something else, but as a subordinate employee of the Institute, you have no right to express any convictions or personal opinions about anything connected with policy.

DR. STOCKMANN.   Now you listen to me. I am a doctor and a scientist—

PETER STOCKMANN.   This has nothing to do with science!

DR. STOCKMANN.   Peter, I have the right to express my opinion on anything in the world!

PETER STOCKMANN.   Not about the Institute—that I forbid.

DR. STOCKMANN.   You forbid!

PETER STOCKMANN.   I forbid you as your superior, and when I give orders you obey.

DR. STOCKMANN.   Peter, if you weren't my brother—

PETRA (*throwing the door at the left open*).   Father! You aren't going to stand for this! (*She enters.*)

MRS. STOCKMANN (*coming in after her*).   Petra, Petra!

PETER STOCKMANN.   What have you two been doing, eavesdropping?

MRS. STOCKMANN.   You were talking so loud we couldn't help . . .

PETRA.   Yes, I was eavesdropping!

PETER STOCKMANN.   That makes me very happy.

DR. STOCKMANN (*approaching his brother*).   You said something to me about forbidding—

PETER STOCKMANN.   You forced me to.

DR. STOCKMANN.   So you want me to spit in my own face officially—is that it?

PETER STOCKMANN.   Why must you always be so colourful?

DR. STOCKMANN.   And if I don't obey?

PETER STOCKMANN.   Then we will publish our own statement, to calm the public.

DR. STOCKMANN.   Good enough! And I will write against

you. I will stick to what I said, and I will prove that I am right and that you are wrong, and what will you do then?

PETER STOCKMANN. Then I simply won't be able to prevent your dismissal.

DR. STOCKMANN. What!

PETRA. Father!

PETER STOCKMANN. Dismissed from the Institute is what I said. If you want to make war on Kirsten Springs, you have no right to be on the Board of Directors.

DR. STOCKMANN (*after a pause*). You'd dare to do that?

PETER STOCKMANN. Oh, no, you're the daring man.

PETRA. Uncle, this is a rotten way to treat a man like Father!

MRS. STOCKMANN. Will you be quiet, Petra!

PETER STOCKMANN. So young and you've got opinions already—but that's natural. (*To* MRS. STOCKMANN.) Catherine dear, you're probably the only sane person in this house. Knock some sense into his head, will you? Make him realize what he's driving his whole family into.

DR. STOCKMANN. My family concerns nobody but myself.

PETER STOCKMANN. His family and his own town.

DR. STOCKMANN. I'm going to show you who loves this town. The people are going to get the full stink of this corruption, Peter, and then we will see who loves his town!

PETER STOCKMANN. You love your town when you blindly, spitefully, stubbornly go ahead trying to cut off our most important industry?

DR. STOCKMANN. That source is poisoned, man. We are getting fat by peddling filth and corruption to innocent people!

PETER STOCKMANN. I think this has gone beyond opinions and convictions, Thomas. A man who can throw that kind of insinuation around is nothing but a traitor to society!

DR. STOCKMANN (*starting toward his brother in a fury*). How dare you to—

MRS. STOCKMANN (*stepping between them*). Tom!

PETRA (*grabbing her father's arm*).   Be careful, Father!

PETER STOCKMANN (*with dignity*).   I won't expose myself to violence. You have been warned. Consider what you owe yourself and your family! Good day! (*He exits.*)

DR. STOCKMANN (*walking up and down*).   He's insulted. *He's* insulted!

MRS. STOCKMANN.   It's shameful, Tom.

PETRA.   Oh, I would love to give him a piece of my mind!

DR. STOCKMANN.   It was my own fault! I should have shown my teeth right from the beginning. He called me a traitor to society. Me! Damn it all, that's not going to stick!

MRS. STOCKMANN.   Please, think! He's got all the power on his side.

DR. STOCKMANN.   Yes, but I have the truth on mine.

MRS. STOCKMANN.   Without power, what good is the truth?

PETRA.   Mother, how can you say such a thing?

DR. STOCKMANN.   That's ridiculous, Catherine. I have the liberal press with me, and the majority. If that isn't power, what is?

MRS. STOCKMANN.   But, for heaven's sake, Tom, you aren't going to—

DR. STOCKMANN.   What am I not going to do?

MRS. STOCKMANN.   You aren't going to fight it out in public with your brother!

DR. STOCKMANN.   What else do you want me to do?

MRS. STOCKMANN.   But it won't do you any earthly good. If they won't do it, they won't. All you'll get out of it is a notice that you're fired.

DR. STOCKMANN.   I am going to do my duty, Catherine. Me, the man he calls a traitor to society!

MRS. STOCKMANN.   And how about your duty toward your family—the people you're supposed to provide for?

PETRA.   Don't always think of us first, Mother.

MRS. STOCKMANN (*to* PETRA).   You can talk! If worst comes to worst, you can manage for yourself. But what about the boys, Tom, and you and me?

DR. STOCKMANN. What about you? You want me to be the miserable animal who'd crawl up the boots of that damn gang? Will you be happy if I can't face myself for the rest of my life?

MRS. STOCKMANN. Tom, Tom, there's so much injustice in the world! You've simply got to learn to live with it. If you go on this way, God help us, we'll have no money again. Is it so long since the north that you've forgotten what it was to live as we lived? Haven't we had enough of that for one lifetime? (*The boys enter.*) What will happen to them? We've got nothing if you're fired!

DR. STOCKMANN. Stop it! (*He looks at the boys.*) Well, boys, did you learn anything in school today?

MORTEN (*looking at them, puzzled*). We learned what an insect is.

DR. STOCKMANN. You don't say!

MORTEN. What happened here? Why is everybody—

DR. STOCKMANN. Nothing, nothing. You know what I'm going to do, boys? From now on I'm going to teach you what a man is. (*He looks at* MRS. STOCKMANN. *She cries as*

THE CURTAIN FALLS

ACT II

SCENE ONE

The editorial office of the People's Daily Messenger. *At the back of the room, to the left, is a door leading to the printing-room. Near it, in the left wall, is another door. At the right of the stage is the entrance door. In the middle of the room there is a large table covered with papers, newspapers, and books. Around it are a few chairs. A writing-desk stands against the right wall. The room is dingy and cheerless, the furniture shabby.*

As the curtain rises, BILLING *is sitting at the desk, reading the manuscript.* HOVSTAD *comes in after a moment from the printing-room.* BILLING *looks up.*

BILLING.   The Doctor not come yet?

HOVSTAD.   No, not yet. You finish it?

> (BILLING *holds up a hand to signal "just a moment." He reads on, the last paragraph of the manuscript.* HOVSTAD *comes and stands over him, reading with him. Now* BILLING *closes the manuscript, glances up at* HOVSTAD *with some trepidation, then looks off.* HOVSTAD, *looking at* BILLING, *walks a few steps away.*)

HOVSTAD.   Well? What do you think of it?

BILLING (*with some hesitation*).   It's devastating. The Doctor is a brilliant man. I swear, I myself never really understood how incompetent those fat fellows are, on top. (*He picks up the manuscript and waves it a little.*) I hear the rumble of revolution in this.

HOVSTAD (*looking toward the door*).   Sssh! Aslaksen's inside.

BILLING.   Aslaksen's a coward. With all that moderation talk, all he's saying is, he's yellow. You're going to print this, aren't you?

HOVSTAD.   Sure, I'm just waiting for the Doctor to give

the word. If his brother hasn't given in, we put it on the press anyway.

BILLING. Yes, but if the Mayor's against this it's going to get pretty rough. You know that, don't you?

HOVSTAD. Just let him try to block the reconstruction— the little businessmen and the whole town'll be screaming for his head. Aslaksen'll see to that.

BILLING (*ecstatically*). The stockholders'll have to lay out a fortune of money if this goes through!

HOVSTAD. My boy, I think it's going to bust them. And when the springs go busted, the people are finally going to understand the level of genius that's been running this town. Those five sheets of paper are going to put in a liberal administration once and for all.

BILLING. It's a revolution. You know that? (*With hope and fear.*) I mean it, we're on the edge of a real revolution!

DR. STOCKMANN (*entering*). Put it on the press!

HOVSTAD (*excited*). Wonderful! What did the Mayor say?

DR. STOCKMANN. The Mayor has declared war, so war is what it's going to be! (*He takes the manuscript from* BILLING.) And this is only the beginning! You know what he tried to do?

BILLING (*calling into the printing-room*). Mr. Aslaksen, the Doctor's here!

DR. STOCKMANN (*continuing*). He actually tried to blackmail me! He's got the nerve to tell me that I'm not allowed to speak my mind without his permission! Imagine the shameless effrontery!

HOVSTAD. He actually said it right out?

DR. STOCKMANN. Right to my face! The trouble with me was I kept giving them credit for being our kind of people, but they're dictators! They're people who'll try to hold power even if they have to poison the town to do it.

(*Toward the last part of* DR. STOCKMANN'*s speech* ASLAKSEN *enters.*)

ASLAKSEN. Now take it easy, Doctor, you—you mustn't always be throwing accusations. I'm with you, you understand, but moderation—

DR. STOCKMANN (*cutting him off*). What'd you think of the article, Hovstad?

HOVSTAD. It's a masterpiece. In one blow you've managed to prove beyond any doubt what kind of men are running us.

ASLAKSEN. May we print it now, then?

DR. STOCKMANN. I should say *so!*

HOVSTAD. We'll have it ready for tomorrow's paper.

DR. STOCKMANN. And listen, Mr. Aslaksen, do me a favour, will you? You run a fine paper, but supervise the printing personally, eh? I'd hate to see the weather report stuck into the middle of my article.

ASLAKSEN (*laughing*). Don't worry, that won't happen this time!

DR. STOCKMANN. Make it perfect, eh? As if you were printing money. You can't imagine how I'm dying to see it in print. After all the lies in the papers, the half-lies, the quarter-lies—to finally see the absolute, unvarnished truth about something important. And this is only the beginning. We'll go on to other subjects and blow up every lie we live by! What do you say, Aslaksen?

ASLAKSEN (*nodding in agreement*). But just remember . . .

BILLING *and* HOVSTAD *together with* ASLAKSEN. Moderation!

ASLAKSEN (*to* BILLING *and* HOVSTAD). I don't know what's so funny about that!

BILLING (*enthralled*). Doctor Stockmann, I feel as though I were standing in some historic painting. Goddammit, this is a historic day! Someday this scene'll be in a museum, entitled, "The Day the Truth Was Born".

DR. STOCKMANN (*suddenly*). Oh! I've got a patient half-bandaged down the street. (*He leaves.*)

HOVSTAD (*to* ASLAKSEN). I hope you realize how useful he could be to us.

ASLAKSEN. I don't like that business about "this is only the beginning." Let him stick to the springs.

BILLING. What makes you so scared all the time?

ASLAKSEN. I have to live here. It'd be different if he were attacking the national government or something, but if he thinks I'm going to start going after the whole town administration—

BILLING. What's the difference? Bad is bad!

ASLAKSEN. Yes, but there is a difference. You attack the national government, what's going to happen? Nothing. They go right on. But a town administration—they're liable to be overthrown or something! I represent the small property owners in this town—

BILLING. Ha! It's always the same. Give a man a little property and the truth can go to hell!

ASLAKSEN. Mr. Billing, I'm older than you are. I've seen fire-eaters before. You know who used to work at that desk before you? Councilman Stensford—*councilman*!

BILLING. Just because I work at a renegade's desk, does that mean—

ASLAKSEN. You're a politician. A politician never knows where he's going to end up. And besides you applied for a job as secretary to the Magistrate, didn't you?

HOVSTAD (*surprised, laughs*). Billing.

BILLING (*to* HOVSTAD). Well, why not? If I get it I'll have a chance to put across some good things. I could put plenty of big boys on the spot with a job like that!

ASLAKSEN. All right, I'm just saying. (*He goes to the printing-room door.*) People change. Just remember when you call me a coward—I may not have made the hot speeches, but I never went back on my beliefs either. Unlike some of the big radicals around here, I didn't change. Of course, I *am* a little more moderate, but moderation is—

HOVSTAD. Oh, God!

ASLAKSEN. I don't see what's so funny about that! (*He glares at* HOVSTAD *and goes out.*)

BILLING. If we could get rid of him we—

HOVSTAD. Take it easy—he pays the printing bill, he's not that bad. (*He picks up the manuscript.*) I'll get the printer on this. (*He starts out.*)

BILLING. Say, Hovstad, how about asking Stockmann to back us? Then we could really put out a paper!

HOVSTAD. What would he do for money?

BILLING. His father-in-law.

HOVSTAD. Kiil? Since when has he got money?

BILLING. I think he's loaded with it.

HOVSTAD. No! Why, as long as I've known him he's worn the same overcoat, the same suit—

BILLING. Yeah, and the same ring on his right hand. You ever get a look at that boulder? (*He points to his finger.*)

HOVSTAD. No, I never—

BILLING. All year he wears the diamond inside, but on New Year's Eve he turns it around. Figure it out—when a man has no visible means of support, what is he living on? Money, right?

(PETRA *enters, carrying a book.*)

PETRA. Hello.

HOVSTAD. Well, fancy seeing you here. Sit down. What—

PETRA (*walking slowly up to* HOVSTAD). I want to ask you a question. (*She starts to open the book.*)

BILLING. What's that?

PETRA. The English novel you wanted translated.

HOVSTAD. Aren't you going to do it?

PETRA (*with deadly seriousness and curiosity*). I don't get this.

HOVSTAD. You don't get what?

PETRA. This book is absolutely against everything you people believe.

HOVSTAD. Oh, it isn't that bad.

PETRA. But, Mr. Hovstad, it says if you're good there's a supernatural force that'll fix it so you end up happy. And if you're bad you'll be punished. Since when does the world work that way?

HOVSTAD.   Yes, Petra, but this is a newspaper, people like to read that kind of thing. They buy the paper for that and then we slip in our political stuff. A newspaper can't buck the public—

PETRA (*astonished, beginning to be angry*).   You don't say! (*She starts to go.*)

HOVSTAD (*hurrying after her*).   Now, wait a minute, I don't want you to go feeling that way. (*He holds the manuscript out to* BILLING.) Here, take this to the printer, will you?

BILLING (*taking the manuscript*).   Sure. (*He goes.*)

HOVSTAD.   I just want you to understand something. I never even read that book. It was Billing's idea.

PETRA (*trying to penetrate his eyes*).   I thought he was a radical.

HOVSTAD.   He is. But he's also a—

PETRA (*testily*).   A newspaperman.

HOVSTAD.   Well, that too, but I was going to say that Billing is trying to get the job as secretary to the Magistrate.

PETRA.   What?

HOVSTAD.   People are—people, Miss Stockmann.

PETRA.   But the Magistrate! He's been fighting everything progressive in this town for thirty years.

HOVSTAD.   Let's not argue about it, I just didn't want you to go out of here with a wrong idea of me. I guess you know that I—I happen to admire women like you. I've never had a chance to tell you, but I—well, I want you to know it. Do you mind? (*He smiles.*)

PETRA.   No, I don't mind, but—reading that book upset me. I really don't understand. Will you tell me why you're supporting my father?

HOVSTAD.   What's the mystery? It's a matter of principle.

PETRA.   But a paper that'll print a book like this has no principle.

HOVSTAD.   Why do you jump to such extremes? You're just like . . .

PETRA.   Like what?

HOVSTAD.   I simply mean that . . .

PETRA (*moving away from him*).   Like my father, you mean. You really have no use for him, do you?

HOVSTAD.   Now wait a minute!

PETRA.   What's behind this? Are you just trying to hold my hand or something?

HOVSTAD.   I happen to agree with your father, and that's why I'm printing his stuff.

PETRA.   You're trying to put something over, I think. Why are you in this?

HOVSTAD.   Who're you accusing? Billing gave you that book, not me!

PETRA.   But you don't mind printing it, do you? What are you trying to do with my father? You have no principles —what are you up to here?

(ASLAKSEN *hurriedly enters from the printing-shop,* STOCKMANN's *manuscript in his hand.*)

ASLAKSEN.   My God! Hovstad! (*He sees* PETRA.) Miss Stockmann.

PETRA (*looking at* HOVSTAD).   I don't think I've been so frightened in my life. (*She goes out.*)

HOVSTAD (*starting after her*).   Please, you mustn't think I—

ASLAKSEN (*stopping him*).   Where are you going? The Mayor's out there.

HOVSTAD.   The Mayor!

ASLAKSEN.   He wants to speak to you. He came in the back door. He doesn't want to be seen.

HOVSTAD.   What does he want? (*He goes to the printing-room door, opens it, calls out with a certain edge of servility.*) Come in, Your Honour!

PETER STOCKMANN (*entering*).   Thank you.

(HOVSTAD *carefully closes the door.*)

PETER STOCKMANN (*walking around*). It's clean! I always imagined this place would look dirty. But it's clean. (*Commendingly.*) Very nice, Mr. Aslaksen. (*He puts his hat on the desk.*)

ASLAKSEN. Not at all, Your Honour—I mean to say, I always . . .

HOVSTAD. What can I do for you, Your Honour? Sit down.

PETER STOCKMANN (*sits, placing his cane on the table*). I had a very annoying thing happen today, Mr. Hovstad.

HOVSTAD. That so?

PETER STOCKMANN. It seems my brother has written some sort of—memorandum. About the springs.

HOVSTAD. You don't say.

PETER STOCKMANN (*looking at* HOVSTAD *now*). He mentioned it . . . to you?

HOVSTAD. Yes. I think he said something about it.

ASLAKSEN (*nervously starts to go out, attempting to hide the manuscript*). Will you excuse me, gentlemen . . .

PETER STOCKMANN (*pointing to the manuscript*). That's it, isn't it?

ASLAKSEN. This? I don't know, I haven't had a chance to look at it, the printer just handed it to me . . .

HOVSTAD. Isn't that the thing in which the printer wanted the spelling checked?

ASLAKSEN. That's it, it's only a question of spelling. I'll be right back.

PETER STOCKMANN. I'm very good at spelling. (*He holds out his hand.*) Maybe I can help you.

HOVSTAD. No, Your Honour, there's some Latin in it. You wouldn't know Latin, would you?

PETER STOCKMANN. Oh, yes. I used to help my brother with his Latin all the time. Let me have it.

(ASLAKSEN *gives him the manuscript.* PETER STOCK-MANN *looks at the title on the first page, then glances up sarcastically at* HOVSTAD, *who avoids his eyes.*)

PETER STOCKMANN. You're going to print this?

HOVSTAD. I can't very well refuse a signed article. A signed article is the author's responsibility.

PETER STOCKMANN. Mr. Aslaksen, you're going to allow this?

ASLAKSEN. I'm the publisher, not the editor, Your Honour. My policy is freedom for the editor.

PETER STOCKMANN. You have a point—I can see that.

ASLAKSEN (*reaching for the manuscript*). So if you don't mind . . .

PETER STOCKMANN. Not at all. (*But he holds on to the manuscript. After a pause*) This reconstruction of the springs—

ASLAKSEN. I realize, Your Honour—it does mean tremendous sacrifices for the stockholders.

PETER STOCKMANN. Don't upset yourself. The first thing a Mayor learns is that the less wealthy can always be prevailed upon to demand a spirit of sacrifice for the public good.

ASLAKSEN. I'm glad you see that.

PETER STOCKMANN. Oh, yes. Especially when it's the wealthy who are going to do the sacrificing. What you don't seem to understand, Mr. Aslaksen, is that so long as I am Mayor, any changes in those springs are going to be paid for by a municipal loan.

ASLAKSEN. A municipal—you mean you're going to tax the people for this?

PETER STOCKMANN. Exactly.

HOVSTAD. But the springs are a private corporation!

PETER STOCKMANN. The corporation built Kirsten Springs out of its own money. If the people want them changed, the people naturally must pay the bill. The corporation is in no position to put out any more money. It simply can't do it.

ASLAKSEN (*to* HOVSTAD). That's impossible! People will never stand for a new tax. (*To the* MAYOR.) Is this a fact or your opinion?

PETER STOCKMANN. It happens to be a fact. Plus another

fact—you'll forgive me for talking about facts in a newspaper office—but don't forget that the springs will take two years to make over. Two years without income for your small businessmen, Mr. Aslaksen, and a heavy new tax besides. And all because—(*his private emotion comes to the surface; he throttles the manuscript in his hand*)—because of this dream, this hallucination, that we live in a pest-hole!

HOVSTAD. That's based on science.

PETER STOCKMANN (*raising the manuscript and throwing it down on the table*). This is based on vindictiveness, on his hatred of authority and nothing else. (*He pounds on the manuscript.*) This is the mad dream of a man who is trying to blow up our way of life! It has nothing to do with reform or science or anything else, but pure and simple destruction! And I intend to see to it that the people understand it exactly so!

ASLAKSEN (*hit by this*). My God! (*To* HOVSTAD.) Maybe . . . You sure you want to support this thing, Hovstad?

HOVSTAD (*nervously*). Frankly I'd never thought of it in quite that way. I mean . . . (*To the* MAYOR.) When you think of it psychologically it's completely possible, of course, that the man is simply out to—I don't know what to say, Your Honour. I'd hate to hurt the town in any way. I never imagined we'd have to have a new tax.

PETER STOCKMANN. You should have imagined it because you're going to have to advocate it. Unless, of course, liberal and radical newspaper readers enjoy high taxes. But you'd know that better than I. I happen to have here a brief story of the actual facts. It proves that, with a little care, nobody need be harmed at all by the water. (*He takes out a long envelope.*) Of course, in time we'd have to make a few minor structural changes and we'd pay for those.

HOVSTAD. May I see that?

PETER STOCKMANN. I want you to *study* it, Mr. Hovstad, and see if you don't agree that—

BILLING (*entering quickly*).   Are you expecting the Doctor?

PETER STOCKMANN (*alarmed*).   He's here?

BILLING.   Just coming across the street.

PETER STOCKMANN.   I'd rather not run into him here. How can I . . .

BILLING.   Right this way, sir, hurry up!

ASLAKSEN (*at the entrance door, peeking*).   Hurry up!

PETER STOCKMANN (*going with* BILLING *through the door at the left.*) Get him out of here right away! (*They exit.*)

HOVSTAD.   Do something, do something!

> (ASLAKSEN *pokes among some papers on the table.*
> HOVSTAD *sits at the desk, starts to "write". DR.*
> STOCKMANN *enters.*)

DR. STOCKMANN.   Any proofs yet? (*He sees they hardly turn to him.*) I guess not, eh?

ASLAKSEN (*without turning*).   No, you can't expect them for some time.

DR. STOCKMANN.   You mind if I wait?

HOVSTAD.   No sense in that, Doctor, it'll be quite a while yet.

DR. STOCKMANN (*laughing, places his hand on* HOVSTAD's *back*). Bear with me, Hovstad, I just can't wait to see it in print.

HOVSTAD.   We're pretty busy, Doctor, so . . .

DR. STOCKMANN (*starting toward the door*).   Don't let me hold you up. That's the way to be, busy, busy. We'll make this town shine like a jewel! (*He has opened the door, now he comes back.*) Just one thing. I—

HOVSTAD.   Couldn't we talk some other time?. We're very—

DR. STOCKMANN.   Two words. Just walking down the street now, I looked at the people, in the stores, driving the wagons, and suddenly I was—well, touched, you know? By their innocence, I mean. What I'm driving at is, when this exposé breaks they're liable to start making a saint out of me or something, and I—Aslaksen, I want you to promise me that you're not going to try to get up any dinner for me or—

ASLAKSEN (*turning toward the* DOCTOR). Doctor, there's no use concealing—

DR. STOCKMANN. I knew it. Now look, I will simply not attend a dinner in my honour.

HOVSTAD (*getting up*). Doctor, I think it's time we—

(MRS. STOCKMANN *enters.*)

MRS. STOCKMANN. I thought so. Thomas, I want you home. Now come. I want you to talk to Petra.

DR. STOCKMANN. What happened? What are you doing here?

HOVSTAD. Something wrong, Mrs. Stockmann?

MRS. STOCKMANN (*levelling a look of accusation at* HOV-STAD). Doctor Stockmann is the father of three children, Mr. Hovstad.

DR. STOCKMANN. Now look, dear, everybody knows that. What's the—

MRS. STOCKMANN (*restraining an outburst at her husband*). Nobody would *believe* it from the way you're dragging us into this disaster!

DR. STOCKMANN. What disaster?

MRS. STOCKMANN (*to* HOVSTAD). He treated you like a son, now you make a fool of him?

HOVSTAD. *I'm* not making a—

DR. STOCKMANN. Catherine! (*He indicates* HOVSTAD.) How can you accuse—

MRS. STOCKMANN (*to* HOVSTAD). He'll lose his job at the springs, do you realize that? You print the article, and they'll grind him up like a piece of flesh!

DR. STOCKMANN. Catherine, you're embarrassing me! I beg your pardon, gentlemen . . .

MRS. STOCKMANN. Mr. Hovstad, what are you up to?

DR. STOCKMANN. I won't have you jumping at Hovstad, Catherine!

MRS. STOCKMANN.   I want you home! This man is not your friend!

DR. STOCKMANN.   He is my friend! Any man who shares my risk is my friend! You simply don't understand that as soon as this breaks everybody in this town is going to come out in the streets and drive that gang of—(*He picks up the* MAYOR's *cane from the table, notices what it is, and stops. He looks from it to* HOVSTAD *and* ASLAKSEN.) What's this? (*They don't reply. Now he notices the hat on the desk and picks it up with the tip of the cane. He looks at them again. He is angry, incredulous.*) What is he doing here?

ASLAKSEN.   All right, Doctor, now let's be calm and—

DR. STOCKMANN (*starting to move*).   Where is he? What'd he do, talk you out of it? Hovstad! (HOVSTAD *remains immobile.*) He won't get away with it! Where'd you hide him? (*He opens the door at the left.*)

ASLAKSEN.   Be careful, Doctor!

> (PETER STOCKMANN *enters with* BILLING *through the door* DR. STOCKMANN *opened.* PETER STOCKMANN *tries to hide his embarrassment.*)

DR. STOCKMANN.   Well, Peter, poisoning the water was not enough! You're working on the press now, eh? (*He crosses to the entrance door.*)

PETER STOCKMANN.   My hat, please. And my stick. (DR. STOCKMANN *puts on the* MAYOR's *hat.*) Now what's *this* nonsense! Take that off, that's official insignia!

DR. STOCKMANN.   I just wanted you to realize, Peter—(*he takes off the hat and looks at it*)—that anyone may wear this hat in a democracy, and that a free citizen is not afraid to touch it. (*He hands him the hat.*) And as for the baton of command, Your Honour, it can pass from hand to hand. (*He hands the cane to* PETER STOCKMANN.) So don't gloat yet. The people haven't spoken. (*He turns to* HOVSTAD *and* ASLAKSEN.) And I have the people because I have the truth, my friends!

ASLAKSEN. Doctor, we're not scientists. We can't judge whether your article is really true.

DR. STOCKMANN. Then print it under my name. Let *me* defend it!

HOVSTAD. I'm not printing it. I'm not going to sacrifice this newspaper. When the whole story gets out the public is not going to stand for any changes in the springs.

ASLAKSEN. His Honour just told us, Doctor—you see, there will have to be a new tax—

DR. STOCKMANN. Ahhhhh! Yes, I see. That's why you're not scientists suddenly and can't decide if I'm telling the truth. Well. So!

HOVSTAD. Don't take that attitude. The point is—

DR. STOCKMANN. The point, the point, oh, the point is going to fly through this town like an arrow, and I am going to fire it! (*To* ASLAKSEN.) Will you print this article as a pamphlet? I'll pay for it.

ASLAKSEN. I'm not going to ruin this paper and this town. Doctor, for the sake of your family—

MRS. STOCKMANN. You can leave his family out of this, Mr. Aslaksen. God help me, I think you people are horrible!

DR. STOCKMANN. My article, if you don't mind.

ASLAKSEN (*giving it to him*). Doctor, you won't get it printed in this town.

PETER STOCKMANN. Can't you forget it? (*He indicates* HOVSTAD *and* ASLAKSEN.) Can't you see now that everybody—

DR. STOCKMANN. Your Honour, I can't forget it, and you will never forget it as long as you live. I am going to call a mass meeting, and I—

PETER STOCKMANN. And who is going to rent you a hall?

DR. STOCKMANN. Then I will take a drum and go from street to street, proclaiming that the springs are befouled and poison is rotting the body politic! (*He starts for the door.*)

PETER STOCKMANN. And I believe you really are that mad!

DR. STOCKMANN. Mad? Oh, my brother, you haven't

even heard me raise my voice yet. Catherine? (*He holds out his hand, she gives him her elbow. They go stiffly out.*)

(PETER STOCKMANN *looks regretfully toward the exit, then takes out his manuscript and hands it to* HOVSTAD, *who in turn gives it to* BILLING, *who hands it to* ASLAKSEN, *who takes it and exits.* PETER STOCKMANN *puts his hat on and moves toward the door. Blackout.*)

THE CURTAIN FALLS

SCENE TWO

A room in CAPTAIN HORSTER's *house. The room is bare, as though unused for a long time. A large doorway is at the left, two shuttered windows at the back, and another door at the right. Upstage right, packing cases have been set together, forming a platform, on which are a chair and a small table. There are two chairs next to the platform at the right. One chair stands downstage left.*

The room is angled, thus making possible the illusion of a large crowd off in the wing to the left. The platform faces the audience at an angle, thus giving the speakers the chance to speak straight out front and creating the illusion of a large crowd by addressing "people" in the audience.

As the curtain rises the room is empty. CAPTAIN HORSTER *enters, carrying a pitcher of water, a glass, and a bell. He is putting these on the table when* BILLING *enters. A crowd is heard talking outside in the street.*

BILLING.   Captain Horster?

HORSTER (*turning*).   Oh, come in. I don't have enough chairs for a lot of people so I decided not to have chairs at all.

BILLING.   My name is Billing. Don't you remember, at the Doctor's house?

HORSTER (*a little coldly*). Oh, yes, sure. I've been so busy I didn't recognize you. (*He goes to a window and looks out.*) Why don't those people come inside?

BILLING. I don't know. I guess they're waiting for the Mayor or somebody important so they can be sure it's respectable in here. I wanted to ask you a question before it begins, Captain. Why are you lending your house for this? I never heard of you connected with anything political.

HORSTER (*standing still*). I'll answer that. I travel most of the year and—did you ever travel?

BILLING. Not abroad, no.

HORSTER. Well, I've been in a lot of places where people aren't allowed to say unpopular things. Did you know that?

BILLING. Sure, I've read about it.

HORSTER (*simply*). Well, I don't like it. (*He starts to go out.*)

BILLING. One more question. What's your opinion about the Doctor's proposition to rebuild the springs?

HORSTER (*turning, thinks, then*) Don't understand a thing about it.

(THREE CITIZENS *enter.*)

HORSTER. Come in, come in. I don't have enough chairs so you'll just have to stand. (*He goes out.*)

FIRST CITIZEN. Try the horn.

SECOND CITIZEN. No, let him start to talk first.

THIRD CITIZEN (*a big beef of a man, takes out a horn*). Wait'll they hear this! I could blow your moustache off with this!

(HORSTER *returns. He sees the horn and stops abruptly.*)

HORSTER. I don't want any roughhouse, you hear me?

(MRS. STOCKMANN *and* PETRA *enter.*)

HORSTER. Come in. I've got chairs just for you.

MRS. STOCKMANN (*nervously*). There's quite a crowd on the sidewalk. Why don't they come in?

HORSTER.   I suppose they're waiting for the Mayor.

PETRA.   Are all those people on his side?

HORSTER.   Who knows? People are bashful, and it's so unusual to come to a meeting like this, I suppose they—

BILLING (*going over to this group*).   Good evening, ladies. (*They simply look at him.*) I don't blame you for not speaking. I just wanted to say I don't think this is going to be a place for ladies tonight.

MRS. STOCKMANN.   I don't remember asking your advice, Mr. Billing.

BILLING.   I'm not as bad as you think, Mrs. Stockmann.

MRS. STOCKMANN.   Then why did you print the Mayor's statement and not a word about my husband's report? Nobody's had a chance to find out what he really stands for. Why, everybody on the street there is against him already!

BILLING.   If we printed his report it only would have hurt your husband.

MRS. STOCKMANN.   Mr. Billing, I've never said this to anyone in my life, but I think you're a liar.

> (*Suddenly the* THIRD CITIZEN *lets out a blast on his horn. The women jump,* BILLING *and* HORSTER *turn around quickly.*)

HORSTER.   You do that once more and I'll throw you out of here!

> (PETER STOCKMANN *enters. Behind him comes the crowd. He pretends to be unconnected with them. He goes straight to* MRS. STOCKMANN, *bows.*)

PETER STOCKMANN.   Catherine? Petra?

PETRA.   Good evening.

PETER STOCKMANN.   Why so coldly? He wanted a meeting and he's got it. (*To* HORSTER.) Isn't he here?

HORSTER.   The Doctor is going around town to be sure there's a good attendance.

PETER STOCKMANN.   Fair enough. By the way, Petra, did

you paint that poster? The one somebody stuck on the Town Hall?

PETRA.   If you can call it painting, yes.

PETER STOCKMANN.   You know I could arrest you? It's against the law to deface the Town Hall.

PETRA.   Well, here I am. (*She holds out her hands for the handcuffs.*)

MRS. STOCKMANN (*taking it seriously*).   If you arrest her, Peter, I'll never speak to you!

PETER STOCKMANN (*laughing*).   Catherine, you have no sense of humour!

> (*He crosses and sits down at the left. They sit right. A* DRUNK *comes out of the crowd.*)

DRUNK.   Say, Billy, who's runnin'? Who's the candidate?

HORSTER.   You're drunk, Mister, now get out of here!

DRUNK.   There's no law says a man who's drunk can't vote!

HORSTER (*pushing the* DRUNK *toward the door as the crowd laughs*).   Get out of here! Get out!

DRUNK.   I wanna vote! I got a right to vote!

> (ASLAKSEN *enters hurriedly, sees* PETER STOCKMANN, *and rushes to him.*)

ASLAKSEN.   Your Honour . . . (*He points to the door.*) He's . . .

DR. STOCKMANN (*offstage*).   Right this way, gentlemen! In you go, come on, fellows!

> (HOVSTAD *enters, glances at* PETER STOCKMANN *and* ASLAKSEN, *then at* DR. STOCKMANN *and another crowd behind him, who enter.*)

DR. STOCKMANN.   Sorry, no chairs, gentlemen, but we couldn't get a hall, y'know, so just relax. It won't take long anyway. (*He goes to the platform, sees* PETER STOCKMANN.) Glad you're here, Peter!

PETER STOCKMANN.   Wouldn't miss it for the world.

DR. STOCKMANN.   How do you feel, Catherine?

MRS. STOCKMANN (*nervously*). Just promise me, don't lose your temper . . .

HORSTER (*seeing the* DRUNK *pop in through the door*). Did I tell you to get out of here!

DRUNK. Look, if you ain't voting, what the hell's going on here? (HORSTER *starts after him.*) Don't push!

PETER STOCKMANN (*to the* DRUNK). I order you to get out of here and stay out!

DRUNK. I don't like the tone of your voice! And if you don't watch your step I'm going to tell the Mayor right now, and he'll throw yiz all in the jug! (*To all.*) What're you, a revolution here?

> (*The crowd bursts out laughing; the* DRUNK *laughs with them, and they push him out.* DR. STOCKMANN *mounts the platform.*)

DR. STOCKMANN (*quieting the crowd*). All right, gentlemen, we might as well begin. Quiet down, please. (*He clears his throat.*) The issue is very simple—

ASLAKSEN. We haven't elected a chairman, Doctor.

DR. STOCKMANN. I'm sorry, Mr. Aslaksen, this isn't a meeting. I advertised a lecture and I—

A CITIZEN. I came to a meeting, Doctor. There's got to be some kind of control here.

DR. STOCKMANN. What do you mean, control? What is there to control?

SECOND CITIZEN. Sure, let him speak, this is no meeting!

THIRD CITIZEN. Your Honour, why don't you take charge of this—

DR. STOCKMANN. Just a minute now!

THIRD CITIZEN. Somebody responsible has got to take charge. There's a big difference of opinion here—

DR. STOCKMANN. What makes you so sure? You don't even know yet what I'm going to say.

THIRD CITIZEN. I've got a pretty good idea what you're going to say, and I don't like it! If a man doesn't like it here, let him go where it suits him better. We don't want any troublemakers here!

> (*There is assent from much of the crowd.* DR. STOCK-MANN *looks at them with new surprise.*)

DR. STOCKMANN.   Now look, friend, you don't know anything about me—

FOURTH CITIZEN.   We know plenty about you, Stockmann!

DR. STOCKMANN.   From what? From the newspapers? How do you know I don't like this town? (*He picks up his manuscript.*) I'm here to save the life of this town!

PETER STOCKMANN (*quickly*).   Now just a minute, Doctor, I think the democratic thing to do is to elect a chairman.

FIFTH CITIZEN.   I nominate the Mayor!

> (*Seconds are heard.*)

PETER STOCKMANN.   No, no, no! That wouldn't be fair. We want a neutral person. I suggest Mr. Aslaksen—

SECOND CITIZEN.   I came to a lecture, I didn't—

THIRD CITIZEN (*to* SECOND CITIZEN).   What're you afraid of, a fair fight? (*To the* MAYOR.) Second Mr. Aslaksen!

> (*The crowd assents.*)

DR. STOCKMANN.   All right, if that's your pleasure. I just want to remind you that the reason I called this meeting was that I have a very important message for you people and I couldn't get it into the press, and nobody would rent me a hall. (*To* PETER STOCKMANN.) I just hope I'll be given time to speak here. Mr. Aslaksen?

> (*As* MR. ASLAKSEN *mounts the platform and* DR. STOCKMANN *steps down,* KIIL *enters, looks shrewdly around.*)

ASLAKSEN.   I just have one word before we start. Whatever is said tonight, please remember, the highest civic virtue is moderation. (*He can't help turning to* DR. STOCKMANN, *then back to the crowd.*) Now if anybody wants to speak—

> (*The* DRUNK *enters suddenly.*)

DRUNK (*pointing at* ASLAKSEN). I heard that! Since when you allowed to electioneer at the polls? (*Citizens push him toward the door amid laughter.*) I'm gonna report this to the Mayor! (*They push him out and close the door.*)

ASLAKSEN. Quiet, please, quiet. Does anybody want the floor?

> (DR. STOCKMANN *starts to come forward, raising his hand, but* PETER STOCKMANN *also has his hand raised.*)

PETER STOCKMANN. Mr. Chairman!

ASLAKSEN (*quickly recognizing* PETER STOCKMANN). His Honour the Mayor will address the meeting.

> (DR. STOCKMANN *stops, looks at* PETER STOCKMANN, *and, suppressing a remark, returns to his place. The* MAYOR *mounts the platform.*)

PETER STOCKMANN. Gentlemen, there's no reason to take very long to settle this tonight and return to our ordinary, calm, and peaceful life. Here's the issue: Doctor Stockmann, my brother—and believe me, it is not easy to say this—has decided to destroy Kirsten Springs, our Health Institute—

DR. STOCKMANN. Peter!

ASLAKSEN (*ringing his bell*). Let the Mayor continue, please. There mustn't be any interruptions.

PETER STOCKMANN. He has a long and very involved way of going about it, but that's the brunt of it, believe me.

THIRD CITIZEN. Then what're we wasting time for? Run him out of town!

> (*Others join in the cry.*)

PETER STOCKMANN. Now wait a minute. I want no violence here. I want you to understand his motives. He is a man, always has been, who is never happy unless he is badgering authority, ridiculing authority, destroying authority. He wants to attack the springs so he can prove that the administration blundered in the construction.

DR. STOCKMANN (*to* ASLAKSEN). May I speak? I—

ASLAKSEN. The Mayor's not finished.

PETER STOCKMANN. Thank you. Now there are a number of people here who seem to feel that the Doctor has a right to say anything he pleases. After all, we are a democratic country. Now, God knows, in ordinary times I'd agree a hundred per cent with anybody's right to say anything. But these are not ordinary times. Nations have crises, and so do towns. There are ruins of nations, and there are ruins of towns all over the world, and they were wrecked by people who, in the guise of reform, and pleading for justice, and so on, broke down all authority and left only revolution and chaos.

DR. STOCKMANN. What are you talking about!

ASLAKSEN. I'll have to insist, Doctor—

DR. STOCKMANN. I called a lecture! I didn't invite him to attack me. He's got the press and every hall in town to attack me, and I've got nothing but this room tonight!

ASLAKSEN. I don't think you're making a very good impression, Doctor.

(*Assenting laughter and cat-calls. Again* DR. STOCK-MANN *is taken aback by this reaction.*)

ASLAKSEN. Please continue, Your Honour.

PETER STOCKMANN. Now this is our crisis. We know what this town was without our Institute. We could barely afford to keep the streets in condition. It was a dead, third-rate hamlet. Today we're just on the verge of becoming internationally known as a resort. I predict that within five years the income of every man in this room will be immensely greater. I predict that our schools will be bigger and better. And in time this town will be crowded with fine carriages; great homes will be built here; first-class stores will open all along Main Street. I predict that if we are not defamed and maliciously attacked we will someday be one of the richest and most beautiful resort towns in the world. There are your choices. Now all you've got to do is ask yourselves a simple question: Has any of us the right, the "democratic right", as they like to call it, to pick at minor flaws in the springs, to exaggerate the most picayune faults? (*Cries of No, No!*) And to attempt to publish these defamations for the whole world to see? We live or die on what the outside world thinks of us. I believe there is a line that must be drawn, and if a man decides to cross that line, we the people must finally take him by the collar and declare, "You cannot say that!"

(*There is an uproar of assent.* ASLAKSEN *rings the bell.*)

PETER STOCKMANN (*continuing*).   All right, then. I think we all understand each other. Mr. Aslaksen, I move that Doctor Stockmann be prohibited from reading his report at this meeting! (*He goes back to his chair, which meanwhile* KIIL *has occupied.*)

(ASLAKSEN *rings the bell to quiet the enthusiasm.* DR. STOCKMANN *is jumping to get up on the platform, the report in his hand.*)

ASLAKSEN.   Quiet, please. Please now. I think we can proceed to the vote.

DR. STOCKMANN.   Well, aren't you going to let me speak at all?

ASLAKSEN.   Doctor, we are just about to vote on that question.

DR. STOCKMANN.   But damn it, man, I've got a right to—

PETRA (*standing up*).   Point of order, Father!

DR. STOCKMANN (*picking up the cue*).   Yes, point of order.

ASLAKSEN (*turning to him now*).   Yes, Doctor.

(DR. STOCKMANN, *at a loss, turns to* PETRA *for further instructions.*)

PETRA.   You want to discuss the motion.

DR. STOCKMANN.   That's right, damn it, I want to discuss the motion!

ASLAKSEN.   Ah . . . (*He glances at* PETER STOCKMANN.) All right, go ahead.

DR. STOCKMANN (*to the crowd*). Now, listen. (*He points at* PETER STOCKMANN.) He talks and he talks and he talks, but not a word about the facts! (*He holds up the manuscript.*)

THIRD CITIZEN. We don't want to hear any more about the water!

FOURTH CITIZEN. You're just trying to blow up everything!

DR. STOCKMANN. Well, judge for yourselves, let me read—

(*Cries of No, No, No! The man with the horn blows it.* ASLAKSEN *rings the bell.* DR. STOCKMANN *is utterly shaken. Astonished, he looks at the maddened faces. He lowers the hand holding the manuscript and steps back, defeated.*)

ASLAKSEN. Please, please now, quiet. We can't have this uproar! (*Quiet returns.*) I think, Doctor, that the majority wants to take the vote before you start to speak. If they so will, you can speak. Otherwise, majority rules. You won't deny that.

DR. STOCKMANN (*turns, tosses the manuscript on the floor, turns back to* ASLAKSEN). Don't bother voting. I understand everything now. Can I have a few minutes—

PETER STOCKMANN. Mr. Chairman!

DR. STOCKMANN (*to his brother*). I won't mention the Institute. I have a new discovery that's a thousand times more important than all the Institutes in the world. (*To* ASLAKSEN.) May I have the platform?

ASLAKSEN (*to the crowd*). I don't see how we can deny him that, as long as he confines himself to—

DR. STOCKMANN. The springs are not the subject. (*He mounts the platform, looks at the crowd.*) Before I go into my subject I want to congratulate the liberals and radicals among us, like Mr. Hovstad—

HOVSTAD. What do you mean, radical! Where's your evidence to call me a radical!

DR. STOCKMANN. You've got me there. There isn't any

evidence. I guess there never really was. I just wanted to congratulate you on your self-control tonight—you who have fought in every parlour for the principle of free speech these many years.

HOVSTAD.   I believe in democracy. When my readers are overwhelmingly against something, I'm not going to impose my will on the majority.

DR. STOCKMANN.   You have begun my remarks, Mr. Hovstad. (*He turns to the crowd.*) Gentlemen, Mrs. Stockmann, Miss Stockmann. Tonight I was struck by a sudden flash of light, a discovery second to none. But before I tell it to you— a little story. I put in a good many years in the north of our country. Up there the rulers of the world are the great seal and the gigantic squadrons of duck. Man lives on ice, huddled together in little piles of stones. His whole life consists of grubbing for food. Nothing more. He can barely speak his own language. And it came to me one day that it was romantic and sentimental for a man of my education to be tending these people. They had not yet reached the stage where they needed a doctor. If the truth were to be told, a veterinary would be more in order.

BILLING.   Is that the way you refer to decent hard-working people!

DR. STOCKMANN.   I expected that, my friend, but don't think you can fog up my brain with that magic word—the People! Not any more! Just because there is a mass of organisms with the human shape, they do not automatically become a People. That honour has to be earned! Nor does one automatically become a Man by having human shape, and living in a house, and eating—and agreeing with one's neighbours. That name *also* has to be earned. Now, when I came to my conclusions about the springs—

PETER STOCKMANN.   You have no right to—

DR. STOCKMANN.   That's a picayune thing, to catch me on a word, Peter. I am not going into the springs. (*To the crowd.*) When I became convinced of my theory about the water, the authorities moved in at once, and I said to myself, I will fight them to the death, because—

THIRD CITIZEN. What're you trying to do, make a revolution here? He's a revolutionist!

DR. STOCKMANN. Let me finish. I thought to myself: The majority, I have the majority! And let me tell you, friends, it was a grand feeling. Because that's the reason I came back to this place of my birth. I wanted to give my education to this town. I loved it so, I spent months without pay or encouragement and dreamed up the whole project of the springs. And why? Not as my brother says, so that fine carriages could crowd our streets, but so that we might cure the sick, so that we might meet people from all over the world and learn from them, and become broader and more civilized. In other words, more like Men, more like A People.

A CITIZEN. You don't like anything about this town, do you?

ANOTHER CITIZEN. Admit it, you're a revolutionist, aren't you? Admit it!

DR. STOCKMANN. I don't admit it! I proclaim it now! I am a revolutionist! I am in revolt against the age-old lie that the majority is always right!

HOVSTAD. He's an aristocrat all of a sudden!

DR. STOCKMANN. And more! I tell you now that the majority is always wrong, and in this way!

PETER STOCKMANN. Have you lost your mind! Stop talking before—

DR. STOCKMANN. Was the majority right when they stood by while Jesus was crucified? (*Silence.*) Was the majority right when they refused to believe that the earth moved around the sun and let Galileo be driven to his knees like a dog? It takes fifty years for the majority to be right. The majority is never right until it *does* right.

HOVSTAD. I want to state right now, that although I've been this man's friend, and I've eaten at his table many times, I now cut myself off from him absolutely.

DR. STOCKMANN.   Answer me this! Please, one more moment! A platoon of soldiers is walking down a road toward the enemy. Every one of them is convinced he is on the right road, the safe road. But two miles ahead stands one lonely man, the outpost. He sees that this road is dangerous, that his comrades are walking into a trap. He runs back, he finds the platoon. Isn't it clear that this man must have the right to warn the majority, to argue with the majority, to fight with the majority if he believes he has the truth? Before many can know something, *one* must know it! (*His passion has silenced the crowd.*) It's always the same. Rights are sacred until it hurts for somebody to use them. I beg you now—I realize the cost is great, the inconvenience is great, the risk is great that other towns will get the jump on us while we're rebuilding—

PETER STOCKMANN.   Aslaksen, he's not allowed to—

DR. STOCKMANN.   Let me prove it to you! The water is poisoned!

THIRD CITIZEN (*steps up on the platform, waves his fist in* DR. STOCKMANN's *face*).   One more word about poison and I'm gonna take you outside!

> (*The crowd is roaring; some try to charge the platform. The horn is blowing.* ASLAKSEN *rings his bell.* PETER STOCKMANN *steps forward, raising his hands.* KIIL *quietly exits.*)

PETER STOCKMANN.   That's enough. Now stop it! Quiet! There is not going to be any violence here! (*There is silence. He turns to* DR. STOCKMANN.) Doctor, come down and give Mr. Aslaksen the platform.

DR. STOCKMANN (*staring down at the crowd with new eyes*). I'm not through yet.

PETER STOCKMANN.   Come down or I will not be responsible for what happens.

MRS. STOCKMANN.   I'd like to go home. Come on, Tom.

PETER STOCKMANN.   I move the chairman order the speaker to leave the platform.

VOICES. Sit down! Get off that platform!

DR. STOCKMANN. All right. Then I'll take this to out-of-town newspapers until the whole country is warned!

PETER STOCKMANN. You wouldn't dare!

HOVSTAD. You're trying to ruin this town—that's all; trying to ruin it.

DR. STOCKMANN. You're trying to build a town on a morality so rotten that it will infect the country and the world! If the only way you can prosper is this murder of freedom and truth, then I say with all my heart, "Let it be destroyed! Let the people perish!"

(*He leaves the platform.*)

FIRST CITIZEN (*to the* MAYOR). Arrest him! Arrest him!

SECOND CITIZEN. He's a traitor!

(*Cries of "Enemy! Traitor! Revolution!"*)

ASLAKSEN (*ringing for quiet*). I would like to submit the following resolution: The people assembled here tonight, decent and patriotic citizens, in defence of their town and their country, declare that Doctor Stockmann, medical officer of Kirsten Springs, is an enemy of the people and of his community.

(*An uproar of assent starts.*)

MRS. STOCKMANN (*getting up*). That's not true! He loves this town!

DR. STOCKMANN. You damned fools, you fools!

(*The* DOCTOR *and his family are all standing together, at the right, in a close group.*)

ASLAKSEN (*shouting over the din*). Is there anyone against this motion! Anyone against!

HORSTER (*raising his hand*). I am.

ASLAKSEN. One? (*He looks around.*)

DRUNK (*who has returned, raising his hand*). Me too! You can't do without a doctor! Anybody'll . . . tell you . . .

ASLAKSEN. Anyone else? With all votes against two, this

assembly formally declares Doctor Thomas Stockmann to be the people's enemy. In the future, all dealings with him by decent, patriotic citizens will be on that basis. The meeting is adjourned.

> (*Shouts and applause. People start leaving.* DR. STOCK-MANN *goes over to* HORSTER.)

DR. STOCKMANN.   Captain, do you have room for us on your ship to America?

HORSTER.   Any time you say, Doctor.

DR. STOCKMANN.   Catherine? Petra?

> (*The three start for the door, but a gantlet has formed, dangerous and silent, except for*)

THIRD CITIZEN.   You'd better get aboard soon, Doctor!

MRS. STOCKMANN.   Let's go out the back door.

HORSTER.   Right this way.

DR. STOCKMANN.   No, no. No back doors. (*To the crowd.*) I don't want to mislead anybody—the enemy of the people is not finished in this town—not quite yet. And if anybody thinks —

> (*The horn blasts, cutting him off. The crowd starts yelling hysterically:* "Enemy! Traitor! Throw him in the river! Come on, throw him in the river! Enemy! Enemy! Enemy!" *The* STOCKMANNS, *erect, move out through the crowd, with* HORSTER. *Some of the crowd follow them out, yelling.*
>
> *Downstage, watching, are* PETER STOCKMANN, BILLING, ASLAKSEN, *and* HOVSTAD. *The stage is throbbing with the chant,* "Enemy, Enemy, Enemy!" *as*

THE CURTAIN FALLS

ACT III

DR. STOCKMANN's *living-room the following morning. The windows are broken. There is great disorder. As the curtain rises.* DR. STOCKMANN *enters, a robe over shirt and trousers— it's cold in the house. He picks up a stone from the floor, lays it on the table.*

DR. STOCKMANN. Catherine! Tell what's-her-name there are still some rocks to pick up in here.

MRS. STOCKMANN (*from inside*). She's not finished sweeping up the glass.

> (*As* DR. STOCKMANN *bends down to get at another stone under a chair a rock comes through one of the last remaining panes. He rushes to the window, looks out.* MRS. STOCKMANN *rushes in.*)

MRS. STOCKMANN (*frightened*). You all right?

DR. STOCKMANN (*looking out*). A little boy. Look at him run! (*He picks up the stone.*) How fast the poison spreads— even to the children!

MRS. STOCKMANN (*looking out the window*). It's hard to believe this is the same town.

DR. STOCKMANN (*adding this rock to the pile on the table*). I'm going to keep these like sacred relics. I'll put them in my will. I want the boys to have them in their homes to look at every day. (*He shudders.*) Cold in here. Why hasn't what's-her-name got the glazier here?

MRS. STOCKMANN. She's getting him . . .

DR. STOCKMANN. She's been getting him for two hours! We'll freeze to death in here.

MRS. STOCKMANN (*unwillingly*). He won't come here, Tom.

DR. STOCKMANN (*stops moving*). No! The glazier's afraid to fix my windows?

MRS. STOCKMANN. You don't realize—people don't like to be pointed out. He's got neighbours, I suppose, and—(*She hears something.*) Is that someone at the door, Randine?

(*She goes to front door. He continues picking up stones. She comes back.*)

MRS. STOCKMANN. Letter for you.

DR. STOCKMANN (*taking and opening it*). What's this now?

MRS. STOCKMANN (*continuing his pick-up for him*). I don't know how we're going to do any shopping with everybody ready to bite my head off and—

DR. STOCKMANN. Well, what do you know? We're evicted.

MRS. STOCKMANN. Oh, no!

DR. STOCKMANN. He hates to do it, but with public opinion what it is . . .

MRS. STOCKMANN (*frightened*). Maybe we shouldn't have let the boys go to school today.

DR. STOCKMANN. Now don't get all frazzled again.

MRS. STOCKMANN. But the landlord is such a nice man. If he's got to throw us out, the town must be ready to murder us!

DR. STOCKMANN. Just calm down, will you? We'll go to America, and the whole thing'll be like a dream.

MRS. STOCKMANN. But I don't want to go to America— (*She notices his pants.*) When did this get torn?

DR. STOCKMANN (*examining the tear*). Must've been last night.

MRS. STOCKMANN. Your best pants!

DR. STOCKMANN. Well, it just shows you, that's all—when a man goes out to fight for the truth he should never wear his best pants. (*He calms her.*) Stop worrying, will you? You'll sew them up, and in no time at all we'll be three thousand miles away.

MRS. STOCKMANN. But how do you know it'll be any different there?

DR. STOCKMANN. I don't know. It just seems to me, in a big country like that, the spirit must be bigger. Still, I suppose they must have the solid majority there too. I don't know, at least there must be more room to hide there.

MRS. STOCKMANN. Think about it more, will you? I'd hate

to go half around the world and find out we're in the same place.

DR. STOCKMANN. You know, Catherine, I don't think I'm ever going to forget the face of that crowd last night.

MRS. STOCKMANN. Don't think about it.

DR. STOCKMANN. Some of them had their teeth bared, like animals in a pack. And who leads them? Men who call themselves liberals! Radicals! (*She starts looking around at the furniture, figuring.*) The crowd lets out one roar, and where are they, my liberal friends? I bet if I walked down the street now not one of them would admit he ever met me! Are you listening to me?

MRS. STOCKMANN. I was just wondering what we'll ever do with this furniture if we go to America.

DR. STOCKMANN. Don't you ever listen when I talk, dear?

MRS. STOCKMANN. Why must I listen? I know you're right.

(PETRA *enters.*)

MRS. STOCKMANN. Petra! Why aren't you in school?

DR. STOCKMANN. What's the matter?

PETRA (*with deep emotion, looks at* DR. STOCKMANN, *goes up and kisses him*). I'm fired.

MRS. STOCKMANN. They wouldn't!

PETRA. As of two weeks from now. But I couldn't bear to stay there.

DR. STOCKMANN (*shocked*). Mrs. Busk fired you?

MRS. STOCKMANN. Who'd ever imagine she could do such a thing!

PETRA. It hurt her. I could see it, because we've always agreed so about things. But she didn't dare do anything else.

DR. STOCKMANN. The glazier doesn't dare fix the windows, the landlord doesn't dare let us stay on—

PETRA. The landlord!

DR. STOCKMANN. Evicted, darling! Oh, God, on the

wreckage of all the civilizations in the world there ought to be a big sign: "They Didn't Dare!"

PETRA. I really can't blame her, Father. She showed me three letters she got this morning—

DR. STOCKMANN. From whom?

PETRA. They weren't signed.

DR. STOCKMANN. Oh, naturally. The big patriots with their anonymous indignation, scrawling out the darkness of their minds onto dirty little slips of paper—that's morality, and *I'm* the traitor! What did the letters say?

PETRA. Well, one of them was from somebody who said that he'd heard at the club that somebody who visits this house said that I had radical opinions about certain things.

DR. STOCKMANN. Oh, wonderful! Somebody heard that somebody heard that she heard, that he heard . . . ! Catherine, pack as soon as you can. I feel as though vermin were crawling all over me.

(HORSTER *enters*.)

HORSTER. Good morning.

DR. STOCKMANN. Captain! You're just the man I want to see.

HORSTER. I thought I'd see how you all were.

MRS. STOCKMANN. That's awfully nice of you, Captain, and I want to thank you for seeing us through the crowd last night.

PETRA. Did you get home all right? We hated to leave you alone with that mob.

HORSTER. Oh, nothing to it. In a storm there's just one thing to remember: it will pass.

DR. STOCKMANN. Unless it kills you.

HORSTER. You mustn't let yourself get too bitter.

DR. STOCKMANN. I'm trying, I'm trying. But I don't guarantee how I'll feel when I try to walk down the street with "Traitor" branded on my forehead.

MRS. STOCKMANN. Don't think about it.

HORSTER.   Ah, what's a word?

DR. STOCKMANN.   A word can be like a needle sticking in your heart, Captain. It can dig and corrode like an acid, until you become what they want you to be—really an enemy of the people.

HORSTER.   You mustn't ever let that happen, Doctor.

DR. STOCKMANN.   Frankly, I don't give a damn any more. Let summer come, let an epidemic break out, then they'll know whom they drove into exile. When are you sailing?

PETRA.   You really decided to go, Father?

DR. STOCKMANN.   Absolutely. When do you sail, Captain?

HORSTER.   That's really what I came to talk to you about.

DR. STOCKMANN.   Why? Something happen to the ship?

MRS. STOCKMANN (*happily, to* DR. STOCKMANN).   You see! We can't go!

HORSTER.   No, the ship will sail. But I won't be aboard.

DR. STOCKMANN.   No!

PETRA.   You fired too? 'Cause I was this morning.

MRS. STOCKMANN.   Oh, Captain, you shouldn't have given us your house.

HORSTER.   Oh, I'll get another ship. It's just that the owner, Mr. Vik, happens to belong to the same party as the Mayor, and I suppose when you belong to a party, and the party takes a certain position . . . Because Mr. Vik himself is a very decent man.

DR. STOCKMANN.   Oh, they're all decent men!

HORSTER.   No, really, he's not like the others.

DR. STOCKMANN.   He doesn't have to be. A party is like a sausage grinder: it mashes up clearheads, longheads, fatheads, blockheads—and what comes out? Meatheads!

> (*There is a knock on the hall door.* PETRA *goes to answer.*)

MRS. STOCKMANN.   Maybe that's the glazier!

DR. STOCKMANN.   Imagine, Captain! (*He points to the window.*) Refused to come all morning!

(PETER STOCKMANN *enters, his hat in his hand. Silence.*)

PETER STOCKMANN. If you're busy . . .

DR. STOCKMANN. Just picking up broken glass. Come in, Peter. What can I do for you this fine, brisk morning? (*He demonstratively pulls his robe tighter around his throat.*)

MRS. STOCKMANN. Come inside, won't you, Captain?

HORSTER. Yes, I'd like to finish our talk, Doctor.

DR. STOCKMANN. Be with you in a minute, Captain.

(HORSTER *follows* PETRA *and* CATHERINE *out through the dining-room doorway.* PETER STOCKMANN *says nothing, looking at the damage.*)

DR. STOCKMANN. Keep your hat on if you like, it's a little draughty in here today.

PETER STOCKMANN. Thanks, I believe I will. (*He puts his hat on.*) I think I caught cold last night—that house was freezing.

DR. STOCKMANN. I thought it was kind of warm—suffocating, as a matter of fact. What do you want?

PETER STOCKMANN. May I sit down? (*He indicates a chair near the window.*)

DR. STOCKMANN. Not there. A piece of the solid majority is liable to open your skull. Here.

(*They sit on the couch.* PETER STOCKMANN *takes out a large envelope.*)

DR. STOCKMANN. Now don't tell me.

PETER STOCKMANN. Yes. (*He hands the* DOCTOR *the envelope.*)

DR. STOCKMANN. I'm fired.

PETER STOCKMANN. The Board met this morning. There was nothing else to do, considering the state of public opinion.

DR. STOCKMANN (*after a pause*). You look scared, Peter.

PETER STOCKMANN. I—I haven't completely forgotten that you're still my brother.

DR. STOCKMANN. I doubt that.

PETER STOCKMANN. You have no practice left in this town, Thomas.

DR. STOCKMANN. Oh, people always need a doctor.

PETER STOCKMANN. A petition is going from house to house. Everybody is signing it. A pledge not to call you any more. I don't think a single family will dare refuse to sign it.

DR. STOCKMANN. You started that, didn't you?

PETER STOCKMANN. No. As a matter of fact, I think it's all gone a little too far. I never wanted to see you ruined, Thomas. This will ruin you.

DR. STOCKMANN. No, it won't.

PETER STOCKMANN. For once in your life, will you act like a responsible man?

DR. STOCKMANN. Why don't you say it, Peter? You're afraid I'm going out of town to start publishing about the springs, aren't you?

PETER STOCKMANN. I don't deny that. Thomas, if you really have the good of the town at heart, you can accomplish everything without damaging anybody, including yourself.

DR. STOCKMANN. What's this now?

PETER STOCKMANN. Let me have a signed statement saying that in your zeal to help the town you went overboard and exaggerated. Put it any way you like, just so you calm anybody who might feel nervous about the water. If you'll give me that, you've got your job. And I give you my word, you can gradually make all the improvements you feel are necessary. Now, that gives you what you want . . .

DR. STOCKMANN. You're nervous, Peter.

PETER STOCKMANN (nervously). I am not nervous!

DR. STOCKMANN. You expect me to remain in charge while people are being poisoned? (He gets up.)

PETER STOCKMANN. In time you can make your changes.

DR. STOCKMANN. When, five years, ten years? You know your trouble, Peter? You just don't grasp—even now—that there are certain men you can't buy.

PETER STOCKMANN.   I'm quite capable of understanding that. But you don't happen to be one of those men.

DR. STOCKMANN (*after a slight pause*).   What do you mean by that now?

PETER STOCKMANN.   You know damned well what I mean by that. Morten Kiil is what I mean by that.

DR. STOCKMANN.   Morten Kiil?

PETER STOCKMANN.   Your father-in-law, Morten Kiil.

DR. STOCKMANN.   I swear, Peter, one of us is out of his mind! What are you talking about?

PETER STOCKMANN.   Now don't try to charm me with that professional innocence!

DR. STOCKMANN.   What are you talking about?

PETER STOCKMANN.   You don't know that your father-in-law has been running around all morning buying up stock in Kirsten Springs?

DR. STOCKMANN (*perplexed*).   Buying up stock?

PETER STOCKMANN.   Buying up stock, every share he can lay his hands on!

DR. STOCKMANN.   Well, I don't understand, Peter. What's that got to do with—

PETER STOCKMANN (*walking around agitatedly*).   Oh, come now, come now, come now!

DR. STOCKMANN.   I hate you when you do that! Don't just walk around gabbling "Come now, come now!" What the hell are you talking about?

PETER STOCKMANN.   Very well, if you insist on being dense. A man wages a relentless campaign to destroy confidence in a corporation. He even goes so far as to call a mass meeting against it. The very next morning, when people are still in a state of shock about it all, his father-in-law runs all over town, picking up shares at half their value.

DR. STOCKMANN (*realizing, turns away*).   My God!

PETER STOCKMANN.   And you have the nerve to speak to me about principles!

DR. STOCKMANN. You mean you actually believe that I . . . ?

PETER STOCKMANN. I'm not interested in psychology! I believe what I see! And what I see is nothing but a man doing a dirty, filthy job for Morten Kiil. And let me tell you—by tonight every man in this town'll see the same thing!

DR. STOCKMANN. Peter, you, you . . .

PETER STOCKMANN. Now go to your desk and write me a statement denying everything you've been saying, or . . .

DR. STOCKMANN. Peter, you're a low creature!

PETER STOCKMANN. All right then, you'd better get this one straight, Thomas. If you're figuring on opening another attack from out of town, keep this in mind: the morning it's published I'll send out a subpoena for you and begin a prosecution for conspiracy. I've been trying to make you respectable all my life; now if you want to make the big jump there'll be nobody there to hold you back. Now do we understand each other?

DR. STOCKMANN. Oh, we do, Peter! (PETER STOCKMANN *starts for the door.*) Get the girl—what the hell is her name—scrub the floors, wash down the walls, a pestilence has been here!

(KIIL *enters.* PETER STOCKMANN *almost runs into him.* PETER *turns to his brother.*)

PETER STOCKMANN (*pointing to* KIIL). Ha! (*He turns and goes out.*)

(KIIL, *humming quietly, goes to a chair.*)

DR. STOCKMANN. Morten! What have you done? What's the matter with you? Do you realize what this makes me look like?

(KIIL *has started taking some papers out of his pocket.* DR. STOCKMANN *breaks off on seeing them.* KIIL *places them on the table.*)

DR. STOCKMANN. Is that—them?

KIIL.   That's them, yes. Kirsten Springs shares. And very easy to get this morning.

DR. STOCKMANN.   Morten, don't play with me—what is this all about?

KIIL.   What are you so nervous about? Can't a man buy some stock without . . . ?

DR. STOCKMANN.   I want an explanation, Morten.

KIIL (nodding).   Thomas, they hated you last night—

DR. STOCKMANN.   You don't have to tell me that.

KIIL.   But they also believed you. They'd love to murder you, but they believe you. (Slight pause.) The way they say it, the pollution is coming down the river from Windmill Valley.

DR. STOCKMANN.   That's exactly where it's coming from.

KIIL.   Yes. And that's exactly where my tannery is.

(Pause. DR. STOCKMANN sits down slowly.)

DR. STOCKMANN.   Well, Morten, I never made a secret to you that the pollution was tannery waste.

KIIL.   I'm not blaming you. It's my fault. I didn't take you seriously. But it's very serious now. Thomas, I got that tannery from my father; he got it from his father; and his father got it from my great-grandfather. I do not intend to allow my family's name to stand for the three generations of murdering angels who poisoned this town.

DR. STOCKMANN.   I've waited a long time for this talk, Morten. I don't think you can stop that from happening.

KIIL.   No, but you can.

DR. STOCKMANN.   I?

KIIL (nudging the shares).   I've bought these shares because—

DR. STOCKMANN.   Morten, you've thrown your money away. The springs are doomed.

KIIL.   I never throw my money away, Thomas. These were bought with your money.

DR. STOCKMANN.   My money? What . . . ?

KIIL. You've probably suspected that I might leave a little something for Catherine and the boys?

DR. STOCKMANN. Well, naturally, I'd hoped you'd . . .

KIIL (*touching the shares*). I decided this morning to invest that money in some stock.

DR. STOCKMANN (*slowly getting up*). You bought that junk with Catherine's money!

KIIL. People call me "badger", and that's an animal that roots out things, but it's also some kind of a pig, I understand. I've lived a clean man and I'm going to die clean. You're going to clean my name for me.

DR. STOCKMANN. Morten . . .

KIIL. Now I want to see if you really belong in a strait jacket.

DR. STOCKMANN. How could you do such a thing? What's the matter with you?

KIIL. Now don't get excited, it's very simple. If you should make another investigation of the water—

DR. STOCKMANN. I don't *need* another investigation, I—

KIIL. If you think it over and decide that you ought to change your opinion about the water—

DR. STOCKMANN. But the water is poisoned! It is poisoned!

KIIL. If you simply go on insisting the water is poisoned —(*he holds up the shares*)—with these in your house, then there's only one explanation for you—you're absolutely crazy. (*He puts the shares down on the table again.*)

DR. STOCKMANN. You're right! I'm mad! I'm insane!

KIIL (*with more force*). You're stripping the skin off your family's back! Only a madman would do a thing like that!

DR. STOCKMANN. Morten, Morten, I'm a penniless man! Why didn't you tell me before you bought this junk?

KIIL. Because you would understand it better if I told you after. (*He goes up to* DR. STOCKMANN, *holds him by the lapels. With terrific force, and the twinkle still in his eye.*) And, goddammit, I think you do understand it now, don't you?

Millions of tons of water come down that river. How do you know the day you made your tests there wasn't something unusual about the water?

DR. STOCKMANN (*not looking at* KIIL). Yes, but I . . .

KIIL. How do you know? Why couldn't those little animals have clotted up only the patch of water you souped out of the river? How do you know the rest of it wasn't pure?

DR. STOCKMANN. It's not probable. People were getting sick last summer . . .

KIIL. They were sick when they came here or they would-n't have come!

DR. STOCKMANN (*breaking away*). Not intestinal diseases, skin diseases . . .

KIIL (*following him*). The only place anybody gets a bellyache is here! There are no carbuncles in Norway? Maybe the food was bad. Did you ever think of the food?

DR. STOCKMANN (*with the desire to agree with him*). No, I didn't look into the food . . .

KIIL. Then what makes you so sure it's the water?

DR. STOCKMANN. Because I tested the water and—

KIIL (*taking hold of him again*). Admit it! We're all alone here. You have some doubt.

DR. STOCKMANN. Well, there's always a possible . . .

KIIL. Then part of it's imaginary.

DR. STOCKMANN. Well, nothing is a hundred per cent on this earth, but—

KIIL. Then you have a perfect right to doubt the other way! You have a scientific right! And did you even think of some disinfectant? I bet you never even thought of that.

DR. STOCKMANN. Not for a mass of water like that, you can't . . .

KIIL. Everything can be killed. That's science! Thomas, I never liked your brother either, you have a perfect right to hate him.

DR. STOCKMANN. I don't do it because I hate my brother.

KIIL. Part of it, part of it, don't deny it! You admit there's some doubt in your mind about the water, you admit there may be ways to disinfect it, and yet you went after your brother as though these doubts didn't exist; as though the only way to cure the thing was to blow up the whole Institute! There's hatred in that, boy, don't forget it. (*He points to the shares.*) These can belong to you now, so be sure, be sure! Tear the hatred out of your heart, stand naked in front of yourself—*are you sure?*

DR. STOCKMANN.   What right have you to gamble my family's future on the strength of my convictions?

KIIL.   Aha! Then the convictions are not really that strong!

DR. STOCKMANN.   I am ready to hang for my convictions! But no man has a right to make martyrs of others; my family is innocent. Sell back those shares, give her what belongs to her. I'm a penniless man!

KIIL.   Nobody is going to say Morten Kiil wrecked this town. (*He gathers up the shares.*) You retract your convictions—or these go to my charity.

DR. STOCKMANN.   Everything?

KIIL.   There'll be a little something for Catherine, but not much. I want my good name. It's exceedingly important to me.

DR. STOCKMANN (*bitterly*).   And charity . . .

KIIL.   Charity will do it, or you will do it. It's a serious thing to destroy a town.

DR. STOCKMANN.   Morten, when I look at you, I swear to God I see the devil!

(*The door opens, and before we see who is there . . .*)

DR. STOCKMANN.   You!

(ASLAKSEN *enters, holding up his hand defensively.*)

ASLAKSEN.   Now don't get excited, please!

(HOVSTAD *enters. He and* ASLAKSEN *stop short and smile on seeing* KIIL.)

KIIL.   Too many intellectuals here: I'd better go.

ASLAKSEN (*apologetically*). Doctor, can we have five minutes of—

DR. STOCKMANN. I've got nothing to say to you.

KIIL (*going to the door*). I want an answer right away. You hear? I'm waiting. (*He leaves.*)

DR. STOCKMANN. All right, say it quick, what do you want?

HOVSTAD. We don't expect you to forgive our attitude at the meeting, but . . .

DR. STOCKMANN (*groping for the word*). Your attitude was weak . . . womanish . . . damnably shameful!

HOVSTAD. All right, call it whatever you—

DR. STOCKMANN. I've got a lot on my mind, so get to the point. What do you want?

ASLAKSEN. Doctor, you should have told us what was in back of it all. You could have had the *Messenger* behind you all the way.

HOVSTAD. You'd have had public opinion with you now. Why didn't you tell us?

DR. STOCKMANN. Look, I'm very tired, let's not beat around the bush!

HOVSTAD (*gesturing toward the door where* KIIL *went out*). He's been all over town buying up stock in the springs. It's no secret any more.

DR. STOCKMANN (*after a slight pause*). Well, what about it?

HOVSTAD (*in a friendly way*). You don't want me to spell it out, do you?

DR. STOCKMANN. I certainly wish you would. I—

HOVSTAD. All right, let's lay it on the table. Aslaksen, you want to . . . ?

ASLAKSEN. No, no, go ahead.

HOVSTAD. Doctor, in the beginning we supported you. But it quickly became clear that if we kept on supporting you in the face of public hysteria—

DR. STOCKMANN. Your paper created the hysteria.

HOVSTAD.   One thing at a time, all right? (*Slowly, to drive it into* DR. STOCKMANN's *head.*) We couldn't go on supporting you because, in simple language, we didn't have the money to withstand the loss in circulation. You're boycotted now? Well, the paper would have been boycotted too, if we'd stuck with you.

ASLAKSEN.   You can see that, Doctor.

DR. STOCKMANN.   Oh, yes. But what do you want?

HOVSTAD.   *The People's Messenger* can put on such a campaign that in two months you will be hailed as a hero in this town.

ASLAKSEN.   We're ready to go.

HOVSTAD.   We will prove to the public that you had to buy up the stock because the management would not make the changes required for public health. In other words, you did it for absolutely scientific, public-spirited reasons. Now what do you say, Doctor?

DR. STOCKMANN.   You want money from me, is that it?

ASLAKSEN.   Well, now, Doctor . . .

HOVSTAD (*to* ASLAKSEN).   No, don't walk around it. (*To* DR. STOCKMANN.) If we started to support you again, Doctor, we'd lose circulation for a while. We'd like you—or Mr. Kiil rather—to make up the deficit. (*Quickly.*) Now that's open and above-board, and I don't see anything wrong with it. Do you?

(*Pause.* DR. STOCKMANN *looks at him, then turns and walks to the windows, deep in thought.*)

ASLAKSEN.   Remember, Doctor, you need the paper, you need it desperately.

DR. STOCKMANN (*returning*).   No, there's nothing wrong with it at all. I—I'm not at all averse to cleaning up my name— although for myself it never was dirty. But I don't *enjoy* being hated, if you know what I mean.

ASLAKSEN.   Exactly.

HOVSTAD.   Aslaksen, will you show him the budget . . .

(ASLAKSEN *reaches into his pocket.*)

DR. STOCKMANN.   Just a minute. There is one point. I hate to keep repeating the same thing, but the water is poisoned.

HOVSTAD.   Now, Doctor . . .

DR. STOCKMANN.   Just a minute. The Mayor says that he will levy a tax on everybody to pay for the reconstruction. I assume you are ready to support that tax at the same time you're supporting me.

ASLAKSEN.   That tax would be extremely unpopular.

HOVSTAD.   Doctor, with you back in charge of the baths, I have absolutely no fear that anything can go wrong.

DR. STOCKMANN.   In other words, you will clean up my name—so that I can be in charge of the corruption.

HOVSTAD.   But we can't tackle everything at once. A new tax—there'd be an uproar!

ASLAKSEN.   It would ruin the paper!

DR. STOCKMANN.   Then you don't intend to do anything about the water?

HOVSTAD.   We have faith you won't let anyone get sick.

DR. STOCKMANN.   In other words, gentlemen, you are looking for someone to blackmail into paying your printing bill.

HOVSTAD (*indignantly*).   We are trying to clear your name, Doctor Stockmann! And if you refuse to co-operate, if that's going to be your attitude . . .

DR. STOCKMANN.   Yes? Go on. What will you do?

HOVSTAD (*to* ASLAKSEN).   I think we'd better go.

DR. STOCKMANN (*stepping in their way*).   What will you do? I would like you to tell me. Me, the man two minutes ago you were going to make into a hero—what will you do now that I won't pay you?

ASLAKSEN.   Doctor, the public is almost hysterical . . .

DR. STOCKMANN.   To my face, tell me what you are going to do!

HOVSTAD.   The Mayor will prosecute you for conspiracy

to destroy a corporation, and without a paper behind you, you will end up in prison.

DR. STOCKMANN. And you'll support him, won't you? I want it from your mouth, Hovstad. This little victory you will not deny me. (HOVSTAD *starts for the door.* DR. STOCKMANN *steps into his way.*) Tell the hero, Hovstad. You're going to go on crucifying the hero, are you not? Say it to me! You will not leave here until I get this from your mouth!

HOVSTAD (*looking directly at* DR. STOCKMANN). You are a madman. You are insane with egotism. And don't excuse it with humanitarian slogans, because a man who'll drag his family through a lifetime of disgrace is a demon in his heart! (*He advances on* DR. STOCKMANN.) You hear me? A demon who cares more for the purity of a public bath than the lives of his wife and children. Doctor Stockmann, you deserve everything you're going to get!

(DR. STOCKMANN *is struck by* HOVSTAD'*s ferocious conviction.* ASLAKSEN *comes toward him, taking the budget out of his pocket.*)

ASLAKSEN (*nervously*). Doctor, please consider it. It won't take much money, and in two months' time I promise you your whole life will change and . . .

(*Offstage* MRS. STOCKMANN *is heard calling in a frightened voice, "What happened? My God, what's the matter?" She runs to the front door.* DR. STOCKMANN, *alarmed, goes quickly to the hallway.* EJLIF *and* MORTEN *enter.* MORTEN'*s head is bruised.* PETRA *and* CAPTAIN HORSTER *enter from the left.*)

MRS. STOCKMANN. Something happened! Look at him!

MORTEN. I'm all right, they just . . .

DR. STOCKMANN (*looking at the bruise*). What happened here?

MORTEN. Nothing, Papa, I swear . . .

DR. STOCKMANN (*to* EJLIF). What happened? Why aren't you in school?

EJLIF.   The teacher said we better stay home the rest of the week.

DR. STOCKMANN.   The boys hit him?

EJLIF.   They started calling you names, so he got sore and began to fight with one kid, and all of a sudden the whole bunch of them . . .

MRS. STOCKMANN (*to* MORTEN).   Why did you answer!

MORTEN (*indignantly*).   They called him a traitor! My father is no traitor!

EJLIF.   But you didn't have to answer!

MRS. STOCKMANN.   You should've known they'd all jump on you! They could have killed you!

MORTEN.   I don't care!

DR. STOCKMANN (*to quiet him—and his own heart*) Morten . . .

MORTEN (*pulling away from his father*).   I'll kill them! I'll take a rock and the next time I see one of them I'll kill him!

>   (DR. STOCKMANN *reaches for* MORTEN, *who, thinking his father will chastise him, starts to run.* DR. STOCKMANN *catches him and grips him by the arm.*)

MORTEN.   Let me go! Let me . . . !

DR. STOCKMANN.   Morten . . . Morten . . .

MORTEN (*crying in his father's arms*).   They called you traitor, an enemy . . . (*He sobs.*)

DR. STOCKMANN.   Sssh. That's all. Wash your face.

>   (MRS. STOCKMANN *takes* MORTEN. DR. STOCKMANN *stands erect, faces* ASLAKSEN *and* HOVSTAD.)

DR. STOCKMANN.   Good day, gentlemen.

HOVSTAD.   Let us know what you decide and we'll—

DR. STOCKMANN.   I've decided. I am an enemy of the people.

MRS. STOCKMANN.   Tom, what are you . . . ?

DR. STOCKMANN.   To such people. who teach their own children to think with their fists—to them I'm an enemy! And my boy . . . my boys . . . my family . . . I think you can count us all enemies.

ASLAKSEN. Doctor, you could have everything you want!

DR. STOCKMANN. Except the truth. I could have everything but that—that the water is poisoned!

HOVSTAD. But you'll be in charge.

DR. STOCKMANN. But the children are poisoned, the people are poisoned! If the only way I can be a friend of the people is to take charge of that corruption, then I am an enemy! The water is poisoned, poisoned, poisoned! That's the beginning of it and that's the end of it! Now get out of here!

HOVSTAD. You know where you're going to end?

DR. STOCKMANN. I said get out of here! (*He grabs* AS-LAKSEN'S *umbrella out of his hand.*)

MRS. STOCKMANN. What are you doing?

(ASLAKSEN *and* HOVSTAD *back toward the door as* DR. STOCKMANN *starts to swing.*)

ASLAKSEN. You're a fanatic, you're out of your mind!

MRS. STOCKMANN (*grabbing* DR. STOCKMANN *to take the umbrella*). What are you doing?

DR. STOCKMANN. They want me to buy the paper, the public, the pollution of the springs, buy the whole pollution of this town! They'll make a hero out of me for that! (*Furiously, to* ASLAKSEN *and* HOVSTAD.) But I'm not a hero, I'm the enemy —and now you're first going to find out what kind of enemy I am! I will sharpen my pen like a dagger—you, all you friends of the people, are going to bleed before I'm done! Go, tell them to sign the petitions! Warn them not to call me when they're sick! Beat up my children! And never let her—(*he points to* PETRA)—in the school again or she'll destroy the immaculate purity of the vacuum there! See to all the barricades—the truth is coming! Ring the bells, sound the alarm! The truth, the truth is out, and soon it will be prowling like a lion in the streets!

HOVSTAD. Doctor, you're out of your mind.

(*He and* ASLAKSEN *turn to go. They are in the door-way.*)

EJLIF (*rushing at them*).   Don't you say that to him!

DR. STOCKMANN (*as* MRS. STOCKMANN *cries out, rushes them with the umbrella*).   Out of here!

(*They rush out.* DR. STOCKMANN *throws the umbrella after them, then slams the door. Silence. He has his back pressed against the door, facing his family.*)

DR. STOCKMANN.   I've had all the ambassadors of hell today, but there'll be no more. Now, now listen, Catherine! Children, listen. Now we're besieged. They'll call for blood now, they'll whip the people like oxen—(*A rock comes through a remaining pane. The boys start for the window.*) Stay away from there!

MRS. STOCKMANN.   The Captain knows where we can get a ship.

DR. STOCKMANN.   No ships.

PETRA.   We're staying?

MRS. STOCKMANN.   But they can't go back to school! I won't let them out of the house!

DR. STOCKMANN.   We're staying.

PETRA.   Good!

DR. STOCKMANN.   We must be careful now. We must live through this. Boys, no more school. I'm going to teach you, and Petra will. Do you know any boys, street louts, hookey-players—

EJLIF.   Oh, sure, we—

DR. STOCKMANN.   We'll want about twelve of them to start. But I want them good and ignorant, absolutely uncivilized. Can we use your house, Captain?

HORSTER.   Sure, I'm never there.

DR. STOCKMANN.   Fine. We'll begin, Petra, and we'll turn out not taxpayers and newspaper subscribers, but free and independent people, hungry for the truth. Oh, I forgot! Petra, run to Grandpa and tell him—tell him as follows: NO!

MRS. STOCKMANN (*puzzled*). What do you mean?

DR. STOCKMANN (*going over to* MRS. STOCKMANN). It means, my dear, that we are all alone. And there'll be a long night before it's day—

> (*A rock comes through a paneless window.* HORSTER *goes to the window. A crowd is heard approaching.*)

HORSTER. Half the town is out!

MRS. STOCKMANN. What's going to happen? Tom! What's going to happen?

DR. STOCKMANN (*holding up his hands to quiet her, and with a trembling mixture of trepidation and courageous insistence*). I don't know. But remember now, everybody. You are fighting for the truth, and that's why you're alone. And that makes you strong. We're the strongest people in the world . . .

> (*The crowd is heard angrily calling outside. Another rock comes through the window.*)

DR. STOCKMANN. . . . and the strong must learn to be lonely!

> (*The crowd noise gets louder. He walks upstage toward the windows as a wind rises and the curtains start to billow out toward him.*)

THE CURTAIN FALLS

THE PLAY'S HISTORY

Unlike *I Remember Mama* and *The Teahouse of the August Moon*, the Broadway production of *An Enemy of the People* was not completely successful. It ran for only thirty-six performances.

Two reasons can be given for the fact that it had only limited success. The first is that on December 28, 1950, when it opened, it was too topical and radical to win popular approval. The Korean War was in progress, and even liberals and progressives were wary about showing enthusiasm for a play which attacked the witch-hunters of the day, even if it did so in the guise of a classic play seventy-two years old. It was not patriotic to like the play!

But a better reason was that this production was not a completely satisfactory one. George Jean Nathan rather savagely remarked that the make-up and costuming would have been laughed off the stage fifty years ago, and that the stage direction emphasized everything with a sledge hammer. The *Theatre Arts* critic said that Fredric March and Florence Eldridge, playing the leads, were best in the final scene, the inflammatory mood of which was more compatible with their "bravura techniques" than the quiet first act.

It is interesting to note that the director of *An Enemy of the People* was Robert Lewis who was responsible, three years later, for an imaginative and altogether successful production of *The Teahouse of the August Moon*!

In February, 1959, *An Enemy of the People* was revived in an off-Broadway production at the Actors' Playhouse.

This time it was successful.

Why?

In the first place, nine years had elapsed and the wave of fear and hysteria that had swept across America at the time of the Korean crisis was almost a forgotten thing. Freed from the topical parallel and climate the play proved that its theme and writing were enduring stuff. It was born of a passionate belief in freedom, justice and truth. These passions are as old and as ever-new as the dreams of men.

The second reason that the play was a success was that the production was far more effective than the original one. It was admirably directed by Gene Frankel and, according to Richard Watts, Jr., revealed "a dynamic power" far beyond that of the Broadway presentation.

Proof of the dynamic power of *An Enemy of the People* is that it was successful in a "theatre-in-the-round" or arena production in Toronto in the spring of 1959. Four of the actors in this production by the Arts Theatre, directed by Basya Hunter, are shown in the illustration of our play. The performance was given in the theatre of the Central Reference Library.

ARTHUR MILLER'S STORY

The story begins like that of an average American boy. Arthur Miller was born in 1915 in the Harlem section of Manhattan, of well-to-do parents. His father, a manufacturer, later lost his fortune in the depression. Arthur Miller was a poor student by school standards; he was interested only in football, hockey and "just plain fooling around". He failed algebra three times.

What changed his life? Reading *The Brothers Karamazov* by Dostoyevsky. Suddenly he believed he was born to be a writer. He was working at a warehouse at the time, having graduated from high school. He began reading on the subway to and from work.

Despite his poor scholastic record, he persuaded the University of Michigan to allow him to enter the university as a student of journalism. His first play, written in the ten days of his spring vacation, won several prizes and gave him confidence as a writer. He wrote two plays a year at Michigan, winning more prizes. Returning to New York, he continued to write plays, radio dramas, short stories, and a novel, *Focus*.

In 1940 he married Mary Grace Slattery. They had two children. The marriage was dissolved, and in 1956 he married Marilyn Monroe.

His most successful plays are *All My Sons*, which won the New York Critics Award in 1947; *Death of a Salesman* which, like *The Teahouse of the August Moon*, won both the Critics Award and the Pulitzer Prize in 1949; *An Enemy of the People*, 1950; *The Crucible*, 1953; *A View From the Bridge* and *A Memory of Two Mondays*, 1955. His *Collected Plays* appeared in 1958.

STAGING THE PLAY

The stage directions call for three realistic settings: the living-room, the newspaper office, and the bare room in Captain

Horster's house where the meeting is held. No unusual demands are made; there are no revolving stages, no bamboo panels!

If you are presenting the play, and have the necessary money and technical help, you can build the three "box" sets. If you do so, you should pay most attention to Dr. Stockmann's living-room; it is used in three of the five scenes. This could be the permanent setting; the other two might be placed in front of it, if you do not wish to "strike" it, or take it down.

The alternative to building the complete sets is to present the play more simply in curtains, with doors and windows inserted, using only basic units of furniture, and creating the changing moods of the play with skilful lighting. This is a less expensive, and in many ways more challenging approach to the presentation of the play.

You will notice from the picture on the end-papers of this book that period costumes were used in the Toronto production by the Arts Theatre. They were also used in the original New York presentation. I have quoted George Jean Nathan's devastating comment on the costumes and make-up of this New York production. The important point is that if you decide to stage a play in a certain period, this period must be uniformly adhered to in all details: hair styles, make-up, costumes, shoes, and furniture. If sideburns or mutton chops are worn, every man in the cast must wear them!

The meeting scene in Captain Horster's house invites powerful staging. Well done, it can lift an audience to a high pitch of excitement which will carry through to the end of the play.

The stage directions suggest that the room in Horster's house should be angled, so that the illusion of a large unseen crowd, off in the wings to the left, can be created. The speakers address this unseen crowd.

This meeting scene was most effective in the Toronto arena performance by the Arts Theatre. Theatre-in-the-round productions, making movement in all directions possible, lend themselves admirably to crowd scenes. Enterprising producers may find that a theatre-in-the-round production of *An Enemy of the People* is an exciting project to undertake. It is difficult to see how *I Remember Mama* or *The Teahouse of the August Moon* could be performed in the round. But *An Enemy of the People has* been successfully staged in this manner.

If you have a hall with plenty of floor space it is possible to seat your audience on three or four sides of a central area. Ramps or platforms are necessary for the seats if the audience is a large one, but two hundred people can easily see a presentation clearly, if there are from two to five rows of seats on the three or four sides of the playing area.

A theatre-in-the-round production is comparatively inexpensive to stage, because there is little if any scenery and only indicative furniture. Lighting is a problem; it is difficult to light an arena stage effectively without having spotlights glaring in the eyes of some members of the audience. Another problem is that actors have to be trained to concentrate at all times on their roles and to live them intensely and with complete absorption. Nothing is more distracting for a player than to have members of the audience quite near him and to know that they are examining him with a critical eye. If an actor is not well trained he will break under this strain and his lapses from character will at once be apparent to the audience.

If you are doing a class reading of the play, why not try an arena production? For the period of rehearsal and performance exchange your English classroom for one that has movable chairs. Put your student audience on three or four sides of the central area. Use simple low furniture. Remember to keep changing the positions of your actors, so that their backs are not turned for too long to any one section of the audience. A good basic position is to have them face one another so that each half of the audience sees the expressions of at least one of the players. Then, whenever possible, move them so that they are turned to a new group of spectators.

Try it! You will find the experiment a fascinating one!

NOTES AND QUESTIONS

FLIGHT INTO DANGER

P. 11, l. 4. Manifest. A passenger list.

P. 17, l. 14. Film insert: airplane . . . night. It is extremely difficult to photograph an airplane in night flight. In the CBC production a model was used; it was moved skilfully against a suitable background.

P. 21, l. 19. Suspense is quickened by the announcement by the Stewardess that *two* passengers are sick. We had feared only that the condition of the *woman passenger* would be worse. Notice the relationship between the two dramatic elements of surprise and suspense.

P. 22, ll. 6-7. The flashlight is used to see whether the pupils of the eye have contracted, or whether they are still open.

P. 27, ll. 17-18. ETA is 0505. Initials of Estimated Time of Arrival. The time is, of course, five minutes after five in the morning.

P. 28, l. 32. . . . fog down to the deck. Deck is Air Force slang for ground.

P. 30, l. 22. The first male passenger has only two lines to speak in this act. The part as written lacks colour and personality. Those who saw the CBC production may remember that this passenger was played by a cheerful, hearty, vigorous actor whose good humour was valuable in relieving the gathering tension of the scene. This shows the contribution that the director can make, particularly when the actor has a good deal of "business"—in this case helping the Stewardess to bring glasses of water to those who are sick. Even a minor part can be handled with such conviction and richness of characterization that we have another figure to add to the gallery of portraits which the play presents.

P. 36, l. 5. Gizmos. Air Force slang for devices or gadgets.

P. 36, l. 34. Mayday! The international verbal SOS signal; it is used only in cases of extreme urgency.

P. 43, l. 12. . . . get him on that heading. Heading is used interchangeably with "course".

P. 46, ll. 2-4. Several times from here until the end of the play the device of the Stewardess calling out the air speed, with fear in her voice as the speed drops below that which we have been told is safe, is used to create almost unbearable excitement.

P. 47, l. 33.   . . . **flaps down.**   The CBC performance showed film clips of a North Star liner flying in the dawn light and lowering first its flaps and then its wheels and landing gear. These sequences were filmed at Trenton on several bitterly cold mornings early in March, 1956, from an RCAF plane whose rear doors had been removed.

P. 51, ll. 19-24.   **No dice, Vancouver . . . Over.**   This speech, and the similar one spoken by Spencer just prior to landing, in which he refuses to make a trial run, are two of the high moments of the play. Their recklessness appeals to us. In our sane moments we may object that this is foolhardy courage, and that it would be better to take an extra three or four minutes and be sure of preventing disaster. But when we read the play and watch the performance we are thrilled and completely caught up by Spencer's courage. We identify ourselves with him—with the hero who does impossibly brave and daring deeds.

P. 53, ll. 3-4.   **. . . cross-wind . . . down-wind leg.**   In order to make the explanation simple let us assume that the plane is proceeding in a westerly direction, cutting across the wind which is from the north. Spencer crosses the runway, which runs north and south, and then makes a left turn on the down-wind leg, with the runway on his left and the wind behind him. He then makes another left turn, crosswind, and finally turns left again into the wind to land on the runway.

P. 55, ll. 15-16.   **. . . propellers to fully fine.**   The angle of the propeller blades is changed in relation to the task they are expected to perform. In the take-off they are "fully fine" to give the maximum lift into the air. In the air they are adjusted to give the maximum thrust. In landing they are changed again to fully fine to secure the maximum lift. This is done so that if the pilot does not wish to complete the landing he can lift the plane quickly and overshoot the runway. For some reason, such as the landing of another plane, the control tower may call for this overshoot procedure.

P. 56, l. 4.   **What a . . . wagon this is!**   It has been said that profanity is effective when seldom used. In the CBC production the word "blasted" was used in place of "miserable" in this line. The playwright saves his strongest language for this line and for the line which follows the climax on page 58 when he uses the phrase "a lousy stinking groundloop". Yet despite this over-all moderation in language we accept the dialogue as completely natural, lifelike and convincing. It is true, we believe, to the language spoken in real life by men in a comparable situation.

1. In the CBC production the airplane belonged to Continental Air Lines Corporation. In our version the plane has been chartered from Maple Leaf Charter, which uses the facilities of Cross-Canada Airlines. Why did the dramatist make this change?

2. On page 13 the Second Agent tells the Stewardess that the plane has been held up because they could not get service from the regular caterers and had to go to "some outfit the other side of town". Can you suggest why these lines were written into the play?

3. What is the purpose of the film insert on page 20, showing an airplane in level flight at night?

4. On page 32 Dr. Baird tells some of the passengers that with modern food-handling methods "the chances of this happening are probably a million to one against". Why did the author make this statement?

5. The foreshadowing of trouble to come is one device that is used in creating suspense. In the scene between the Stewardess, the Captain and the First Officer on page 18 the First Officer says, "It's in the quiet times that trouble brews." His next comment is rich in dramatic irony. "I'll bet you right now that somebody's getting ready to be sick." Find another example of such foreshadowing and irony, in which the speaker makes a remark in one mood and we in the audience, because of our foreknowledge, receive it in a contrasting mood.

6. In the scene just referred to, the First Officer is well characterized. How does the dramatist establish the following facts: (a) that his table manners could be improved, (b) that he has a big appetite, (c) that he is young, (d) that he is superstitious?

7. In the sequence in the Control Room in the opening minutes of Act III the author has written a scene which is packed with tension and excitement. In the CBC production the director decided that the mood of confusion was all-important. Consequently, there was a general hubbub; the speeches overlapped, and it was difficult to distinguish the words that were spoken. In the NBC production the Control Room was tense and generally quiet. The author wrote unimportant but natural background lines for the actors who were required to be talking, but these were spoken in sufficiently low tones that the words of the principal speakers were easily heard.

If you were directing the play, which plan would you follow in interpreting this scene? Why?

8. On page 16 we hear the voice of the First Officer, talking to the Stewardess, telling her that the Captain will have the lamb. Then he reports that the Captain has changed his mind and will take the

halibut instead. The First Officer goes along with this. "Make it two fish, Janet," he says. Why does the dramatist have the Captain waver in his choice and then take the fish?

9.   The opening pages of the play, before we learn of sickness among the passengers, are skilfully written. Comment on these pages, scene by scene, showing how our interest is maintained, and what we learn in each scene which is important as background information or exposition.

10.   Do you like the way *Flight Into Danger* ends? What would be your opinion had it ended with Spencer and the Stewardess happy and relieved to find that they have landed safely? What do Treleaven's words contribute to rounding off the situation and leaving us pleased with what has happened? Why are they characteristic of Treleaven, or, as we say, "in character"?

11.   *Flight Into Danger* is interesting because it uses a great many film clips or inserts. Arthur Hailey told the editor that some directors are opposed in principle to film clips, considering them "gimmicks" which a good script should be able to do without. Hailey himself now makes his film clips optional, and is careful to make sure that there is continuity in the story in the event that they are not used.

What is your opinion about this? Are the film inserts not essential to the success of *Flight Into Danger*? When television and film are such closely allied arts is there any reason why their techniques should not be mingled?

If you were a director, would you use film clips? Give a reasoned answer, based on your study of *Flight Into Danger* and on television plays which you have seen.

12.   Perhaps the biggest difference in the Canadian and American productions was in the interpretation of the hero, George Spencer. In the CBC production Spencer (played by James Doohan) was nervous and tense almost to the point of sickness once he found he had no alternative but to take the controls. His snatches of humour were delivered with a kind of wild bravado. It was a high-strung, nerve-wracking, gripping performance. Macdonald Carey, in the NBC production, played the role with much greater assurance and self-control, and with a genuine feeling for comedy despite the fearful pressure he was under. Jack Gould, television critic of the *New York Times*, said "The touches of humour in the characterization of the passenger-turned-pilot particularly enhanced the sense of danger."

Which interpretation of the part would you prefer? Give your reasons.

13.   On page 34 Dr. Baird tells the Stewardess to send George Spencer to the flight deck and then to ask the other passengers if any

of them have had flying experience. In order to avoid a panic she is to say only that the First Officer is sick and that the Captain wants someone to assist him. This device pays rich dramatic dividends in the following scene with the entrance of Spencer and the re-entrance of the Stewardess. Analyse these results, showing how the urgency of the situation is sharply increased. If the playwright had not had the Doctor follow this course of action, what would the alternative action have had to be? Why would it be less desirable?

14. In talking to the editor, the dramatist said that comedy was not his specialty. He has written one comedy only, *The Change in Chester*; he did not think he would write another. However, he said that he tries to put a "seasoning" of humorous lines in his plays. "Nothing helps suspense along like a laugh in a tense moment."

Choose five lines which you think have genuine comic value. Try to analyse the humour in each, showing why it is funny; suggest whether the laugh which it provokes serves any dramatic purpose, including the one referred to by the playwright.

15. Hailey urges would-be television writers to tell their story from all points of view, using the "intimacy" and "fluidity" which the medium affords.

Discuss these two characteristics of television drama, illustrating your remarks by referring to *Flight Into Danger*. Comment on the difference between TV and stage drama which are suggested by Hailey's advice.

16. Analyse *Flight Into Danger* act by act to show the firm construction of the plot, the tightening of suspense and the increasing sense of peril. Show how this tension is broken and heightened by quiet passages and by humorous situations and dialogue.

I REMEMBER MAMA

NOTES

P. 74, l. 12. **Traveller curtains.** A term used for curtains; they are usually upstage of the main curtains and move horizontally.

P. 74, l. 22. **Prologue.** An opening speech or scene. Here it consists of the four paragraphs spoken by Katrin before the lights come up on the kitchen. These paragraphs contain the preliminary exposition—the information we must have before we can follow the play.

P. 75, l. 28. **Flat.** A stage flat consists of canvas stretched over a wooden frame, and painted.

P. 78, l. 10. **English "laddie" actor type.** The actor who, although too old, fancies himself in debonair younger roles.

P. 83, l. 27. **Feather boa.** A neckpiece of feathers, fashionable at this time.

P. 89, ll. 32-3. **The Three Graces.** In classical mythology the Three Graces were lovely goddesses who were able to bring the gifts of charm and beauty to mortals.

P. 90, l. 14. **Fenimore Kipling.** It is an amusing idea of the playwright to have Mama confuse Fenimore Cooper and Rudyard Kipling.

P. 92, l. 6. **Bead portières.** Curtains made of long strings of beads, serving as a screen or for ornament.

P. 92, ll. 28-9. **A cat draws breath from a sleeping child.** An old superstition.

P. 94, l. 21. **Conciergerie.** A prison belonging to the Palace of Justice in Paris.

P. 99, ll. 2-3. **He has a strong accent ... children's names.** Enlist the help of someone in your community who speaks Norwegian in acquiring this accent, and in the proper pronunciation of the children's names and of other Norwegian terms used throughout the play.

P. 129, l. 24. **Lille Ven.** Norwegian for "little friend".

P. 131, ll. 28-9. **'Tis true, 'tis pity ... true.** *Hamlet*, Act II, Scene 2. Polonius speaking to the Queen.

P. 132, l. 8. **Ave Atque Vale!** Catullus, Carmina CI.

P. 133, l. 7. **cable-car.** San Francisco's famous streetcars operate on cables because of the steepness of the grades.

P. 162, l. 27. **Soirée.** An evening party or gathering.

P. 169, l. 24. **Lutefisk.** A special fish dish.

QUESTIONS

1. List five facts that we learn about Katrin and her family from the prologue which she speaks before the play begins.

2. In the description of the kitchen, we are told that the table has a low bench below it. Why are chairs not used, rather than a bench? Why is the bench low?

3. What do we learn about the character of Christine in the scene in the kitchen in which Mama gets down on her knees and scrubs the floor?

4. It is an example of irony that the playwright should have Mr. Hyde call the three aunts the Three Graces. Why? Why is it characteristic of Mr. Hyde that he should call them this?

5. The scene between Katrin and Mama at the drugstore gives us important background information (exposition) about Mama. List some of the details which we learn about her life in Norway and her arrival in San Francisco. What are some of the ideas about life that emerge from her experiences?

6. In *Mama's Bank Account* Uncle Chris is described as a giant. No such description is given in the stage directions of the play. Why must the dramatist be careful about the physical characteristics of his people?

7. The scene in the kitchen in the late evening after Katrin's graduation has an attractive "shape" because Papa labels or ticks off in turn each of the older members of his family with a telling phrase. What has Christine done to deserve his comment, "Christine is the stubborn one"? How then, in turn, does he label each of Nels, Katrin and Mama? What has each done to deserve the epithet?

8. The novel has a great advantage over the play in that the novelist can describe a scene in detail. In *Mama's Bank Account* we are very much aware of the beauty of San Francisco, one of the most romantically picturesque cities in the world. Aside from the play's stage setting, showing San Francisco in the background, what has van Druten done to keep us aware that the action is happening in this unusual and unique hill city?

9. In play-writing, the most important rule is that you must keep your audience continuously interested. If the speech is too long, the attention of the audience is apt to waver. One way to keep interest in a long story is to have the story-teller ask a question. This alerts both the listener and the audience.

In the scene in Jenny's kitchen in Act I, the dramatist has Sigrid break her account of Arne's knee injury with the question, "And what do you think?" The reply given to Jenny is an example of very skilful play-writing. Why?

10. Another important principle of play-writing is that every significant action should be prepared for, so that it seems natural when it occurs. This is called "planting" an idea. In the first scene in the hospital corridor, how is the audience prepared for Mama scrubbing the floors in order to see Dagmar in the final scene of the act? Can you think of other examples of "planting"?

11. The scene in the hospital in which Uncle Chris sings to little Arne is an excellent one because of its humour and because it tells us a good deal about Uncle Chris. Discuss this scene, showing how the words and actions of Uncle Chris reveal both the kindly and gentle, and the hearty and rough aspects of his nature.

12. In addition to its comment on the writer's life and art, *I Re-*

member Mama praises another great profession—that of medicine. On his death-bed, Uncle Chris says, "Is the greatest thing in the world. It is to have a little of God in you."

How did Uncle Chris come to believe this? Write something about his life and activities to explain his deep interest in medicine. What part does Nels play in his thinking on the subject?

13. Discuss under the headings of plot, character and theme, the scene between Katrin and Christine in Christine's closet or "boodwar" in Act I. Indicate at least two purposes it serves in telling the story or increasing our interest in the play. Show what it reveals about the characters of the two girls. What theme or idea about the writer's approach to life is developed?

14. The New York newspaper *P.M.* had this interesting comment to make on the play. "For this story . . . adds to homely warmth just enough humour and colour to take the kinks out of reality without altogether removing the kernel. It prettifies family life, that is, without arrantly falsifying it; and at its best, it is really touching or really funny." Choose a scene that you like and show how humour and colour add to its reality; point out two or three of the high moments at which it is "really touching or really funny".

15. A crisis is a period of extreme suspense, when the characters are doubtful about the outcome of the situation in which they find themselves. For the final scenes in Act I, the crisis begins when Mama finds that she is not allowed to see Dagmar, and extends over the period in which she seeks a way to do so. The climax is the moment when the issue is resolved. Here it is her appearance after her floor-mopping expedition, successful in having seen Dagmar. The denouement or period of falling action is the sequence between the climax and the curtain. Our interest here is sustained in the scene between Uncle Chris and Mama because he is such a forceful, turbulent character, and because we like him and are as much concerned as Mama is about him. The curtain line closes the scene. Here we have a new light on Mama, showing how unscrupulous and witty she can be. She would not try to see Dagmar again. "That would be against the rules."

Comment on the crisis, climax, denouement and curtain line in the final scene of the play.

16. Some critics in reviewing the Broadway production had reservations about the structure of the play. They were enthusiastic about its warm and human qualities but they felt that its construction was a little too leisurely and episodic. They felt there were some static moments, and some over-long parts where it could be cut. Discuss these criticisms. Are there any static moments? Are there any scenes which would benefit from cutting?

17.   If you are interested in writing, here are two projects: (a) Compare the style of *Mama's Bank Account* with that of *I Remember Mama*, scene by scene. Examine particularly the scenes written entirely by John van Druten. See if you can come to any conclusion about the contributions that each author made to the success of *I Remember Mama*. (b) If they are available, read the two short stories which appeared in the Toronto *Star Weekly* and compare them with the stories as they appear in permanent form in *Mama's Bank Account*. Analyse the changes that were made. Decide for yourself why they were made and whether they represent an improvement.

THE TEAHOUSE OF THE AUGUST MOON

NOTES

P. 186, l. 2.   **House curtain.**   The main stage curtain, which separates the house or auditorium from the stage.

P. 186, l. 9.   **G.I.**   The common name for the American soldier. Initials of *General Issue* or *Government Issue*.

P. 227, ll. 16-17.   **"They not beat your time."**   They are not taking advantage of you by using your time to do something else.

P. 231, l. 31.   A chrysanthemum bud has a special romantic significance to the Okinawans. In the novel on which the play is based, First Flower, the leading geisha, who is in love with Seiko, the painter, tries to find a chrysanthemum bud to send to him as a sign that her heart is opening to him and that he should come to the village. Unfortunately, one cannot be found.

In the big party at the teahouse in Act III, Scene 1, Lotus Blossom gives a yellow chrysanthemum to Fisby on his birthday. When, later, he returns it to her with a flourish, Sakini explains that this means that he has given his heart to her.

P. 234, ll. 6-7.   **". . . you not take money from her."**   In Japan it was the custom for geisha owners to go from village to village and, from poor families, to buy beautiful young girls six to seven years of age. They would then send them to school where they were trained in dancing, singing, playing an instrument, arranging flowers, the tea ceremony and the conversational arts. The owners expected and secured a large share of the earnings of their geisha protégées.

P. 248, l. 16.   **Squawk box.**   The inter-com set with its loudspeaker.

P. 274, ll. 8-16. **Then tell her . . . beautiful.** These lines may have a double meaning. Not only is Fisby telling Lotus Blossom why it would be wrong for him to marry her and take her to America; he may also be stating a general principle, perhaps the most important in the play. We of the West must not impose our way of life on the people of the East. What is beautiful in the East we must leave beautiful.

P. 280, ll. 15-26. The re-building of the teahouse before our very eyes, to the accompaniment of music, is the perfect climax for the play. We are pleased with the child-like cunning of the villagers, who have been invaded before and who know how to bide their time. We share their naïve delight in their triumph. It is all in the fairy-tale mood of magic and wonder.

P. 280, ll. 33-4. **Colonel . . . poetry.** We remember that Colonel Purdy has said this to Captain Fisby in Act I, Scene 1; the repetition gives us the same pleasure that we derive from a musical phrase when it is repeated by another instrument; moreover, we are delighted that the tables are turned and that Purdy himself is aware of poetry. The total effect is one of high comedy, drawing not only upon situation but also on character, idea and turn of phrase.

P. 281, l. 24. **May . . . sleep.** Sakini's final line brings the play to a serene and lovely conclusion.

QUESTIONS

1. Point out how the author has used cricket cages for (i) comedy and (ii) an effective climax to a scene.

2. The playwright finds an hilarious opportunity in which to use the fancy name he has given to the goat, "Lady Astor". What is this opportunity? Do you think he chose this name with this moment in mind? If you don't know who the famous Lady Astor is, try to find out from reference books at your disposal.

3. Why did the playwright vary Sakini's introduction in Act III, Scene 3, and have him appear and say practically nothing? Why is it both amusing and fitting that he should do so?

4. In Act I, Scene 3, when Fisby asks whether the villagers want to be ignorant, they reply "Yes!", and Sakini explains that in Luchuan "yes" means "no" and that they say "Yes, that they do *not* want to be ignorant." Later in the play the author provides moments of high comedy by carrying on this topsy-turvy native logic. Find these moments and comment on this type of humour.

5. The last line spoken by Captain McLean as he leaves the stage in Act III, Scene 2, is, "Please take care of my beans." In a paragraph,

give your opinion as to why this line is funny. In your answer, consider not only the line itself, but the situation, the speaker, and those to whom it is addressed.

6. One of the funniest scenes in the play is the telephone conversation that closes Act II, Scene 3, in which McLean tells the unbelieving Purdy about his gardening hopes. Analyse the humour in this scene. Remember that in Shakespeare's time, people used to pay admission to watch the lunatics in the asylum. Examine what is comic, not only in the situation and in the personalities of the two characters, but in the ideas and expressions that are used.

7. From Sakini's opening speech, select and discuss an example of each of: (a) irony; (b) parallel structure; (c) balanced clauses or sentences; (d) humorous internal rhyme; (e) humorous misuse of language.

8. One critic has objected that the natives are "uniformly lovable". Discuss this objection.

9. Mr. Oshira's speech at the end of Act II, Scene 1, urging Fisby to allow the villagers to have a teahouse, is a moving piece of pleading. Why? How does it build to its climax of appeal? Identify and comment on the order in which the following are arranged: facts, a lovely picture, a personal poignant statement, a philosophical idea, a final appeal that combines both philosophy and personal longing. Comment also on the effectiveness of the language with which these ideas are expressed.

10. An important question in considering whether a work of literature will survive the years is whether it is too topical in its material. Do you consider that *The Teahouse of the August Moon* is "dated" because it deals with a specific situation in World War II? What permanent values does it possess? Do you think it will be as popular in twenty-five years as it is now? Construct your answer as a reasoned statement, admitting the arguments on the opposite side and supporting your conclusion as effectively as you can.

11. One New York critic, Louis Kronenberger, had reservations about *The Teahouse of the August Moon*. While giving it full marks as entertainment, he claimed that it sticks "resolutely to surfaces"; that the writing never rises to actual brilliance; that it lacks real beauty and has only "a tinkly charm"; and that it is no closer to art than to life.

Compare this minority opinion with those expressed in the quotations from William Hawkins and Brooks Atkinson and with the editor's opinion in the notes on the play. What is your own conclusion?

AN ENEMY OF THE PEOPLE

NOTES

P. 300, ll. 25-9. The two boys and Horster go along the hallway up stage and directly into the dining-room. We see them only as they pass the door and seat themselves at the table. They do not appear on the stage until after the scene between Peter and Dr. Stockmann.

Arthur Miller does not state the ages of the two boys, but Ibsen tells us that Ejlif is thirteen and Morten ten.

Pp. 314-16. The playwright has Kiil use ungrammatical constructions like "It better be true" and unpleasant-sounding words like "Ya" in order to show his lack of education and culture. Kiil does not know the word bacteria—he calls them cockroaches. His lack of table manners and his furtive pocketing of apples and tobacco in the opening scene of the play are further indications of his manners and character.

P. 343. The difference between the two plays by Ibsen and Miller is nowhere so sharp and interesting as in the treatment of this scene in which Dr. Stockmann picks up the mayor's cane and hat and puts them on. Arthur Miller has Dr. Stockmann deadly serious as he does so. In Ibsen's play it is a moment of high comedy. Dr. Stockmann bursts out laughing when he sees the cane and hat. He puts them on, clowning in an impudent and mock-serious manner. Striding up and down, he demands that Peter be properly respectful to the "chief authority in the town".

P. 362, ll. 21-6. When Petra tells her father that she has been given notice of dismissal, Dr. Stockmann is shocked. When Ibsen's hero hears the news, he laughs and rubs his hands. "She didn't dare do otherwise, either," he says. "It's delicious."

P. 380, ll. 21-2. **And the strong must learn to be lonely!** This is the most famous line in the play. In our version the words are spoken above the voices of a crowd that grows angrier and more threatening as the curtains close.

In Ibsen's play there is no danger from the crowd. The family are together. Dr. Stockmann lowers his voice and tells them that he has made a great discovery. Mrs. Stockmann asks, "Another one?" He replies "Yes." He then gathers them round him and tells them his secret, confidentially: ". . . the strongest man in the world is he who stands most alone." Mrs. Stockmann smiles and shakes her head. "Oh Thomas, Thomas!" she says. But Petra encourages him, crying out "Father!" as the curtains close.

Which ending do you like better?

QUESTIONS

1. What do Kiil's actions and words concerning the apples in the opening scene of the play reveal about his character?

2. The closing moments of Act I, Scene 1 are rich in irony. Why?

3. In the list of characters for Ibsen's play Morten Kiil is described as Mrs. Stockmann's adoptive father. Arthur Miller does not follow Ibsen in this. Mrs. Stockmann *is* Kiil's daughter. State the pros and cons of each relationship. From the standpoint both of plot and of character, which has the greater dramatic value?

4. Captain Horster is one of the most appealing figures in the play. Suggest some of the mental and spiritual qualities which draw us to him, illustrating each trait with a detailed reference.

5. Comment on the scene on pages 341-2 in which Dr. Stockmann talks to Aslaksen and Hovstad before Mrs. Stockmann enters. Discuss the interest and appeal of the scene from the standpoint of (a) its ironic values; (b) its suspense; (c) its revelation of Dr. Stockmann's character.

6. Contrast the characters of Petra and Mrs. Stockmann. Stress particularly their relationship to Dr. Stockmann; account for their differing reactions to him and to the problems he faces as the play progresses.

7. Re-read carefully the scene between Kiil and Dr. Stockmann in Act III. Do the language, behaviour, and reasoning of Kiil in this scene correspond at all points with his language, actions and reasoning in the opening scene of the play? If there is a divergence, how would you justify it?

8. Write a character sketch of Aslaksen. First describe him as you imagine him physically: his appearance, mannerisms, and voice. Then consider his actions and his role in the play. Next examine his own words, justifying these actions. Then comment on what others say about him. Finally make your own estimate of him and of his importance to the plot and ideas of the play.

9. The author does not hold the two liberals, Billing and Hovstad, in high regard. Sketch their characters and discuss their philosophies as revealed in the first scene; show their relationship to Dr. Stockmann and his family. Then show how they reveal their true selves and the weakness of their political convictions as Dr. Stockmann's difficulties increase and his enemies triumph.

10. Invent a situation in which a scientist or doctor today finds himself at odds with municipal, provincial, or national authorities. Here are two suggestions: fluoridation and the pollution of water at our beaches. You may think of other ideas. Develop your situation into a short story or one-act play.

A THEATRE LIBRARY

HISTORY OF THE THEATRE

Cheney, Sheldon, *The Theatre*. New York: Longmans, Green and Company, 1928.

Freedley, George, and John A. Reeves, *A History of the Theatre*, Revised Edition. New York: Crown Publishers, 1955.

PLAY PRODUCTION

Dean, Alexander, *Fundamentals of Play Directing*. New York: Farrar and Rinehart, Inc., 1941.

Dolman, John, *The Art of Play Production*, Revised Edition. New York: Harper and Brothers, 1946.

Hewitt, Barnard, J. F. Foster and Muriel Sibell Wolle, *Play Production Theory and Practice*. New York: J. B. Lippincott Company, 1952.

Jones, Leslie Allen, *Painting Scenery*. Boston: Baker, 1935.

McCandless, S. R., *A Method of Lighting the Stage*, Third Edition. New York: Theatre Arts, 1947.

Melville, Harald, *Magic of Make-up for the Stage*. London: Rockliff, 1957.

Napier, Frank, *Curtains for Stage Settings*. London: Frederick Muller, 1937.

Philippi, Herbert, *Stagecraft and Scene Design*. Boston: Houghton Mifflin, 1953.

Selden, Samuel, and Hunton D. Sellman, *Stage Scenery and Lighting*. New York: F. S. Crofts & Company, 1945.

Smith, Milton, *Play Production for Little Theatres, Schools and Colleges*. New York: D. Appleton-Century-Crofts, Inc., 1948.

PLAYWRITING

Baker, George Pierce, *Dramatic Technique*. Boston: Houghton Mifflin Company, 1919.

Egri, Lajos, *The Art of Dramatic Writing*. New York: Simon and Schuster, 1946.

398

Raphaelson, Samson, *The Human Nature of Playwriting*. New York: The Macmillan Company, 1949.

Wilde, Percival, *The Craftsmanship of the One-Act Play*. New York: Crown, 1951.

DRAMATIC THEORY

Clark, Barrett H., *A Study of the Modern Drama*. New York: D. Appleton and Company, 1925.

ANTHOLOGIES OF PLAYS

Dickinson, Thomas H., *Chief Contemporary Dramatists*, Series 1, 2 and 3. Boston: Houghton Mifflin Company, 1915, 1921, 1930.

Gassner, John, *A Treasury of the Theatre*, Vols. I and II. New York: Simon and Schuster, 1950 & 1951.

Whitman, Charles H., *Representative Modern Dramas*. New York: The Macmillan Company, 1939.

76 86 96 07 17 27 37 47 57 THB 16 15 14 13 12 11 10 9 8 7

Top Left AN ENEMY OF THE PEOPLE
Photo Pegasus Films Limited

Bottom Left THE TEAHOUSE OF THE AUGUST MOON
Photo Nina Leen, Life

Top Right FLIGHT INTO DANGER
Photo Page Toles

Bottom Right I REMEMBER MAMA
Photo Vandamm